VIVA PRACTICE FOR THE
FRCS(Urol) EXAMINATION

VIVA PRACTICE FOR THE FRCS(Urol) EXAMINATION

Edited by

MANIT ARYA, IQBAL S SHERGILL, JAS S KALSI, ASIF MUNEER AND ANTHONY R MUNDY

Forewords by

DEREK FAWCETT
FRCS, FEBU
Consultant Urological Surgeon, Royal Berkshire NHS Foundation Trust
President, British Association of Urological Surgeons
President, Federation of Surgical Specialty Associations

and

HASHIM U AHMED
MRCS, BM, BCh, BA
Medical Research Council Fellow
Institute of Urology, University College London
Specialist Registrar in Urology
University College London Hospitals

Radcliffe Publishing
Oxford • New York

Radcliffe Publishing Ltd
18 Marcham Road
Abingdon
Oxon OX14 1AA
United Kingdom

www.radcliffe-oxford.com
Electronic catalogue and worldwide online ordering facility.

British Library Cataloguing in Publication Data

A catalogue record for this book is available from the British Library.

ISBN-13: 978 184619 317 0

The paper used for the text pages of this book is FSC certified. FSC (The Forest Stewardship Council) is an international network to promote responsible management of the world's forests.

Mixed Sources
Product group from well-managed forests and other controlled sources
www.fsc.org Cert no. SGS-COC-2482
© 1996 Forest Stewardship Council

Typeset by Phoenix Photosetting, Chatham, Kent
Printed and bound by TJI Digital, Padstow, Cornwall

Contents

Foreword

The trainee urologist is the future of Urology and the final intercollegiate FRCS(Urol) examination is the test of knowledge and clinical acumen that allows progression to independent practice.

The British Association of Urological Surgeons (BAUS) is a charity whose mission is to promote the highest standard in the practice of Urology for the benefit of patients by fostering education, research and clinical excellence through the dissemination of information.

As President of BAUS, it is therefore a great privilege and pleasure to introduce this excellent book – whose clear intention is to promote excellence by providing an educational and revision resource surrounding common clinical scenarios, not only to candidates sitting the FRCS(Urol) but to all Urologists.

The authors and contributors are all recognised experts in their fields and have either taken the FRCS(Urol) examination themselves or been involved in teaching the candidates. It is necessarily a difficult examination, designed to test the candidate and ensure that only those with sufficient knowledge and clinical expertise become Consultants in Urology in the NHS.

The second part of the exam is based on clinical scenarios in a viva setting, such as any Urologist might meet in everyday outpatient practice or multidisciplinary team meetings. This part is designed to assess their clinical acumen and understanding of common clinical issues. The inclusion of seminal references in this book is of particular value, as candidates in the exam are required to support their answers with appropriate evidence.

This book replicates those scenarios and provides sample answers to common questions – thus also providing a reference book for any Urologist, confronted by clinical situations outside their normal area of practice or expertise. This book is to be welcomed and will become essential reading for all trainees (and examiners) in preparation for the FRCS(Urol), FEBU and other Urological examinations.

BAUS is committed to the development of excellence in Urology and this book supports that aspiration.

Derek Fawcett FRCS, FEBU
Consultant Urological Surgeon, Royal Berkshire NHS Foundation Trust
President, British Association of Urological Surgeons
President, Federation of Surgical Specialty Associations
January 2010

Foreword

The greatest challenge for trainees sitting postgraduate exams is to determine the depth and breadth of knowledge that they must acquire during their training. Despite the training in Urology being more structured and dictated by a syllabus, the final examination can still seem daunting if the level of factual discussion that occurs in *viva voce* exams is vague.

This book is a precious and timely resource for Urology trainees approaching the FRCS(Urol). The editors have the experience and gravitas to put together such a book and they have recruited chapter authors who are experts and recent successful candidates in the FRCS(Urol) examination. This combination makes each of the chapters both sound in terms of fact and relevant for the reader about to sit in front of the viva panels.

I think we will find that no Urology trainee should be without this important and valuable contribution to the training of future consultants.

Hashim U Ahmed MRCS, BM, BCh, BA
Medical Research Council Fellow
Institute of Urology, University College London
Specialist Registrar in Urology
University College London Hospitals
January 2010

Preface

The FRCS(Urol) examination has recently undergone a change in format, and the examination is now divided into two parts. The first part is devoted entirely to MCQs and EMQs which are aimed at testing the entire urology syllabus in depth. The second part uses clinical scenarios to form the basis of the *viva voce* section of the examination. The aim of this book is to provide a selection of common clinical scenarios together with a guide to answering these questions. Each chapter has been written by consultant urological surgeons or senior urology trainees who have already successfully passed the examination. This book is intended primarily to be used as a revision tool in conjunction with a larger urology textbook, supplemented by lectures and urology journals. In order to avoid an exhaustive list of references, only selected references are included together with suggested further reading. In a few chapters (e.g. those on prostate cancer and benign prostatic hyperplasia), a longer list of references has been included as, in the editors' experience, the candidate is expected to be able to quote the literature, particularly in these subjects.

We hope that this book will be useful not only to those preparing for the FRCS(Urol) examination, but also to individuals sitting the FEBU (Fellowship of the European Board of Urology), MSc/Diploma in Urology examination. In addition, established consultants may find the book useful as a 'refresher' in areas outside their subspecialist interest.

Viva Practice for the FRCS(Urol) Examination is unique in that this is the first revision book to be published specifically for candidates sitting the FRCS(Urol) examination. The journey from initial conception of the idea to final publication has involved hard work, frustration and commitment, but has nonetheless been both exciting and challenging. We would like to thank all of the authors and contributors for their time and hard work.

Finally, to the candidates: 'Good luck!'

Manit Arya
Iqbal S Shergill
Jas S Kalsi
Asif Muneer
Anthony R Mundy
January 2010

About the editors

Manit Arya FRCS, FRCS(Urol)

Manit Arya is an Honorary post-CCT Fellow in laparoscopic and minimally invasive surgery at King's College Hospital, London. He has published extensively throughout the urology literature, particularly in uro-oncology, as well as being an editor of four further books. He completed his higher surgical training in London, and has since organised a number of local and national teaching courses for both medical students and trainees.

Iqbal S Shergill BSc(Hons), MRCS(Eng), FRCS(Urol)

Iqbal S Shergill is a Senior Specialist Registrar in London. He was among one of the first candidates to pass the new-format FRCS(Urol) examination. During his urology training he has organised a number of practical skills courses for fellow trainees, as well as career advice courses for medical students. He has published on all aspects of urology in the medical literature, editing four teaching textbooks, and continues to be involved in teaching and training of medical/surgical education.

Jas S Kalsi BSc(Hons), MRCS(Eng), FRCS(Urol)

Jasjit S Kalsi is a post-CCT Fellow in Urology at University College London Hospitals. He undertook a period of research at the Wolfson Institute of Biomedical Research, based at University College London, followed by higher surgical training in London. His main areas of interest are endourology and andrology.

Asif Muneer BSc(Hons), MB, MD, FRCS(Ed), FRCS(Urol)

Asif Muneer is a Consultant Urological Surgeon and Honorary Senior Lecturer at University College London Hospitals and University College London. While completing his higher surgical training in Oxford, he was awarded the prestigious Keith Yeates Gold Medal by the intercollegiate specialty board for his outstanding performance in the FRCS(Urol) examination. His continued interest in teaching and education and experience of the FRCS(Urol) examination have enabled him to relay his own expertise to the readers of this book.

Anthony R Mundy MS, FRCP, FRCS

Anthony R Mundy is Professor of Urology at University College London Hospitals. He is also a past President of the British Association of Urological Surgeons and Civilian Consultant Urological Surgeon for the Royal Navy. He has edited numerous urology textbooks and is internationally respected for his contributions to urology.

List of contributors

Aruna Abhyankar
MCh, FRCS, FRCS(Paed)
Specialist Registrar in Paediatric
  Urology
Evelina Children's Hospital
Guys and St Thomas' NHS Trust,
  London

Jim Adshead
MA, MD, FRCS(Urol)
Consultant Urological Surgeon
Lister Hospital
East and North Hertfordshire NHS
  Trust, Stevenage

Manit Arya
FRCS, FRCS(Urol)
Honorary post-CCT Fellow
King's College Hospital, London

Jane Boddy
MD, FRCS(Urol)
Specialist Registrar
Department of Urology
University Hospital Birmingham

Emma Bromwich
FRCS(Urol)
Specialist Registrar in Urology
Bournemouth and Christchurch NHS
  Foundation Trust

John A Bycroft
BSc, FRCS(Urol)
Specialist Registrar in Urology
Whipps Cross University Hospital,
  London

Alan Doherty
MD, FRCS(Urol)
Consultant Urological Surgeon
Department of Urology
University Hospital Birmingham

Mark Emberton
FRCS(London), FRCS(Urol), MD
Reader in Interventional Oncology
Honorary Consultant Urologist
University College London Hospitals

Lyndon Gommersall
MD, FRCS(Urol)
Specialist Registrar
Department of Urology
University Hospital Birmingham

Rizwan Hamid
MBBS, FRCS, FRCS(Urol)
Fellow in Female and Reconstructive
  Urology
University College London Hospitals

Dominic Hodgson
MSc, FRCS(Urol), Keith Yeates Gold Medal
  winner
Consultant Urological Surgeon
Solent Department of Urology
Portsmouth Hospital NHS Trust

Jas Kalsi
BSc(Hons), FRCS(Urol)
Post-CCT Fellow in Andrology and
    Genital Surgery
University College London Hospitals

Vinay Kalsi
MRCS
Specialist Registrar
Guy's Hospital, London

Farooq A Khan
BSc (Hons), FRCS(Urol)
Specialist Registrar
Norfolk & Norwich University NHS
    Foundation Trust, Norwich

Ciaran Lynch
FRCS(Urol), MD
Specialist Registrar
Department of Urology
University Hospital Birmingham

William J McAllister
MB, BChir, FRCS, FRCS(Urol), Keith Yeates
    Gold Medal winner
Consultant Urological Surgeon
Broomfield Hospital, Chelmsford

Suks Minhas
MD, FRCS(Urol)
Consultant Urological Surgeon
University College London Hospitals

Vibhash Mishra
MS, FRCS(Urol)
Specialist Registrar
University College London Hospitals

Asif Muneer
BSc(Hons), FRCSEd, MD, FRCS(Urol), Keith
    Yeates Gold Medal winner
Consultant Urological Surgeon
University College London Hospitals

David E Neal
FMed Sci, MS, FRCS
Professor of Surgical Oncology
Honorary Consultant Urological
    Surgeon
Addenbrookes NHS Foundation Trust,
    Cambridge

Mark Rochester
MA, MD, FRCS(Urol)
Specialist Registrar in Urology
Addenbrookes NHS Foundation Trust,
    Cambridge

Julian Shah
FRCS
Senior Lecturer
Honorary Consultant Urological
    Surgeon
University College London Hospitals

Davendra M Sharma
MB, BCh, BAO, MRCS, MSc(Urol),
    FRCS(Urol), RAF
Specialist Registrar
King's College Hospital, London
Squadron Leader, Royal Air Force

Deendyal P Sharma
MB, BCh, BAO, MD, FRCS
Consultant Urologist
Woodlands Hospital, Georgetown,
    Guyana
President, Caribbean Association of
    Urology

Iqbal S Shergill
BSc(Hons), MRCS(Eng), FRCS(Urol)
Specialist Registrar in Urology
Colchester General University Hospital
    NHS Foundation Trust, Colchester

Arash K Taghizadeh
MSc, FRCS(Urol)
Consultant Paediatric Urological
  Surgeon
Evelina Children's Hospital
Guys and St Thomas' NHS Trust,
  London

Oliver Wiseman
MA, FRCS(Urol)
Consultant Urological Surgeon
Addenbrookes NHS Foundation Trust,
  Cambridge

To Maanvii Arya and Krishan Arya, who light up my life.

To Navroop, Mehtaab and Partap for their support and motivation.

To Harwinder, Serena, Sian and Hari, I thank you for enriching my life and all the love and support you give me every day.

To Iaisha, Adam and Jemima for all your patience and support.

Chapter 1

Prostate cancer

Lyndon Gommersall, Jane Boddy and Alan Doherty

PROSTATE-SPECIFIC ANTIGEN (PSA) AND PROSTATE CANCER DETECTION

Q. **A 66-year-old man with a PSA of 5.3 is referred to you. This test was performed during a routine health check with his GP. He has mild lower urinary tract symptoms, but is otherwise fit and well. Examination revealed a small benign-feeling prostate. How would you assess this patient?**

A. A full urological history should be taken with an emphasis on lower urinary tract symptoms (LUTS), age, racial origin, family history and history of urine infections. If advanced disease is suspected, a history of bone pain, leg swelling, anorexia, weight loss, coagulopathy and new-onset peripheral neurology is important. A general urology examination should be performed along with a digital rectal examination. Transrectal ultrasound (TRUS)-guided prostate biopsy should be offered, quoting a 1% risk of severe bleeding and/or severe sepsis. Almost all patients experience some bleeding (rectal bleeding, haematuria and/or haematospermia) following this procedure. Treatment is dependent on the grade and stage of the tumour as well as any comorbidity.

Q. **What is PSA?**

A. PSA is a 34kD serine protease. This glycoprotein was first discovered in 1970. Also known as human kallikrein 3 (HK3), it has 261 amino acids. HK2 and HK1 also exist. PSA is encoded by a gene on chromosome 19. It is secreted uniquely by prostatic ductal epithelial cells, and its biological effect is to liquefy the seminal coagulum within the ejaculate. It is synthesised as pre-pro PSA which is converted to pro-PSA and then PSA. PSA exists in three forms in serum:

- *free*: unbound with a half-life of 2–3 hours
- *bound to alpha-1-antichymotrypsin (ACT)* (a serine protease inhibitor or serpin): this form has some epitopes exposed which affects free to total PSA measurement. It has a half-life of 4–5 days
- *bound to alpha-2-macroglobulin (AMG)*: all five PSA epitopes are covered, making this more difficult to quantitate. It has a half-life of 4–5 days.

Overall PSA has a half-life of 2–3 days. Total PSA therefore equates to:

Total PSA = free PSA + complexed PSA (ACT-bound PSA not including AMG-bound PSA)

The measurement of PSA is now automated, using a monoclonal antibody assay technique and commercially produced antibodies.

Q. **What is a normal PSA?**

A. No normal PSA cut-off value can be attributed. However, in clinical practice a normal PSA can be defined either as being lower than an absolute figure (generally considered to be 4 ng/ml) or as a range of values related to the patient's age. Oesterling described the most commonly used age-specific reference ranges for PSA.[1] These are reproduced in Table 1.1. More recently, Sun *et al.* have reported on 12 078 patients who were retrospectively reviewed following prostate biopsy.[2] In this study, receiver operating characteristic (ROC) analysis of the PSA results demonstrated a normal PSA cut-off value of 2.3 ng/ml.

PSA is prostate-specific but not prostate cancer-specific. It is also elevated in benign prostatic hyperplasia, prostatitis, catheterisation and other non-malignant conditions. The Prostate Cancer Prevention Trial (PCPT) has shown a high incidence of prostate cancer in patients with a PSA of < 4 ng/ml, with positive biopsies in almost 25% of patients with a PSA of < 4 ng/ml (see below).

Table 1.1 Osterling's age-specific reference range[1]

Age (years)	PSA (ng/ml)
40–50	2.5
50–60	3.5
60–70	4.5
70–80	6.5

Note:
The figure of 4 ng/ml was defined on the basis of ROC analysis, a technique that was used in radar detection of enemy aircraft during the Second World War. From the 1970s this approach was applied to medical testing in general. For a range of values this technique originally delineated when a given signal was more likely to be enemy aircraft than radar artefact, and when applied to PSA readings it can distinguish between benign disease and malignancy.

The original clinical work on PSA was performed by Catalona *et al.* in the early 1990s.[3] This study investigated men who were invited to attend for a PSA blood test. They were stratified into three groups according to their PSA. The first group had a PSA in the range 0–4 ng/ml, in the second group it was in the range 4–10 ng/ml, and in the third group it was > 10 ng/ml. Each patient with a PSA greater than 4 ng/ml was offered a prostate biopsy. Prostate cancer was detected in 26% of the patients with a PSA in the range 4–10 ng/ml and in 53% of patients with a PSA higher than 10 ng/ml. More recently the Prostate Cancer Prevention Trial (PCPT) has provided further insight into the percentage of positive biopsies for a 'normal' PSA.[4] These data are reproduced in Table 1.2. This landmark study reveals the high proportion of patients with prostate cancer with low PSA readings. A criticism of the PCPT is the over-diagnosis of prostate cancer, i.e. a man's lifetime risk of developing prostate cancer is approximately 16%, whereas in the PCPT, prostate cancer was detected in 24.4% of patients analysed.

Table 1.2 Prevalence of prostate cancer among men with a prostate-specific antigen level of less than 4 ng/ml[4]

PSA range (ng/ml)	Prevalence of prostate cancer
< 0.5	6.6%
0.6–1.0	10.1%
1.1–2.0	17.0%
2.1–3.0	23.9%
3.1–4.0	26.9%

Gerstenbluth et al. reported on the positive predictive value of PSA, and found that a PSA concentration higher than 20 ng/ml relates to an 87% chance of prostate cancer being detected on biopsy. Table 1.3 lists the positive predictive value for PSA ranges from their paper.[5]

Table 1.3 Positive predictive value for various PSA ranges from Gerstenbluth et al.[5]

PSA range (ng/ml)	Positive predictive value (PPV)
20–29	74%
30–39	90%
50–99	100%
> 20	87%

Q. **What do you know about PSA velocity (PSAV)?**

A. PSA is not a specific test. To improve the accuracy of detection of prostate cancer, many adaptations of PSA have been described (see Table 1.4). PSAV is defined as the rise in PSA per year, expressed in ng/ml/year. A rise in PSA of greater then 0.75 ng/ml per year is associated with an increased risk of prostate cancer.[6] Sun et al. utilised a PSAV cut-off value of 0.6 ng/ml/year.[2] Ideally at least three PSA results are required to produce a PSAV reading, due to the variability of the test. This is calculated using the following equation:

$$PSAV = 0.5 \times (PSA2 - PSA1/time_1 + PSA3 - PSA2/time_2)$$

where $time_1$ and $time_2$ are expressed in years.

Table 1.4 PSA derivatives and normal values

PSA derivative	Normal value
PSA velocity	< 0.6–0.75 ng/ml/year
PSA doubling time	> 3 years
PSA density	< 0.15 ng/ml/ml
PSA transitional zone density	< 0.35 ng/ml/ml
Free to total PSA	> 20%
Supersensitive PSA	< 0.01 ng/ml

Q. **What do you know about PSA doubling time (PSADT)?**
A. PSADT is defined as the length of time that a patient's PSA takes to double in months or years. PSADT is useful in patients under surveillance for high PSA readings with negative prostate biopsies, for active monitoring, and for patients with a rising PSA following radical treatment. It is calculated using regression analysis of the PSA tests recorded. The Marsden experience with active monitoring uses a PSADT of less than 2 years. The data on active monitoring provide useful information on how to follow up patients with a high PSA who have negative biopsies. Following radical prostatectomy, biochemical progression can be due to local recurrence, lymph-node-positive disease or metastatic disease. Calculation of the PSA doubling time can discriminate between these two scenarios. In one study, a PSADT of < 4.3 months suggested metastatic disease and a PSADT of > 11.7 months suggested local recurrence.[7] This is important in deciding whether adjuvant local treatment is appropriate. Similar data exist for post-radiotherapy biochemical progression.

Q. **What do you know about PSA density (PSAD)?**
A. PSAD is defined as the serum PSA level per ml of prostate tissue. Prostate volume can be measured using the ellipsoid volume formula:

$$\text{Prostate volume} = \text{height} \times \text{width} \times \text{length} \times 0.52$$

A PSAD of > 0.15 ng/ml/ml of prostate tissue is more likely to lead to a diagnosis of prostate cancer.[8] Other authors have not demonstrated the utility of PSAD. This may be due to the inability to measure prostate volume accurately, and the considerable variability of PSA production from benign prostate epithelium.

The PSA transitional zone density (PSATZD) can also be quantified. This is defined as the amount of PSA per ml of transitional zone tissue. Djavan *et al.* described a normal value of 0.35 ng/ml and published a PPV of 74% for PSA levels less than 10 ng/ml.[9] This result has not been replicated.

Q. **What do you know about free to total PSA (FTPSA)?**
A. FTPSA is defined as the percentage of free PSA compared with the total PSA in serum. PSA exists in serum either as free PSA or bound to ACT and AMG. Prostate cancer has a significantly lower free to total PSA value compared with BPH in the PSA range 4–10 ng/ml.[10] A cut-off value of greater than 20% suggests benign disease. Despite several meta-analyses, the clinical utility of FTPSA has not been clearly defined.

Q. **What do you know about supersensitive PSA (sPSA)?**
A. sPSA enables PSA to be detected to a threshold of 0.003 ng/ml. Around 10–40% of patients will develop biochemical relapse following radical prostatectomy. An undetectable PSA is defined as less than 0.01 ng/ml. In a study of 200 patients following radical prostatectomy, if the PSA nadir was less than 0.01 ng/ml, biochemical progression occurred in only 3% of patients, compared with 75% if this level was not attained.[11] This assay therefore allows the early detection of biochemical relapse after radical prostatectomy, and can expedite the use of secondary interventions.

Q. Does DRE change the PSA results?

A. In a study of 202 patients, digital rectal examination (DRE) significantly changed the PSA by only 0.26 ng/ml, and the authors concluded that PSA elevation due to DRE was clinically insignificant.[12]

Q. What is uPM3?

A. The uPM3 test detects prostate cancer antigen 3 (PCA3), a non-coding segment of mRNA. It is a gene specifically produced by prostate epithelial cells 60–100 times more in prostate cancer than in benign prostatic disease.[13] A uPM3 test is performed by collecting the first 20–30 ml of urine voided following vigorous prostatic massage. The ratio of PCA3 to PSA mRNA can then be calculated. The test is claimed to have a specificity of 70%.

Q. Is screening for prostate cancer evidence based?

A. Prostate cancer screening is not evidence based, and is therefore not currently undertaken in the UK or Europe as a whole. In the USA the American Urology Association and the American Cancer Society both recommend prostate cancer screening after 50 years of age. In the UK a policy of early detection through case finding is recommended via the Prostate Cancer Risk Management Programme (www.cancerscreening.nhs.uk/prostate). This aims to ensure that concerned individuals receive clear and balanced information about the advantages and disadvantages of the PSA blood test and treatment of prostate cancer before undergoing the test.

Prostate cancer screening is controversial and does not fulfil Wilson and Junger's criteria for a good screening programme. Table 1.5 lists the criteria developed in 1968 with the World Health Organization. Prostate cancer is an important health problem with a lifetime risk of 16% and a 3% mortality risk. In the UK in 2004 the incidence was 31 923 (Office of National Statistics data). Although localised prostate cancer can be aggressively treated with surgery, radiation or more novel techniques, no randomised controlled trial data have been reported on the benefit of these treatments. Bill-Axelson *et al.* reported on the success of radical prostatectomy vs. watchful waiting at 10 years. They found that radical prostatectomy significantly improves local progression, and reduces the rate of metastatic disease and death from prostate cancer.[14] However, radical treatment can have side-effects, with both surgical and radiotherapy studies reporting significant problems with erectile dysfunction, incontinence, lower urinary tract symptoms and rectal toxicity.[15] The disease has a long latent period, which means that the patient often dies of other causes rather than prostate cancer. PSA is an acceptable screening test for patients, but lacks sensitivity and specificity. A significant proportion of men who are offered screening would have to be subjected to a transrectal ultrasound and prostate biopsy which is not only an invasive procedure but also has a 1% risk of significant sepsis. The multidisciplinary team framework and recent NICE guidelines reinforce the indication for treatment at all stages of prostate cancer. The ProtecT (Prostate testing for cancer and Treatment) Study will report on the success of treatment of screen-detected prostate cancer. Without definitive evidence that prostate cancer screening decreases prostate cancer-specific mortality, the cost per life year saved is difficult to quantify. Overall it seems unlikely that such a programme will be introduced in the near future.

Table 1.5 Wilson and Junger's criteria for a screening programme*

1. The condition sought should be an important health problem for the individual and community.
2. There should be an accepted treatment or useful intervention for patients with the disease.
3. The natural history of the disease should be adequately understood.
4. There should be a latent or early symptomatic stage.
5. There should be a suitable and acceptable screening test or examination.
6. Facilities for diagnosis and treatment should be available.
7. There should be an agreed policy on whom to treat as patients.
8. Treatment started at an early stage should be of more benefit than treatment started later.
9. The cost should be economically balanced in relation to possible expenditure on medical care as a whole.
10. Case finding should be a continuing process and not a once-and-for-all project.

*Wilson JMG, Junger G. *Principles and Practice of Screening for Disease*. Public Health Paper No. 34. Geneva: World Health Organization; 1968.

In terms of the evidence for prostate cancer screening, three studies are repeatedly quoted, namely the Quebec Study, the Tyrol Study and the Seattle and Connecticut Study.

- In the Quebec Study patients were randomised to screened and non-screened populations. Initial reports showed a 70% decrease in prostate cancer death rates in the screened population. However, this trial has been widely criticised due to cross-contamination of the patient groups. Further analysis on an intention-to-screen basis has shown no difference in mortality.
- The Tyrol Study is a natural experiment comparing two areas of Austria. In Tyrol, free PSA testing was introduced and a 70% uptake was achieved. This resulted in a 44% decrease in prostate cancer mortality in 2000. However, this effect was too rapid to explain this outcome. Elucidation of the efficacy of localised disease treatment would take a far longer period of time, and therefore these results probably represent aggressive treatment of locally advanced and metastatic disease.
- Seattle and Connecticut have very disparate socio-economic populations. Seattle is prosperous and there is more PSA screening and aggressive treatment of prostate cancer than in Connecticut. However, no difference in prostate cancer mortality was demonstrated in these two populations.

Several studies investigating the screening and treatment of prostate cancer will report in the next 5 years. The key trials are the European Randomized Study of Screening for Prostate Cancer (ERSPC), the Prostate, Lung, Colon and Ovary (PLCO) trial in the USA, and the ProtecT study comparing radical prostate cancer treatments and active monitoring in screen-detected prostate cancer.

Q. **What do you know about the Prostate Cancer Prevention Trial (PCPT)?**

A. The Prostate Cancer Prevention Trial reported on 18 882 men randomised to receive prostate cancer chemoprevention with finasteride 5 mg od or placebo for 7 years.[16] The entry criteria was simply a PSA level of less than 3 ng/ml. Prostate biopsies were performed if an abnormal DRE or PSA > 4 ng/ml were found. All patients were offered an end-of-study biopsy. The study closed 15 months early due to significant results being achieved. It was then published in the *New England Journal of Medicine* in 2003. The study found a relative risk reduction of 24.8% in the finasteride group. However, a higher incidence of high-grade cancer (Gleason score of 7, 8, 9 or 10) was detected in the finasteride arm (6.4%) compared with the placebo arm (5.1%) of the trial. This worrying effect has been discussed at length in the urological literature. The main issues are first that cancer was detected in four times as many patients as was expected, and secondly that the cancers were low or intermediate grade. Possible explanations for these findings have been discussed by Grover et al.,[17] among others. They concluded that:

- finasteride may induce histological changes that mimic those seen in high-grade cancer
- high-grade tumours are resistant to androgen deprivation and are unaffected by finasteride
- treatment created an environment that promotes the growth of high-grade tumours
- these results may be an artefact due to increased detection.

The REDUCE (Reduction by Dutasteride of Prostate Cancer Events) trial is an international, multi-centre, double-blind, placebo-controlled chemoprevention study using dutasteride, the dual inhibitor of 5-alpha-reductase subtypes I and II. In this trial patients were enrolled with a negative prostate biopsy within 6 months of entry and a PSA in the range 2.5–10 ng/ml (50–60 years) or 3–10 ng/ml (> 60 years). Repeat biopsy is performed at 2 and 4 years. This trial has yet to report its findings.[18]

MANAGEMENT OF THE PATIENT WITH AN ELEVATED PSA

Q. A 62-year-old man is referred urgently by his GP with a raised PSA of 6.4 ng/ml. He had the PSA blood test performed because of a deterioration in his urinary symptoms. An MSU was negative and he is otherwise well. He is concerned and anxious about further assessment. How would you assess this patient in clinic?

A. A full urological history should be taken, including the patient's age, racial origin, lower urinary tract symptoms (LUTS), urinary tract infection, bone pain and family history of prostate cancer. A general examination would precede examination of his external genitalia and a digital rectal examination. If advanced disease is suspected, one should also look for leg swelling, anorexia, weight loss, bone tenderness and neurological signs suggesting spinal cord compression. This relatively young patient has an abnormal PSA result and should therefore be counselled about undergoing a TRUS prostate biopsy with an explanation that we are concerned about a diagnosis of prostate cancer. Explain the procedure to him, and discuss the risks of severe bleeding (1%), severe infection (1%), pain and urinary retention. Many men will experience haematospermia, rectal and/or urethral bleeding following this procedure. If his biopsy results are negative, one would continue to follow him up with a further PSA blood test in 6 months time. If his biopsy is positive, he should be counselled about all the treatment options available. He may need further investigation of his lower urinary tract symptoms prior to treatment.

Q. **How do you perform a prostate biopsy?**

A. Prostate biopsy is performed using a 7.5 MHz transrectal ultrasound probe. Many of these are now bidirectional, allowing multi-planar views. Antibiotic prophylaxis is required. Regimes vary between hospitals, but commonly intravenous gentamicin, rectal metronidazole and three doses of a quinolone are prescribed. After obtaining informed consent, including a discussion of the risks of bleeding, infection, pain and acute urinary retention, a digital rectal examination is first performed to assess the prostate for size and consistency. The ultrasound probe is then inserted into the rectum. The prostate is scanned to detect any capsular breach or hypoechoic areas within the periphery of the prostate. The prostate volume can be calculated using the ellipsoid volume formula (height × breadth × width × 0.52). The PSAD can then be calculated. Local anaesthetic peri-prostatic injections have been shown to reduce the pain associated with a prostate biopsy in a randomised controlled trial.[19] A total of 12 biopsy cores is now considered standard, and is an acceptable compromise between increased cancer detection and the morbidity from the procedure. Targeting of the periphery of the prostate is essential due to the higher proportion of prostate cancers diagnosed in this anatomical location (approximately 85% of prostate cancers are found in the peripheral zone of the prostate and 15% in the transition zone).

Q. **What are the chances of finding prostate cancer in further biopsies?**

A. Djavan *et al.* looked at prostate biopsies in a series of 1051 men with a normal DRE and a PSA in the range 4–10 ng/ml. This study reported that the probabilities of finding a prostate cancer on the first, second, third and fourth biopsy were 22%, 10%, 5% and 4%, respectively.[20] The more biopsies that are taken, the lower the Gleason score of the cancer when it is detected. Therefore a second biopsy is often considered in patients with serial abnormal PSAs, but the more biopsies that are taken the more confident the clinician can be that the disease will be insignificant.

Q. **How would you manage a patient with high-grade prostatic intra-epithelial neoplasia (HGPIN) on biopsy?**

A. It has been suggested that HGPIN is a precursor to prostate cancer, but this remains unproven. If HGPIN is found on one core, the patient has a 20% probability of having prostate cancer on further biopsies. If more than one core identifies HGPIN, the next biopsy can be positive for prostate cancer in up to 70% of cases. Around 82% of radical prostatectomy specimens have HGPIN, but only 40% of BPH specimens show HGPIN after TURP. *HGPIN does not secrete PSA.* With an overall positive biopsy rate of 24% on second biopsy, this is very similar to the detection of prostate cancer in the PCPT trial. Clinically, the European Association of Urology (EAU) guidelines recommend repeat biopsy, but the interval is unclear.

Q. **How would you manage a patient with abnormal small acinar proliferation (ASAP) on biopsy?**

A. ASAP is associated with a 40% detection of prostate cancer on repeat biopsy, compared with 24% for HGPIN. The EAU guidelines recommend repeat biopsy, but the interval is unclear. Due to the higher rate of detection of prostate cancer on subsequent biopsy with ASAP, a more aggressive approach to repeat biopsy is often undertaken.

Q. **What do you know about epidemiology, diet and chemoprevention in prostate cancer?**

A. Prostate cancer affects 100 in 100 000 men in the Western world. Post-mortem studies suggest that the prevalence is very high, with 30% of 50-year-olds having the disease, increasing to 80% at 80 years. However, only a small proportion of these patients develop clinically significant, life-threatening cancer. In the UK, in 2004 a total of 31 923 men developed prostate cancer, making the disease a significant health problem.

Dietary factors have been shown to affect the risk of prostate cancer. The factors that increase the risk of prostate cancer include obesity (relative risk 1.1), meat (few data available) and dairy products (higher risk). A reduced risk of prostate cancer has been publicised for many components of a man's diet, with limited evidence. These include fruit and vegetables (no benefit), beta-carotene 50 mg (no benefit), lycopene (possible benefit), vitamin D (no benefit), vitamin E (no benefit) and selenium (secondary end point for selenium vitamin D trial). In addition, the PCPT trial has shown the possible chemoprevention benefit of finasteride compared with placebo in decreasing the incidence of prostate cancer, although this may be at the cost of an increase in higher-grade cancers (see previous discussion).

Q. **What do you know about hereditary prostate cancer?**

A. Familial prostate cancer represents about 9% of prostate cancer patients, and relates to a clustering of prostate cancer cases within a family. Hereditary prostate cancer by definition must have three generations affected with three first-degree relatives or three relatives under the age of 55 years. In addition, prostate cancer in a family infers an increased risk of prostate cancer. If one relative is affected, a two- to threefold increase in risk is transferred, if two relatives are affected, a fivefold increase in risk is transferred, and if three relatives are affected, an 11-fold increased risk is transferred. Familial breast cancer confers a greater risk of prostate cancer within a particular family. The BRCA1 gene has been implicated in this relationship.

LOCALISED PROSTATE CANCER

Q. **A 65-year-old man is referred to your clinic with an elevated PSA of 11.1 ng/ml, which has been found during a routine medical check. How would you assess this patient in your clinic?**

A. A full history and clinical examination including a digital rectal examination (DRE) to assess the prostate gland is required.

Q. **What features in the clinical history would you be interested in and why?**

A. The important factors are discussed in Table 1.6.

Table 1.6 Important factors in the history of patients with suspected prostate cancer

Age	The risk of prostate cancer increases with age
Racial origin	Afro-Caribbean patients are at higher risk of prostate cancer than Caucasian patients,[21] who are at higher risk than Asian patients
Previous urological history	A history of inflammation (i.e. prostatitis) or infection (i.e. urinary tract infection) may account for an elevated PSA. Previous surgery (i.e. TURP) may affect potential treatment
Family history	The risk of familial prostate cancer increases with the number of first-degree relatives affected Hereditary prostate cancer accounts for approximately 9% of cases, and may be related to a single gene defect on Chr1q24–25 (HPC-1)
Past medical history	The presence of comorbidities is important in helping to determine life expectancy and therefore the most appropriate management and treatment options
Drug history	Identifying whether the patient is on warfarin or clopidogrel is important if requesting a transrectal ultrasound biopsy

Q. He has no preceding urinary symptoms and is otherwise fit and well. DRE reveals a 40 g prostate with a firm irregular left lobe. You organise a TRUS prostate biopsy. What does the histology slide in Figure 1.1 show?

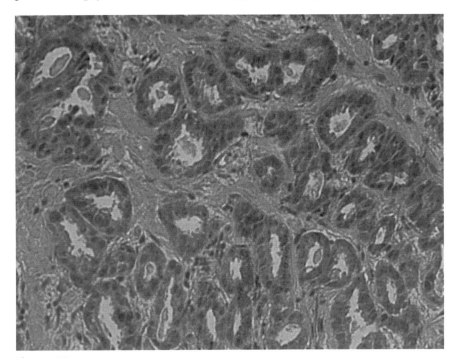

Figure 1.1

A. Figure 1.1 is a histological slide of a prostate biopsy demonstrating prostatic acinar and stromal tissue. (We are grateful to Dr Rupali Arora, Consultant Histopathologist, University College Hospitals, London, for providing this image.)

Q. **Can you determine the Gleason score in Figure 1.1?**

A. The glands demonstrate an irregular shape with irregular spacing in between and loss of the basal-cell layer, consistent with a Gleason grade 3. As there is only one predominant pattern, the Gleason score is 3+3.

Note:

The Gleason scoring system was described by Donald Gleason in 1974[22] after he compared tumour architecture with clinical outcome. The Gleason score is derived by assigning a score to the most common and also the second most common tumour pattern within a specimen. The tumour pattern is assessed by examining the glandular architecture at low magnification. The glandular features that determine the Gleason grade are shown in Table 1.7.

Table 1.7 Gleason's grading system for prostate cancer[22]

Grade 1	Well-demarcated nodule (the whole periphery must be seen)
Grade 2	Irregular spacing between glands and irregular outline (cannot be diagnosed on biopsy)
Grade 3	Variability in gland shape and spacing
Grade 4	Gland fusion
Grade 5	Diffuse solid sheet of undifferentiated cells

Q. **What is the clinical stage of this tumour using the 2002 TNM classification?**

A. The clinical stage is T2bNxMx. It is T2b as the whole of the left lobe is involved, and Nx Mx as investigations have not been performed to assess for lymph node involvement or metastases.

The prefix 'c' is used to describe clinical staging, and the prefix 'p' is used to describe pathological stage following radical prostatectomy. The TNM scoring system for prostate cancer is reproduced in Table 1.8.

Table 1.8 The 2002 TNM classification of prostate cancer

T	Primary tumour
Tx	Primary tumour cannot be assessed
T0	No evidence of primary tumour
T1	Clinically inapparent tumour not palpable or visible by imaging
T1a	Tumour incidental histological finding in 5% or less of tissue resected
T1b	Tumour incidental histological finding in more than 5% of tissue resected
T1c	Tumour identified by needle biopsy following elevated PSA (neither palpable nor visible)
T2	Tumour confined within the prostate
T2a	Tumour involves one half of one lobe or less
T2b	Tumour involves more than half of one lobe, but not both lobes
T2c	Tumour involves both lobes
T3	Tumour extends through the prostatic capsule
T3a	Extracapsular extension (unilateral or bilateral)
T3b	Tumour invades seminal vesicle(s)

continued

Table 1.8 *Continued*

T4	Tumour is fixed or invades adjacent structures other than seminal vesicles (bladder neck, external sphincter, rectum, levator muscles or pelvic wall)
N	Regional lymph nodes
Nx	Regional lymph nodes cannot be assessed
N0	No regional lymph node metastasis
N1	Regional lymph node metastasis
M	Distant metastasis
Mx	Distant metastasis cannot be assessed
M0	No distant metastasis
M1	Distant metastasis
M1a	Non-regional lymph node(s)
M1b	Bone(s)
M1c	Other site(s)

Q. Are you aware of a risk stratification system for prostate cancer? What is its role?

A. The National Institute for Health and Clinical Excellence (NICE) guidelines 2008 describe a stratification system for dividing patients into three groups according to their risk of having metastatic disease – low-, intermediate- and high-risk groups (*see* Table 1.9). The patients are assigned to a group on the basis of their PSA level, Gleason score and clinical stage. Establishing the risk group for a particular patient enables you to determine the most appropriate staging investigations and treatment for that individual.

Table 1.9 Risk stratification system reproduced from NICE guidelines, 2008

Risk group	PSA level (ng/ml)	Gleason score	Clinical stage
Low	< 10	≤ 6	T1–T2a
Intermediate	10–20	7	T2b–T2c
High	> 20	8–10	T3–T4

Q. What is this patient's risk group?

A. His PSA is 11.1 ng/ml, his Gleason score is 6 and his clinical tumour stage is T2b, putting him in the intermediate-risk group.

Q. What should happen next in the management of this patient?

A. This is a newly diagnosed cancer and therefore it should be discussed at the local multi-disciplinary team (MDT) meeting with the aim of confirming the histology, determining the need for staging investigation and identifying the most appropriate treatment options.

Q. What factors need to be considered when discussing a case at the MDT meeting?

A. The factors that influence the need for staging investigations and treatment options include the following:
- disease profile (risk group):
  - baseline PSA level

- clinical 2002 TNM stage
- Gleason score
- patient profile:
  - age
  - comorbidities
  - life expectancy
  - quality of life
  - associated urinary symptoms/urological pathology.

Q. **What is a nomogram?**

A. A nomogram is a statistically derived tool or two-dimensional diagram that can be used to help to predict risk.

Q. **What are Partin tables and what is their role?**

A. Partin tables are a group of nomograms, based upon the outcomes of several thousand radical prostatectomies, which were designed to help to predict the post-operative pathological T and N stage.[23] Four clinical risks can be assessed, namely organ-confined disease, capsular penetration, seminal vesicle involvement and positive lymph nodes. These tables use three clinical variables, namely PSA level (pre-operative), Gleason score (on biopsy) and clinical T stage.

It is important to acknowledge that nomograms are only as strong as the variables that are used to calculate them. For example, Partin tables are based on radical prostatectomies where only a limited lymph node dissection (obturator fossa and external iliac vein) was performed. It has been shown that prostate cancer can metastasise outside of this area, and therefore the risk of having positive lymph nodes may in fact be higher than that calculated using Partin tables.

Q. **What staging investigations would you perform in this case and why?**

A. This is a 65-year-old man who is otherwise fit and well, and therefore curative treatment is an option. If curative treatment is being considered, the need for staging investigations must be addressed. MRI scanning in this patient is controversial. The recently published NICE prostate cancer guidelines do not require radiological T staging unless the patient is high risk and being considered for radical treatment options. In high-risk cases the presence or absence of extracapsular spread will determine whether a radical prostatectomy is a viable treatment option or whether radical radiotherapy would be more appropriate. As the PSA is less than 20 ng/ml and this patient has clinical stage T2b, Gleason 6 disease, he is intermediate risk and therefore an MRI is not required according to the NICE guidelines. (*However, one must also consult local guidelines, which may differ.*) In addition, the risk of having bone metastases is less than 2% (0.5% if the PSA is less than 10 ng/ml,[24] and therefore one would not perform a bone scan; again one must also refer to local guidelines).

Determining lymph node status is important when planning radiotherapy for potentially curative treatment of high-risk cases. Assessment is thought to be unnecessary in those patients with stage T2 disease or less, PSA < 20 ng/ml and a Gleason score of 6 or lower, as their risk of lymph node involvement is less than 10% according to Partin tables.[23] MRI or CT can be used to identify suspicious nodes over 1 cm in diameter. CT is particularly useful in high-risk patients, and for those with locally advanced tumours who are being considered for curative radiotherapy.

Q. Look at Figure 1.2. On this occasion an MRI has been performed. What does Figure 1.2 show?

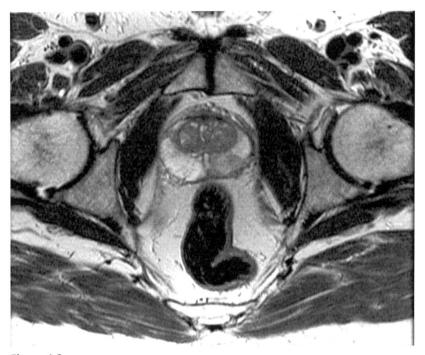

Figure 1.2

A. This MRI (T2-weighted) demonstrates a hypoechoic lesion in the peripheral zone of the left lobe causing a bulge to the capsule but no obvious capsular breach.

On MRI, T1-weighted images are best for assessing the anatomy of the prostate gland, and T2-weighted images for identifying tumours of the prostate, which appear as low-signal areas. A period of 4 weeks should be allowed before performing an MRI post biopsy, as haemorrhage can mimic a prostate tumour.

Q. Your MRI confirms an apparently localised tumour to the left lobe. What treatment options are available for this man with intermediate-risk disease?

A. The NICE 2008 recommendations for the preferred treatment of intermediate-risk disease include radical prostatectomy and conformal deep X-ray therapy (DXT) (*see* Table 1.10). Other options include watchful waiting (WW) and active surveillance. Brachytherapy may also be considered if the criteria for prostate size are met. Cryotherapy and high-intensity focused ultrasound (HIFU) are currently only recommended as part of a clinical trial (*see* Table 1.10).

Table 1.10 Treatment options as recommended by NICE guidelines according to the risk stratification group

	Low risk	Intermediate risk	High risk
Watchful waiting	Option	Option	Option
Active surveillance	Preferred	Option	Not recommended
Prostatectomy	Option	Preferred	Preferred*
Brachytherapy	Option	Option	Not recommended
Conformal DXT†	Option	Preferred	Preferred*
Cryotherapy	Not recommended‡	Not recommended‡	Not recommended‡
HIFU	Not recommended‡	Not recommended‡	Not recommended‡

*Offer if there is a realistic prospect of long-term disease control.
†Conformal DXT should be given at a minimum dose of 74 Gy (maximum of 2 Gy per fraction),
‡Unless part of a clinical trial.

Q. What is watchful waiting (WW) and why is it offered?

A. Watchful waiting is the conscious decision to avoid treatment in a patient until it is required, usually when symptoms of progressive disease develop or the PSA level rises above an arbitrary cut-off value. WW is offered to men with well-differentiated or moderately differentiated tumours who have a life expectancy of less than 10–15 years, as it has been shown that the majority of these men will die from other causes due to competing comorbidities.[25]

The indications for WW include:
- life expectancy less than 10–15 years
- low-grade cancer
- low-stage cancer
- significant comorbidities.

Q. What is active surveillance?

A. Active surveillance is a management option for men who have potentially curable prostate cancer but who wish to avoid the complications associated with intervention (*see* Table 1.11). However, the patient should be suitable for radical treatment if there is evidence of disease progression. The aim is to avoid treatment in those men with indolent cancers, by only treating those whose cancers show signs of progression. It requires regular reassessment of their risk category. It is reported that this management option may avoid radical intervention in up to 60–80% of patients.

Table 1.11 Summary of the differences between watchful waiting and active surveillance

	Watchful waiting	Active surveillance
Aim	Avoid treatment	Treat only if necessary
Protocol	Occasional PSA No biopsies	Frequent PSA Frequent biopsies
Treatment indication	Symptoms	Increase in PSA level (PSADT) Upgrading of Gleason score
Treatment timing	Late	Early
Treatment aim	Palliative	Radical

Q. What criteria are needed for active surveillance to be considered?

A. In order for active surveillance to be offered, the patient should be suitable for radical treatment if they show signs of disease progression. Therefore they need to be medically fit for radical intervention, with a life expectancy of over 10–15 years. They also need to have localised disease which is low to moderately differentiated.

The Royal Marsden criteria for active surveillance include:[26]

- age 50–80 years
- fitness for radical treatment
- PSA level of < 15 ng/ml
- stage T1–2
- Gleason score of ≤ 3+4
- < 50% positive cores.

The NICE guidelines recommend active surveillance of all men at low risk who are considered suitable for radical treatment, particularly those with features that match the Epstein 1994 criteria for 'insignificant' disease, namely T1c, Gleason score of 6, PSAD level of < 0.15 ng/ml, less than three positive cores, and no core more than 50% positive or over 10 mm.[27] A potential drawback of active surveillance is that it is a valid treatment option without long-term data. Young men with a long life expectancy may also miss the opportunity for curative intervention. Active surveillance is also advised for men with intermediate-risk disease, but it is not recommended for those at high risk. All men for whom this option is considered should have had an initial minimum of a 10-core prostate biopsy protocol.

Q. How would you follow up a patient on active surveillance?

A. One would actively monitor their PSA level. Different regimens are described, one of which is the Royal Marsden regime[26] which involves performing a PSA blood test every month for the first year, every 3 months for the second year and every 6 months thereafter. In this regime one would also arrange a repeat TRUS biopsy at 18–24 months and 2-yearly thereafter. One would not perform routine imaging unless signs of disease progression developed. This protocol is seen as the ideal, and it may not be possible to implement it in many urology departments. One of the dilemmas when offering active surveillance is the lack of consensus about the ideal follow-up regime and when to intervene.

Q. What are the indicators for disease progression on active surveillance?

A. PSADT and grade progression on repeat biopsy are the primary factors used to assess disease progression. A PSADT of less than 2 years and a re-biopsy primary Gleason grade 4 or above, or more than 50% positive cores, are the main indicators for initiating treatment.

Q. Can you quote any outcomes for active surveillance?

A. Klotz has published an update of the original Canadian active surveillance series in 2005.[28] At 8 years follow-up the overall survival was 85% and the disease-specific survival was 99%, with only two patients succumbing to prostate cancer.

This is a series of favourable-risk prostate cancer patients (stage pT1b to pT2b N0 M0, Gleason score of 7 or less and PSA level of 15 ng/ml or less). Of the total cohort, 34% of patients came off active surveillance because of rapid biochemical progression (15%), clinical progression (3%), histological progression (4%) or patient preference (12%).

Q. **The patient asks you whether there is any evidence about which treatment option is best. How will you answer this?**

A. There is only one randomised controlled trial that has assessed the role of primary therapy in prostate cancer, and this compared radical prostatectomy (RP) with watchful waiting (WW). This study was published by the Scandinavian study group, SPCG-4, initially by Holmberg in 2002[29] and most recently by Bill-Axelson in 2005.[14] It included 695 men (348 RP and 347 WW) with a mean age of 65 years with localised (T2 or less), well or moderately differentiated prostate cancer. Patients were followed up for a mean period of 8.2 years. The primary end point was death due to prostate cancer, while secondary end points included death from any cause, metastasis and disease progression. Deaths were reported in 83 patients in the RP group and 106 patients in the WW group. Prostate cancer deaths accounted for 30 (8.6%) and 50 (14.4%) of these deaths, respectively. The results demonstrated that RP provided a 44% relative risk reduction in prostate cancer death at 10 years, and an improvement in disease-specific and *overall survival* at 10 years.

This study has a number of limitations which should be acknowledged. Firstly, only 5% of the patients had T1c tumours (PSA detected), whereas 75% were T2 tumours, which is in contrast to present-day practice, where only 15% of cases are T2 tumours. The study excluded high-grade disease, and the criteria for local progression included DRE and bladder outflow symptoms requiring TURP, which itself could have resulted from BPH as opposed to prostate cancer. In addition, the pathological data were limited, so it is not known how many were up-staged secondary to positive margins. The overall number of deaths in the study was small. Finally, the cancer-specific survival was only improved in men under 65 years of age.

The Medical Research Council (MRC) previously attempted to evaluate primary treatment options by comparing RP with external beam radiation therapy (EBRT) and active surveillance in the PR06 study.[30] Unfortunately, this had to close after 2 years due to poor recruitment. PIVOT (Prostate cancer Intervention Versus Observation Trial), an American study that is comparing watchful waiting with surgery, has managed to recruit successfully, and the results are currently awaited.[31]

Q. **The patient would like to know what complications may occur if they undergo a radical prostatectomy.**

A. The complications which may occur as listed on the British Association of Urological Surgeons (BAUS) consent form are reproduced in Table 1.12. Complication rates are lower when the surgery is performed in high-volume centres.

Table 1.12 Complications of radical prostatectomy (reproduced from the BAUS consent form)

Mortality	0–1.5%
Infection	5–10%
Bleeding	5–10%
Rectal injury	5%
Impotence (and no ejaculation)	40–60%
Incontinence	50% early (5–10% long-term)
Anastomotic stricture, stenosis	10%
Anaesthetic (chest infection, deep vein thrombosis and pulmonary embolism, myocardial infarction, death)	5–10%

Q. **The patient is particularly concerned about urinary incontinence and would like to know whether there is any treatment for this.**

A. All patients should be taught to perform pelvic floor exercises before surgery. Despite this, up to 50% of patients experience mild urinary incontinence, which tends to improve over a period of 12–18 months. Approximately 5–10% of patients will have severe, long-term incontinence that requires the use of more than one pad per day. If severe incontinence persists for longer than 12 months, invasive intervention can be considered. Options include urethral bulking agents, the bulbourethral sling and the artificial urinary sphincter (AUS). The AUS, which has an 80% success rate, is currently the only option recommended by NICE.

   Bladder neck stenosis and detrusor overactivity may also present with incontinence and therefore must be excluded with a flow rate, post-micturition residual volume and urodynamics prior to intervention.

Q. **The patient, who has an active sex life, is also concerned about the risk of impotence and asks whether this risk can be reduced.**

A. This patient has palpable disease on one side and is therefore eligible for a unilateral nerve-sparing (NS) RP. He does need to be aware that there is no guarantee that the right neurovascular bundle can be preserved, and that sometimes it does have to be sacrificed to enable a curative operation to be performed. His risk of impotence with a unilateral NS procedure is approximately 50% (over 60% if bilateral). This patient can be advised to start a PDE5 inhibitor (PDE5I) at his first post-operative visit at 6 weeks, although there is some evidence to suggest that treatment is more beneficial if it is started pre-operatively. Post-operative alternatives to PDE5I include intraurethal and intracavernosal prostaglandin E1. The vacuum pump can also be considered, and recently it has been reported that its use may prevent post-operative shortening of the penis while awaiting the return of normal erectile function. Following surgery all patients should have access to a specialist clinic for follow-up of their erectile dysfunction (ED).

   Contraindications to a NS-RP include palpable disease (although the contralateral side can be spared if this is unilateral), apical tumour extension and a high-risk Gleason score of 8 or more.

Q. The patient asks about the advantages and disadvantages of having a lapa-roscopic as opposed to an open RP.

A. Both the laparoscopic and open technique for radical prostatectomy have similar oncological outcomes. The technical advantages of a laparoscopic RP include a field magnification of × 10–15, allowing for better nerve sparing and a more pre-cise anastomosis. The clinical advantages include less blood loss, early catheter removal and early continence. The disadvantage of laparoscopic RP is a longer learning curve.

Q. The patient undergoes a successful RP. Histology confirms that the cap-sule is not breached by the tumour and that the resection margins are negative. How will you follow this patient up?

A. Following discharge one would arrange for the patient to attend for a trial with-out a catheter 7–14 days following surgery. Assuming that there are no com-plications, the patient would then be reviewed in the outpatient department at 6 weeks. This visit is primarily to assess the patient's recovery, exclude early complications and discuss the histology. At this visit it is also important to ensure that the patient is performing pelvic floor exercises. A PDE5I can also be offered to begin rehabilitation of erectile function. The second review occurs 3 months post-operatively, and it is at this point that the PSA level is checked to ensure that it is undetectable. At this visit it is also important to review the degree of incontinence and impotence, in order to provide appropriate ongoing specialist care and follow-up. Assuming that the PSA level is undetectable and the patient has made a good recovery, follow-up then takes place on a 6-monthly basis with a PSA check at each visit.

Q. The patient attends their 3-month visit and asks you about their chances of survival. Can you briefly outline the 10-year survival figures for a radical prostatectomy?

A. The 10-year survival figures following a radical prostatectomy are as follows:
- PSA-free survival   65–75%
- metastasis-free survival 85–90%
- overall survival   > 95%.

The 10-year PSA progression rate following RP is approximately 30%. Of these, 80% will fail within 3 years of their RP. Without additional treatment, the aver-age time to development of clinical disease after PSA progression is 8 years.[32]

Q. Is there any role for neoadjuvant hormone treatment prior to RP for localised disease?

A. Neoadjuvant hormone treatment, which is defined as the administration of hor-mone treatment prior to definitive local curative treatment, has been shown to reduce the prostate volume and positive surgical margin rate. However, there is no evidence that it improves overall survival or disease-free survival compared with RP alone. Currently it is not recommended except as part of a clinical trial.

Q. A 73-year-old man is found to have a PSA of 15 ng/ml. His past medical history includes hypertension, atrial fibrillation and a previous TURP. His DRE reveals a 30 g suspicious-feeling prostate. He undergoes a prostate biopsy which confirms bilateral adenocarcinoma Gleason 4 + 4. A staging MRI suggests bilateral disease which is organ confined. His bone scan is negative for metastatic disease.

What treatment options would you advise for this patient?

A. This patient has high-risk disease with a Gleason score of 8. The treatment options therefore include radical radiotherapy, radical prostatectomy (if there is a realistic prospect of long-term disease control) and hormone treatment. Active surveillance and brachytherapy are not recommended for high-risk disease, whilst HIFU and cryotherapy should only be offered as part of a clinical trial.

Q. **What is radiotherapy and how does it work?**

A. Radiotherapy involves the use of ionising radiation to cause fatal damage to neoplastic cells. When X-rays are passed through proliferating tissue, a proportion of the energy is absorbed and results in DNA damage. Radiotherapy utilises high-energy photons (produced by linear accelerators) which have excellent tissue penetration. The interaction between photons (packets of energy) and outer atoms lead to the formation of free radicals (e.g. OH–). These result in DNA damage and double-strand breakage which are both irreparable. The optimisation and effects of radiation can be summarised as follows:

1. *Repair.* DNA repair occurs following the delivery of radiotherapy. Cells are more radiosensitive in the G2 or S phase of cell division. Fractionation results in more cells entering the sensitive phases of the cell cycle, as well as arresting the repair process.

2. *Reoxygenation.* Oxygen is important for free radical formation. As cells die, more oxygen becomes available for free radical formation.

3. *Reassortment.* Cells are more sensitive to radiotherapy in the G2 and S phase of the cell cycle. Damage may not be appreciable until cell division has occurred.

4. *Repopulation.* Further cell division results in tumour growth, which compromises efficacy.

Q. **What types of radiation can be used for prostate cancer?**

A. The two types of radiation therapy that are used in prostate cancer treatment are external beam radiation therapy (EBRT) and brachytherapy:

- EBRT uses a linear accelerator to produce high-energy X-rays which are directed in a beam towards the prostate. Conformal radiotherapy was introduced in the 1990s, and intensity-modulated radiotherapy (IMRT) was developed more recently. IMRT utilises computer-controlled linear accelerators to deliver precise radiation to a specified area. Like conformal radiotherapy it shapes the beam to fit the target area, but unlike conformal radiotherapy it can alter the dose depending upon the shape of the prostate. This enables the dose administered to be increased to 80 Gy within the target volume, while reducing bladder and rectal toxicity.

- Brachytherapy involves the placement of small 'seeds' containing radioactive material (such as iodine-125 or palladium-103) with multiple needles through the perineum directly into the prostate. The seeds, which eventually become inert, emit lower-energy radiation that is only capable of travelling short distances, thereby limiting damage to the bladder and rectum.

Q. What are the complications associated with external beam radiotherapy to the prostate?

A. The complications of external beam radiotherapy are listed in Table 1.13.

Table 1.13 Complications of radiotherapy to the prostate

Cystitis	20%
Haematuria	18%
Proctitis	30% (severe long-term complication in 3%)
Urethral stricture	4–8%
Urinary incontinence	1% severe long-term
Lower limb oedema	6%
Erectile dysfunction	25–60% (occurs over several years)
Secondary cancer	1 in 300 (1 in 70 in long-term survivors)

Q. Are you aware of any contraindications to EBRT to the prostate?

A. There are a number of contraindications to radiotherapy, including severe lower urinary tract symptoms, inflammatory bowel disease and previous pelvic irradiation.

Q. What is the role of neoadjuvant and adjuvant hormone treatment with EBRT in a patient with high-risk localised disease?

A. There has been a large EORTC randomised controlled trial by Bolla *et al.*[33] which clearly demonstrated a benefit of *adjuvant* hormone treatment (3 years) in terms of disease-free survival and overall survival in patients with high-risk localised and locally advanced disease (see below).

The NICE 2008 guidelines advise that *neoadjuvant* hormones should be given for 3–6 months to all patients with localised and locally advanced disease who are receiving radiotherapy. *Adjuvant* hormones are recommended for at least 2 years after radiotherapy if the Gleason score is 8 or above.

The EORTC 22863 study by Bolla *et al.*[33] addressed the role of adjuvant hormone treatment in conjunction with external beam radiotherapy. The study included 415 patients with T1–2 high-grade disease or stage T3–4 N0–N1 M0 with a median follow-up period of 4.5 years. Patients were randomised to 3 years of hormone ablation with EBRT (195 patients) versus EBRT alone (190 patients). The disease-free survival (DFS) figures for those with and without adjuvant treatment were 74% and 40%, respectively, and the overall survival (OS) figures were 78% and 62%, respectively. This demonstrated that an LHRH analogue given during and for 3 years after EBRT improves both DFS and OS.

Q. The patient undergoes radiotherapy without any significant complications. How will you monitor this patient in clinic and how do you define treatment failure?

A. After their initial follow-up has been completed, the patient would be seen in the outpatient department every 4–6 months to assess their symptoms and monitor their PSA level. There are two main definitions of PSA recurrence following radiotherapy. The American Society of Therapeutic Radiation Oncologists

(ASTRO) 1996 definition[34] is three consecutive PSA increases measured 4 months apart. Time to recurrence is midway through the three PSA measurements. Recently, the RTOG-ASTRO Consensus Conference[35] created a new definition, with failure being an increase in PSA level of 2 ng/ml above the post-treatment PSA nadir (lowest value).

Q. **What treatment options are available if the patient does develop disease recurrence after radiation therapy?**

A. Hormone therapy is the mainstay of treatment, although local salvage is an option in the absence of metastatic disease. The patient must understand the significant additional complications associated with salvage RP, which is also technically demanding. Cryotherapy is also an option, as is HIFU, although these techniques are still regarded as experimental.

Local failure after radiation therapy is confirmed by a positive prostate biopsy and negative imaging studies. However, this is only necessary if salvage prostatectomy is being considered.

Q. **A 70-year-old man with a PSA of 13 ng/ml is diagnosed with adenocarcinoma of the prostate, with a Gleason score of 4 + 5. He has undergone a previous TURP and suffers from chronic obstructive pulmonary disease (COPD). Staging MRI confirms localised disease. The patient has a friend who has undergone brachytherapy, and he would like to know whether this is an option for him.**

A. Brachytherapy is not an option for this patient due to his previous TURP and high-risk disease. The contraindications to brachytherapy include the following:
- life expectancy less than 5 years
- coagulation disorder
- previous pelvic irradiation
- Gleason grade 5 disease
- previous TURP (high risk of incontinence)
- large prostate (> 50 cm³) or large median lobe (difficult seed implantation) (LHRH agonists can be used to decrease prostate volume)
- moderate to severe LUTS (risk of retention and worsening LUTS).

Q. **Which patients would be suitable for brachytherapy?**

A. The NICE guidelines advise that brachytherapy is an option for patients with low- and intermediate-risk disease:
- stage T2c or less
- Gleason score of 7 or less
- PSA level of 20 ng/ml or less.

Q. **If the patient had been a suitable candidate for brachytherapy, what complications would they need to be warned about?**

A. The complications associated with brachytherapy include the following:
- development of irritative voiding symptoms
- urinary incontinence (particularly if the patient requires TURP following brachytherapy for urine retention)
- acute urinary retention
- erectile dysfunction (in 50% of patients over several years)

- perineal haematoma
- proctitis (usually mild).

Q. **What do you understand by the term PSA 'bounce'?**

A. PSA 'bounce' refers to the benign rise in the PSA level that occurs after its initial fall following radiotherapy (this can occur with either EBRT or brachytherapy). However, the level should remain below 1.5 ng/ml. The mean time to a PSA bounce is approximately 9 months. It can be seen in up to 30% of patients after brachytherapy, but tends to occur later following this treatment, often in the second year following therapy.

Q. **The patient has also read an article in the newspaper about high-intensity focused ultrasound (HIFU). He would like to know whether this treatment is available.**

A. NICE does not currently recommend HIFU as a treatment option for localised prostate cancer unless it is being performed as part of a clinical trial. HIFU treatment uses focused ultrasound waves (emitted from a rectal transducer) to cause coagulative necrosis through both mechanical and thermal effects. HIFU requires general or spinal anaesthesia and can be time-consuming.

LOCALLY ADVANCED PROSTATE CANCER

Q. **A fit and well 68-year-old man is referred to your clinic with an elevated PSA of 14.3 ng/ml. Examination reveals a nodule in the left lobe of the prostate. A TRUS biopsy is performed and confirms Gleason 3 + 4 disease in the left lobe. An MRI scan raises the possibility of a capsular breach on the left side. What treatment options are available for this patient?**

A. This is an intermediate-risk patient with possible high-risk disease, given the potential capsular extension. The preferred treatment options for intermediate-risk disease are conformal EBRT and RP. For high-risk disease these options are only recommended if there is considered to be a good chance of cure. In this otherwise fit and well patient an RP is an option, but the risk of residual disease must be carefully explained. Alternative non-curative options include watchful waiting and hormone treatment if the patient cannot accept the side-effects associated with curative treatment.

Q. **The patient elects to undergo an RP despite the potential risk of residual disease. Histology confirms a capsular breach on the left with a positive resection margin but negative lymph nodes. You see the patient in the out-patient department at 6 weeks and explain the histology result. He wants to know his risk of developing tumour recurrence.**

A. Studies have shown that 30–60% of patients with T3 disease will develop bio-chemical progression at 5 years.[36]

Q. **The patient is concerned about the possible risk of residual cancer, and asks whether there is any further treatment that can be given.**

A. The adjuvant treatment options available to the patient following RP include adjuvant radiotherapy and adjuvant hormone treatment. Adjuvant hormone therapy following an RP for localised disease has not been shown to be of additional benefit.[37] The role of adjuvant radiotherapy is less clear. In particular it is not known whether immediate radiotherapy is more beneficial than delayed radiotherapy when PSA relapse occurs. Currently one would follow the NICE guidelines and advise close PSA surveillance every 3 months, offering radiotherapy if the PSA relapses, ideally before it reaches 1 ng/ml.

The only randomised controlled trial that has been conducted to assess the role of immediate postoperative radiotherapy in positive surgical margins and T3 disease is the EORTC 22911 study by Bolla et al.[38] This assessed immediate postoperative EBRT (502 patients) compared with delayed EBRT at the time of biochemical progression (503 patients) in those with pT3N0M0 disease but with one or more risk factors suggesting stage T3. The study found that immediate EBRT was well tolerated and that it improves biological free survival at 5 years from 51.8% to 72.2%. However, there was no evidence that it improves overall survival, and therefore its role remains controversial.

The EAU guidelines advise that those patients with stage T2/T3 disease with positive margins or capsular breach can be offered immediate EBRT or clinical monitoring and salvage EBRT when the PSA is > 0.5 ng/ml but < 1 ng/ml. In contrast, the NICE 2008 guidelines do not recommend immediate radiotherapy for margin positive disease after RP, favouring PSA surveillance and salvage radiotherapy on relapse. The role of adjuvant radiotherapy may be clarified when the results of the RADICALS (Radiotherapy and Androgen Deprivation In Combination After Local Surgery) study are available. This randomised controlled trial is assessing adjuvant vs. salvage EBRT after RP with or without adjuvant short- and long-term hormones.[39]

Adjuvant androgen deprivation therapy (ADT) has been assessed in the Early Prostate Cancer (EPC) studies by McLeod et al.[40] The EPC programme consists of three randomised controlled trials involving 23 countries and 8113 patients. The studies evaluate the efficacy and tolerability of high-dose bicalutamide (150 mg/day) vs. placebo given in addition to standard care (RP, EBRT, AS). For localised disease, no benefit to progression-free survival (PFS) was achieved by adding bicalutamide to standard care, although there was a trend towards decreased survival in patients otherwise undergoing watchful waiting. In those with locally advanced disease there was a significantly improved PFS for those given EBRT, and a trend for those treated with watchful waiting ($P = 0.06$), but it was not significant for those who underwent an RP.

Q. **The patient was reviewed in the outpatient department at 3 months and his PSA was < 0.1 ng/ml. He was kept under regular surveillance over the next 3 years and his PSA remained < 0.1 ng/ml. When he attends your outpatient department you find that his latest PSA has increased to 0.3 ng/ml. What do you tell the patient and how would you manage this?**

A. This PSA level indicates PSA recurrence. There are a number of definitions of PSA recurrence following an RP, but a widely accepted definition is a PSA above 0.2 ng/ml. One would therefore explain to the patient that this is likely to indicate residual local disease, following which potential treatment options would be discussed. If they wish to try to cure the cancer, salvage radiotherapy is an option, assuming that there are no contraindications. An alternative technique, although it is still under investigation, is cryotherapy. If the patient wishes to avoid the complications of radical treatment, androgen deprivation treatment (ADT) can be given. ADT is best given early in the presence of systemic relapse, as it has been shown to decrease the frequency of clinical metastases.[41] With localised recurrence, delaying ADT until the development of clinically evident metastatic disease is more appropriate, as the median time for the development of metastasis is 8 years and the median time from metastasis to death is a further 5 years.[32]

Q. **A fit and well 71-year-old man is referred to your clinic with an elevated PSA of 19.1 ng/ml and an abnormal DRE. TRUS biopsy confirms Gleason 4 + 4 disease. An MRI reveals capsular breach bilaterally and invasion of the left seminal vesicle. What treatment options are available for this patient?**

A. This man has locally advanced high-risk disease. Curative treatment can be attempted with the use of conformal EBRT, but RP is contraindicated in the presence of seminal vesicle invasion. Alternative options include hormone treatment and watchful waiting.

Q. **What is the role of adjuvant hormone therapy if this patient elects to undergo radiotherapy?**

A. In the EORTC 22863 study, Bolla *et al.* clearly demonstrated the benefit of 3 years of adjuvant hormone treatment following radiotherapy for high-risk localised and locally advanced disease.[33]

An unresolved issue regarding adjuvant hormone therapy in conjunction with radiotherapy is whether radiotherapy provides any additional benefit to the hormone treatment. This question is being addressed by the MRC PRO7 trial, which is investigating whether the addition of EBRT (66 Gy) to ADT improves survival in patients with high-risk, localised and locally advanced disease (cT2 N0/NX M0 PSA > 40 or cT2 N0/NX M0 PSA > 20 + Gleason sum score ≥ 8 or T3/T4 N0/NX M0). The study has now closed and the results are awaited.

Q. **A 70-year-old man who had radiotherapy for G3pT1 bladder cancer 2 years ago was found to have an elevated PSA of 24 ng/ml and clinically T3 prostate cancer. The biopsy confirms Gleason 3 + 4 disease, and his MRI scan demonstrates capsular penetration and seminal vesicle invasion bilaterally. His bone scan is negative. What treatment options are available to him?**

A. This man has locally advanced disease, which is not curable with RP. Conformal radiotherapy is also not an option, given his previous pelvic irradiation. The treatment options therefore include hormone treatment or watchful waiting.

Q. **What is androgen deprivation therapy and how does it work?**

A. ADT refers to any treatment that lowers androgen activity. Prostate cells are physiologically dependent on androgens which stimulate growth and proliferation. Testosterone, although not tumorigenic, is essential for the growth and perpetuation of tumour cells. When androgen deprivation occurs, androgen-sensitive prostate cancer cells undergo apoptosis.

Q. Can you briefly outline the physiology behind androgen secretion?

A. Approximately 90–95% of androgens are produced by the Leydig cells of the testes, with only 5–10% being derived from the adrenal cortex. Testosterone secretion is regulated by the hypothalamic–pituitary–gonadal axis as shown in Figure 1.3.

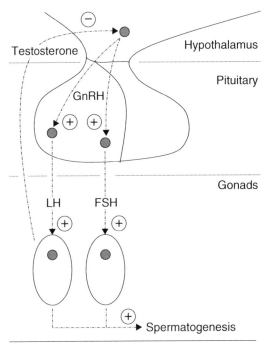

Figure 1.3 Hypothalamic–pituitary–gonadal axis.

The hypothalamic gonadotropin-releasing hormone (GnRH) stimulates the anterior pituitary gland to release luteinising hormone (LH) and follicle-stimulating hormone (FSH). LH stimulates the Leydig cells of the testes to secrete testosterone. Within prostate cells, testosterone is converted by the enzyme 5-alpha-reductase into dihydrotestosterone (DHT), which is approximately 10 times more biologically active. Once bound to the androgen receptor in the cytoplasm, the androgen-receptor complex enters the nucleus, where it interacts with DNA to influence cell growth and division. Peripheral aromatisation of testosterone into oestrogens, together with circulating androgens, exerts negative feedback control on hypothalamic LH secretion.

Q. What are the different mechanisms used to induce androgen deprivation and what hormone treatment options are available for each of them?

A. Androgen deprivation can be induced by suppressing the secretion of testicular androgens, either medically or surgically, or by inhibiting their action at the androgen receptor using anti-androgens. Some, including oestrogen and steroidal anti-androgens, have more than one mechanism of action. These actions are summarised in Table 1.14.

Both surgical and medical forms of castration have equivalent efficacy.

Table 1.14 The actions of hormonal manipulation in prostate cancer

Reduced androgen production	
Surgical castration	Removes Leydig cells
Medical castration	Reduces LH production
• LHRH agonists	Down-regulate pituitary GnRH receptors
• LHRH antagonists	Inhibit GnRH receptor
Blocks androgen effect	
Non-steroidal anti-androgens (e.g. bicalutamide, flutamide)	Block androgen at receptor level
Combined effect	
Oestrogen	Down-regulates LHRH secretion Inactivates androgen Suppresses Leydig cells
Steroidal anti-androgens (e.g. cyproterone acetate)	Down-regulate LHRH secretion Block androgen at receptor level

Q. **What are LHRH agonists and how do they work?**

A. LHRH agonists are long-acting synthetic analogues of GnRH. Chronic exposure to LHRH agonists eventually results in down-regulation of GnRH-receptors, with subsequent suppression of pituitary LH and FSH secretion and testosterone production. The level of testosterone decreases to castrate levels, usually within 2 to 4 weeks. Two examples of LHRH agonists are goserelin and leuprorelin. They are delivered as depot injections on a 1- or 3-monthly basis.

Over 70–80% of patients will respond to ADT. However, the development of androgen independence is inevitable, with a mean time to disease progression of 14–36 months after commencement of treatment.

Q. **What are the side-effects of LHRH agonists?**

A. Typical side-effects of LHRH agonists include the following:
- flushing (vasomotor) (occurs in 80% of patients)
- erectile dysfunction
- osteoporosis
- hyperlipidaemia
- gynaecomastia
- cognitive decline
- diabetes
- anaemia
- loss of muscle mass
- reduced quality of life.

Q. **What are the two types of anti-androgens and how do they differ?**

A. The two classes of anti-androgens are steroidal (cyproterone acetate) and non-steroidal (bicalutamide, flutamide). Non-steroidal anti-androgens act purely as competitors of androgens at the receptor level, enabling the testosterone level to be maintained or increased. Steroidal anti-androgens also compete at the receptor level, but have additional progesterogenic activity which causes central inhibition of LH secretion by the pituitary gland and hence a reduced testosterone level.

Q. **The patient denies any urinary symptoms and has a good quality of life. He asks you whether there are any benefits to starting the hormone treatment early.**

A. Hormone treatment tends to be reserved for patients with symptomatic metastatic disease. One argument against early hormones is their associated side-effects, particularly in patients who are clearly asymptomatic from their disease. However, studies have suggested that in locally advanced and metastatic disease, early hormone treatment results in slower disease progression and reduced disease morbidity. These issues therefore need to be discussed with the patient and the risk–benefit ratio assessed for each individual.

Q. **The patient enjoys an active sex life and asks whether there is any treatment that can be given which does not interfere with his sex life?**

A. In those men who wish to avoid erectile dysfunction and reduced libido, bicalutamide 150 mg od has been shown to be an alternative to LHRH agonists, although its equivalence has not been proven.[40]

Q. **The patient is commenced on bicalutamide treatment and his PSA falls to less than 0.1 ng/ml. He returns to your clinic 6 months later distressed about the painful breast swellings that he has developed. He would like to know whether anything can be done about this.**

A. Around 75–80% of patients develop gynaecomastia when taking non-steroidal anti-androgens, and 50% develop pain. The condition occurs as a result of the peripheral aromatisation of testosterone to oestradiol. Prevention of gynaecomastia can be achieved with radiotherapy (8–10 Gy to each breast), but such treatment does not prevent pain or tenderness. An alternative is tamoxifen 20 mg od, particularly if there is no response to RT. However, once gynaecomastia has already developed, or in the presence of severe pain, the most effective treatment is a bilateral mastectomy.

Q. **The patient has a successful bilateral mastectomy. When he returns to your clinic 18 months later, his PSA has increased on several occasions and is currently 1.2 ng/ml. What do you do now?**

A. The patient has developed androgen-independent disease. Having been on anti-androgens alone, the patient would require the addition of an LHRH agonist and his bicalutamide would have to be reduced to 50 mg daily.

Q. **What is the aim of maximum androgen blockade (MAB)?**

A. MAB aims to inhibit all androgen stimulation by suppressing the production of androgens by the testes and also inhibiting the action of androgens from the adrenal glands at the androgen receptor level.

Q. **What is the role of intermittent hormone treatment?**

A. Intermittent ADT is becoming an increasingly popular way of treating patients with localised disease, particularly those patients who wish to limit the side-effects of treatment.

    The primary aim of intermittent ADT is to delay the development of an androgen-independent state. Androgen independence may begin early after the initiation of hormonal treatment, due to the arrest of androgen-induced differentiation of the prostatic epithelium. If ADT is stopped prior to the progression of androgen-independent cells, any subsequent tumour growth may remain androgen dependent, so will potentially be susceptible once again to androgen withdrawal. Although superiority over continuous ADT has not been demonstrated, it does have three clinical benefits, namely reduced side-effects during the off-therapy periods, decreased bone loss and reduced cost. However, side-effects may be slow to resolve after stopping treatment, as the serum testosterone level can take up to 9 months to recover.

Q. **A 76-year-old man who underwent radiotherapy for Gleason 4 + 3, T2/3 disease has developed PSA recurrence 2 years after completing his 3 years of adjuvant hormone treatment. His PSA is currently 2.7 ng/ml, and PSADT is 2.5 years. The patient has read about cryotherapy in the newspapers, and asks whether this treatment would be an option for him.**

A. Cryotherapy has been shown to have a role in salvage therapy for organ-confined prostate cancer. In this case the time to PSA recurrence and the PSADT suggest localised disease and, assuming that this is confirmed on re-staging scans, cyrotherapy is an option for this patient.

Cryotherapy is one of two minimally invasive treatment options, the other being HIFU. Both techniques have been proposed as treatment options for localised prostate cancer, although current NICE guidelines only recommend their use in this group as part of a clinical trial. Both also have a potential role in salvage therapy for organ-confined recurrent disease following radical radiotherapy.

Q. **What does the technique of cryotherapy involve?**

A. Cryotherapy involves the insertion of trans-perineal ultrasound-guided cryoprobes which are used to deliver argon or liquid nitrogen at temperatures between –20 and –40° Celsius. Two freeze–thaw cycles are administered, resulting in cellular necrosis. The diameter of the ice ball is monitored on ultrasound. A urethral warming catheter and thermosensors are used during the procedure to protect the urethra, external sphincter and rectal wall.

Q. **What is the mechanism of cell death during cryotherapy?**

A. The two freeze–thaw cycles result in:
- cellular dehydration and protein denaturation
- direct rupture of cellular membranes by ice crystal formation
- vascular stasis and microthrombi resulting in ischaemia and coagulative necrosis.

The complications of cryotherapy include erectile dysfunction, incontinence, urinary symptoms/urethral sloughing/urinary retention, pelvic pain, transient perineal numbness and recto-urethral fistula. All of these complications are more common in the salvage setting.

METASTATIC AND HORMONE-REFRACTORY PROSTATE CANCER

Q. **A 75-year-old man is referred to your clinic with an elevated PSA of 62 ng/ml and an abnormal DRE. TRUS biopsy confirms Gleason 4 + 4 disease. Figure 1.4 illustrates an investigation that this patient subsequently underwent. What investigation does Figure 1.4 show and what does it demonstrate?**

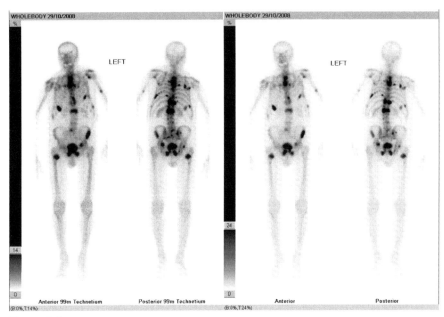

Figure 1.4

A. Figure 1.4 shows a radionuclide whole body isotope bone scan. It demonstrates several scattered hot spots within the ribs, thoracic spine, iliac bone and proximal long bones which, given the patient's history, are consistent with bone metastases.

Q. The patient asks what treatment options are available.

A. The mainstay of treatment for metastatic prostate cancer is ADT, i.e. medical castration (with anti-androgens or LHRH analogues) or surgical castration (bilateral subcapsular orchidectomy). In advanced disease this should be commenced at the time of diagnosis rather than at the time of symptomatic progression, as it has been shown to reduce both disease progression and its complications.[41] Clinical disease progression after androgen deprivation will tend to occur after a median interval of about 12–18 months. Contemporary practice will result in this time being considerably longer, but data are awaited.

Q. What is tumour flare and how would you prevent it?

A. When first administered, LHRH agonists stimulate the pituitary LHRH receptors, resulting in a transient increase in LH and FSH release. Consequently, testosterone levels are temporarily increased, and this is referred to as a testosterone 'surge' or 'flare.' The flare occurs within 2 or 3 days after the first injection, and continues for approximately 1 week. It can have severe consequences, such as spinal cord compression or acute urinary retention.

Q. Who is at risk of tumour flare and what are its consequences?

A. Patients at risk of clinical flare are those with high-volume, symptomatic, bone disease, which accounts for only 4–10% of metastatic patients. The typical consequences include spinal cord compression, fatal cardiovascular events due to hypercoagulation, ureteric obstruction, acute bladder outlet obstruction and increased bone pain.

Q. **How can tumour flare be prevented?**

A. Concomitant therapy with an anti-androgen, commencing on the same day or preferably a week before the first depot injection of LHRH agonist and continuing for 2 weeks following it, can prevent tumour flare by blocking the androgen receptor. An alternative option in patients at high risk is to use LHRH *antagonists*, although this has been associated with significant side-effects resulting from histamine release. Surgical castration (subcapsular orchidectomy) has the advantage that no concomitant therapy is required (i.e. there is no tumour flare with surgical castration), and is extremely effective in rapidly reducing circulating testosterone levels, which is useful in emergency situations.

Q. **The patient would like to know about his prognosis.**

A. With asymptomatic disease the average survival is 2–3 years, which decreases to 12 months with symptomatic disease. The overall 5-year survival rate for a patient with metastatic disease is approximately 25%. However, these figures are historical, and with contemporary interventions patients are clearly living longer.

Q. **The patient responds to ADT initially, but 22 months later his PSA starts to increase. His latest PSA is 54 ng/ml, and he is now complaining of severe pain in his ribs. What options are available for the management of bone pain secondary to metastases?**

A. In addition to analgesia, alternative options include:
- radiotherapy, which is particularly useful when the pain is localised
- radioisotopes (e.g. strontium-89), which are useful for widespread disease
- bisphosphonates (e.g. zoledronic acid), which can both reduce pain and decrease the incidence and time to skeletal-related complications
- oestrogens/steroids.

Bisphosphonates act by inhibiting osteoclast-mediated bone resorption. Saad *et al.* studied the role of bisphosphonates in 643 men with hormone-resistant prostate cancer and bone metastases.[42] The men were randomised to receive either zoledronic acid for 15 consecutive months or placebo. At 15 months and 24 months follow-up, there was a significant reduction in skeletal-related events in the zoledronic-acid-treated group compared with the placebo group (33% vs. 44%), as well as a significant reduction in the frequency of pathological fractures (13.1% vs. 22.1%). Furthermore, zoledronic acid significantly prolonged the time to first skeletal-related event.

Q. **A 70-year-old man is diagnosed with Gleason 3 + 4 disease (PSA 12 ng/ml). His bone scan is negative, and the MRI suggests possible capsular breach on the left. The patient elects to undergo an RP. The histology report shows a positive margin in the left lobe with one positive obturator lymph node. What management options are available for this patient?**

A. This patient has lymph-node-positive disease, and therefore the treatment options include early hormone therapy or delayed hormone therapy when he develops clinically symptomatic disease.

   Messing *et al.* assessed the use of immediate hormonal therapy compared with observation after radical prostatectomy in 98 men with node-positive prostate cancer.[43] The men were randomly assigned to receive immediate ADT, with either goserelin or bilateral orchidectomy, or to be followed until disease progression. After a median follow-up of 7.1 years, 7 of 47 men who received immediate ADT had died, compared with 18 of 51 men in the observation group. Prostate cancer was the cause of death in 3 men in the immediate-treatment group and in 16 men in the observation group. At the time of the last follow-up, 36 men in the immediate-treatment group (77%) and 9 men in the observation group (18%) were alive and had no evidence of recurrent disease. The authors concluded that immediate ADT after radical prostatectomy with positive lymph node disease improves survival and reduces the risk of recurrence in patients with node-positive prostate cancer. With the use of supersensitive PSA, an argument could be made for observation followed by the introduction of delayed ADT when progression occurs, in order to limit the side-effects of treatment.

Q. **What are the complications associated with metastatic prostate cancer?**
A. The common complications include:
- spinal cord compression
- ureteric obstruction/renal failure
- sepsis
- hypercalcaemia
- anaemia
- hepatotoxicity
- skeletal fractures
- urinary retention.

Q. **An 82-year-old man is admitted as an emergency, complaining of increasing lethargy and difficulty passing urine. Abdominal examination confirms an enlarged palpable bladder. DRE reveals a non-tender, malignant-feeling prostate, cT3/4. What is your diagnosis?**
A. This patient has chronic urinary retention, which is likely to be due to prostate cancer. The history of lethargy raises concerns that he may have also developed renal failure.

Q. **After completing a basic assessment, you insert a urinary catheter and 1.5 litres of urine are drained. The patient's renal function results are as follows: urea 18.1 mmol/l; creatinine, 364 μmol/l; potassium, 5.2 mmol/l. Six months ago his renal function was normal. What is the diagnosis and how will you manage this patient now?**
A. This patient has acute renal failure which may be secondary to high-pressure chronic urinary retention or ureteric obstruction. Given his large residual and renal impairment, he is at risk of a post-obstructive diuresis, and therefore his urine output should be monitored every hour, and 4-hourly observations should be performed, including blood pressure measurements to assess for postural hypotension. His weight and renal function should also be checked on a daily basis. An ultrasound scan of his renal tract will confirm the presence of hydronephrosis and exclude any other renal pathology. In order to confirm the diagnosis of prostate cancer, he needs to have his PSA repeated (it may be artificially elevated secondary to retention), and a biopsy should be performed. If the PSA

is very high (> 100 ng/nl) a biopsy may not be necessary, and a bone scan can be requested instead.

If the patient's renal function does not return to normal and the hydronephrosis persists despite catheter insertion, ureteric obstruction must be considered and percutaneous nephrostomy tubes should be inserted.

Q. **A 78-year-old man on ADT for metastatic prostate cancer who has been complaining of back pain for the last 2 months is admitted to the A&E department with a sudden exacerbation of his pain, 'off legs' and difficulty in passing urine. What is the likely diagnosis and how will you confirm this?**

A. The likely diagnosis is spinal cord compression. A thorough history and clinical examination need to be performed to assess for signs of cord compression and determine its level. The diagnosis is confirmed with an urgent MRI.

Q. **What investigation does Figure 1.5 show and what does it demonstrate?**

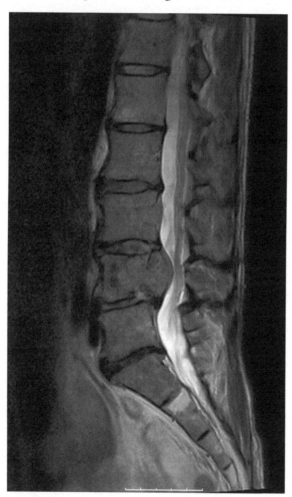

Figure 1.5

A. Figure 1.5 shows an MRI of the spine. It demonstrates compression of the spinal cord at the level of L5. In fact, spinal cord compression most commonly occurs in the thoracic or upper lumbar regions of the spine. It is due either to vertebral collapse secondary to tumour invasion, or to extradural tumour growth. Symptoms include radicular pain and peripheral neurological symptoms such as motor and/or sensory loss, including urinary retention.

Q. How would you manage spinal cord compression?

A. Spinal cord compression is an acute surgical emergency. Steroid treatment should be administered immediately, followed by definitive treatment with either radiotherapy or surgical decompression, depending upon the patient and the nature of the cord compression. ADT should also be started on an urgent basis with anti-androgen cover to prevent tumour flare.

Q. What is the role of chemotherapy in androgen-independent prostate cancer?

A. Systemic chemotherapy is indicated in men with androgen-independent prostate cancer with proven metastatic disease. It is contraindicated in patients with significant renal, haematological or bone disease and poor performance status. Docetaxel-based regimens have been shown to give a median survival advantage of 2–3 months.[44] What is not clear is when to initiate cytotoxic treatment. The EAU guidelines currently recommend that at least two consecutive increases in PSA should have occurred, with the level exceeding 5 ng/ml.

REFERENCES

1. Oesterling JE *et al.* Serum prostate-specific antigen in a community-based population of healthy men. Establishment of age-specific reference ranges. *JAMA* 1993; **270:** 860–64.
2. Sun L *et al.* Prostate-specific antigen (PSA) and PSA velocity for prostate cancer detection in men aged < 50 years. *BJU Int* 2007; **99:** 753–7.
3. Catalona WJ *et al.* Comparison of digital rectal examination and serum prostate-specific antigen in the early detection of prostate cancer: results of a multicenter clinical trial of 6,630 men. *J Urol* 1994; **151:** 1283–90.
4. Thompson IM *et al.* Prevalence of prostate cancer among men with a prostate-specific antigen level < or =4.0ng per milliliter. *NEJM* 2004; **350:** 2239–46.
5. Gerstenbluth RE *et al.* The accuracy of the increased prostate-specific antigen level (greater than or equal to 20 ng/ml) in predicting prostate cancer: is biopsy always required? *J Urol* 2002; **168:** 1990–93.
6. Carter HB *et al.* Longitudinal evaluation of prostate-specific antigen levels in men with and without prostate disease. *JAMA* 1992; **267:** 2215–20.
7. Trapasso JG *et al.* The incidence and significance of detectable levels of serum prostate-specific antigen after radical prostatectomy. *J Urol* 1994; **152:** 1821–5.
8. Benson MC *et al.* Prostate-specific antigen density: a means of distinguishing benign prostatic hypertrophy and prostate cancer. *J Urol* 1992; **147:** 815–16.
9. Djavan B *et al.* Prostate-specific antigen density of the transition zone for early detection of prostate cancer. *J Urol* 1998; **160:** 411–18.
10. Lee R *et al.* A meta-analysis of the performance characteristics of the free prostate-specific antigen test. *Urology* 2006; **67:** 762–8.

11. Doherty AP *et al*. Undetectable ultrasensitive PSA after radical prostatectomy for prostate cancer predicts relapse-free survival. *Br J Cancer* 2000; **83**: 1432–6.

12. Internal Medicine Clinic Research Consortium. Effect of digital rectal examination on serum prostate-specific antigen in a primary care setting. *Arch Intern Med* 1995; **155**: 389–92.

13. Hessels D *et al*. DD3(PCA3)-based molecular urine analysis for the diagnosis of prostate cancer. *Eur Urol* 2003; **44**: 8–15.

14. Bill-Axelson A *et al*. Radical prostatectomy versus watchful waiting in early prostate cancer. *NEJM* 2005; **352**: 1977–84.

15. Stanford JL *et al*. Urinary and sexual function after radical prostatectomy for clinically localized prostate cancer: the Prostate Cancer Outcomes Study. *JAMA* 2000; **283**: 354–60.

16. Thompson IM *et al*. The influence of finasteride on the development of prostate cancer. *NEJM* 2003; **349**: 215–24.

17. Grover S *et al*. Do the benefits of finasteride outweigh the risks in the prostate cancer prevention trial? *J Urol* 2006; **175**: 934–8.

18. Andriole G *et al*. Chemoprevention of prostate cancer in men at high risk: rationale and design of the reduction by dutasteride of prostate cancer events (REDUCE) trial. *J Urol* 2004; **172**: 1314–17.

19. Pareek G *et al*. Periprostatic nerve blockade for transrectal ultrasound-guided biopsy of the prostate: a randomized, double-blind, placebo-controlled study. *J Urol* 2001; **166**: 894–7.

20. Djavan B *et al*. Prospective evaluation of prostate cancer detected on biopsies 1, 2, 3 and 4: when should we stop? *J Urol* 2001; **166**: 1679–83.

21. Ben Shlomo Y *et al*. The risk of prostate cancer amongst black men in the United Kingdom: the PROCESS cohort study. *Eur Urol* 2008; **53**: 99–105.

22. Gleason DF *et al*. Prediction of prognosis for prostatic adenocarcinoma by combined histological grading and clinical staging. *J Urol* 1974; **111**: 58–64.

23. Partin AW *et al*. Combination of prostate-specific antigen, clinical stage, and Gleason score to predict pathological stage of localized prostate cancer. A multi-institutional update. *JAMA* 1997; **277**: 1445–51.

24. Oesterling JE *et al*. The use of prostate-specific antigen in staging patients with newly diagnosed prostate cancer. *JAMA* 1993; **269**: 57–60.

25. Albertsen PC *et al*. Competing risk analysis of men aged 55 to 74 years at diagnosis managed conservatively for clinically localized prostate cancer. *JAMA* 1998; **280**: 975–80.

26. van As NJ *et al*. Active surveillance with selective radical treatment for localized prostate cancer. *Cancer J* 2007; **13**: 289–94.

27. Epstein JI *et al*. Pathologic and clinical findings to predict tumor extent of nonpalpable (stage T1c) prostate cancer. *JAMA* 1994; **271**: 368–74.

28. Klotz L. Active surveillance with selective delayed intervention is the way to manage 'good-risk' prostate cancer. *Nat Clin Pract Urol* 2005; **2**: 136–42.

29. Holmberg L *et al*. A randomized trial comparing radical prostatectomy with watchful waiting in early prostate cancer. *NEJM* 2002; **347**: 781–9.

30. MRC PR06 collaborators. Early closure of a randomized controlled trial of three treatment approaches to early localised prostate cancer: the MRC PR06 trial. *BJU Int* 2004; **94**: 1400–1.

31. Wilt TJ *et al*. The Prostate Cancer Intervention Versus Observation Trial: a randomized trial comparing radical prostatectomy versus expectant management for the treatment of clinically localized prostate cancer. *J Urol* 1994; **152**: 1910–14.

32. Pound CR *et al*. Natural history of progression after PSA elevation following radical prostatectomy. *JAMA* 1999; **281**: 1591–7.

33. Bolla M *et al*. Long-term results with immediate androgen suppression and external irradiation in patients with locally advanced prostate cancer (an EORTC study): a phase III randomised trial. *Lancet* 2002; **360**: 103–6.

34. Shipley WU. PSA following irradiation for prostate cancer: the upcoming ASTRO symposium. *Int J Radiat Oncol Biol Phys* 1996; **35**: 1115.

35. Roach M III *et al*. Defining biochemical failure following radiotherapy with or without hormonal therapy in men with clinically localized prostate cancer: recommendations of the RTOG-ASTRO Phoenix Consensus Conference. *Int J Radiat Oncol Biol Phys* 2006; **65**: 965–74.

36. Heidenreich A *et al*. EAU guidelines on prostate cancer. *Eur Urol* 2008; **53**: 68–80.

37. Sternberg CN. Apples and oranges. Re: 7.4-year update of the ongoing bicalutamide Early Prostate Cancer (EPC) trial programme. *BJU Int* 2006; **97**: 435–8.

38. Bolla M *et al*. Postoperative radiotherapy after radical prostatectomy: a randomised controlled trial (EORTC trial 22911). *Lancet* 2005; **366**: 572–8.

39. Parker C *et al*. Radiotherapy and androgen deprivation in combination after local surgery (RADICALS): a new Medical Research Council/National Cancer Institute of Canada phase III trial of adjuvant treatment after radical prostatectomy. *BJU Int* 2007; **99**: 1376–9.

40. McLeod DG *et al*. Bicalutamide 150 mg plus standard care vs standard care alone for early prostate cancer. *BJU Int* 2006; **97**: 247–54.

41. Medical Research Council Prostate Cancer Working Party Investigators Group. Immediate versus deferred treatment for advanced prostatic cancer: initial results of the Medical Research Council Trial. *Br J Urol* 1997; **79**: 235–46.

42. Saad F *et al*. Long-term efficacy of zoledronic acid for the prevention of skeletal complications in patients with metastatic hormone-refractory prostate cancer. *J Natl Cancer Inst* 2004; **96**: 879–82.

43. Messing EM *et al*. Immediate hormonal therapy compared with observation after radical prostatectomy and pelvic lymphadenectomy in men with node-positive prostate cancer. *NEJM* 1999; **341**: 1781–8.

44. Tannock IF *et al*. Docetaxel plus prednisone or mitoxantrone plus prednisone for advanced prostate cancer. *NEJM* 2004; **351**: 1502–12.

Chapter 2
Testicular cancer

Farooq A Khan and David E Neal

CLINICAL ASSESSMENT OF TESTICULAR SWELLINGS, IMAGING AND STAGING

Q. A 26-year-old previously healthy man is referred to the urology clinic on the 2-week wait pro forma with a right-sided testicular mass. How would you assess this patient in clinic?

A. I would take a pertinent history and perform a physical examination with specific reference to the following points:

History related to the mass

- Duration of symptoms.
- Painful or painless mass.
- Change in size of mass.
- Any previous history of surgery on the genitalia.
- Sexual history: recent sexual contact or penile discharge.
- Associated urinary symptoms.
- Trauma (does not cause testicular cancer, but may be the cause of the testicular swelling).

Previous relevant history and risk factors

- *History of cryptorchidism* (on either side) increases the risk of testicular cancer in the undescended testicle by 4–13 times, [1] with 7–10% of testicular tumours arising in an undescended testis.[2] There still remains a 5–10% risk of developing testicular cancer in the contralateral testis in those with a history of cryptorchidism.[3,4]
- *Family history of testicular cancer*, especially in fathers and brothers, increases the risk by 6 and 8 times, respectively, with 1.35% of cases providing a positive family history.[5,6]
- *Racial origin* – testicular cancer is three times more common in Caucasians and in Northern Europe, with the highest incidence in Scandinavia (11 per 100 000 men in Norway and Denmark). In the UK, the incidence is 7.1 per 100 000 men.
- *Maternal oestrogen exposure* – fetal exposure to diethylstilboestrol increases the risk of testicular cancer in the male offspring (relative risk is 2.8–5.3%). This is a difficult history to elicit.[4]

- *History of subfertility* and poor semen analysis increases the risk of testicular cancer in some studies by 1.6 times, and from the SEER (Surveillance, Epidemiology and End Results) database by 20 times.
- *Contralateral history of testicular tumour* – there remains a 5–10% risk of testis cancer in the remaining testicle.
- *HIV* is associated with an increased risk of seminoma. The cause is unknown.

Q. **What features are of particular interest on physical examination?**

A. I would perform a general examination to include palpation of the supraclavicular nodes, chest examination and an abdominal examination to palpate for a retroperitoneal nodal mass and to ensure there are no inguinal scars from childhood orchidopexy that the patient has failed to mention. I would complete my examination by examining the testicle for the mass, its size and whether it is painful or painless. I would also examine the contralateral testicle.

The presence of pain does not unequivocally discriminate infection from a neoplastic process, as 10% of men who present with a painful testicle that clinically resembles epididymo-orchitis have a testicular tumour, and up to 20% can present with testicular pain as their first symptom.[1]

Q. **The patient's right testicle has a hard, irregular and painless mass arising from the upper pole. What would you do?**

A. I would arrange an urgent scrotal ultrasound scan, and in our department we would walk the patient to the radiology department for this the same day (using a minimum of a 7.5 MHz transducer).

Q. **The ultrasound scan shows the following image (Figure 2.1)? What do you see and how would you describe this?**

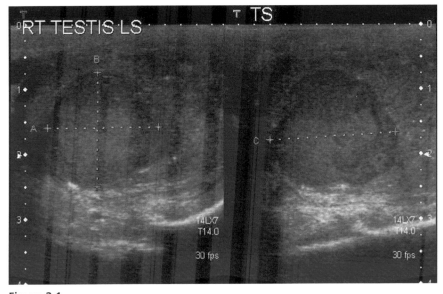

Figure 2.1

A.   Figure 2.1 shows a heterogenous, irregular mass in the upper pole of the right testis. Radiologically this is a testicular tumour.

Q.   **Are there any other investigations that you would like to do in clinic?**
A.   I would organise a blood test to check the tumour markers, namely α-fetoprotein (AFP) (half-life 5 days), β-human chorionic gonadotrophin (βhCG) (half-life 36 hours) and lactate dehydrogenase (LDH), and arrange a chest X-ray in clinic to look for pulmonary metastases. (Note that the presence of widespread testicular metastases on chest X-ray is an oncological emergency, and the patient must be referred urgently to an oncologist. Immediate chemotherapy may be necessary prior to radical inguinal orchidectomy in these cases.)

Q.   **Do all patients have raised tumour markers at presentation?**
A.   No. Across the board, 51% of all testicular tumours will have raised tumour markers. This varies according to the type of tumour present. For germ-cell tumours, 5–10% of pure seminomas will have a raised βhCG level (produced by syncytiotrophoblast elements). Pure seminomas do not secrete AFP.

For non-seminomatous germ-cell tumours (NSGCT), elevated tumour markers can be found in up to 90% of cases, with 50–70% having a raised AFP (produced by yolk sac elements) and around 40% having a raised βhCG level. All choriocarcinomas and 40–60% of embryonal carcinoma have elevated βhCG levels.

Q.   **What is the role of tumour markers in this case?**
A.   The role is both diagnostic and prognostic. Measurement of tumour markers following orchidectomy and their half-life decline is useful when assessing the likelihood of retroperitoneal and metastatic disease. Given the half-life of the markers, we would expect the βhCG level to halve every 36 hours and the AFP level to halve every 5 days.

The presence of normal markers prior to orchidectomy does not exclude metastatic disease, and equally normalisation of markers post-orchidectomy does not necessarily indicate the absence of distant disease.

Q.   **What is the significance of measuring LDH?**
A.   This is useful for determining tumour burden, and is a surrogate marker for tumour volume and cell necrosis. This is usually helpful for seminomas and to the oncologist as a measure of tumour response. LDH levels are raised in approximately 10% of seminomas.

Q.   **Are there any other conditions apart from testicular cancer in which the above tumour markers may be raised?**
A.   Yes. Other malignancies can raise the βhCG level, such as pancreatic, liver, stomach, lung, breast, kidney and bladder cancers, and, strangely, it may be raised in marijuana smokers. AFP levels can be raised in patients with liver, pancreas, stomach and lung malignancies and with benign liver dysfunction. In addition, raised levels of luteinising hormone in hypo-gonadotrophic patients may cross-react with some radioimmunoassay techniques for βhCG, resulting in spuriously high results.

Q. **Is there any other pre-operative imaging that you might wish to undertake, in addition to an ultrasound scan and a chest X-ray?**

A. No, not pre-operatively.

Post-operatively, once the germ-cell tumour has been confirmed, a staging CT of the abdomen/pelvis is performed, and in the case of NSGCT a chest CT is undertaken. A chest CT is not mandatory for stage I seminoma, according to European Association of Urology (EAU) guidelines published in 2008, but practically all men with germ-cell tumours undergo a staging CT of the chest, abdomen and pelvis while awaiting histological confirmation.

There is no role for the routine use of pre-operative magnetic resonance imaging (MRI) or positron emission tomography (PET), as these do not alter the initial treatment plan. They may have a role in select cases in assessing the retroperitoneal nodes – in the case of MRI in patients with a contrast allergy that prevents the use of CT, or in the case of PET in assessing whether a residual retroperitoneal mass after chemotherapy (in seminomas) can be safely watched, or whether it requires active treatment.

Q. **What would you do with this young man?**

A. I would arrange for an urgent radical inguinal orchidectomy (generally within 1 week) and assess whether a contralateral testis biopsy is required at the same time.

Q. **How would you perform a radical inguinal orchidectomy?**

A. The tumour-bearing testicle is removed through an inguinal incision, along with the epididymis and spermatic coverings and cord. Prior to manipulation of the testis the cord is isolated and clamped to allow control of the draining lymphatics, in order to minimise tumour spill and metastatic release into the lymphatics towards the landing retroperitoneal nodes. The tumour-bearing testicle and cord are mobilised to the deep inguinal ring, and the cord is transected and secured with one heavy tie (0 or 1 vicryl) and an additional transfixation suture. Some authors suggest that a prolene suture should be used at the cut end of the cord to act as a marker for possible future nodal dissection.

I would warn the patient about the common complications of bleeding, infection and specifically loss of sensation on the inner thigh and ipsilateral scrotal wall or chronic groin pain as a consequence of damage to the ilio-inguinal nerve.

Q. **Is there anything else that you would offer the patient or consider prior to inguinal orchidectomy?**

A. I would offer him the opportunity to firstly bank his sperm and secondly to consider the insertion of a testicular prosthesis. The EAU recommends cryopreservation of sperm prior to orchidectomy. However, sometimes it is not possible for adequate specimens to be banked and therefore banking happens after orchidectomy in most units. If there is a history of sub-fertility or a small contralateral testicle, and fertility is an issue for the patient, banking sperm prior to orchidectomy is advisable. I would offer the patient a prosthesis at the same sitting, but caution should be advised with regard to those who are likely to need early post-operative chemotherapy (pulmonary metastases, markedly raised markers), because prosthesis-related infection (which occurs in 0.6–2% of cases)[7] may delay this. Some oncologists would therefore prefer not to offer a prosthesis in this setting, but at a later date instead.

Q. **How does a patient bank sperm? Are there any issues that the patient needs to be aware of?**

A. The patient is asked to attend a designated fertility clinic to provide three semen samples with a 2- to 3-day period of abstinence. A brief assessment of sperm quality is undertaken microscopically, and the sample is then frozen in liquid nitrogen at –196°C. The patient should be made aware of the following as part of the consent process for banking sperm:

- The quality of sperm is not guaranteed if and when it is thawed.
- Illness prior to or at the time of banking sperm may affect the quality of the sperm. If chemotherapy is planned, sperm banking can still be done in the first week or so following its initiation, as sperm produced prior to the start of chemotherapy will still be healthy and usable.
- There is some evidence that the quality of semen in men with germ-cell tumours is poor compared with that of similarly matched healthy males, and assisted conception techniques may be required.[8]
- The maximum storage period is 10 years (up to 55 years of age).
- The Human Fertilisation and Embryology Authority (HFEA) requires all men who bank sperm to be screened for HIV and for hepatitis B and C prior to transfer of the sperm to a long-term storage facility. Men with HIV can bank sperm in separate storage vessels.
- At present the cost of initial consultations, blood tests and storage for the first year is met by the NHS. Discussions for further funding are currently under way, but for most centres this is approximately £200 per year of storage, which at present is met by the patient.
- The patient may need to travel some distance to the nearest facility to be able to bank sperm.

Q. **The patient decides that he wishes to have a testicular prosthesis. What complications should you warn him about with regard to prosthesis insertion?**

A. Based on a review of 2500 prostheses for a variety of indications,[7] the complications include the following:

- extrusion from the scrotum (3–8%)
- scrotal contraction and migration (3–5%)
- chronic pain (1–3%)
- haematoma (0.3–3%)
- infection (0.6–2%).

Q. **You mentioned a little earlier that you would consider a contralateral testis biopsy. How would you decide this for individual patients?**

A. The purpose of a contralateral biopsy is to identify the presence of carcinoma *in situ* or intratubular germ-cell neoplasia (ITGCN), the risk of which is around 5–9% of patients with testicular cancer. The EAU recommends that men under the age of 40 years with a contralateral testis volume of < 12 ml (for which the relative risk of developing ITGCN is 3.78) have a 34% risk of ITGCN on biopsy.[9] Contralateral testicular biopsy should also be considered in men with a history of undescended testis (normal volume testis) and subfertility, as these conditions are associated with ITGCN.[9,10]

Q. **How would you biopsy the contralateral side?**

A. The testicle is delivered through a scrotal incision and the tunica vaginalis is opened. Small incisions in the tunica albuginea at each pole (5 mm) are made with a scalpel, allowing extrusion of the seminiferous tubules. These are then cut with a pair of scissors or taken flush to the albuginea with a scalpel and placed into Bouin's solution (not formalin). Using a double-biopsy open technique (i.e. biopsies from each pole), it can be anticipated that 99% of ITGCN will be identified.[11]

There is evidence that using a biopsy gun and Tru-Cut needle (with the testis delivered through a scrotal incision) provides the same quality of biopsy and detection rate for a diagnosis of ITGCN as an open technique.

Q. **Are there any occasions when an immediate orchidectomy is not undertaken?**

A. Yes. In rare cases patients may present with extensive life-threatening metastatic disease (e.g. respiratory compromise from widespread metastases, severe back pain from retroperitoneal disease). In such cases an immediate orchidectomy is not required, but urgent chemotherapy under the care of an oncologist is needed. A later orchidectomy may be required, which may reveal the original tumour or often a residual scar in the testis.

In men who have no obvious testicular tumour, but have widespread disease of unknown origin, the diagnosis of a germ-cell tumour should be considered, and raised tumour markers can be diagnostic. As it will be some time before the results of marker estimation become available, a urine pregnancy test can be considered to confirm the presence of urinary βhCG, which would be an indication that the widespread metastatic disease is in fact a germ-cell tumour. Initial chemotherapy can then be given without delay.

Q. **You perform the radical inguinal orchidectomy and your patient goes home the same day. What information do you want your pathologist to give you about the orchidectomy specimen?**

A. Macroscopically we want to know the size of the testicle and tumour and any macroscopic invasion of the epididymis, tunica vaginalis and cord structures.

Microscopically we would want to know the following:
- histological type of tumour (germ-cell tumour, sex cord tumours)
- size
- multiplicity
- rete testis involvement
- pathological stage
- presence of ITGCN
- presence of microvascular invasion.

If there is a seminoma, it is important to determine whether there are any non-seminomatous elements, which would then dictate how the patient is managed in the long term.

Specifically, seminoma tumour size greater than 4 cm and rete testis invasion have been shown to be important prognostic factors for relapse for stage I disease.

For NSGCT, the presence of vascular and lymphatic invasion, the percentage of embryonal carcinoma (> 50%) and the proliferation rate (> 70%) predict metastatic disease.

Note should be made of the pathological classification of testicular tumours, which divides tumours into those of germ-cell origin (subdivided into those with one histological type and those with more than one histological type) and the less common sex cord and paratesticular tumours (*see* Table 2.1).

Table 2.1 Pathological classification of testicular tumours and comparison of the World Health Organization (WHO) and British Testicular Tumour Panel and Registry (BTTP&R) pathological classifications of testicular germ-cell tumours

WHO	BTTP&R
Germ-cell tumours	*Germ-cell tumours*
Seminoma	Seminoma
Spermatocytic seminoma	Spermatocytic seminoma
Non-seminomatous germ-cell tumour	Teratoma
1. Mature teratoma	1. Malignant teratoma differentiated (MTD)
2. Embryonal carcinoma with teratoma (teratocarcinoma)	2. Malignant teratoma intermediate (MTI)
	3. Malignant teratoma undifferentiated (MTU)
3. Embryonal carcinoma	4. Yolk sac tumour
4. Yolk sac tumour	5. Malignant teratoma trophoblastic (MTT)
5. Choriocarcinoma	
Sex cord stromal tumours	
Leydig cell tumour	
Sertoli cell tumour	
Granulosa cell tumour	
Mixed	
Unclassified	
Mixed germ cell/sex cord stromal tumours	
Other tumours	
Adenocarcinoma of rete testis	
Lymphoma	
Metastatic	

Q. **Microscopically the specimen appears as shown in Figure 2.2. Can you describe the likely histological diagnosis?**

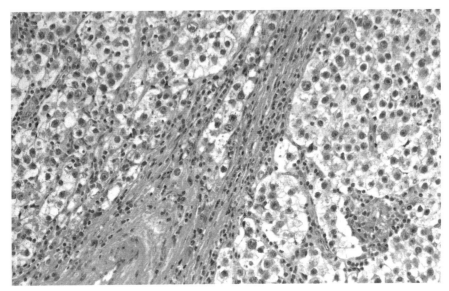

Figure 2.2

A. In Figure 2.2 there are islands and sheets of large cells with clear cytoplasm and densely stained nuclei of varying sizes with prominent nucleoli, consistent with the appearance of a seminoma. In addition, there are fibrous glands traversing the tumour and an associated lymphocytic infiltrate, which are also characteristic of a seminoma.

Q. The pathologist agrees with you and reports that the specimen is a seminoma. What would you do now?

A. I would complete the staging of the patient by means of a contrast abdominal and chest CT. In our department, all patients with seminoma undergo this investigation along with NSGCTs. I am aware that the EAU guidelines do not mandate the chest CT in this setting, but in our department and most units, all testicular tumour patients undergo both abdominal and chest CT while awaiting histological confirmation of the tumour.

In addition, if there had been any elevated tumour markers pre-operatively I would repeat these and document the post-operative tumour marker kinetics.

SUMMARY AND KEY FACTS
- When asked 'how you would assess a patient', always start with a history and examination, and specifically tell them what things you want to know in the history (i.e. risk factors for testicular cancer).
- Ultrasound scanning has almost 100% sensitivity for testicular tumour detection. MRI is just as good, but is expensive and therefore not cost-effective.
- Tumour markers: overall 51% of new testicular tumours have raised markers.
- AFP is made by yolk sac elements and its level is not raised with seminoma.
- βhCG levels are raised in all choriocarcinomas but in only around 10% of seminomas. βhCG is produced by the giant syncytiotrophoblastic cells.
- AFP has a half-life of 3–5 days. βhCG has a half-life of 36 hours.

- EAU recommendations for staging CT for germ-cell tumours are as follows: chest X-ray and abdominal/pelvic CT for seminoma; chest, abdominal and pelvic CT for NSGCTs.
- Always offer the patient the opportunity to bank sperm prior to orchidectomy, especially if there is a history of subfertility or a small contralateral testis and the patient wishes to maintain fertility.
- The EAU guidelines for contralateral testis biopsy are as follows:
  - < 40 years of age
  - testicular volume < 12 ml
  - consider in men with a history of undescended testis and subfertility.
- Contralateral biopsy technique – open two-pole technique will detect 99% of ITGCN.
- Pathological prognostic factors for relapsing disease are as follows:
  - *seminoma*: rete testis invasion, tumour size > 4 cm
  - *NSGCTs*: microvascular/lymphatic invasion, embryonal cancer content > 50%, proliferation rate > 70%.

INTRATUBULAR GERM-CELL NEOPLASIA (ITGCN) AND MICROLITHIASIS

Q. **What do you understand by the term testicular intra-epithelial neoplasia (TIN) or intratubular germ-cell neoplasia (ITGCN)?**

A. Intratubular germ-cell neoplasia (ITGCN) is a pre-invasive testicular germ-cell lesion also known as carcinoma *in situ*. It is believed to be the precursor of all germ-cell tumours except spermatocytic seminoma.

Q. **Why is ITGCN important?**

A. Its presence denotes that there is a 50% probability of progression to germ-cell tumours over a 5-year period, and a cumulative probability of 70% of developing cancer at 7 years.[12]

Q. **Pathologically how would you describe ITGCN? (Figure 2.3)**

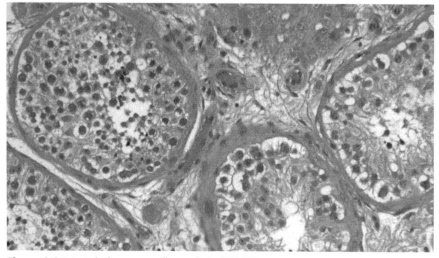

Figure 2.3 Intratubular germ-cell neoplasia (ITGCN).

A. Histologically, ITGCN is characterised by malignant germ cells lining seminiferous tubules containing Sertoli cells in a single row with nuclear pleomorphism with an intact basement membrane. The tubules are usually of smaller diameter than normal, with thickened walls, and show decreased or absent spermatogenesis. The atypical cells are usually aligned along the basement membrane and are similar in appearance to seminoma tumour cells, having clear cytoplasm and large round or irregular nuclei, with prominent nucleoli.

Q. **How often do we see ITGCN in testicular tumours? Are there any other conditions associated with this condition?**

A. ITGCN is present in the contralateral testis in around 5–9% of patients. This figure rises to 34% in those under 40 years of age and with testicular volumes of less than 12 ml – hence the recommended criteria for contralateral testis biopsy in this group of patients.[9] The presence of ITGCN in the tumour-bearing testicle has no bearing on the overall prognosis. In the general population the overall incidence is around 0.8%.

Other risk factors for the development of ITGCN are:
* cryptorchidism (3%)
* extra-gonadal germ-cell tumour (40%)
* 45XO karyotype
* subfertility (0.4–1.1%).

Q. **Does ITGCN raise tumour markers?**

A. No.

Q. **What would you tell the patient who has had an orchidectomy with ITGCN in the contralateral testis?**

A. I would tell him that there is a 50% risk of progression to invasive germ-cell tumour over the following 5 years.

Q. **The patient asks you what can be done about this.**

A. This poses a difficult problem. The options for the patient are surveillance, treatment by radiotherapy, or orchidectomy, rendering the patient anorchic and reliant on testosterone replacement.

The case should be discussed with the patient. For those men who have not completed their family it is entirely reasonable to encourage them to do so naturally or by assisted conception techniques, if they wish, with a close surveillance programme. This will require regular physical self-examinations and an annual ultrasound scan of the testis.

Radiation treatment consists of a total dose of 20 Gy delivered at single 2 Gy doses over 5 days per week. This dose seems to be adequate to eliminate all foci of ITGCN, but possibly at the cost of losing Leydig cell function, necessitating regular follow-up serum testosterone levels. There is evidence that a smaller dose of 16 Gy is not sufficient to completely eradicate ITGCN.[13]

Undertaking an orchidectomy for ITGCN requires long-term testosterone replacement therapy and loss of fertility.

Q. **Is there any role for chemotherapy in patients with ITGCN?**

A. The answer to the question 'Will chemotherapy eradicate ITGCN in some patients?' is yes, but we would not use it routinely unless otherwise indicated.

Two-thirds of patients with ITGCN who need post-orchidectomy chemotherapy will have their ITGCN eradicated on follow-up biopsy. Any follow-up biopsy should be performed no earlier than 2 years after the completion of chemotherapy in order to minimise the risk of missing the ITGCN. If the biopsies show persistent ITGCN, the above options can still be used, although the likelihood of developing hypogonadism is increased with radiation therapy at this stage.

Q. **A young patient is referred by his GP with a testicular ultrasound scan showing widespread testicular microlithiasis. What is microlithiasis?**

A. Microlithiasis is the presence of widespread calcifications throughout the testicular parenchyma. Strictly it is defined as the presence of more than 5 calcifications per image field on ultrasound scan, with each calcification being less than 2 mm in diameter, with no change in testicular shape or volume.[14] Its incidence in the population is 2–6%.

Q. **Is microlithiasis important? What would you tell the patient?**

A. We now believe that microlithiasis is not as important as it was once thought to be. The finding of microlithiasis in association with in some cases up to 74% of testicular cancer, led to the belief that this might be a premalignant marker lesion and in some way involved in the development of testicular cancer. It is now clear that the rate of testicular cancer in patients with microlithiasis on long-term follow-up is no different to the rate of developing testicular cancer in the general population,[15] and for this reason we would not follow up such patients in the urology clinic. Advice is given about self-examination and that there is early referral of any palpable abnormality, rather than the annual testicular ultrasound scan that was until recently the norm in many departments.

Q. **Is this advice true across the board for all patients?**

A. Yes, although there is a suggestion that the risk of testicular cancer should be stratified according to risk factors that the patient may have and the initial reason for the ultrasound scan.

Q. **How would you stratify this risk?**

A. For those without any risk factors for testicular cancer, advice on self-examination by the patient is given without urology follow-up. For those with risk factors, an annual ultrasound scan is reasonable, along with self-examination and possibly review with a urologist.[16]

Q. **What do you do in your department with a patient with microlithiasis?**

A. We advise and educate patients to self-examine, and we do not undertake regular follow-up, but will provide ultrasound testing for those patients who seek the additional reassurance that this may provide, especially those who in the past may have been told that regular follow-up was recommended.

STAGING AND TREATMENT: CLINICAL STAGE I, II AND ADVANCED SEMINOMA

Q. **What do you understand by the term 'staging' and why is it important in testicular cancer? What imaging modalities do we commonly use to stage testicular cancer?**

A. Staging is a process by which clinically, radiologically and pathologically the extent of the disease is defined in order to prognosticate for relapse and survival for the patient, and the need for additional treatments.

The mainstay of radiological staging is abdominal CT to assess retro-peritoneal nodes, and chest CT to assess the lungs and mediastinum. The EAU recommends that chest CT is not mandatory for a seminoma although it is for NSGCTs. Occasionally there can be a role in special select cases for MRI (in those with a contrast allergy, for whom a CT cannot be used) and PET scanning (in re-staging residual masses following chemotherapy, specifically in seminoma). CT scans of the head for brain metastases and liver imaging are used where clinically indicated.

Q. **What staging systems do you know for testis cancer?**

A. There are clinical and pathological staging systems. We use primarily the American Joint Committee on Cancer (AJCC) staging classification of TNM and serum markers (*see* Table 2.2).

The AJCC TNM stage grouping classification of testicular germ-cell tumours (*see* Table 2.3) is similar to the Royal Marsden Staging System (*see* Table 2.4). Stage I disease is that confined to the testis, stage II disease has varying degrees of retroperitoneal nodal involvement depending on size (stage IIA, B and C), and stage III disease indicates supra-diaphragmatic and visceral metastatic disease with varying degrees of raised tumour markers. The use of tumour markers in the TNM staging is unique to testis cancer.

Other staging systems include the Boden–Gibbs classification and the previously mentioned Royal Marsden Staging System, which are similar to the AJCC TNM stage grouping classification.

Table 2.2 TNM classification of testicular cancer

pT	*Primary tumour*	
	pTX	Primary tumour cannot be assessed (see note 1, T-primary tumour)
	pT0	No evidence of primary tumour (e.g. histological scar in testis)
	pTis	Intratubular germ-cell neoplasia (carcinoma *in situ*)
	pT1	Tumour limited to testis and epididymis without vascular/lymphatic invasion; tumour may invade tunica albuginea but not tunica vaginalis
	pT2	Tumour limited to testis and epididymis with vascular/lymphatic invasion, or tumour extending through tunica albuginea with involvement of tunica vaginalis
	pT3	Tumour invades spermatic cord with or without vascular/lymphatic invasion
	pT4	Tumour invades scrotum with or without vascular/lymphatic invasion
	Note 1: Except for pTis and pT4 where radical orchidectomy is not always necessary for classification purposes.	
N	*Regional lymph nodes clinical*	
	NX	Regional lymph nodes cannot be assessed
	N0	No regional lymph node metastasis
	N1	Metastasis in a lymph node mass 2 cm or less in greatest dimension or multiple lymph nodes, none more than 2 cm in greatest dimension
	N2	Metastasis in a lymph node mass more than 2 cm but not more than 5 cm in greatest dimension or multiple lymph nodes, any one mass more than 2 cm but not more than 5 cm in greatest dimension
	N3	Metastasis in a lymph node mass more than 5 cm in greatest dimension

pN	Pathological			
	pNX	Regional lymph nodes cannot be assessed		
	pN0	No regional lymph node metastasis		
	pN1	Metastasis in a lymph node mass 2 cm or less in greatest dimension and 5 or fewer positive nodes, none more than 2 cm in greatest dimension		
	pN2	Metastasis with a lymph node mass more than 2 cm but not more than 5 cm in greatest dimension; or more than 5 nodes positive, none more than 5 cm; or evidence of extranodal extension of tumour		
	pN3	Metastasis in a lymph node mass more than 5 cm in greatest dimension		
M	Distant metastasis			
	MX	Distant metastasis cannot be assessed		
	M0	No distant metastasis		
	M1	Distant metastasis		
	M1a	Non-regional lymph node(s) or lung		
	M1b	Other sites		
S	Serum tumour markers			
	SX	Serum tumour markers not available or not performed		
	S0	Serum marker study levels within normal limits		
		LDH (U/l)	*hCG (mU/ml)*	*AFP (ng/ml)*
	S1	< 1.5 x N and	<5000 and	< 1000
	S2	< 1.5–10 x N or	5000–50 000 or	1000–10 000
	S3	> 10 x N or	> 50 000 or	>10 000

N indicates the upper limit of normal for the LDH assay.
LDH, lactate dehydrogenase; hCG, human chorionic gonadotrophin; AFP, alpha-fetoprotein.

Table 2.3 AJCC stage groupings for testicular tumours

Stage	TNM classification
Stage I	pT1–4, N0, M0, SX
Stage II	Any pT/Tx, N1–3, M0, SX
IIA	Any pT/Tx, N1, M0, SX
IIB	Any pT/Tx, N1, M0, S1
IIC	Any pT/Tx, N2, M0, S0
	Any pT/Tx, N2, M0, S1
	Any pT/Tx, N3, M0, S0
	Any pT/Tx, N3, M0, S1
Stage III	Any pT/Tx, any N, M1, SX
IIIA	Any pT/Tx, any N1, M1a, S0
IIIB	Any pT/Tx, any N1, M1a, S1
IIIC	Any pT/Tx, N1–3, M1a, S0
	Any pT/Tx, any N, M1a, S2
	Any pT/Tx, N1–3, M0, S3
	Any pT/Tx, any N, M1a, S3
	Any pT/Tx, any N, M1b, any S

Table 2.4 Comparison of several staging systems for testicular cancer

Royal Marsden system	TNM system	Description
I	Tx, N0, M0	Disease confined to testis and peritesticular tissue

continued

Table 2.4 *continued*

II	Tx, N1 or N2a, M0	Fewer than six positive lymph nodes without
A < 2 cm	Tx, N2b,M0	extension into retroperitoneal fat; no node >
B 2–5 cm	Tx, N3, M0	2 cm (infradiaphragmatic)
C > 5–10 cm		Six or more positive lymph nodes, well-
D > 10 cm		encapsulated and/or retroperitoneal fat
		extension; any node > 2 cm
		Any node > 5 cm
III	Tx, Nx, M1	Supradiaphragmatic and infradiaphragmatic lymphadenopathy (no extralymphatic metastasis)
IV		Disseminated disease (lungs, liver, bone)

Q. **A patient has an orchidectomy, and histologically this is a seminoma that is confined to the testicle. His chest X-ray and abdominal/pelvic CT are normal and he has normal tumour markers. What stage of disease does he have?**

A. This is clinical stage I disease. Stage I is disease confined to the testicle and surrounding structures without nodal spread or metastatic deposits (T1–4, N0, M0).

Stage I disease can be subdivided further into IA, where the T stage is T1 (confined to testis with no involvement of tunica vaginalis and no vascular invasion), stage IB (where the tumour stage is T2–T4 but there are normal markers) and stage IS (where any T stage is accompanied by elevated serum tumour markers).

Q. **Does this man require follow-up and, if so, by whom?**

A. Such patients are normally followed up by the oncologist. The purpose of follow-up is to detect distant disease relapse, especially in the retroperitoneum, and to initiate early treatment.

For clinical stage I seminoma, around 15–20% of men have subclinical metastatic disease, usually in the retroperitoneum, and will subsequently relapse after orchidectomy alone.[17] To minimise this rate of relapse, an informed discussion with the patient about the need for adjuvant treatment is undertaken that reduces this risk, balanced with the risks of treatment.

Q. **What options does this young man have for clinical stage I seminoma following radical inguinal orchidectomy?**

A. The options are surveillance, single-dose adjuvant chemotherapy (carboplatin) following orchidectomy, or adjuvant radiotherapy to the retroperitoneum.

Q. **This man is interested in surveillance, given that you have indicated to him that he has an approximately 80–85% chance of being cured by orchidectomy alone. What would you tell him in view of the above information about surveillance?**

A. I would tell him that patients who choose surveillance have an 80–85% cure rate with orchidectomy alone, but will need close regular follow-up (with which they must be compliant) to look for relapse. If relapse were to occur, it can be treated with adjuvant treatment, resulting in an overall cancer-specific survival rate of 97–100%. Given that around 16% of cases will relapse[18] over a 5-year follow-up period, an intensive programme of clinic visits and imaging of the ret-roperitoneum by undertaking biannual CT scans for the first 2 years along with 6-monthly chest X-ray, physical examination and tumour marker assessment is required. Patients have to be committed to this extensive surveillance approach.

In addition to the above, I would warn this patient that although the majority of relapses occur in the first few years of follow-up, around 20% of late relapses occur after 4 years,[17] and therefore there is a necessity for prolonged follow-up, which in some cases can be lifelong, with the attendant anxiety and psychologi-cal stress that this may generate in some patients. Any relapse following a period of observation requires a more intensive treatment schedule of radiotherapy or chemotherapy.

Q. **Are there any prognostic factors that you are aware of for clinical stage I seminoma that may guide you in counselling this patient?**

A. Yes. Data from a retrospective meta-analysis of surveillance studies suggests that tumour size (> 4 cm) and invasion of the rete testis represent a group of men that are at higher risk for future relapse for stage I seminoma. Together, the presence of both these factors can represent a relapse rate of 32%, compared with 16% for the presence of one risk factor, and 12% when both of these risk factors are absent.[19] For this reason the notion of a risk-adapted approach has developed, whereby patients at higher risk of failure are encouraged to undergo adjuvant therapy, and those at lower risk can safely choose surveillance as a reasonable option in the first instance. Early data for this risk-adapted approach suggests that it can safely be used in this setting.

Q. **What other options are available to this patient?**

A. For stage I seminoma, he can consider adjuvant radiotherapy or chemotherapy. Radiotherapy and chemotherapy are equally effective and reduce the risk of relapse in the retroperitoneum to 3–4% (compared with the 15–20% risk with surveillance alone).

Radiotherapy is administered in a 'hockey-stick' fashion to the para-aortic field and ipsilateral iliac nodes to a total dose of 20 Gy over a 2-week period. Chemotherapy consists of a single dose of carboplatin (EORTC trial AUC 7, MRC trial TE 19). After a 4-year follow-up period both have been shown to be equally effective.[20]

Q. **What do the oncologists in your unit now generally advise?**

A. Given the equal efficacy of single-dose chemotherapy (i.e. one cycle of carbo-platin) and radiotherapy, there is a general trend towards offering the former as the preferred adjuvant modality due to its ease of administration, shorter time to delivery, and to avoid the recognised late secondary pelvic malignancy rate associated with the use of radiotherapy (albeit small and unquantified).

Q. **This patient decides to have adjuvant chemotherapy. How would you then follow him up?**

A. I would arrange 3-monthly clinic appointments in order to perform a physical examination, tumour markers and organise biannual chest X-rays and CT scans for the first 2 years, eventually stretching out at year 5 to annual assessments.

The follow-up regime is more intensive in the first 2 years, as this is the time when relapses are more likely to occur.

Q. **Why do you think that follow-up needs to be extended in such cases?**

A. Although most disease relapse occurs within the first few years, with seminoma there remains a 20% risk of relapse after 4 years, with some cases presenting after 10 years, therefore some clinicians would advocate a lifelong follow-up schedule.

Q. **Suppose that following his staging investigations, this patient presented with a CT like that shown in Figure 2.4. What does this indicate?**

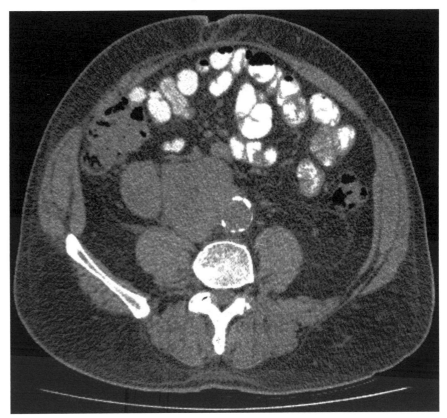

Figure 2.4

A. The unenhanced axial abdominal CT scan in Figure 2.4 shows the presence of enlarged retroperitoneal nodes encasing the inferior vena cava, which is highly suggestive of metastatic disease in the retroperitoneum. This indicates that the patient has stage II disease or nodal metastatic disease.

In general, metastatic disease can be classified into low-volume metastatic disease, which includes stages IIA and IIB (stage II disease which can be divided into A (< 2 cm nodal mass) and B (2–5 cm nodal mass)) and advanced metastatic disease, which encompasses stage IIC (nodal mass > 5 cm) and stage III disease (supradiaphragmatic or visceral metastases).

Q. **How would you manage this patient?**

A. The mainstay of treatment for seminoma in this group (stage IIA/B) is 3 cycles of BEP (bleomycin, etoposide and cisplatin) chemotherapy or 4 cycles of EP (etoposide and cisplatin) for those in whom bleomycin should be avoided (i.e. age > 40 years, and smokers). However, there are some centres that would still offer radiotherapy (30–36 Gy) – although this is not commonly practised in the UK it is popular in European centres, especially for stage IIA disease (EAU guidelines published in 2008).

Treatment of metastatic germ-cell tumours is based on the prognostic groups defined by the International Germ Cell Cancer Consensus Group (IGCCCG), which has validated a model for germ-cell tumours that divides patients into good, intermediate and poor prognostic groups based on histology, location of primary tumour, location of metastases and post-orchidectomy tumour marker levels (*see* Table 2.5). Treatment and specifically chemotherapy is tailored according to this classification, allowing high cure rates with minimal toxicity for the good prognostic group, while more aggressive chemotherapy is reserved for the poor prognostic group.

Table 2.5 The International Germ Cell Cancer Collaborative Group (IGCCCG) prognostically based staging system for metastatic seminoma

Good prognosis group	
(90% of cases)	*All of the following criteria*
5-year PFS 82%	Any primary site
5-year survival 86%	No non-pulmonary visceral metastases
	Normal AFP
	Any hCG
	Any LDH
Intermediate prognosis group	
(10% of cases)	*Any of the following criteria*
5-year PFS 67%	Any primary site
5-year survival 72%	Non-pulmonary visceral metastases
	Normal AFP
	Any hCG
	Any LDH
Seminoma	
No patients classified as poor prognosis	

PFS, progression-free survival.

Q. **Following from the above, the patient has induction chemotherapy and undergoes a follow-up CT scan 3 months later, which shows the persistence of a retroperitoneal mass. What would you do now?**

A. I would check his tumour markers in the first instance. Seminomatous residual masses following chemotherapy or radiation therapy are not common, and can be observed by serial imaging without the need to resort to immediate resection of the retroperitoneal mass irrespective of size. PET scanning has been found to be particularly useful in this group of patients in separating retroperitoneal masses that contain active tumour. It is generally agreed that residual masses > 3 cm that do not regress after therapy should undergo this imaging modality in order to look for evidence of active tumour. A positive PET scan after an interval of 4–6 weeks following the end of chemotherapy/radiotherapy is a very reliable predictor of viable tumour tissue in this group of patients. For such patients, confirmation by biopsy may require further treatment, such as retroperitoneal lymph node dissection (RPLND) or salvage chemotherapy (or radiotherapy in those who did not receive this initially). In general, a residual mass after primary treatment in seminoma is rare. Surgery after treatment for seminoma is generally more difficult, and is restricted to patients with 'globular' masses rather than a retro-peritoneal fibrosis type of picture.

Q. **If the patient had presented with advanced seminoma from the outset (stage IIC or higher), what would the mainstay of treatment have been?**

A. The mainstay of treatment is three or four cycles of chemotherapy with BEP or EP if contraindications to bleomycin exist (i.e. smoker, > 40 years of age, high burden of pulmonary metastases), which again is based on the IGCCCG classification grouping system (*see* Table 2.5). The final regime that the patient receives is guided by the prognostic group within which they are classified. For the good prognosis group this is three cycles of BEP, and for the intermediate group it is four cycles. There is no poor prognosis group for seminomatous disease.

STAGING AND TREATMENT: CLINICAL STAGE I, II NSGCT

Q. **If the tumour was an NSGCT but still stage I disease, would you do anything different compared with clinical stage I seminoma?**

A. Again, a number of options exist, namely radical orchidectomy with surveillance or adjuvant chemotherapy or, for those who are not prepared to consider the first two options, RPLND remains an option.

Across all NSGCTs surveillance alone is associated with a 30% relapse rate (the majority in the retroperitoneum and then the lungs) if orchidectomy is the sole treatment. The majority of such relapses (around 80%) occur in the first year of follow-up.

Q. **Is there anything that can guide you in determining and counselling the patient about the most appropriate option?**

A. For NSGCTs, the presence of vascular invasion is the most important prognostic indicator for distant relapse. The presence of vascular invasion portends a 48% risk of developing metastatic disease, compared with 14–22% without vascular invasion. Once again a risk-adapted approach can be used to stratify patients into low-risk and high-risk groups based on the absence and presence of vascular invasion, respectively.

Q. **What would you advise the patient?**

A. The patient can choose adjuvant treatment, but in the absence of vascular invasion we would advocate a surveillance programme with regular CT scans at 0, 3 and 12 months. This means that 78–86% of patients are cured following orchidectomy alone and do not require further treatment.

However, if there are difficulties with patient compliance with this regime, adjuvant chemotherapy with two cycles of BEP is recommended.

In the presence of vascular invasion, we would advise adjuvant chemotherapy with two cycles of BEP. Surveillance can be used but, in view of the 48% risk of relapse and the anxiety that this can generate, adjuvant chemotherapy is advised.

Q. Is there anything else that can be offered in clinical stage I NSGCT with vascular invasion in this group of patients?

A. Occasionally, patients who are unwilling to undergo surveillance or adjuvant chemotherapy can be offered an RPLND. This exposes patients to surgery and its associated side-effects in about 50% of cases who may never have relapsed. At the same time, RPLND does not eliminate the possibility of late distant recurrence, often in the lungs (around 10%). Around 30% of such patients who undergo an RPLND have disease in the retroperitoneum that upstages their disease to pathological stage II, and will require additional chemotherapy with two cycles of BEP to reduce the 30% risk of relapse to 2%, although in some centres surgery alone will be used. In the USA it is normal practice to offer all stage I NSGCTs an RPLND to achieve accurate pathological staging of the disease. In the UK, first-line treatment consists of surveillance or two cycles of BEP chemotherapy. If the patient is unwilling to follow an intensive surveillance programme or undergo chemotherapy, an RPLND can be advised.

Q. In general what would the follow-up be for these patients?

A. The follow-up schedule varies depending on the treatment modality that is chosen. For those who choose surveillance, this is more intensive and regimens vary, but in general patients require 3-monthly clinic visits with tumour marker assessment, twice-yearly chest X-rays and twice-yearly abdomino-pelvic CT scans for the first 2 years, with the frequency of these reducing after 10 years of follow-up. For those who choose RPLND or adjuvant chemotherapy the follow-up is less intensive, with the above applicable in general, but with the CT scan being undertaken annually.

Q. If instead the patient at first presentation on his staging CT had the appearances shown in Figure 2.5, with elevated tumour markers, what would you do?

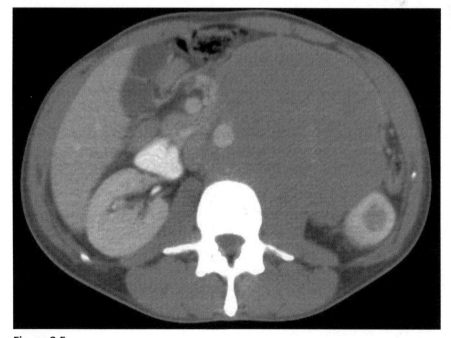

Figure 2.5

A. He has clinical stage II disease and I would therefore offer the patient induction chemotherapy based on the IGCCCG prognostic classification (*see* Table 2.6). Patients in the good prognosis group would normally receive three cycles of BEP (22-day cycle), and those in whom bleomycin needs to be avoided would receive four cycles of EP. Patients in the intermediate and poor prognosis groups would receive four cycles of BEP, or if bleomycin is to be avoided, they would receive four cycles of cisplatin, etoposide and ifosfamide (PEI/VIP) with a follow-up repeat CT scan to look for regression of the retroperitoneal nodes at 4–6 weeks. Occasionally, a rare situation arises where small retroperitoneal nodes are detected, which may well be benign in the absence of raised tumour markers (marker-negative stage IIA disease). The problem is deciding whether such nodes are pathological. For marker-negative stage IIA disease with small 1–2 cm nodes, a policy of surveillance, especially if the nodes are shrinking on serial scans, is acceptable, although this also depends on the original histology of the orchidectomy specimen. The EAU recommends that in clinical stage IIA disease with negative markers, patients with pure embryonal carcinoma in the orchidectomy specimen should undergo immediate chemotherapy. If the histology is teratoma or mixed tumour, surveillance or a RPLND can be undertaken. In the UK, most centres would either give chemotherapy or perform an early CT scan, and if the nodes were still present would proceed with chemotherapy. Patients with marker-negative stage IIA disease who are unwilling to undergo chemotherapy have the option of undergoing RPLND with adjuvant chemotherapy (two cycles of BEP) if nodal disease is present on RPLND histology.

Table 2.6 The International Germ Cell Cancer Collaborative Group (IGCCCG) prognostic-based staging system for metastatic NSGCT

Good prognosis group	
(56% of cases)	*All of the following criteria*
5-year PFS 89%	Testis/retroperitoneal primary
5-year survival 92%	No non-pulmonary visceral metastases
	AFP < 1000 ng/ml
	hCG < 5000 IU/l (1000 ng/ml)
	LDH < 1.5 x ULN
Intermediate prognosis group	
(28% of cases)	*Any of the following criteria*
5-year PFS 75%	Testis/retroperitoneal primary
5-year survival 80%	No non-pulmonary visceral metastases
	AFP > 1000 and < 10 000 ng/ml or
	hCG > 5000 and < 50 000 IU/l or
	LDH > 1.5 and < 10 x ULN
Poor prognosis group	
(16% of cases)	*Any of the following criteria*
5-year PFS 41%	Mediastinal primary
5-year survival 48%	Non-pulmonary visceral metastases
	AFP > 10 000 ng/ml or
	hCG > 50 000 IU/l (10 000 ng/ml) or
	LDH > 10 x ULN

PFS, progression-free survival; ULN, upper limit of normal.

Q. This patient's CT after induction chemotherapy appears as shown in Figure 2.6. What would you do now?

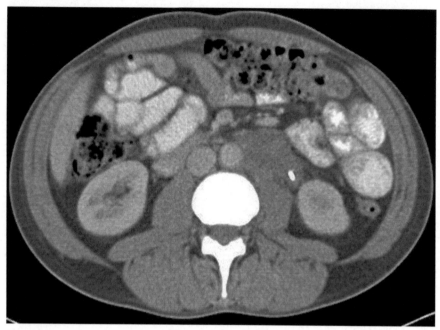

Figure 2.6

A. There still remains a large para-aortic retroperitoneal mass that has regressed considerably following the chemotherapy. At this point we would check the patient's tumour markers again. If these have normalised he has potentially resectable disease by way of an RPLND. However, if his markers remained elevated but at a plateau, we would watch them a little longer with further markers taken at variable times in the next 4–12 weeks. If at this stage these remained stable, we would offer him an RPLND. If they continued to rise then, instead of surgery, salvage chemotherapy would be needed with PEI/VIP or paclitaxel, ifosfamide and cisplatin (TIP) regimes.

There is no reliable model for predicting whether such masses harbour active tumour, so RPLND is mandatory with residual masses in excess of 1cm as the likelihood of significant residual disease increases. In contrast to stage II seminoma, there is no role for PET scanning in this group. In general, for those patients who undergo RPLND for a residual mass after primary induction BEP chemotherapy, the histology will show necrosis in 50% (around 30% in most studies), mature teratoma in 35% and viable cancer in 15%, although there are few predictors of this. Such masses have an increased risk of harbouring teratoma in the final histology if the original orchidectomy specimen had teratoma.

Q. Another patient had initially presented with clinical stage I NSGCT disease with vascular invasion, and completed two cycles of primary BEP chemotherapy. He has a follow-up CT scan at 12 months, which appears as shown in Figures 2.7 and 2.8. What does this show?

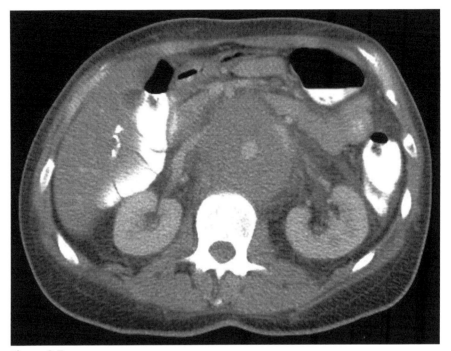

Figure 2.7

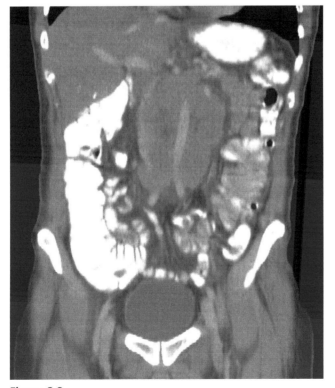

Figure 2.8

A.   These are axial (Figure 2.7) and coronal (Figure 2.8) abdominal/pelvic CT images showing bulky nodes in the retroperitoneum encasing the great vessels, indicating clinical relapse.

Q.   **What would you do with the patient now?**

A.   In this instance, where there is a residual mass following induction chemotherapy, the patient requires second-line or salvage chemotherapy. This normally takes the form of four cycles of PEI/VIP (cisplatin, etoposide and ifosfamide) or four cycles of TIP (cisplatin, ifosfamide and paclitaxel). The response to this salvage chemotherapy depends on a variety of factors, such as the original histology and location of the tumour, the response to first-line treatment, the duration of remission and the level of tumour markers at relapse. There is some early evidence that treatment-refractory germ-cell tumours may benefit from a combination of taxol and gemcitabine chemotherapy, and referral to centres that have expertise in this area as well as entering such patients into clinical trials is advised.

Q.   **If the retroperitoneal mass persisted despite salvage chemotherapy (Figure 2.9), is there anything else that could be offered?**

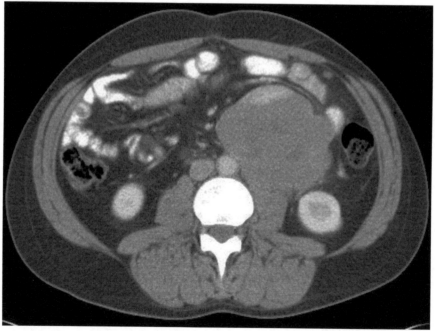

Figure 2.9 Persistent retroperitoneal mass despite salvage chemotherapy.

A.   Yes. Salvage RPLND 4–6 weeks after normalisation of tumour markers or achievement of their plateau could be offered. The outlook is poor for those patients who after second- or third-line chemotherapy still harbour undifferentiated tumour in the surgical specimen.

Q. **What are the principles of post-chemotherapy RPLND surgery?**

A. Through a transabdominal or thoraco-abdominal approach, the retroperitoneal great vessels are completely cleared, removing all lymphatic tissue out to the ureters, extending from the renal artery down to the ipsilateral external iliac vessels. Nodal tissue is dissected out in an attempt to cure the patient (if this is the only site of metastatic disease), but one must minimise morbidity and particularly attempt to preserve antegrade ejaculation, if possible. With unilateral disease it may be possible to preserve the contralateral hypogastric plexus and postganglionic sympathetic fibres (and thus antegrade ejaculation). In pre-chemotherapy cases, nerve-sparing RPLND can be performed, leading to an antegrade ejaculation rate as high as 90%.

Q. **What would you warn the patient about prior to performing an RPLND?**

A. RPLND is a major undertaking that has an associated mortality (1–3%) and morbidity (5–25%) rate. With the use of modern dissection templates it is designed to minimise the complications mainly associated with ejaculation and subsequent fertility in young men.

The main complications are as follows:
- overall complication rate of around 10%
- major complications (around 1–5%)
  – chylous ascites (1–3%)
  – renovascular injury and nephrectomy (higher incidence in post-chemotherapy cases) – it is not 'injury', but a planned nephrectomy in around 5–8% of cases
  – small bowel obstruction (1–3%)
  – spinal cord ischaemia (< 1%)
- minor complications (around 15%)
  – wound infections
  – anejaculation
  – paralytic ileus
  – lymphocele
  – transient hyperamylasaemia
  – pneumonitis/atelectasis.

Q. **How would you follow up a patient after RPLND?**

A. For the poor prognosis group, no further adjuvant treatment is required, as the relapse rate in this group of patients is low (around 5–10%), but for viable tumour further salvage chemotherapy is advised with second-line chemotherapy.[21] In completely resected tumours with viable tumour, 70% of patients remain disease-free, compared with none of those who did not receive further chemotherapy. Furthermore, patients with complete resection, good IGCCCG prognostic grouping and less than 10% viable tumour tend to fare well following RPLND, and therefore may not need further salvage chemotherapy.

With regard to chemotherapy, caution is used in those who have already received bleomycin, as this cumulative dose increases the risk of 'bleomycin lung' (a pneumonitis and fibrotic condition of the lung interstitium). Occasionally, if a further residual mass persists despite this, a second RPLND can be considered, but this is rare.

Q. If the patient had first presented with stage III NSGCT disease, how would the treatment differ, broadly speaking?

A. Again the treatment would be similar to that for advanced seminoma based on the IGCCCG classification system. In essence this consists of three cycles of BEP chemotherapy in the first instance for the good prognosis group, and four cycles for the intermediate group. For the poor prognostic group the standard remains four cycles of BEP or PEI (cisplatin, etoposide and ifosfamide), but referral to a centre for inclusion in trials is recommended, as the optimum treatment has yet to be established.

Q. If at first presentation a patient has a CT of the brain that shows a metastatic deposit, does that confer a poor prognosis compared with a later relapse to the brain following initial successful treatment (*see* Figure 2.10)?

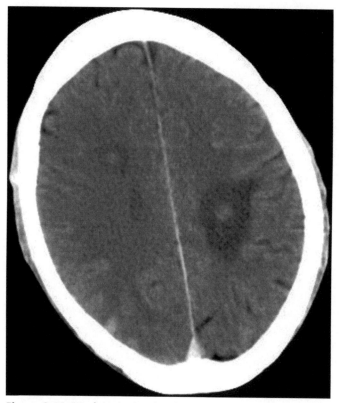

Figure 2.10 CT of the brain, showing a metastatic deposit.

A. No. Around 10% of all patients with germ-cell tumours present with brain metastases, and overall they have a long-term survival rate of 30–40%. In patients who show relapse in the brain following initial treatment this is part of a systemic relapse pattern, and they have a poor 5-year survival rate, of the order of 2–5%.

KEY FACTS AND SUMMARY
Relapse rates for surveillance

- Clinical stage I seminoma:
  - relapse after surveillance: 15–20%
  - relapse after adjuvant chemotherapy: 3–4%
  - relapse after adjuvant radiotherapy: 3–4%.
- Relapse with poor prognostic factors:
  - tumour > 4 cm
  - rete testis involvement.
- Clinical stage I NSGCT:
  - surveillance relapse: 30% (higher if there is vascular invasion)
  - adjuvant chemotherapy: 2%
  - poor prognostic factor: vascular invasion.

Metastatic germ-cell tumour
Treatment based on IGCCCG prognostic classification

- Stage IIA/B disease: seminoma:
  - chemotherapy (three cycles of BEP or four cycles of EP) (occasionally radiotherapy).
- Stage IIA/B NSGCT:
  - good prognosis group: three cycles of BEP
  - intermediate and poor prognosis group: four cycles of BEP
  - if there is a residual mass, RPLND is performed, and if histology is positive, salvage chemotherapy is used.
- Stages IIC and III:
  - based on IGCCCG grouping
  - good prognosis group: three cycles of BEP
  - intermediate prognosis group: four cycles of BEP
  - poor prognosis group: four cycles of BEP or PEI/VIP (it is recommended that these patients are enrolled in trials).

Drainage of nodes to retroperitoneum

- Defined drainage (landing sites) to retroperitoneum based on site of tumour.
- *Right-sided testicular tumours*: first landing zone is the interaortocaval area, followed by the precaval and pre-aortic nodes, and finally the right common iliac and external iliac nodes.
- *Left-sided testicular tumours*: first landing zone is the para-aortic and pre-aortic nodes, followed by the interaortocaval nodes, and finally the left common iliac and external iliac nodes.
- It is rare for left-sided tumours to have positive right-sided nodes (around 1% of cases), but more common for the reverse situation to occur.

ACKNOWLEDGEMENTS

We are very grateful to Dr Matthew Gaskarth (Consultant Radiologist, Addenbrookes Hospital, Cambridge) and Dr Anne Warren (Consultant Pathologist, Addenbrookes Hospital, Cambridge) for providing the radiology and histopathological images to complement this chapter.

REFERENCES

1. Schottenfeld D *et al.* The epidemiology of testicular cancer in young adults. *Am J Epidemiol* 1980; **112:** 232–46.
2. Whitaker RH. Neoplasia in cryptorchid men. *Semin Urol* 1988; **6:** 107–9.
3. Berthelsen JG *et al.* Screening for carcinoma in situ of the contralateral testis in patients with germinal testicular cancer. *BMJ (Clin Res Ed)* 1982; **285:** 1683–6.
4. Henderson BE *et al.* Risk factors for cancer of the testis in young men. *Int J Cancer* 1979; **23:** 598–602.
5. Dieckmann KP *et al.* The prevalence of familial testicular cancer: an analysis of two patient populations and a review of the literature. *Cancer* 1997; **80:** 1954–60.
6. Westergaard T *et al.* Cancer risk in fathers and brothers of testicular cancer patients in Denmark. A population-based study. *Int J Cancer* 1996; **66:** 627–31.
7. Marshall S. Potential problems with testicular prostheses. *Urology* 1986; **28:** 388–90.
8. Dieckmann KP *et al.* Spermatogenesis in the contralateral testis of patients with testicular germ-cell cancer: histological evaluation of testicular biopsies and a comparison with healthy males. *BJU Int* 2007; **99:** 1079–85.
9. Harland SJ *et al.* Intratubular germ-cell neoplasia of the contralateral testis in testicular cancer: defining a high-risk group. *J Urol* 1998; **160:** 1353–7.
10. Dieckmann KP *et al.* Prevalence of contralateral testicular intraepithelial neoplasia in patients with testicular germ-cell neoplasms. *J Clin Oncol* 1996; **14:** 3126–32.
11. Dieckmann KP *et al.* Diagnosis of contralateral testicular intraepithelial neoplasia (TIN) in patients with testicular germ-cell cancer: systematic two-site biopsies are more sensitive than a single random biopsy. *Eur Urol* 2007; **51:** 175–83.
12. Skakkebaek NE *et al.* Carcinoma in situ of the undescended testis. *Urol Clin North Am* 1982; **9:** 377–85.
13. Classen J *et al.* Radiotherapy with 16 Gy may fail to eradicate testicular intraepithelial neoplasia: preliminary communication of a dose-reduction trial of the German Testicular Cancer Study Group. *Br J Cancer* 2003; **88:** 828–31.
14. Hobarth K *et al.* Incidence of testicular microlithiasis. *Urology* 1992; **40:** 464–7.
15. DeCastro BJ *et al.* A 5-year follow-up study of asymptomatic men with testicular microlithiasis. *J Urol* 2008; **179:** 1420–3.
16. Rashid HH *et al.* Testicular microlithiasis: a review and its association with testicular cancer. *Urol Oncol* 2004; **22:** 285–9.
17. Warde P *et al.* Surveillance for stage I testicular seminoma. Is it a good option? *Urol Clin North Am* 1998; **25:** 425–33.
18. Groll RJ *et al.* A comprehensive systematic review of testicular germ-cell tumor surveillance. *Crit Rev Oncol Hematol* 2007; **64:** 182–97.
19. Warde P *et al.* Prognostic factors for relapse in stage I seminoma managed by surveillance: a pooled analysis. *J Clin Oncol* 2002; **20:** 4448–52.
20. Oliver RT *et al.* Radiotherapy versus single-dose carboplatin in adjuvant treatment of stage I seminoma: a randomised trial. *Lancet* 2005; **366:** 293–300.
21. Donohue JP *et al.* Integration of surgery and systemic therapy: results and principles of integration. *Semin Urol Oncol* 1998; **16:** 65–71.

Chapter 3
Penile cancer

Asif Muneer and Suks Minhas

PENILE CANCER: AETIOLOGY AND EPIDEMIOLOGY

Q. A 45-year-old man attends your outpatient clinic as he is worried about developing penile cancer when he is older. He wants to have a circumcision performed, as he believes that this will be protective.

Approximately how many cases of penile cancer are reported annually in the UK?

A. The incidence is between 1.2 and 1.4 cases per 100 000 inhabitants, which amounts to approximately 400 new cases per year.

Q. Which parts of the world have a higher incidence of penile cancer?

A. There is a higher incidence in South America, East Africa and South East Asia, where this disease can account for 10% of all male malignancies, compared with 0.6% in North America and Europe.

Q. Do you know any risk factors for this disease?

A. It has been shown that neonatal circumcision virtually eliminates the risk of developing penile cancer. Therefore the presence of a foreskin increases the risk, as does phimosis, poor penile hygiene, smoking, exposure to ultraviolet (UV) radiation, and human papillomavirus (HPV) infection. The risk of penile cancer also increases with age.

Q. Would circumcision at his age be of any benefit in protecting this patient against penile cancer?

Although neonatal circumcision does offer protection against the development of penile cancer, it is unlikely that adult circumcision when the foreskin is normal offers the same benefit. However, in the presence of phimosis, circumcision would be of benefit to ensure good penile hygiene and also prevent the accumulation of smegma.

Q. What is the commonest histological subtype?

A. Squamous-cell carcinoma accounts for the majority of penile cancers (95%), and is sub-divided into usual type (60-70%), papillary (7%), condylomatous (7%), basaloid (4-10%), verrucous (7%) or sarcomatoid (1-4%). The basaloid and sarcomatoid subtypes are aggressive and have a poor prognosis.

Rarer tumours are malignant melanoma (2%), basal-cell carcinoma (2%) and extra-mammary Paget's disease (which is essentially adenocarcinoma arising in the penile skin). Sarcomas account for less than 1% of penile cancers.

Q. **Do you think that HPV status is a good prognostic marker?**

A. Although HPV infection has been found to be a risk factor in penile cancer with approximately 50% of cases linked to HPV infection, its role as a prognostic marker is still unclear. Alternative markers are under investigation, including p53, SCC antigen, P16^{INK4a}, Ki-67, E-cadherin and MMP-2.[1]

ASSESSMENT AND MANAGEMENT OF PREMALIGNANT PENILE LESIONS

Q. **A 79-year-old diabetic is referred to you with a non-retractile foreskin. What is the term used for this condition?**

A. Phimosis.

Q. **What are the key points to ascertain from the history?**

A. (1) What is the duration of the phimosis?
(2) How well controlled is his diabetes?
(3) Does he have problems with splitting of the foreskin or bleeding?
(4) Lower urinary tract symptoms.
(5) Smoking history.
(6) Sexual history, including number of partners and any previous HPV infection.
(7) Exposure to UV radiation.

Q. **How would you conduct an examination of this patient?**

A. I would conduct a general examination to assess the general health of the patient. A more focused assessment would include an examination of the penis and scrotum in order to identify any skin lesions or palpable lumps. If the foreskin is partially retractable, I would conduct a visual examination of the glans penis. If it is not retractable, I would palpate the glans penis in order to identify any palpable lesion on it. I would then palpate both inguinal regions to determine whether there are any palpable inguinal lymph nodes.

With regard to the foreskin, I would assess whether there was any change in colour and evidence of scarring or thickening.

Q. **The foreskin is completely non-retractable with extensive scarring and fissuring similar to that shown in Figure 3.1. What does this show and what would you advise the patient?**

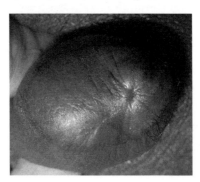

Figure 3.1 Phimosis developing secondary to BXO.

A. Figure 3.1 shows phimosis developing secondary to balanitis xerotica obliterans (BXO). Therefore I would advise the patient to undergo a circumcision.

Q. If there was mild scarring and the foreskin was retractable, are there any other treatment options available?

A. A trial of topical corticosteroids for 4–6 weeks can resolve scarring associated with BXO, but treatment must be administered under medical supervision.

Q. How would you consent a patient for a circumcision?

A. The consent would include the risks and side-effects specifically associated with circumcision, and also the general risks associated with undergoing any operative procedure.

Specific risks and side-effects associated with circumcision include the following:
- bleeding (early or late; 1–2% of patients require a return to theatre for haemostasis)
- infection (1–2% require antibiotics)
- altered sensitivity of the glans
- meatal stenosis (reported in the literature in up to 10% of patients)
- the need for a further biopsy of any suspicious lesion
- in childhood circumcision, approximately 4% of parents are not happy with the cosmetic appearance.

General risks, which would be low in this procedure, include (if performed under general anaesthetic):
- deep vein thrombosis
- pulmonary embolism
- cardiorespiratory complications
- anaesthetic complications.

Q. On the day of surgery the patient has been consented. Describe how you would perform a circumcision.

A. (There are several techniques, so be familiar with your own technique.)

I would ensure that the patient is consented and fully informed about the risks, and that their expectations have been discussed. I would prepare the patient in the supine position. At the beginning of the procedure I would perform a penile block.

As the foreskin is completely non-retractable in this case, I would initially make a midline dorsal slit in order to visually assess the meatus and ensure that the glans penis does not have an unexpected lesion, and also to ensure that there is no hypospadius present. I use a scalpel technique which involves making a circumcoronal incision in the inner prepuce and outer skin. The foreskin is then removed between these two incisions. Meticulous haemostasis is ensured using bipolar diathermy or absorbable ties. The skin is sutured using interrupted absorbable sutures.

Q. The foreskin is sent for histology and the pathologist shows you the slide (*see* Figure 3.2). What is the diagnosis?

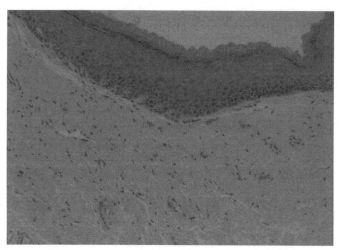

Figure 3.2

A. This histology slide shows balanitis xerotica obliterans (BXO), otherwise known as lichen sclerosus et atrophicus.

Q. What are the histological features of this condition?
A. The typical pathological features of BXO or lichen sclerosus et atrophicus are loss of rete pegs, epidermal atrophy and chronic inflammatory changes. There is perivascular infiltration of the dermis and homogenisation of collagen in the upper dermis.

Q. This same patient is referred again to the outpatient clinic having undergone an uncomplicated procedure. He has noticed a small red area on the glans penis which has persisted despite the fact that he underwent circumcision several months ago. How would you manage this patient?
A. An area of residual BXO can persist on the glans penis even after circumcision. I would take a culture swab of the area and treat the area with a combination of topical steroid and anti-fungal cream, followed by an early review (after 2 weeks).

Q. The culture swab is negative. The patient is reviewed again and the red area is found to have increased in size as shown in Figure 3.3. What would you do now?

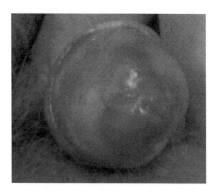

Figure 3.3

A. I would arrange an urgent biopsy.

Q. **The biopsy is performed and the histology is as shown in Figure 3.4. What is the diagnosis?**

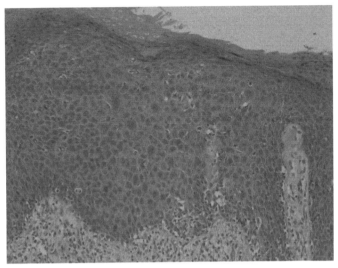

Figure 3.4

A. This histology slide shows carcinoma in situ (CIS) of the glans penis, also known as erythroplasia of Queyrat.

Note: Erythroplasia of Queyrat is CIS affecting the glans or inner surface of the prepuce (non-keratinising CIS).

Bowen's disease is CIS affecting the penile shaft or scrotal skin (keratinising CIS).

Erythroplasia of Queyrat is 10 times more likely to progress to invasive squamous-cell carcinoma (SCC) than is Bowen's disease. The lesions are slightly raised and erythematous and can be single or multifocal. Characteristically, the texture can be smooth, scaly, verrucous or velvety.

Q. **What is the definition of CIS?**

A. It is a lesion that has all the characteristics of malignancy except for invasion (i.e. it does not cross the basement membrane).

Q. **What are the histological features that characterise this lesion?**

A. The mucosa is replaced by atypical hyperplastic cells. These show disorientation, with multiple hyperchromatic nuclei and multi-level mitotic figures. The rete is elongated and bulbous. The submucosa shows proliferation of capillaries with an inflammatory infiltrate rich in plasma cells.

Q. **Specifically with regard to the penis, which other pre-malignant lesions are you aware of?**

A. These include Erythroplasia of Queyrat, Bowen's disease, Bowenoid papulosis, leukoplakia, cutaneous horns, pseudoepitheliomatous and micaceous balanitis, extramammary Paget's disease, and condyloma acuminatum.

Q. **How would you treat this patient with CIS?**

A. If the lesion is small, he can be prescribed topical treatment in the form of either 5-FU or imiquimod. Topical 5-FU is structurally similar to thymine and therefore DNA synthesis is blocked by inhibiting thymidylate synthetase. In contrast, imiquimod is an imidazoquinonin tetracyclicamine which alters the immune response by possibly inducing interferon alpha.

Q. **What are the side-effects of 5-FU?**

A. There is commonly discomfort in the area of application due to an inflammatory reaction. Erythema, crusting and weeping of the area may also occur.

Q. **Do you know of any other penile-preserving therapies, excluding surgery, which have been described for the treatment of CIS?**

A. Various therapies have been reported but they have not gained widespread popularity due to the higher recurrence rate. These include laser therapy (CO_2, Nd-YAG or KTP), photodynamic therapy, cryotherapy and Mohs micrographic surgery.

Q. **Having been successfully treated with topical 5-FU, the patient re-presents several months later with multiple red areas affecting most of the glans penis, which are confirmed as CIS on a further biopsy. What surgical option would you offer him?**

A. As the CIS is affecting a large surface area of the glans penis, I would offer a total glans resurfacing of the glans penis and use a split skin graft to cover the area that is excised. At the same time deeper biopsies would be taken to ensure that there is no corpus spongiosum involvement (i.e. to check that it has not developed into an invasive carcinoma).

Q. **What are the advantages of penis-preserving surgery?**

A. Penile-preserving surgery allows preservation of length, so that the patient can void standing up, as well as maintenance of sexual function. There is also a reduction in the psychological impact related to this type of surgery, as it avoids the need for penile amputation.

Q. **What is the disadvantage of undertaking penile-preserving surgery?**

A. There is a higher local recurrence rate, and therefore close surveillance is required post-operatively.

Q. **What is a Buschke–Löwenstein tumour (also known as a verrucous carcinoma or giant condyloma acuminatum)?**

A. This is a *locally* invasive penile lesion of viral aetiology. Although tumours in extragenital sites can metastasise, penile verrucous carcinoma does *not* metastasise unless there has been malignant degeneration of the primary lesion.

MANAGEMENT OF INVASIVE PENILE CARCINOMA

Q. **A 60-year-old patient who is an ex-smoker presents with a large lump on his glans penis and a palpable lump in the left groin.**
   A picture of the lump is shown in Figure 3.5. What is the likely diagnosis?

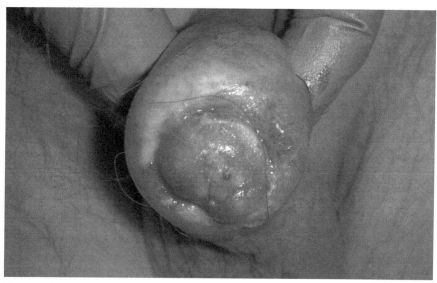

Figure 3.5

A. The likely diagnosis is a penile tumour. The picture shows an extensive carcinoma affecting the glans penis.

Q. What is the most common type of cancer that affects the penis?
A. Squamous-cell carcinoma (SCC).

Q. Which region of the penis does SCC most commonly affect?
A. The glans penis. The primary tumour is localised to the glans penis in approximately 48% of cases.

Q. What are the risk factors for SCC of the penis?
A. They include smoking, increasing age, previous HPV infection (type 16 and 18), uncircumcised males, poor penile hygiene and retained smegma. There is an association with exposure to psoralen and ultraviolet A photochemotherapy (PUVA) and BXO.
    (Pre-malignant lesions are mentioned in a previous question above.)

Q. Which HPV subtypes are commonly implicated in penile SCC?
A. HPV 16 and 18.

Q. In this particular case, what would you do next?
A. I would perform a biopsy of the lesion in order to confirm the diagnosis, and I would organise further imaging to stage the tumour.

Q. How would you stage the tumour?
A. The penile lesion can be imaged using penile MRI with an injection of intracavernosal prostaglandin (resulting in an artificial erection) in order to assess whether the lesion is invading the corpus cavernosum or urethra. A CT scan of the chest, abdomen and pelvis will identify enlarged lymph nodes.

Q. **Does CT imaging detect all pathological lymph nodes?**

A. No. The CT criteria for metastatic lymph nodes rely mainly on the size of the lymph nodes and abnormal features of the hilum or shape of the lymph nodes. CT imaging will not detect small foci of metastatic disease.

Q. **Describe the image shown in Figure 3.6.**

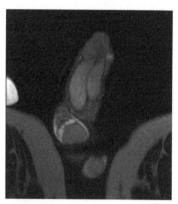

Figure 3.6

A. This is an MRI of the penis demonstrating a penile tumour on the glans penis that is extending into the corpus spongiosum and cavernosum.

Q. **What is the likely T stage of this tumour?**

A. The tumour is extending into the corpus spongiosum and cavernosum, and therefore it is at least a T2 lesion according to the 2002 TNM classification (*see* Table 3.1).

Table 3.1 TNM 2002 classification of penile cancer

TX	Primary tumour cannot be assessed
T0	No evidence of primary tumour
Tis	Carcinoma *in situ*
Ta	Non-invasive verrucous carcinoma
T1	Tumour is invading subepithelial connective tissue
T2	Tumour is invading corpus spongiosum or cavernosum
T3	Tumour is invading urethra or prostate
T4	Tumour is invading other adjacent structures
NX	Regional lymph nodes cannot be assessed
N0	No evidence of lymph node metastasis
N1	Metastasis in a single superficial inguinal lymph node
N2	Metastasis in multiple or bilateral superficial inguinal lymph nodes
N3	Metastasis in deep inguinal or pelvic lymph node(s), unilateral or bilateral
MX	Distant metastases cannot be assessed
M0	No evidence of distant metastases
M1	Distant metastases

Q. How accurate is MRI in predicting invasion into the corpus cavernosum?

A. It is very accurate, and has been shown to predict corpus cavernosum/spongiosum invasion in all cases analysed.[2]

Q. What would be the surgical treatment option?

A. As the tumour is based distally, adequate clear margins can be achieved by performing a partial penectomy.

Q. Would you advise any other surgical treatment if the tumour had involved the glans without extension to the corpus cavernosum?

A. Tumours of the glans penis can be managed by performing a glansectomy and reconstruction of a neoglans using a split skin graft.

Q. How would you perform a partial penectomy?

A. Ensure that appropriate consent has been obtained, and then place the patient in a supine position. Cover the tumour with a glove finger or condom, and then deglove the penis and mark the extent of tumour-free margins. Mobilise the neurovascular bundle and ligate. Mobilise the urethra and then transect the penis. (Several techniques are described for this procedure, e.g. straight transection or 'fish mouth.' It is important to be familiar with at least one of them.) Send the proximal shavings of the corpus cavernosum and urethra for frozen-section analysis. Oversew the corpora and Buck's fascia with absorbable sutures. Spatulate the urethra and either cover the corpora with penile skin or use a split skin graft to reconstruct the neoglans. Leave a catheter *in situ*.

Q. How would you follow up a patient who has undergone penile-preserving surgery with no inguinal lymph node disease?

A. Most recurrences will occur within 3 years. Therefore the follow-up should be on a 2- to 3-monthly basis. I would examine the penis and inguinal lymph nodes for local or distant recurrence. The patient should also self-examine and request an urgent follow-up if any new lesion is palpable.

Q. The patient underwent reconstruction of a neoglans using a split skin graft. At a follow-up visit he reports a small lesion on the neoglans which is biopsied and found to be consistent with BXO. What is this phenomenon called?

A. This is known as the Koebner phenomenon, whereby BXO can recur on the split skin graft.

Q. What is the local recurrence rate following a partial or total penectomy?

A. This varies according to the initial stage. Studies have generally reported a local recurrence rate of 0–8%.

Q. How does this compare with the recurrence rates following penile-preserving surgery?

A. Although early studies reported a local recurrence rate of up to 40%, more recent studies have shown a local recurrence rate of 11%. As a number of different techniques are incorporated in the same series, this is an approximate recurrence rate. One series has reported a local recurrence rate of 2.5% in patients undergoing a glansectomy and split skin grafting.[3]

Q. How would you manage the palpable lump in the groin?

A. This is likely to be an enlarged lymph node. Bearing in mind the size and the stage of the primary tumour, I would recommend an inguinal lymphadenectomy.

Q. If this is the only node found to be involved in this patient, what is the N stage according to the 2002 TNM classification?

A. As this is the only lymph node that is involved, it is N1.

Q. Assuming that this patient was found to have a single node in each groin, what would be the N stage according to the 2002 TNM classification?

A. Regardless of the number involved, bilateral nodal involvement is classified as N2.

Q. What percentage of *palpable* inguinal lymph nodes are involved with metastatic disease?

A. This is controversial. In previous studies, mainly from Brazil, it was suggested that only 50% of palpable inguinal lymph nodes were involved with tumour, and the remaining 50% were enlarged as a result of associated sexually transmitted or other infections. Therefore traditionally a short course of antibiotics was given in an attempt to differentiate between the two. However, recent data have suggested that over 90% of palpable inguinal nodes are actually involved with metastases and thus require lymphadenectomy. As a result, in our unit we do not routinely give antibiotics for palpable inguinal nodes.

Q. What is the procedure shown in Figure 3.7?

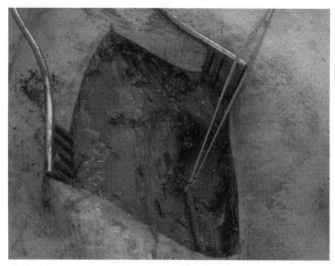

Figure 3.7

A. Figure 3.7 shows an inguinal lymphadenectomy. The saphenous vein has been preserved.

Q. What are the anatomical boundaries of the femoral triangle?

A. The femoral triangle is bordered by the inguinal ligament superiorly, the medial border of the sartorius muscle laterally, and the lateral border of the adductor longus and adductor longus tendon medially. The floor comprises the pectineus muscle medially and the iliopsoas muscle laterally, together with the femoral artery and vein.

Q. **What is the difference between a superficial (modified) and radical inguinal lymph node dissection?**

A. The superficial lymph node dissection is less extensive and the boundaries are reduced by 1–2 cm compared with a radical lymph node dissection. The saphenous vein is preserved and the femoral vessels do not have to be skeletonised deep to the fascia lata.

(Note that if any nodes are found to be positive in a modified superficial inguinal node dissection, one then proceeds to a radical inguinal node dissection. Also, if two or more inguinal lymph nodes are found to be involved on histology, one should proceed to a pelvic lymph node dissection.)

Q. **Where are the deep inguinal nodes located?**

A. They are located mainly medial to the femoral vein.

Q. **What are the complications of a radical inguinal lymph node dissection?**

A. The morbidity associated with this procedure is 30–50%. The complications include early haemorrhage, wound infection, flap necrosis, lymphoedema of the lower limb, lymphocele, prolonged lymph drainage and patchy sensory loss of the thigh.

Q. **What is the advantage of performing a superficial modified inguinal node dissection compared with a radical inguinal node dissection?**

A. The superficial inguinal node dissection reduces the morbidity of the procedure by utilising a smaller incision and less extensive mobilisation of skin flaps. The saphenous vein is preserved in order to reduce lower limb lymphoedema. The procedure also avoids the need to use a sartorius flap for femoral vessel coverage.

Q. **Does superficial (modified) lymphadenectomy reduce the lymphoedema rate?**

A. Yes. Approximately 20% of patients will suffer from lymphoedema, with a very small proportion developing persistent lower limb lymphoedema.

Q. **Can you describe what has happened in Figure 3.8?**

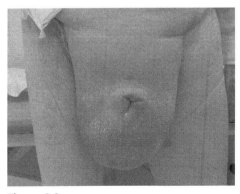

Figure 3.8

A. This shows extensive scrotal lymphoedema. This patient has had surgery to the penis combined with bilateral inguinal node dissections as indicated by the groin scars. There is extensive genital lymphoedema which has developed following the surgery.

Q. **How would you manage this post-operative complication?**

A. Initially I would opt for conservative management, including supportive underwear and ensuring that the patient avoids trauma to the skin (e.g. scratches, pressure sores). Once the patient is mobile, the lymphoedema may reduce. However, for troublesome and persistent scrotal lymphoedema a scrotoplasty can be performed.

Q. **In patients with impalpable inguinal lymph nodes, what is the risk of lymph node metastases?**

A. Approximately 20%.

Q. **There appears to be overtreatment of the *impalpable* inguinal nodes in approximately 80% of patients. Do you know of any other techniques that are currently utilised to reduce the number of individuals with impalpable inguinal nodes undergoing inguinal lymph node dissections?**

A. Yes. Dynamic sentinel lymph node biopsy.

Q. **Which radioisotope is used in this technique?**

A. ^{99m}Tc nanocolloid.

Q. **What is the false-negative rate of dynamic sentinel lymph node biopsy for penile cancer?**

A. Approximately 5%.[4]

Q. **Do you know of any modifications to the original technique which have reduced the false-negative rate to 5%?**

A. The false-negative rate has been reduced by incorporating ultrasonography combined with fine-needle aspiration of suspicious nodes pre-operatively. The rationale for this was to locate nodes that have extensive tumour and which are therefore unlikely to have normal lymph drainage and so will not be identified by the ^{99m}Tc nanocolloid. In addition, the use of a blue dye has assisted localisation of the lymph nodes.

Q. **Which pathological features correlate with lymph node metastases and prognosis?**

A. T stage (≥T2), lymphovascular and perineural invasion, histological grade of tumour and histological subtype (e.g. basaloid features). Other factors include depth of primary tumour, positive margins following resection and urethral invasion. Of all these factors the most important appear to be perineural invasion, vascular invasion and high-grade tumours.

Q. **What is the 5-year survival rate for a T2 penile SCC with no evidence of metastatic disease in the inguinal lymph nodes bilaterally?**

A. Around 66%.

Q. **An 83-year-old patient with a 2 cm primary SCC on the glans penis opts for radiotherapy to this lesion as opposed to surgical excision, as he is worried**

about the perioperative risks and complications. What would you quote as the response rate and recurrence rate of external beam radiotherapy?

A. The response rate is approximately 56% and the local failure rate is 40%.

Q. **What are the main complications of external beam radiotherapy for penile SCC?**

A. There is a risk of meatal stenosis and urethral stricture (up to 30%), and telangiectasia (90%). Note that the patient must be circumcised prior to radiotherapy, otherwise the prepuce will become fused to the glans.

Q. **Is there a role for radiotherapy for clinically impalpable nodes?**

A. Currently there is no evidence to suggest that radiotherapy prevents the development of metastatic lymph nodes. However, there is a possible role in patients who have undergone inguinal lymphadenectomy for metastatic lymph nodes showing extracapsular spread.

ADVANCED PENILE CANCERS AND PRIMARY URETHRAL TUMOURS

Q. **A 55-year-old patient who has previously been treated with a partial penectomy and modified bilateral inguinal node dissection presents with a large mass in the right groin fixed to the skin. What are your surgical treatment options?**

A. Large masses presenting on follow-up after inguinal lymphadenectomy represent metastatic disease. The prognosis is poor, and the treatment is directed at palliation and improvement of the patient's quality of life. If the performance status is good, resection combined with coverage of the defect is an option. As the defect is large, this is performed using a pedicled flap, e.g. vertical rectus abdominis (VRAM) or tensor fasciae latae (TFL).

Q. **He is brought in acutely as he is suffering from dehydration, feeling unsteady and confused. Can you give any metabolic reason why this might occur?**

A. This patient is likely to have hypercalcaemia related to the bulk of the disease, as opposed to metastatic bone disease. A study from Memorial Sloan-Kettering Cancer Center reported that approximately 20% of patients with penile cancer develop hypercalcaemia, possibly due to parathyroid hormone or parathyroid hormone-like secretion.

Q. **A 67-year-old man has noticed a palpable lump in the mid shaft of his penis which is getting progressively larger. The lump is not attached to the skin, and he presents with haematuria. How would you investigate this patient?**

A. The salient points of the history and examination are as previously stated above. I would also examine the inguinal lymph nodes and the external urethral meatus. I would then organise a cystoscopy and biopsy the lesion. My suspicion would be a neoplasm of the urethra. Therefore the patient requires CT staging of the abdomen, pelvis and inguinal regions together with an MRI scan of the penis.

Q. **The cystoscopy shows an obvious tumour in the mid urethra which is biopsied. What is the commonest primary urethral tumour in males?**

A. Squamous-cell carcinoma accounts for 80% of primary urethral tumours.

Q. Where in the urethra do these tumours most commonly arise?

A. Around 60% of these tumours are located in the bulbomembranous urethra, with the majority (80%) being squamous-cell carcinomas.

Q. What are the risk factors for a urethral tumour?

A. Chronic stricture disease, inflammatory conditions, HPV infection and sexually transmitted diseases.

Q. How would you manage this patient?

A. As these tumours are very rare, the management also varies, but it involves a multi-modality approach. A tumour of the mid shaft with no synchronous tumour elsewhere can be managed by performing a wide local excision of the urethra together with the adjacent tunica albuginea. Urethral reconstruction is then performed either by bringing the urethra out as a perineal urethrostomy or, if the length is adequate, a hypospadiac urethra can be refashioned. For more aggressive tumours a total urethrectomy is required and further adjuvant treatment is guided by the histology and margins. The inguinal lymph nodes are managed as for a penile cancer, although the majority of patients will undergo a radical lymphadenectomy rather than a sentinel lymph node biopsy.

ACKNOWLEDGEMENTS

We are grateful to Dr Alex Freeman, Consultant Histopathologist, University College London Hospitals, for providing the histology slides for this chapter.

REFERENCES

1. Muneer A *et al*. Molecular prognostic factors in penile cancer. *World J Urol* 2009; **27:** 161–7.
2. Kayes O *et al*. The role of magnetic resonance imaging in the local staging of penile cancer. *Eur Urol* 2007; **51:** 1313–18.
3. Pietrzak P *et al*. Organ sparing surgery for invasive penile cancer: early follow-up data. *BJU Int* 2004; **94**(2):1253–7.
4. Hadway P *et al*. Evaluation of dynamic lymphoscintigraphy and sentinel lymph-node biopsy for detecting occult metastases in patients with penile squamous-cell carcinoma. *BJU Int* 2007; **100:** 561–5.

FURTHER READING

Arya M, Shergill IS, Silhi N *et al*. *Essential Urology in General Practice*. London: Quay Books; 2009.

Wein AJ, Kavoussi LR, Novick AC *et al*. (eds) *Campbell-Walsh Urology*, 9th edn. Philadelphia, PA: Saunders Elsevier; 2006.

Chapter 4
Bladder cancer

Ciaran Lynch and Lyndon Gommersall

HAEMATURIA

Q. **How common is haematuria?**

A. Haematuria is a common finding. In the paediatric population the incidence is as low as 1%, rising to 5% in young adults and increasing to 10% in patients over the age of 50 years.

Q. **A 65-year-old woman is referred with dipstick haematuria. A midstream specimen of urine (MSU) has been sent for microscopy, culture and sensitivity. Microscopy shows a normal white cell count (WCC) and 18 red blood cells (RBCs) per high-powered field, and no growth has been found on culture. The patient has moderate irritative voiding lower urinary tract symptoms (LUTS), and is otherwise well. No other investigations have been performed. How would you assess this woman?**

A. Assessment would involve a focused history, examination and investigations. A full urological history would include exposure to cigarette smoking. Enquiry into environmental carcinogens is a complicated and lengthy undertaking if done properly. It confers a less than 1% risk of developing bladder cancer. Blood pressure should be included as well as a full abdominal and pelvic examination. Investigations should include an MSU for culture and sensitivity, urine for cytology, routine bloods (including FBC, renal function, coagulation profile), an ultrasound scan (USS) of the patient's renal tract, and a flexible cystoscopy. It should be noted that with the advent of novel molecular urinary markers, such as NMP22, urine cytology is increasingly excluded. If a bladder cancer is found, further staging investigations are required. If these tests are negative with high-grade malignant cells on urine cytology, a CT urogram (CTU) should be performed (contemporary radiological practice clearly favours the CTU over IVU). If this does not reveal an upper tract tumour, an examination under anaesthetic, rigid cystoscopy with biopsies, ureteroscopy and retrograde studies need to be undertaken.

Q. **What is the most likely presentation of a patient with bladder cancer?**

A. The most common presentation of bladder cancer is with macroscopic painless haematuria. Almost all patients who are diagnosed with bladder cancer will have had either macroscopic or microscopic haematuria. The degree of bleeding is *not* proportional to the disease stage. Irritative voiding symptoms are a worrying feature, and can occur in approximately 20% of patients with either bladder cancer or carcinoma *in situ*. Urological bleeding associated with urinary tract infection cannot be solely attributed to inflammation, as a proportion of patients will have necrotic infected elements within the bladder tumour and therefore must be fully investigated. Patients who receive imaging or a cystoscopy for another reason make up the remainder of patients.

Q. **What are the causes of haematuria?**

A. The causes of haematuria can be divided into urological or nephrological, benign or malignant, macroscopic or microscopic, or based upon the anatomical location of the bleeding (i.e. renal, ureteric, bladder, prostatic or urethral). Table 4.1 lists the causes of haematuria based on the anatomical location.

Table 4.1 Causes of haematuria based on anatomical location

Anatomical location	Cause
Renal	Renal malignancy: TCC, adenocarcinoma, SCC or other
	Trauma: penetrating or blunt
	Nephrological: IgA nephropathy (Berger's disease), diabetes, Alport's syndrome, thin basement membrane disease
	Renal stones
	Infective: TB, pyelonephritis
Ureteric	Ureteric malignancy: TCC, adenocarcinoma, SCC or other
	Ureteric stone
	Trauma: penetrating or blunt
	Infective: TB
Bladder	Bladder malignancy: TCC, adenocarcinoma, SCC or other
	Bladder stone
	Trauma: blunt or penetrating and pelvic fracture
	Infective: bacterial, TB, schistosomiasis
Prostate	Prostate cancer
	Benign prostatic hypertrophy
	Infective: bacterial prostatitis, granulomatous prostatitis (e.g. TB)
Urethra	Infective: urethritis
	Urethral tumours (SCC, TCC)
Penile tumours	Stricture
	Trauma: blunt or penetrating and catheterisation
Other	Epididymitis
	Menses

TCC, transitional-cell carcinoma; SCC, squamous-cell carcinoma.

Q. **What is the definition of haematuria?**

A. The recent Joint Consensus Statement on the Initial Assessment of Haematuria, prepared on behalf of the Renal Association and the British Association of Urological Surgeons (and published in July 2008), establishes a clear definition of haematuria. According to this document, blood in the urine is either visible haematuria (VH) (i.e. macroscopic or gross haematuria) or non-visible haematuria (NVH) (microscopic haematuria). The NVH is then sub-classified into symptomatic non-visible haematuria (s-NVH) (i.e. with voiding LUTS) or asymptomatic non-visible haematuria (a-NVH) (i.e. without voiding LUTS).

The definition of NVH varies between different guidelines (as do the recommended investigations that are performed), and these definitions are summarised in Table 4.2. The quantification of microscopic haematuria depends on two key techniques, namely the sediment count and the chamber count. The sediment count consists of urine that has been spun down in a centrifuge with the supernatant removed. The pellet of cells is then re-suspended in saline and examined under the microscope. The chamber count detects the number of RBCs per ml of urine. The American Urological Association (AUA) definition of haematuria utilises the sediment count and defines > 3 RBCs per high-powered field as abnormal. Most nephrologists will utilise the threshold of 5 RBCs per microlitre. In 1990, the *Journal of the American Medical Association (JAMA)* defined microscopic haematuria as > 2–3 RBCs per high-powered field.[1] *Campbell-Walsh Urology* defines haematuria as > 5 RBCs per high-powered field for spun urine (sediment count) and > 2 RBCs per high-powered field for unspun urine (chamber count). Table 4.3 shows the relationship between the dipstick positive result and the RBC count per high-powered field. A trace result is generally considered to be negative, and + or more is regarded as a positive result.

Table 4.2 Summary of the various definitions of microscopic haematuria

Authority	Definition
AUA	> 3 RBCs per high-powered field on a spun specimen
Nephrologists	> 5 RBCs per microlitre
JAMA	> 2–3 RBCs per high-powered field[2]
Campbell-Walsh Urology	> 5 RBCs per high-powered field for spun urine and > 2 RBCs per high-powered field for unspun urine

Table 4.3 Equivalent dipstick and microscopy results for non-visible haematuria (NVH)

Dipstick result	RBCs per high-powered field
+/–	1–10
+	10–40
++	40–100
+++	100–200

Khadra has also reported on the percentage of patients who would have had a cancer diagnosis missed for 10, 5 and 3 RBCs per high-powered field. This equates to a missed cancer diagnosis in 20%, 14.8% and 10% of cases, respectively.[2]

Q. **What do you know about dipstick testing for haematuria?**
A. Dipstick testing for haematuria is commonplace. It is based on the alteration of a chromogen by the peroxidase activity of haemoglobin. This results in a colour change that is compared with a set of known standards. Electronic strip readers overcome the subjective nature of the test and eradicate reader error. False-positive results can occur with myoglobinuria, oxidising agents and peroxidases.

A false-negative result can also occur with high levels of ascorbic acid, nitrite, pH < 5.0 and high specific gravity of the urine specimen. *There is no substitute for urine microscopy performed by a competent laboratory.*

Q. How would you set up a haematuria clinic?

A. Haematuria is well suited for investigation using a one-stop clinic. Each patient requires a full history and examination. This should include a detailed report of the haematuria, the duration and any associated symptoms. Smoking exposure must be recorded. Examination should include a general abdominal examination, external genital examination and a digital rectal examination in men. Occasionally in older women vaginal bleeding is mistaken as haematuria and therefore a vaginal examination should also be performed. An MSU and urine cytology are required. An USS of the renal tract is required as well as a flexible cystoscopy. Further imaging of the undiagnosed patient with IVU or CTU is widely used. Interpretation of this data can then lead to immediate discharge of the patient, or to organisation of further investigations if indicated. For example, in a patient with positive cytology, negative MSU, normal USS/ CTU and normal urothelium on flexible cystoscopy, retrograde studies and ureteroscopy are required to elucidate the cause of the high-grade malignant cells detected.

From a referral perspective the recent Joint Consensus Statement on the Initial Assessment of Haematuria, prepared on behalf of the Renal Association and the British Association of Urological Surgeons (and published in July 2008), establishes clear guidelines for referral to a urologist running a haematuria clinic. These include all patients with visible haematuria at any age, all patients with s-NVH at any age and all patients with a-NVH aged over 40 years.

Q. How do you perform urine cytology?

A. Urine cytology is performed on a random or, ideally, a mid-morning urine sample. Early-morning urine samples provide degenerative specimens for cytological examination. The sample should be the whole voided urine, as a midstream urine is the most acellular fraction. The sample needs to be rapidly transferred to the laboratory for processing. If a short delay occurs, refrigeration is recommended. If longer delays are expected, prompt fixation with an equal amount of 50% alcohol can be utilised. The sensitivity of urine cytology increases with the number of specimens examined. Ideally at least three mid-morning or random specimens should be submitted for examination, but this is often impractical. Catheter specimens can be utilised, but cellular changes can be seen with this method of collection. Saline washouts may also be utilised (saline barbotage), and need to be recorded on the request form. The laboratory will then centrifuge the sample, perform fixation in formalin and stain with Papanicolaou or haematoxylin and eosin dyes. The resulting slides are then analysed under the microscope for morphological changes consistent with malignancy.

Cytology is most useful for the detection of high-grade malignancy, and is positive in 90% of these cases. In low-grade tumours it is positive in only 10% of patients. It is often used as a safety system for the detection of malignancy in the investigation-negative group of individuals.

Q. **Can you describe any alternatives to urine cytology?**

A. Urine cytology has been the predominant method of urine testing to detect urothelial cancer for many decades. With a reported specificity of 95% and sensitivity of 30–50% it is an adequate test for detecting high-risk disease, but lacks the sensitivity for detecting low-grade disease. Several novel urine markers for urothelial carcinoma have been developed, including NMP22 (nuclear matrix protein 22), BTA (bladder tumour-associated antigen), BTA stat, UroVysion and telomerase.

The specificity and sensitivity of these bladder cancer urinary markers are reviewed in Table 4.4.

Table 4.4 Summary of novel urinary marker sensitivity and specificity in detecting urothelial carcinoma (reproduced from Konety et al.[3])

	Sensitivity (%)	Specificity (%)
Cytology	49	96
NMP22 (Bladder Chek)	70	75
BTA stat	66	76
Telomerase (TRAP)	74	79

NMP22 (nuclear matrix protein 22) is promoted as the 'NMP22 Bladder Chek' test. It is reported to have increased sensitivity compared with cytology, and has been used during surveillance. The BTA stat test identifies overproduction of the complement protective peptide known as complement factor H related protein (CFHrp) in the urine. This is known as the bladder tumour-associated antigen (BTA). The UroVysion test utilises fluorescent *in situ* hybridisation (FISH) to test for aneuploidy of chromosomes 3, 7 and 17 and loss of chromosome 9p21. This complicated test requires intact cells, expensive equipment and a dedicated laboratory. Telomerase is over-expressed in many cancers, and can be detected in the urine with the telomerase repeat amplification (TRAP) assay. Telomerase adds telomeres to chromosomal terminal DNA sequences, preventing cell senescence.

Q. **What is the evidence for your haematuria investigation regime?**

A. Two studies have provided the evidence for the investigation of haematuria, the first by Khadra *et al.*, published in the *Journal of Urology* in 2000, and the other by Edwards *et al.*, published in the *British Journal of Urology International* in 2006. Khadra *et al.* studied 1930 patients who attended a haematuria clinic between 1994 and 1997.[2] All of the patients underwent a history and examination, routine blood tests, urinalysis, cytology, plain abdominal radiography, renal ultrasound, IVU and flexible cystoscopy. In total, 61% of patients in this cohort had no pathology identified, 12% were diagnosed with bladder cancer, 13% had urinary tract infection and 2% had stone disease. The key message of this paper is that if only ultrasound or IVU had been performed, four cases of upper tract malignancy would have been missed (therefore the use of both imaging modalities is recommended). Overall, macroscopic and microscopic haematuria resulted in a cancer diagnosis in 24% and 9.4% of patients, respectively. Bladder cancer was found in more patients with microscopic haematuria than the 5% or less reported within the urological literature. Edwards *et al.* studied 4020 patients attending a haematuria clinic.[4] Macroscopic haematuria resulted in a fourfold increase in the diagnosis of cancer compared with microscopic haematuria (19% vs. 5%), and 75% had no underlying pathology identified. Three upper tract tumours were identified after a normal ultrasound scan, with 46% of this cohort also undergoing an IVU.

Q. **Is screening for bladder cancer effective?**

A. In 1992, Britton *et al.* investigated the use of dipstick testing for haematuria in 2356 men over 60 years of age.[5] In total, 20% (*n* = 474) of these patients had dipstick haematuria on recurrent testing, of whom 319 patients agreed to undergo urological examination. In this cohort, 17 asymptomatic patients (5.3%) were diagnosed with bladder cancer. However, this approach would lead to large numbers of asymptomatic patients requiring investigation. The cost per bladder cancer diagnosis is therefore prohibitively high at the present time. More recently targeted screening of a population of smokers has reported a 3.3% detection rate for malignancy using urine cytology, urine dipstick and the urinary markers UroVysion and NMP22 (Bladder Chek).[6]

Q. **If all of the patient's investigations are negative, what should be done next?**

A. The key patient in this scenario is the one with negative cystoscopy and imaging but who has positive urine cytology. This patient should be offered a CTU if this had not been performed as part of the initial haematuria investigations. This should be followed by a general anaesthetic cystoscopy combined with bladder biopsies looking for carcinoma *in situ*. At the same time bilateral retrograde studies and if necessary a ureteroscopy can also be performed.

Q. **Who should be referred to a nephrologist?**

A. The Joint Consensus Statement on the Initial Assessment of Haematuria, prepared on behalf of the Renal Association and the British Association of Urological Surgeons (and published in July 2008), establishes clear guidelines for referral to nephrology. Essentially all patients who have negative investigations from a urological perspective need a referral, as well as those patients with microscopic haematuria who did not meet the criteria listed earlier in this section for urological referral. Additional factors that indicate the need to seek nephrological advice include the following:
- evidence of declining GFR (by > 10 ml/min at any stage within the previous 5 years or by > 5 ml/min within the last 1 year)
- stage 4 or 5 chronic kidney disease (eGFR < 30 ml/min)
- significant proteinuria (albumin to creatinine ratio of ≥ 30 mg/mmol or protein to creatinine ratio of ≥ 50 mg/mmol)
- isolated haematuria (i.e. in the absence of significant proteinuria) with hypertension in those aged < 40 years
- visible haematuria coinciding with intercurrent (usually upper respiratory tract) infection.

Q. **What are the common renal (nephrological) causes of microscopic haematuria?**

A. Microscopic haematuria from a nephrological perspective is either glomerular or non-glomerular (*see* Table 4.5).

Table 4.5 Nephrological disorders that result in microscopic haematuria

Glomerular	Non-glomerular
IgA nephropathy	Cystic disease
Alport's syndrome	Inflammatory disorders of the urothelium
Thin basement membrane disease	Interstitial nephritis
Henoch–Schönlein purpura	Papillary necrosis
Vasculitis (e.g. lupus)	Renal artery stenosis
Goodpasture's syndrome	
Nephrotic syndrome	
Diabetic glomerulosclerosis	

Glomerular disease is a common cause of microscopic haematuria. IgA nephropathy is also known as Berger's disease and results in mesangial deposition of IgA. This often occurs after an upper respiratory tract infection. Macroscopic or microscopic haematuria can be present. Around 10–20% of cases will develop renal failure within 10–20 years. The prognosis is worse if the patient develops hypertension or has proteinuria or fibrosis on biopsy. Treatment depends on the strict control of blood pressure, and occasionally requires steroids and immunosuppression.

Alport's syndrome is an X-linked collagen mutation that causes blindness, deafness and nephritis, resulting in chronic renal failure.

Thin basement membrane disease is an asymptomatic disease that results in a-NVH. It is non-progressive and can be diagnosed only by electron microscopy of a renal biopsy.

Nephrotic syndrome results from a non-inflammatory injury to the glomerulus. Patients classically have hypoalbuminaemia, hypercholesterolaemia and hyperlipidaemia due to excessive hepatic lipoprotein synthesis. Considerable proteinuria may exist. Treatment is with steroids.

Causes of non-glomerular microscopic haematuria include interstitial nephritis, which results from an inflammatory infiltrate affecting nephron function. Acute interstitial nephritis occurs 4 days to 5 weeks after starting a new drug, commonly a penicillin. Symptomatically the patient develops a fever and generalised rash with oliguria, increased creatinine levels and hypertension.

Papillary necrosis is characterised by coagulative necrosis of the renal papillae resulting from pyelonephritis, obstructed uropathy, sickle-cell disease, TB, trauma, cirrhosis, analgesic nephropathy, renal vein thrombosis or diabetes (the acronym POSTCARD is used). Urological management involves resolution of urinary obstruction, treatment of infection and resuscitation.

A renal artery stenosis can result in renin-mediated hypertension, and occurs only with a stenosis greater than 70%. Clinically a bruit may be auscultated.

NON-MUSCLE-INVASIVE BLADDER CANCER

Q. **What are the histological types of primary bladder carcinoma?**

A. Almost 95% of patients with bladder cancer have a transitional-cell carcinoma (TCC). The remaining patients have squamous-cell carcinoma (SCC) (4%) or, rarely, adenocarcinoma of the bladder.

Q. **What proportion of patients present with non-muscle-invasive disease?**

A. Over 80% of patients with TCC present with non-muscle-invasive Ta or T1 disease, and the remaining patients present with muscle-invasive malignancy (T2 to T4).

Q. **A 67-year-old man has been assessed in the haematuria clinic. Flexible cystoscopy is performed and reveals a 2 cm papillary lesion on the posterior wall of his bladder. A CTU has been performed which shows normal upper tracts. He is concerned about this diagnosis. How would you treat this man?**

A. This man requires an examination under anaesthetic and transurethral resection of bladder tumour (TURBT). On his consent form I would consent him for the risk of bleeding, infection and bladder perforation as well as further adjuvant treatment with the risk of recurrent disease. He will require catheterisation following his operation.

A TURBT is performed under either a general or a spinal anaesthesia. If the tumour is located on the postero-lateral aspects of the bladder wall, a general anaesthetic is preferable in order to avoid an 'obturator kick' and the almost inevitable risk of bladder perforation. The bladder should be emptied prior to a bimanual examination to assess for a bladder mass indicating invasive disease. The cystoscope is then inserted to examine the urethra and bladder. A 70-degree lens allows for a more complete examination of the bladder urothelium. A continuous-flow resectoscope can then be introduced to perform the operation. A monopolar diathermy loop is used to resect the exophytic tumour in order to obtain a histological diagnosis. Further deep muscle resection specimens from the base of the tumour should be sent separately to fully stage the lesion. Rollerball monopolar diathermy is then utilised to provide haemostasis and fulgurate the edge of the lesion to destroy any potentially malignant urothelium. If any other abnormal areas of urothelium are seen, these sites need separate sampling with a cold cup biopsy and diathermy in order to detect CIS. Random biopsies of normal mucosa are rarely performed in Ta or T1 disease, as the likelihood of detecting CIS is less than 2%. A three-way irrigating catheter can then be inserted to wash out any malignant cells and blood following the procedure. Generally this can be removed the next day, but with larger resections it may be necessary to wait 48 hours. Care must be taken when resecting deep lesions that a perforation of the bladder does not occur. Following the resection, a further bimanual examination can then be performed to assess whether any bladder mass is still palpable. A residual mass strongly suggests residual invasive disease (T3).

There is a significant risk of residual disease after TURBT (in some studies up to 27% and 53% in patients with Ta and T1 tumours, respectively). In those patients with TI disease, upstaging to T2 disease occurs in approximately 21–25% of patients following a second resection, which should be performed 4–6 weeks later.

Post-operatively, clinically superficial lesions should receive adjuvant intravesical mitomycin C (MMC) or epirubicin. In a meta-analysis by Sylvester *et al.* this has shown a 39% decrease in the relative risk of recurrence.[7]

Q. **What do you know about fluorescent cystoscopy?**

A. Fluorescent cystoscopy, photodynamic diagnosis (PDD) or blue light cystoscopy relies on the molecular handling of 5-aminolevulinic acid (5-ALA) by tumour cells. 5-ALA is instilled into the bladder prior to cystoscopy and is taken up by the urothelium. It is converted to protoporphyrin, which is preferentially taken up by malignant cells. When blue light (wavelength 375–440 nm) is used to illuminate the bladder, this results in higher-intensity fluorescence from abnormal mucosa compared with the surrounding normal bladder mucosa (i.e. when illuminated with blue light, malignant tissue appears red). In practice this results in an approximately 30% increase in the diagnosis of bladder cancer and a 67% increase in the diagnosis of CIS compared with white light cystoscopy. Fluorescent TURBT (as compared with white light TURBT) also decreases the incidence of residual tumour on follow-up, as well as improving recurrence-free survival.

Q. **What factors predispose this man to superficial bladder cancer?**

A. The main risk factors for bladder cancer are cigarette smoking (this increases the risk by threefold, particularly in slow hepatic acetylators), industrial carcinogens used in the rubber and paint industries (aniline dyes, α-naphthylamine), phenacetin and cyclophosphamide (used in chemotherapy of many haematological cancers). Carcinogenesis in bladder cancer has been extensively reported. The main karyotypic changes involve aberrations of chromosome 9 (> 50% of tumours), chromosome 17 (p53 loci) and chromosome 13 (retinoblastoma gene loci). A loss of retinoblastoma gene expression, Ha-ras activation and over-expression of telomerase are early genetic changes in superficial bladder cancer, with p53 mutations, FGF and VEGF over-expression leading to invasive or metastatic disease. Two key theories govern the development of bladder cancer. The clonal theory argues that multifocal and recurrent tumours evolve from one single transformed cell from which all cells share identical genetic mutations. The field change or oligoclonal theory suggests that there is a global change in the urothelium. Genetically pre-malignant cells are then transformed into clinically detectable tumours which are genetically unrelated.

Q. **Can you name any lesions that would predispose a patient to bladder cancer?**

A. Several clinically detected lesions can predispose individuals to malignancy. These are summarised in Table 4.6.

Table 4.6 Lesions arising from the urothelium, and their malignant potential

Keratinising squamous metaplasia	This is seen in exstrophy, chronic bladder inflammation and schistosomiasis. It is pre-malignant
Non-keratinising squamous metaplasia	Not pre-malignant
Urothelial dysplasia	A flat non-invasive lesion typified by nuclear clustering. Can be seen with or without malignancy
Cystitis cystica	Non pre-malignant enfolding of normal bladder lining cells
Cystitis glandularis	Associated with adenocarcinoma
Papillary urothelial neoplasm of low malignant potential	Difficult to define. Histology reveals exaggeration of normal glandular rests in bladder urothelium

continued

| Leukoplakia | Clinically seen as thick raised white plaques of squamous metaplasia on bladder surface. It is associated with chronic urinary infections. There is a weak association with malignancy. Histology shows keratinisation of metaplastic squamous metaplasia |
| Malakoplakia | Similar to if not the same as leukoplakia, malakoplakia is histologically characterised by Michaelis–Gutmann bodies with distinctive basophilic inclusions and foamy histiocytes. Clinically seen as soft yellow plaques on the urothelium |

Q. This 67-year-old man (mentioned earlier) attended for a TURBT. EUA revealed no mass. A 2 cm papillary-looking tumour was resected from the posterior wall of his bladder. Deep muscle samples were sent separately. He received a single dose of MMC intravesical chemotherapy post-operatively. The histology shows grade 1 disease invading sub-epithelial tissue. The deep muscle biopsies are clear of tumour. He attends clinic to have the histology explained to him. What is the TNM stage of this man's disease?

A. This man has G1 pT1 disease. The TNM bladder cancer staging system is reproduced in Table 4.7.

Table 4.7 TNM staging of bladder cancer, 2002

Tx	Primary tumour cannot be assessed
Ta	Non-invasive papillary carcinoma
Tis	Carcinoma in situ
T1	Tumour is invading subepithelial connective tissue
T2	a. Tumour is invading superficial detrusor muscle b. Tumour is invading deep detrusor muscle
T3	a. Tumour is invading perivesical tissue microscopically b. Tumour is invading perivesical tissue macroscopically
T4	a. Tumour is invading prostate or uterus and vagina b. Tumour is invading pelvic wall and abdominal wall
Nx	Regional lymph nodes cannot be assessed
N0	No regional lymph node metastasis
N1	Metastasis in a single lymph node, 2 cm or less in greatest dimension
N2	Metastasis in a single lymph node, 2–5 cm, or multiple lymph nodes, none > 5 cm in greatest dimension
N3	Metastasis in a lymph node or multiple lymph nodes > 5 cm in greatest dimension
Mx	Distant metastasis cannot be assessed
M0	No distant metastasis
M1	Distant metastasis

Q. Do you know of any risk stratification for bladder cancer?

A. Several authorities have proposed a risk stratification for superficial bladder cancer. The British Association of Urological Surgeons (BAUS) has published guidelines on bladder cancer, and proposes three risk groups for superficial bladder cancer. These are reproduced in Table 4.8.

Table 4.8 BAUS risk groups for superficial bladder cancer

Low risk	pTa G1/G2 and tumour < 3 cm in diameter and solitary
Intermediate risk	pTa G1/G2 and tumour > 3 cm in diameter or multiple or frequently recurring, pT1 G2 and tumour < 3 cm in diameter and solitary
High risk	pT1 G2 and tumour > 3 cm in diameter or multiple or chemoresistant, pTa/pT1 G3 or CIS

- The European Organization for Research and Treatment of Cancer (EORTC) and the European Association of Urology (EAU) have also published risk categories based on a scoring system utilising the following pathological features: number of tumours (i.e. multifocality); tumour diameter; prior recurrence rate; stage; concomitant CIS and grade. This scoring system is derived from seven trials involving superficial bladder cancer, organised by the EORTC.[8] It calculates a percentage risk of recurrence and progression at 1 and 5 years, as well as defining scores for low-, intermediate- and high-risk disease. The tables are reproduced in the EAU guidelines on Ta/T1 (non-muscle-invasive) bladder cancer.
- By stage Ta, disease has a 50% chance of never recurring, but if tumour is detected at the 3-month flexible check cystoscopy, further recurrent disease will be found in 90% of patients during follow-up.
- Progression occurs in only 15% of Ta disease.
- Around 20% of patients with T1 disease will have died within 5 years.
- G3pT1 disease is under-staged at radical cystectomy in 30% of patients and has a very high risk of progression if concomitant CIS is found.
- CIS leads to invasive disease within 2 years if left untreated.
- Progression will occur in less than 5% of patients with G1pTa disease, 10% of those with multifocal G1pT1, 30% of those with G3pT1, more than 50% of those with CIS, and 50–80% of those with G3 disease with CIS.

Q. **What is the evidence for using mitomycin C intravesical chemotherapy in superficial bladder cancer, and how would you consent a patient for and administer mitomycin C?**

A. Mitomycin C (MMC) is an anti-tumour antibiotic that cross-links complementary DNA strands and alkylates single DNA strands in bladder tumour cells. It has been extensively investigated in the treatment of Ta T1 bladder cancer. Following on from work in the UK for the Medical Research Council by Parmar and Tolley in the late 1980s,[9] a meta-analysis in 2004 by Sylvester *et al.* reported on seven trials studying the use of single-dose intravesical chemotherapy post TURBT. This showed a 39% decrease in the relative risk of *recurrence* with adjuvant treatment.[7] Its use is therefore 'standard of care' post TURBT. For higher-risk disease, a six-dose (weekly) course is necessary. MMC does not prevent *progression* of recurrent TCC, and in high-risk cases BCG is optimal. Sylvester *et al.* have published three meta-analyses for adjuvant treatment of bladder cancer, which are summarised in Table 4.9.

MMC is given at a dose of 40 mg in 40 ml of saline via a urinary catheter. The catheter is then clamped and the patient is left with the solution in the bladder for 1 hour. The catheter is then removed or unclamped. The patient should be aware of the risks of extravasation post-operatively, irritative voiding symptoms, and a chemical dermatitis of the palms of the hands.

Table 4.9 Summary of the three meta-analyses published by Sylvester et al. for the use of adjuvant intravesical treatment following TURBT in superficial bladder cancer and bladder CIS[7,10,11]

1. Meta-analysis of TURBT plus BCG vs. TURBT alone or another adjuvant treatment[10]	24 randomised controlled trials involving 4863 patients with superficial bladder cancer. Resulted in an absolute risk reduction of progression of 4%, and a relative risk reduction of progression of 27%. Therefore BCG reduces the risk of progression
2. Meta-analysis comparing TURBT plus single-dose adjuvant chemotherapy vs. TURBT[7]	7 randomised controlled trials involving 1476 patients with superficial bladder cancer. Resulted in an absolute risk reduction of recurrence of 12% (NNT = 8.5), and a relative risk reduction of recurrence of 39%. Therefore single-dose MMC reduces the risk of recurrence
3. Meta-analysis comparing intravesical chemotherapy and BCG in CIS of the bladder[11]	9 randomised controlled trials involving 700 patients with superficial bladder cancer. Resulted in an absolute risk reduction of recurrence of 20.5%, and a relative risk reduction of recurrence of 59%. Therefore BCG is more effective than intravesical chemotherapy in CIS

Q. **Tell me about the use of BCG in patients with bladder cancer.**

A. BCG or Bacillus Calmette–Guérin was first used by Morales in 1976.[12] It is live attenuated *Mycobacterium bovis*. Connaught, Tice and RIVM are the three strains used. No difference in efficacy has been reported between these strains. The mechanism of action of BCG is still poorly understood. It is known that it attaches to the urothelium via the fibronectin receptor and is internalised within the cell. Glycoproteins remain on the surface membrane of epithelioid cells, and these antigens mediate the immune response by macrophage chemotaxis and cytokine production. Histologically BCG granulomas consist of epitheloid cells, Langerhan's giant cells and lymphocytes. Increasingly, 27 mg of BCG is thought to give the same efficacy as 81 mg with potentially less toxicity.

Q. **How would you consent a patient for and administer BCG intravesical immunotherapy?**

A. Patients who receive intravesical BCG must be at least 2 weeks post TURBT or bladder biopsy. The instillation is performed via a catheter, which is immediately removed, and the BCG is held within the bladder for up to 2 hours. Precautions such as sitting down to void in order to avoid splashing, hand washing after voiding, as well as rinsing the toilet with undiluted bleach are recommended. Patients should be encouraged to increase their fluid intake and void regularly. Common side-effects include dysuria, urinary frequency and malaise, with a mild fever for up to 24 hours expected. More serious symptoms of a high fever for 48 hours, arthralgia, headaches, rash and increased malaise suggest BCG sepsis. This requires hospitalisation, resuscitation, blood cultures and commencement of antituberculous treatment. Steroids should be considered. Seek expert help and continue medication for a period of at least 6 months. Many of the agents used are hepatotoxic, so regular monitoring of liver function is required.

The treatment regime consists of once-weekly instillations for 6 weeks, followed by a 6-week break and three further instillations once a week for 3 weeks. If maintenance treatment is instigated, this consists of once-weekly instillations for 3 weeks every 6 months for up to 3 years. This is the basis of Lamm's regime.[13]

Thus maintenance BCG treatment consists of the following:

- initial post TURBT: 6-week course
- at 3 months: 3-week course
- at 6 months: 3-week course
- every 6 months thereafter: a 3-week course up to 3 years.

Quinolones have some antituberculous activity, so should be avoided in order to maintain efficacy. A meta-analysis by Sylvester *et al.* shows an absolute risk reduction of progression of 4%, with a relative risk reduction of progression of 27%. BCG also significantly reduces recurrence in high-risk superficial bladder cancer.

Q. Do you know of any alternatives to intravesical BCG?

A. In patients who fail a course of BCG, intravesical immunotherapy combination with 50 mega-units of interferon alpha with 1/3 dose of BCG has shown an increased response rate of 50%. Electromotive MMC has also been used in combination with BCG. The inflammatory reaction induced by BCG is thought to increase the absorption of MMC into the transformed urothelium.

Q. How would you manage G3pT1 disease?

A. High-grade T1 bladder cancer presents significant difficulties with regard to management. For G3pT1 disease, 30% of patients will never have a recurrence, 30% will undergo deferred cystectomy and 30% will die of metastatic disease. Adjuvant intravesical immunotherapy (BCG) following TURBT remains the mainstay of treatment to avoid cystectomy. Radiotherapy has shown no increase in progression-free interval, progression-free survival or overall survival. If intravesical strategies fail, cystectomy in carefully chosen individuals results in a 5-year survival rate of 90%. However, 5–10% of these patients will still have positive lymph nodes.

Note: The mainstay of treatment of superficial bladder cancer is TURBT and adjuvant intravesical chemotherapy to prevent recurrence and progression. Accurate staging at TURBT is essential. Follow-up should be tailored to the risk of recurrence. Table 4.10 summarises the investigation, treatment and follow-up of superficial bladder cancer according to the BAUS guidelines.

Table 4.10 BAUS guidelines for the investigation, treatment and follow-up of superficial bladder cancer by risk group

BAUS risk group	Investigation	Treatment	Follow-up
Low (pTa G1/G2 and tumour < 3 cm in diameter and solitary)	Cystoscopy Histopathology	Adjuvant single instillation of intravesical chemotherapy within 6 hours of first resection	If a single new tumour, follow-up cystoscopy at 3 and 9 months and then annually Discharge at 5 years If recurrent, see intermediate-risk group

continued

Intermediate (pTa G1/G2 and tumour > 3 cm in diameter or multiple or frequently recurring, pT1 G2 and tumour < 3 cm in diameter and solitary)	Cystoscopy Histopathology CTU Cytology	Adjuvant single instillation of intravesical chemotherapy within 6 hours of first resection Consider re-resection if incomplete TUR or no muscle in specimen Consider intravesical chemotherapy course	Regular cystoscopic follow-up is required Consider high-risk management options if recurrences occur despite intravesical chemotherapy
High risk (pT1 G2 and tumour > 3 cm in diameter or multiple or chemoresistant, pTa/pT1 G3 or CIS)	Cystoscopy Histopathology CTU Cytology Random biopsies Biopsy of prostatic urethra Re-resection	Adjuvant single instillation of intravesical chemotherapy within 6 hours of first resection Consider early re-resection if grade 3, if incomplete TUR or no muscle in specimen Give BCG intravesical immunotherapy induction and observe If disease is recurrent, consider cystectomy	Regular cystoscopic follow-up is essential, as well as maintenance BCG (if tolerated)

Q. What about re-resection of high-risk disease?

A. Re-resection after an initial TURBT should be considered in all patients with high-grade (G3) or T1 disease. Re-resection with a second TURBT at 4–6 weeks post-operatively for T1 disease has demonstrated residual disease in up to 50% of patients and, importantly, the disease is upstaged (> T1 or concomitant CIS) in approximately 25% of individuals. At the MDT it is important to identify in high-risk patients with superficial disease that adequate bladder muscle has been included in the specimen to exclude invasive disease. These approaches are important in the accurate staging of bladder cancer to decide on appropriate definitive treatment and follow-up.

Q. How would you manage carcinoma *in situ* of the bladder?

A. CIS is a histological diagnosis and is a flat, non-invasive (i.e. not crossing the basement membrane), high-grade malignancy of the bladder (*see* Figure 4.1).

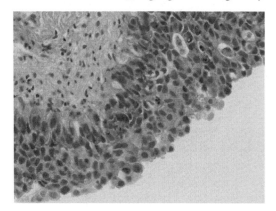

Figure 4.1 H and E of carcinoma *in situ* of bladder displaying flat, non-invasive, full-thickness, disordered proliferation of atypical cells with loss of cell polarity and cell cohesion (changes do not cross the basement membrane). (The authors are grateful to Dr Rupali Arora, Consultant Histopathologist, University College Hospitals, London, for providing this image.)

CIS leads to invasive disease within 2 years if not treated. In addition, if untreated, progression occurs in more than 50% of patients with CIS alone and in 50–80% of patients who have G3 disease with CIS.

Primary CIS of the bladder is defined as CIS without any concomitant or previous TCC. Secondary CIS is defined as CIS with a TCC of the urothelium. Primary disease represents about 5% of CIS diagnosed. It occurs most commonly in men over the age of 50 years. Secondary disease often occurs in association with high-grade invasive lesions. Urine cytology has a very high sensitivity and specificity for the detection of CIS (94% and 96%, respectively). Fluorescent cystoscopy has been used to detect carcinoma *in situ*, but does have a 35% false-positive rate on biopsy. CIS cells show a high percentage of p53 mutations. The mainstay of treatment of CIS is intravesical immunotherapy with BCG. A meta-analysis by Sylvester *et al.* shows that BCG is superior to MMC in the treatment of CIS.[11] With maintenance BCG up to 3 years, 75% of patients show an initial complete response, with 50% remaining disease-free at 5 years and 30% at 10 years. For BCG-refractory disease, other novel approaches have been used, including BCG with electromotive MMC, combination BCG with interferon alpha and photodynamic therapy. Upper-tract CIS is a very dangerous condition, and BCG treatment is associated with a higher degree of BCG-related complications due to increased systemic absorption.

Q. **What do you know about squamous-cell carcinoma of the bladder?**

A. Squamous-cell carcinoma of the bladder accounts for 3–7% of all bladder tumours. It is often associated with long-term inflammation and irritation in the bladder due to catheterisation, stone disease or schistosomiasis (in sub-Saharan Africa). It generally presents with haematuria, as advanced disease, and carries a poor prognosis. Cystoscopy reveals an invasive ulcerative lesion, often on the trigone or lateral walls of the bladder. Treatment is with cystectomy for loco-regional control. At presentation, only 8–10% of patients will have metastatic disease. The 5-year survival rate is 50% in patients whose aetiology is schistosomiasis.

Q. **What do you know about adenocarcinoma of the bladder?**

A. Adenocarcinoma of the bladder is rare, and accounts for less than 1% of all bladder tumours. It is either primary (*de novo* carcinoma, often on the trigone or posterior wall of the bladder) or secondary (metastatic or associated with an urachal remnant). There is an association with cystitis glandularis rather than with CIS. Adenocarcinoma also has an increased incidence in bladder exstrophy patients and bowel augmentation/bladder substitution into the urinary tract (after 10–20 years).

In urachal adenocarcinoma the urachal remnant is patent in one-third of patients. These patients often present with both haematuria and a mucous discharge from the umbilicus. Histology shows mucus-secreting cells in a glandular, colloid or signet-ring pattern. Clinically, an important consideration is to identify a colonic tumour extending into the bladder. Treatment consists of radical cystectomy with excision of the urachus and umbilicus, but with aggressive management the 5-year survival rate is only 40%. There is no proven role for chemotherapy in the treatment of this rare tumour, which often presents with muscle-invasive disease at diagnosis.

MUSCLE-INVASIVE BLADDER CANCER

Q.   70-year-old man has been seen in the haematuria clinic. His renal tract has been imaged with a CTU which shows normal upper tracts, a filling defect in his bladder and no lymphadenopathy (*see* Figure 4.2).

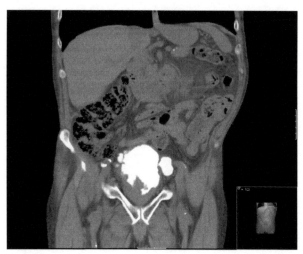

Figure 4.2 CTU (coronal view) demonstrating large filling defect in base of bladder (bladder diverticulae are also present).

Flexible cystoscopy shows a large invasive-looking bladder tumour on the posterior wall of the bladder. The patient has attended for his TURBT. Outline how you would stage bladder cancer if you thought at TURBT it was muscle-invasive.

A.   Staging of bladder cancer is undertaken through a combination of clinical, histological and radiological means. An examination under anaesthetic is performed both before and after TURBT to assess whether there is any palpable disease. Histological staging depends on the pathological evidence of muscle invasion. Radiologically, the bladder is staged locally and also for evidence of loco-regional lymph nodes and metastatic disease.

Q.   Outline how you would perform a TURBT on a solid, 6 cm tumour that appeared to be muscle invasive.

A.   I would begin with a bimanual examination of the bladder under anaesthetic, and would resect the exophytic tumour flat and send it as the superficial specimen. I would then resect the underlying muscle to assess muscle invasion and send this separately. Some authorities favour 'near and far' biopsies as well as biopsies of the prostatic urethra, especially if radical treatment is likely to be contemplated. I would then complete haemostasis and perform a post-TURBT bimanual examination under anaesthesia. A three-way irrigating catheter should be inserted.

Q.   What is N1 disease? What is N2 disease? What is N3 disease?

A.   The 2002 TNM staging of bladder cancer is reproduced in Table 4.7. N1 disease is metastasis in a single lymph node < 2 cm in greatest dimension, N2 is a metastasis in a single lymph node 2–5 cm or multiple lymph nodes < 5 cm in greatest dimension, and N3 is a single lymph node or multiple lymph nodes > 5 cm in greatest dimension.

Q. **What criteria are used to differentiate between normal and involved lymph nodes on imaging (CT or MRI)?**

A. Dimensions of 8 mm in pelvic nodes and 10 mm in abdominal nodes are regarded as significant. This is measured as the maximum short-axis diameter (MSAD). However, size criteria alone are inaccurate, ranging from 50–80% in overall accuracy in detecting metastatic disease.

Q. **How is muscle-invasive bladder cancer staged? For local staging do you use CT or MRI, or both? Is there any advantage to using one or the other?**

A. The majority of units use CT scan of the pelvis, abdomen and chest (CT scan of the chest is preferred to chest X-ray for thoracic staging). A bone scan is also performed to look for distant metastatic disease, as this can be positive in 5–15% of patients with muscle-invasive TCC.

   MRI is superior to CT for determining depth of bladder wall involvement, as CT cannot differentiate between the layers of the bladder wall and thus cannot distinguish between tumours invading the lamina propria and those invading superficial and deep muscle. MRI and CT have similar accuracy in detecting perivesical extension (i.e. in differentiating between T2 and T3 disease). However, MRI certainly shows more promise in detecting nodal metastases. Therefore when MRI is readily available, CT for local staging is not needed. Unfortunately, due to limited resources and a lack of readily available MRI, CT is much more commonly used for local staging.

Q. **At TURBT the 70-year-old man mentioned above has a palpable mass, and histology confirms high-grade (G3) muscle-invasive disease. A bone scan was negative, and a CT scan of his pelvis, abdomen and chest is normal except for the bladder mass, which suggests T2 disease. You are about to see this man in your clinic. What is his TNM staging?**

A. He is stage T2, at least N0 M0.

Q. **Is this man suitable for radical treatment? How would you decide between radical treatment options?**

A. Following a multi-disciplinary team discussion with radiological and oncological colleagues, an agreed management plan based on the available information should be drawn up. The patient should be seen together with a specialist nurse and preferably a family member.

   An assessment of his fitness, including his cardiac and respiratory status and exercise tolerance, should be made and a recent eGFR ascertained. His treatment options are radical cystectomy (with ileal conduit or neobladder formation) or radical radiotherapy.

   Although the 5-year survival rates are better with radical cystectomy, this may be because radical radiotherapy is likely to be given to patients with significant comorbidity. Importantly, no direct randomised comparisons are available between these two treatment options, and therefore the patient should have the opportunity to discuss each treatment option in detail, including the risk profile of each procedure. Manual dexterity is essential if a neobladder is being considered, in order to be able to perform intermittent self-catheterisation. Table 4.11 reviews the benefits, risks and outcomes of radical treatment options for muscle-invasive bladder cancer.

Table 4.11 Benefits, risks and outcomes of radical treatment options for muscle-invasive bladder cancer

	Radiotherapy	Cystectomy
Benefits	Avoids major surgery Preserves functioning bladder	Full staging available with bladder and lymph node histology
Risks	Irritative voiding symptoms Dysuria Small bladder capacity Lethargy Nausea Proctitis Second malignancy	Major surgery Bleeding Chest infection Wound infection Deep vein thrombosis Pulmonary embolism Post-operative pelvic collections Anastomotic leak Stomal stenosis Anastomotic stricture Hyperchloraemic metabolic acidosis
Outcome	Although the 5-year survival rates are better with radical cystectomy, this may be because radical radiotherapy is likely to be given to patients with significant comorbidity. Importantly, there are no direct comparisons to date using these two modalities. There is a proven survival benefit for neoadjuvant chemotherapy in both groups.	

Q. **In which situations is radical cystectomy the treatment of choice as opposed to radical radiotherapy?**

A. In the following situations radical cytectomy is advocated as opposed to radical radiotherapy:
- presence of CIS (radiotherapy does not treat CIS)
- upper tract obstruction
- presence of inflammatory bowel disease
- presence of severe irritative urinary symptoms
- previous extensive abdominal surgery
- previous pelvic radiotherapy
- ?young patient.

However, if it is important to the patient to preserve sexual function, and particularly if the patient has significant comorbidity, radical radiotherapy is preferred.

Q. **How would you consent a patient for a radical cystectomy?**

A. Cystectomy is associated with mortality in 3% of patients and morbidity in 30%. It carries a significant risk of bleeding requiring blood transfusion. In addition, infection in the surgical wound, chest and pelvis can occur. Complications such as ileo-ileal anastamotic leakage, uretero-ileal anastamotic leakage, deep vein thrombosis, pulmonary embolism, stroke, myocardial infarction and death must be discussed with the patient, as well as disease recurrence. Patients who require an ileal conduit need to be aware of the late complications, including risks of stomal stenosis, anastamotic stricture, herniation and metabolic sequelae such as a hyperchloraemic metabolic acidosis. For patients receiving an ileal neobladder, the operation carries risks of impotence, incontinence or retention. Female surgical candidates should be aware of the risk of shortening and narrowing of the vagina. A rare risk of rectal injury should also be explained to the patient.

Q. **Is there any advantage to lymphadenectomy and to what extent should it be carried out?**

A. There is some evidence that the pattern of nodal spread is predictable, i.e. that there are rarely positive nodes outside the pelvis if the pelvic nodes are uninvolved. Therefore most surgeons confine themselves to the obturator, internal and external iliac nodes, but some authors favour including obturator, internal, external and common iliac as well as pre-sacral and aortic bifurcation nodal dissection. As yet, no agreed optimal lymph node dissection has been established, but both progression-free survival and overall survival are thought to be improved with the number of lymph nodes removed at cystectomy. Herr *et al*.[14] looked at 322 patients who underwent cystectomy, and concluded that at least nine lymph nodes needed to be sampled to accurately define lymph node status. They also found an association between the number of lymph nodes excised and survival (i.e. the more lymph nodes that were removed, the longer the survival).

Q. **Is there any advantage to laparoscopic radical cystectomy?**

A. NICE has recently published guidelines on laparoscopic radical cystectomy. As laparoscopic experience has grown, there has been increasing interest in this approach. There is no consensus on the oncological outcomes, and the urinary diversion is usually performed extracorporeally. It is likely that in future it will become the standard approach.

Q. **What proportion of men will have prostate cancer detected in a cystoprostatectomy sample?**

A. Incidentally found prostate cancer is detected in approximately one-third of male patients undergoing a cystoprostatectomy. Of these, 20% have a Gleason score of 7 or more. Careful follow-up of these patients with PSA testing is therefore required.

Q. **Is there any evidence for the use of adjuvant or neoadjuvant chemotherapy in muscle-invasive (non-metastatic) bladder cancer?**

A. The usefulness of adjuvant chemotherapy in muscle-invasive (non-metastatic) bladder cancer is unproven, but neoadjuvant chemotherapy is now used as standard in many units. A Cochrane review of neoadjuvant chemotherapy in 2005 concluded that platinum-based combination neoadjuvant chemotherapy showed a significant benefit in terms of overall survival, with a 14% reduction in the risk of death. The overall survival increased from 45% to 50%[15] at 5 years. This is a modest increase in survival, and the numbers are relatively small in the relevant trials. There is an associated morbidity and a potential inbuilt delay in definitive treatment related to neoadjuvant treatment.

Q. **Do you know of any trials relating to the treatment of muscle-invasive bladder cancer?**

A. The SPARE trial was initiated by Cancer Research UK and involves randomising patients with non-metastatic bladder cancer (T2 or T3) to radical external beam radiotherapy or radical cystectomy after neoadjuvant chemotherapy. If there has been a good response to chemotherapy in the radiotherapy arm of the trial, they will have radiotherapy, otherwise they will have cystectomy. It is hoped that this trial will help to answer several questions about the relative efficacy of radiotherapy and cystectomy as well as the benefits of neoadjuvant chemotherapy.

Q. **Tell me what options are available for urinary diversion following radical cystectomy.**

A. The most commonly used method of diversion in the UK is the ileal conduit. This is formed by anastamosing the ureters to an isolated piece of distal ileum 20 cm from the ileo-caecal valve. The distal end is brought out as a stoma on the right side of the abdomen. This is then managed with a stoma bag.

   Neo-bladder formation or uretero-colic diversion (ureterosigmoidostomy) is less commonly used in the UK.

Q. **What are the potential problems with ileal conduit formation?**

A. (The complications have already been outlined in the section on consent for cystectomy.) The complications can be classified in a number of ways, namely early or late, mechanical and metabolic. Early complications include those associated with any bowel operation, such as ileus, bowel obstruction, anastomotic leakage or ischaemia of the conduit. Late complications include stomal stenosis, para-stomal herniation and uretero-ileal stenosis. Some of these complications are due to chronic ischaemia. Metabolic problems are less common with an ileal conduit than with a neo-bladder (as the ileal conduit does not act as a storage reservoir for urine), but can include absorption of acid and chloride, leading to a hyperchloraemic metabolic acidosis. This responds well to sodium bicarbonate (1 g od). Macrocytic anaemia can be a consequence of vitamin B_{12} deficiency or it may result from a loss of iron absorption from the terminal ileum.

Q. **What are the advantages and disadvantages of neo-bladder construction?**

A. Neo-bladder formation is increasingly being offered to patients, particularly the young, at the time of cystectomy. It has the advantage of dispensing with the need for a stoma, and approximately 90% of patients are continent by day and approximately 70–80% by night. The disadvantages are that it requires a larger segment of small bowel than does an ileal conduit (60 cm in the Studer neo-bladder vs. 15 cm), and therefore the rate of metabolic complications is proportionally higher. A morbidity rate of approximately 22% is reported. The oncological outcomes have been shown to be similar for the two procedures.

Q. **Under what circumstances would a primary urethrectomy be considered?**

A. Traditionally, urethrectomy in female patients formed a routine part of radical cystectomy. For male patients, cystectomy with urethrectomy was commonly offered. More recently, with the growing use of neo-bladders, this approach is being questioned. It appears that the risk of urethral recurrence is decreased with the use of a neo-bladder compared with an ileal conduit. It has been reported that the incidence of urethral recurrence decreases from 8% to 4% if a neo-bladder is anastamosed to the native urethra, which suggests that urine is protective in this setting to the development of recurrent disease. If urethrectomy is not performed at the time of cystectomy, long-term follow-up of the urethra is required.

In summary, a urethrectomy should be considered if there are positive margins at the urethral resection margin (frozen section can be performed), if the primary tumour is located at the bladder neck or in the urethra (in women), if tumour extensively infiltrates the prostate or if there is extensive CIS and/or multifocal disease.

Q. **What treatment options are available for patients who present with metastatic bladder cancer?**

A. Approximately 10% of patients will present with metastatic bladder cancer. The mainstay of treatment, after thorough assessment, is a debulking TURBT to obtain histology and decrease the risk of further haematuria and voiding symptoms. After discussion with the multi-disciplinary team, the patient should then be offered palliative chemotherapy if they have good performance status and adequate renal function. The current gold standard is combination chemotherapy using MVAC (although a combination of gemcitabine and cisplatin is increasingly being used). The overall response rate is 38–73%, with long-term survival in 5–10% of patients.

TRANSITIONAL-CELL CANCER OF THE RENAL PELVIS AND URETER

Q. **What percentage of urothelial malignancies does cancer of the renal pelvis and ureter constitute?**

A. Urothelial cancer of the renal pelvis and ureter is an uncommon finding, accounting for 5% of urothelial malignancies and less than 10% of renal malignancies.

Q. **A 65-year-old woman presents to your haematuria clinic with macroscopic haematuria. Her cytology shows high-grade malignant cells, and flexible cystoscopy is normal. A CT urogram has been performed which shows a filling defect in the right renal pelvis and right ureter. She has no other comorbidities and a normal glomerular filtration rate (GFR). How would you assess this patient?**

A. I am concerned that this woman has a TCC of her renal pelvis. A full urological history, including exposure to cigarette smoking, is required. The case should be discussed at the local multi-disciplinary team meeting and the opinion of a radiologist sought. Uretero-renoscopy is required to visualise an equivocal filling defect before deciding on definitive treatment. A biopsy can also be performed if necessary via the ureteroscope.

Q. **What are the risk factors and genetics for the development of ureteric cancer?**

A. The aetiology is similar to that of bladder cancer, including exposure to cigarette smoking, industrial carcinogens, phenacetin and cyclophosphamide. Smoking has a long latent period of up to 20 years, whereas cyclophosphamide has a much shorter latent period of around 12 years. Phenacetin is a historically used non-steroidal anti-inflammatory agent. More recently its use with cocaine has been reported. The genetic aberrations involved in ureteric cancer are similar to those for bladder cancer, i.e. chromosome 9, chromosome 17 (p53 loci) and chromosome 13 (retinoblastoma gene loci). However, in upper ureteric TCC a higher level of microsatellite instability compared with bladder tumours is reported.

Q. **What treatment options does the patient have?**

A. The likely treatment options for this woman are open nephro-ureterectomy (NU), including excision of a cuff of bladder tissue at the ureteric orifice, or laparoscopic NU with open excision of a cuff of bladder wall. This is essential because with nephrectomy alone a high rate of ipsilateral ureteric recurrence occurs as the whole of the urothelium is susceptible to recurrent lesions.

The traditional approach for the open technique is the loin incision. This often requires a second Pfannenstiel or lower midline incision to facilitate excision of the bladder cuff. The entire renal unit and collecting system can be removed through a midline abdominal incision.

A laparoscopic NU can be performed with either the transperitoneal or retroperitoneal approach. It can also be performed hand assisted.

Both approaches must tackle the distal ureter, ureteric orifice and cuff of bladder. This can be performed through a variety of incisions. The ureter can be dissected free with either an intravesical or extravesical technique. With the extravesical approach care must be taken to complete the ureteric resection to the ureteric orifice. The intravesical approach is the most precise in terms of ureteric resection, but requires an extra cystotomy.

In addition to formal open ureteric excision, the 'rip and pluck' technique has also been described. This involves the resection or cystoscopic dissection of the distal ureter to perivesical fat. The ureter is then 'plucked' during the distal ureteric dissection. Concern remains that tumour cells may extravasate into the retroperitoneum. This approach avoids the morbidity associated with a second incision.

Q. **Do you know of any minimally invasive treatment options for upper tract transitional-cell carcinoma?**

A. Uretero-renoscopic fulguration of small superficial-looking TCCs as well as percutaneous nephroscopic surgery have a place in the treatment of superficial tumours. The patient may have significant comorbidities that preclude major abdominal surgery or laparoscopy. In addition, a solitary kidney or poor global renal function may necessitate renal-preserving surgery. The EAU guidelines on renal-cell carcinoma divide the indications for renal-preserving surgery into absolute (anatomical or functional solitary kidney), relative (functioning opposite kidney which is affected by a condition that might impair renal function in future) and elective (localised unilateral renal-cell carcinoma with a healthy contralateral kidney). Due to the significant annual mortality rate and the considerable morbidity associated with dialysis, rendering a patient anephric is considered to be a last resort.

The uretero-renoscopic approach requires tissue sampling with cold cup biopsy forceps or a stone basket. Fulguration of the base can then be achieved with either the holmium YAG laser (0.5 mm tissue penetration) or the neodymium:yttrium-aluminium-garnet YAG laser (5 mm tissue penetration). Retrograde stenting is required as part of the procedure. The perforation rate is less than 10% in large studies, and can be treated with the placement of a retrograde ureteric stent. The stricture rate is also around 10%.

The percutaneous approach is more invasive and disrupts urothelial integrity. However, it does allow excellent access to the renal pelvis with a 30F sheath and the use of biopsy forceps, loop resection and base sampling to fully stage the lesion resected. The tract can also serve as a conduit for delivering adjuvant therapy following initial resection. Complications associated with this approach include bleeding, infection and injury to adjacent organs or pleura, and potentially seeding along the tract.

Both of these approaches require long-term close surveillance. Imaging and direct inspection of the collecting system with the uretero-renoscope is necessary to identify new lesions or recurrent disease.

Using these approaches, recurrence rates of 33% for pelvic tumours and 31% for ureteric tumours have been reported. The commonest site of recurrence is in the bladder.

Q. **What options are available for an isolated distal ureteric tumour (*see* Figure 4.3)?**

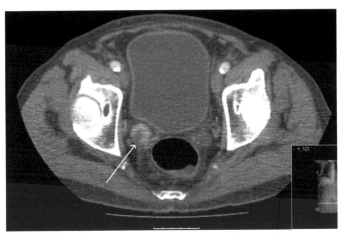

Figure 4.3 CTU (axial view) demonstrating right ureteric tumour.

A. The gold standard for this lesion would be either an open NU or a laparoscopic NU with open excision of a cuff of bladder tissue. However, segmental resection has a role in the elderly patient with significant comorbidity. This can be performed as a direct excision and spatulated tension-free uretero-ureteral anastamosis, or in the lower third of the ureter with a Boari flap or psoas hitch. Comparable oncological failure rates to those for NU are reported.

Q. **The 65-year-old patient mentioned above is treated with an uncomplicated laparoscopic NU with open excision of a cuff of bladder urothelium. The pathologist reports that the lesion is a grade 3 transitional-cell carcinoma**

which is invading the renal parenchyma, and the nodes removed are negative for tumour spread. The surgical margins are clear of tumour. What is the TNM stage for this patient?

A. The TNM stage for this patient is pT3N0Mx. The TNM staging of renal pelvic and ureteric cancer is reproduced in Table 4.12.

Table 4.12 The American Joint Committee on Cancer (AJCC) TNM clinical classification for renal pelvis and ureteric tumours

Tx	Tumour not assessed
T0	No tumour
Ta	Non-invasive papillary carcinoma
Tis	Carcinoma *in situ*
T1	Invading subepithelial connective tissue
T2	Tumour invading muscularis propria
T3	Tumour invading beyond muscularis propria into perinephric or periureteric fat or renal parenchyma
T4	Tumour invading adjacent organs or through kidney into perinephric fat
Nx	Lymph nodes not assessed
N0	No nodes
N2	Single node 2–5 cm or multiple nodes < 5 cm
N3	Single or multiple nodes > 5 cm
Mx	Distant metastasis not assessed
M0	No distant metastasis
M1	Distant metastasis present

Q. What is the prognosis of TCC of the renal pelvis?

A. Hall *et al.* have reported the 5-year survival rates for upper tract TCC.[16] The results are shown in Table 4.13.

Table 4.13 Actuarial disease-specific 5-year survival rates by tumour grade[16]

Stage	Actuarial disease-specific 5-year survival rate (%)
Ta/CIS	100
T1	91.7
T2	72.6
T3	40.5
T4	< 5.0

Q. What percentage of patients develop bladder cancer following upper tract TCC?

A. Up to 50% of patients will develop bladder cancer following a ureteric or renal pelvic tumour. If high-grade upper tract malignancy is resected, the patient has a higher probability of developing high-grade bladder cancer at recurrence.

Q. What percentage of patients develop synchronous and metachronous upper tract TCC?

A. Synchronous tumours of the upper tract have been reported in 3% of patients. Metachronous upper tract TCC has been reported in approximately 6% of patients. This highlights the importance of cystoscopic, ureteroscopic and radio-logical surveillance of these patients following definitive treatment.

Q. **How would you follow-up a patient after an upper tract TCC had been treated (with nephro-ureterectomy)?**

A. Close follow-up of upper tract TCC is essential. This should consist of regular flexible cystoscopy (we recommend 3-monthly for 2 years, followed by 6-monthly for 2 years, and yearly thereafter), due to the high proportion of patients who develop subsequent bladder cancer. Cytology has been used to detect high-grade malignant cells, but has poor sensitivity for low-grade lesions. In addition, these patients require a CT scan of the abdomen and pelvis and a chest X-ray every 6 months for the first 2 years.

Q. **Several years later this patient returns with weight loss, anorexia and loin pain. A repeat CT scan is performed and shows a local recurrence in the renal bed (*see* Figure 4.4). How would you assess this patient?**

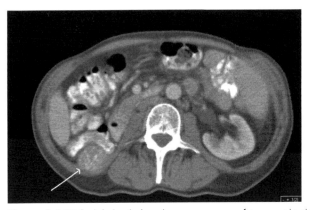

Figure 4.4 CT (axial view) showing recurrence of tumour in right renal bed.

A. This patient requires restaging with a CT scan of her chest, abdomen and pelvis. In addition, a bone scan is required. She is symptomatic and clearly needs further treatment. Palliative chemotherapy with cisplatin and gemcitabine should be discussed at the multi-disciplinary team (MDT) meeting. Palliative care team involvement will aid symptom control and support for this patient during this phase of her illness. Most of the data concerning the use of chemotherapy in upper ureteric and renal pelvic TCC have been extrapolated from bladder cancer TCC trials such as those of the Advanced Bladder Cancer (ABC) Meta-Analysis Trialists Group. Chemotherapy is occasionally used in high-risk patients after discussing the patient at the MDT meeting, as well as in patients with symptomatic recurrent and metastatic disease. No randomised controlled trials have reported on the use of chemotherapy in this setting. Trial design is limited by the low number of patients who develop this disease.

ACKNOWLEDGEMENTS

The authors are grateful to Mr DMA Wallace for his help and advice with the preparation of this chapter.

REFERENCES

1. Sutton JM. Evaluation of hematuria in adults. *JAMA* 1990; **263**: 2475–80.
2. Khadra MH *et al.* A prospective analysis of 1,930 patients with hematuria to evaluate current diagnostic practice. *J Urol* 2000; **163**: 524–7.
3. Konety BR *et al.* Urine-based markers of urological malignancy. *J Urol* 2001; **165**: 600–11.
4. Edwards TJ *et al.* A prospective analysis of the diagnostic yield resulting from the attendance of 4020 patients at a protocol-driven haematuria clinic. *BJU Int* 2006; **97**: 301–5.
5. Britton JP *et al.* A community study of bladder cancer screening by the detection of occult urinary bleeding. *J Urol* 1992; **148**: 788–90.
6. Steiner H *et al.* Early results of bladder-cancer screening in a high-risk population of heavy smokers. *BJU Int* 2008; **102**: 291–6.
7. Sylvester RJ *et al.* A single immediate postoperative instillation of chemotherapy decreases the risk of recurrence in patients with stage Ta T1 bladder cancer: a meta-analysis of published results of randomized clinical trials. *J Urol* 2004; **171**: 2186–90.
8. Sylvester RJ *et al.* Predicting recurrence and progression in individual patients with stage Ta T1 bladder cancer using EORTC risk tables: a combined analysis of 2596 patients from seven EORTC trials. *Eur Urol* 2006; **49**: 466–77.
9. Parmar MK *et al.* Prognostic factors for recurrence and follow-up policies in the treatment of superficial bladder cancer: report from the British Medical Research Council Subgroup on Superficial Bladder Cancer (Urological Cancer Working Party). *J Urol* 1989; **142**: 284–8.
10. Sylvester RJ *et al.* Intravesical bacillus Calmette–Guerin reduces the risk of progression in patients with superficial bladder cancer: a meta-analysis of the published results of randomized clinical trials. *J Urol* 2002; **168**: 1964–70.
11. Sylvester RJ *et al.* Bacillus Calmette-Guerin versus chemotherapy for the intravesical treatment of patients with carcinoma *in situ* of the bladder: a meta-analysis of the published results of randomized clinical trials. *J Urol* 2005; **174**: 86–91.
12. Morales A *et al.* Intracavitary bacillus Calmette–Guerin in the treatment of superficial bladder tumors. *J Urol* 1976; **116**: 180–83.
13. Lamm DL *et al.* Maintenance bacillus Calmette–Guerin immunotherapy for recurrent TA, T1 and carcinoma in situ transitional-cell carcinoma of the bladder: a randomized Southwest Oncology Group Study. *J Urol* 2000; **163**: 1124–9.
14. Herr HW *et al.* Impact of the number of lymph nodes retrieved on outcome in patients with muscle-invasive bladder cancer. *J Urol* 2002; **167**: 1295–8.
15. Neoadjuvant chemotherapy for invasive bladder cancer. *Cochrane Database Syst Rev* 2005; **2**: CD005246.
16. Hall MC *et al.* Prognostic factors, recurrence, and survival in transitional-cell carcinoma of the upper urinary tract: a 30-year experience in 252 patients. *Urology* 1998; **52**: 594–601.

Chapter 5
Renal cancer

Emma Bromwich and Dominic Hodgson

RENAL MASS PRESENTATION

Q. **What does the CT in Figure 5.1 show?**

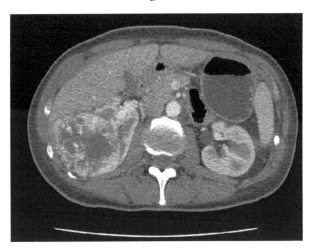

Figure 5.1

A. This is an axial post-contrast abdominal CT scan. There is a heterogeneous tumour arising from the right kidney. This is most probably a renal-cell carcinoma.

Q. **How does renal-cell carcinoma (RCC) present?**
A. Over 50% of cases are found incidentally. Of the remainder, only 10% have the classic triad of haematuria, loin pain and a mass. One-third present with metastases.

Q. **How would you assess a fit 55-year-old man who presents with a large renal mass on ultrasound scan?**
A. I would first take a full medical history from him. I would then examine him for a palpable mass and lymph nodes, a varicocele (for left-sided renal tumours) and lower limb oedema. Finally, I would send blood samples to look for anaemia, a raised ESR, abnormal liver function tests, and calcium and creatinine levels.

Q. **What further imaging would you request?**

A. So long as his renal function was normal, I would arrange an abdominal and pelvic CT with IV contrast to establish the morphology of the contralateral kidney, and to assess the primary tumour, extra-renal spread, and venous, adrenal, liver and lymph node involvement. I would assess the lungs with a chest X-ray or a chest CT. An MRI scan may be indicated if there is contrast allergy or renal insufficiency, and potentially for assessing IVC involvement. Similarly, Doppler ultrasound scanning can also be useful for demonstrating venous extension. Extra-pulmonary metastatic disease is normally symptomatic, so a bone scan or a CT of the brain would be reserved for those with symptoms.

Q. **What prognostic factors are there for RCC patients?**

A. There are three types of factors:
- anatomical factors – those of the TNM staging system
- histological factors – high Fuhrman grade is associated with worsening prognosis. Clear cell tumours have a worse outcome than the chromophobe type, which in turn have a poorer prognosis than the papillary type. The presence of necrosis also confers a poorer prognosis
- clinical factors – cachexia, a poor performance status, anaemia and a low platelet count are all associated with higher risk. Increasingly, molecular markers such as VEGF, HIF, Ki67, p53 and E-cadherin will be used to predict progression more accurately.

Q. **What paraneoplastic syndromes are associated with RCC?**

A. Paraneoplastic syndromes are found in approximately 25% of patients with RCC. The kidney produces 1,25-dihydroxycholecalciferol, renin, erythropoietin and various prostaglandins, all of which can precipitate symptoms.

Hypercalcaemia secondary to the production of parathyroid-like peptides has been reported in 13% of cases. Osteolytic breakdown in metastatic disease may also play a role.

Hypertension secondary to renin production by the primary tumour is more common than polycythaemia due to erythropoietin production. Anaemia is seen in over 30% of patients.

Stauffer's syndrome is non-metastatic hepatic dysfunction in RCC patients, and is seen in approximately 5% of cases. Thrombocytopenia, neutropenia, fever, weight loss and discrete regions of hepatic necrosis are seen. Elevated serum levels of IL-6 and other cytokines may be implicated. Hepatic function will normalise in the majority of cases post-nephrectomy.

Systemic symptoms of cachexia, weight loss and pyrexia are recognised in 15–30% of RCC patients.

TREATMENT OPTIONS

Q. **When would you perform an adrenalectomy concurrently with a radical nephrectomy?**

A. In addition to those patients in whom pre-operative imaging suggests adrenal involvement, concurrent adrenalectomy should be performed for upper pole tumours, T2 cancers (greater than 7 cm) and multifocal disease.

Q. **What are the indications for nephron-sparing surgery?**

A. Absolute indications are bilateral synchronous RCC, and an anatomical or functionally solitary kidney.

Relative indications are unilateral RCC with a reduced or poorly functioning contralateral kidney, unilateral RCC in patients with comorbidity associated with potential renal impairment (diabetes, renovascular disease), and patients with an increased risk of a second renal malignancy (hereditary RCC such as von Hippel–Lindau (VHL) disease).

Elective indications include localised unilateral RCC with a normal contralateral kidney.

Q. **How would you consent someone for a laparoscopic radical nephrectomy?**

A. I would review the imaging prior to consent to confirm the suspected pathology and side. I would introduce myself and check the patient's name and date of birth. I would then describe the procedure and explain that the intended benefit was to remove the kidney which is thought to contain cancer, but explain that there is a chance that the lesion may be benign.

I would describe and explain the potential complications of the procedure, including bleeding, wound infection, the potential need to convert to an open procedure, damage to adjacent organs, chest infection and the small chance of complications from the pneumo-peritoneum (namely impaired venous return and gas embolism, leading to thrombosis or respiratory compromise).

I would state that follow-up is required and further therapy may be indicated. The patient would be told that they would have a catheter after the procedure and possibly a drain, and that the operation would take place under general anaesthetic. I would sign the consent form and ask the patient if they had any further questions. I would then ask them to read and sign the document.

Policies on marking patients differ between departments, but it is my practice to draw a cross with indelible ink on the side for surgery.

Q. **With regard to trans-peritoneal and retro-peritoneal laparoscopic nephrectomy, which is best?**

A. Randomised trials have failed to show a significant advantage for either procedure in terms of blood loss, complication rates and hospital stay. I personally feel that a laparoscopic surgeon should have the ability to perform both procedures. A surgeon may, for example, favour the retroperitoneal approach for obese patients and for those who have had extensive previous abdominal surgery, but may prefer a trans-peritoneal route for an anterior or superiorly placed tumour.

Q. **How would your consent for a partial nephrectomy differ from that for a radical nephrectomy?**

A. I would explain that the aim of the procedure is to remove cancer while at the same time preserving kidney function, and I would warn the patient about the potential need to perform a nephrectomy. I would explain that the risk of local recurrence (5%) and complications (including bleeding and urinary leakage) is greater than with radical nephrectomy (this is particularly so with larger tumours), and that a drain would be routinely placed. Follow-up would be more intensive.

Q. **With regard to laparoscopic and open partial nephrectomy, which technique is superior?**

A. Laparoscopic (and robotic) techniques are improving in an attempt to reproduce the warm ischaemic times and complication rates of the open procedure, which is still considered to be the standard of care.

Q. **How would you follow up patients after a nephrectomy for RCC?**

A. The purpose of follow-up is to assess complications and renal function, and to monitor for local recurrence, contralateral tumours and metastases. The occurrence of contralateral tumours and local recurrence is rare (< 5% for both), but early detection of these (and metastatic disease) increases the likelihood of them being surgically resectable. In addition, if novel systemic treatments are to be used, a lower tumour burden potentially increases their efficacy.

Individual follow-up protocols need to reflect the risk of recurrence. There are anatomical, histological, molecular and clinical factors that influence the prognosis. Using these, nomograms can be consulted (such as the Leibovich scoring system). A low-risk patient will not necessarily require CT follow-up unless they are symptomatic, and ultrasound and chest X-ray will suffice. Intermediate- and high-risk patients will require an abdominal and pelvic CT and chest imaging for at least 5 years. The benefits of an intense and prolonged follow-up need to be balanced against the radiation exposure associated with the scans.

Q. **What are your thoughts about the role of nephrectomy in the presence of metastases?**

A. Based on data from prospective randomised trials, cytoreductive nephrectomy appears to significantly improve overall survival in patients with metastatic renal cancer treated with interferon immunotherapy, independent of patient performance status, the site of metastases and the presence of measurable disease. The European Organisation for Research and Treatment of Cancer (EORTC) study showed that median survival with interferon-α (IFN-α) and nephrectomy (18 months) was significantly better than that with IFN-α alone (11 months).[1] The Southwest Oncology Group (SWOG) also reported that nephrectomy followed by interferon therapy resulted in significantly longer median survival among patients with metastatic renal-cell cancer than interferon therapy alone (11 months vs. 8 months).[2] Subsequently, a combined analysis of the SWOG and EORTC trials was published in the *Journal of Urology*.[3] Data were available for 331 patients randomised to nephrectomy followed by interferon as opposed to interferon alone. The median survival rates were 13.6 and 7.8 months, respectively. This difference represented a 31% decrease in the risk of death ($P = 0.002$).

Q. **What do you think is the role of biopsy in RCC?**

A. I think that biopsy for renal masses will become of increasing importance.

We are diagnosing a greater number of small renal masses which present management dilemmas. However, approximately 10% of these will be benign. In addition to this, we now have the ability to assess the potential progression of small tumours not only from their histological grading, but also from novel histological and molecular analyses, which may influence treatment strategies. With the development of minimally invasive and targeted molecular therapies, information obtained from such sampling will further guide decisions, and will also potentially inform follow-up.

Traditionally there has been reluctance to perform biopsies because of sampling errors and the risk of complications. With better imaging and pathological assessment, sensitivities and specificities of approximately 90% can be achieved. Similarly, there has been a fear of complications in the form of seeding, haemorrhage and pneumothorax. However, there are less than 10 reports of tumour seeding in the literature. Biopsy would not be recommended for cystic lesions, and would only be recommended for large infiltrative tumours if lymphoma was suspected. The risk of haemorrhage requiring transfusion or hospital admission is 2%, and the risk of significant pneumothorax is less than 1%.

VON HIPPEL–LINDAU (VDL) CASE PRESENTATION

Q. **A 28-year-old man with a history of cerebellar surgery has an abdominal CT. What is the diagnosis (*see* Figures 5.2a and Figure 5.2b)?**

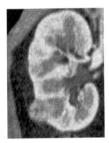 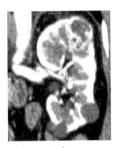

Figure 5.2a   Figure 5.2b

A. Figure 5.2a shows contrast CT demonstrating right kidney and Figure 5.2b shows contrast CT demonstrating left kidney. There are multiple bilateral renal cysts with a malignant-looking lesion in the upper pole of the left kidney and possibly the lateral aspect of the lower pole of the right kidney. Given this and the history of cerebellar surgery, I suspect that this patient has Von Hippel–Lindau disease.

Q. **What is Von Hippel–Lindau (VHL) disease?**
A. It is an autosomal dominant disorder characterised by the development of various benign and malignant tumours and cysts. The VHL tumour suppressor gene is located on the short arm of chromosome 3, and the inactivation of this leads to the development of the disease. The major tumours and cysts are haemangioblastoma in the central nervous system, retinal haemangioblastoma, phaeochromocytoma, renal-cell carcinoma, renal cysts, pancreatic neuro-endocrine tumours, and pancreatic and epididymal cystadenomas.

Q. **Explain how this leads to the development of renal (and other) carcinomas.**
A. Inactivation of the VHL suppressor protein results in subsequent loss of function of the VHL protein and the VBC complex. This complex normally targets transcription factors such as hypoxia-inducible factor (HIF-1α), resulting in their destruction. In cells that lack VHL function, or in hypoxic conditions, HIF-1α

accumulates, resulting in over-expression of many genes, especially those related to angiogenesis, such as vascular endothelial growth factor (VEGF) and platelet-derived growth factor (PDGF), as well as cell division, via transforming growth factor-α and PDGF. Importantly, the VHL gene has also been demonstrated to be inactivated in sporadic renal-cell carcinomas.

Q. What new drug therapies are you aware of for VHL and renal cancer?

A. The VHL/HIF-1α growth factor pathway has become a major area for targeting of drug development.

Sunitinib is a tyrosine kinase inhibitor (TKI) that inhibits all three iso-forms of the VEGF receptor. In a recent phase III trial, 750 patients (previously untreated) with metastatic renal cancer were randomised to sunitinib or IFN-α. Patients who received sunitnib had significantly longer progression-free survival (11 months vs. 5 months) and higher response rates (31% vs. 6%) than those who received IFN-α.[4] Sorafenib, which is another TKI, has been shown to prolong progression-free survival in patients with advanced renal cancer in whom previous therapy has failed. This was demonstrated in a randomised phase III study that compared sorafenib with placebo.[5] Further high-quality studies have potentially shown the benefit of temsirolimus and everolimus, the mammalian target of rapamycin (mTOR) inhibitors,[6,7] and bevacizumab, a humanised monoclonal antibody to VEGF-A,[8] as medical therapies in advanced renal-cell cancer. Although not a uniform policy, one approach to medical therapy is initially to stratify patients according to low, intermediate or high risk, depending on whether they possess none, one, or two or more of the following risk factors: Karnofsky performance status ≤ 80%; anaemia; elevated serum calcium levels; absence of prior nephrectomy; elevated lactate dehydrogenase levels.[9] Low- and intermediate-risk patients should initially be treated with sunitinib or bevacizumab plus IFNα. Selected high-performance-status patients with clear cell tumours can be considered for high-dose IL-2. Second-line therapy after progression could include sorafenib, everolimus, or a different VEGF pathway inhibitor. High-risk patients, especially those with non-clear cell histology, should initially be considered for treatment with temsirolimus. Importantly, with several ongoing clinical trials in progress, treatment options are likely to change.

Q. Describe the course of the renal manifestations of the disease.

A. Typically RCC evolves in multiple sites in the kidney after 20 years of age. Kidneys usually develop a spectrum of lesions ranging from small benign cysts to large renal-cell cancers. Smaller lesions are difficult to evaluate, but a cut-off diameter of 2–3 cm is thought to represent increasing risk of malignant transformation.

Q. Describe the management of RCC in VHL patients.

A. Initially, urological management is in the form of surveillance with annual ultrasound scan. Once cysts or lesions reach 2 cm in diameter, intensive CT/MRI follow-up, either 6- or 12-monthly depending on the size and/or number and growth rate of lesions, will be required.

All management should aim to maintain nephrons and reduce the risk of metastasis. Cryo-ablation, radio-frequency ablation and perhaps HIFU should be considered for treating smaller lesions (< 3 cm). Once lesions are > 3 cm, partial nephrectomy may be more appropriate. For larger lesions, nephrectomy is indicated.

Ultimately, as the disease progresses, the patient may require renal replacement therapy. The evidence for the role of transplantation and subsequent immunosuppression in this population of patients is limited.

BENIGN KIDNEY MASSES

Q. **A 55-year-old patient presents with symptoms suggestive of biliary colic. An ultrasound scan reveals, in addition to gallstones, a large right renal cyst. What would be the initial urological management of this patient?**

A. After confirming normal renal function, I would arrange a pre- and post- contrast CT scan.

Q. **What features are you looking for on the CT (*see* Figures 5.3a and 5.3b)?**

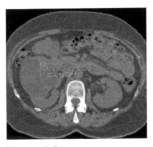

Figure 5.3a   Figure 5.3b

A. Figure 5.3a shows a non-contrast axial CT of the abdomen and Figure 5.3b shows a contrast axial CT of the abdomen. The relevant radiological features include calcification, septations, irregular margins, solid elements and evidence of contrast enhancement.

According to the Bosniak classification, a type I cyst is benign with smooth margins, and no contrast enhancement, calcification or septations.

A type II cyst has simple septations and/or minimal calcification. This type includes hyper-dense cysts which contain old, degenerated or clotted blood, so CT attenuation of their contents is increased. These cysts do not enhance with contrast.

Type III cysts are complicated with irregular margins, moderate calcification and thick septations and, most importantly, enhance with contrast.

Type IV cysts are cystic malignant lesions with irregular margins and solid enhancing elements.

The cyst shown in Figure 5.3a and Figure 5.3b does not enhance with contrast and is therefore a type II cyst.

Q. **What is the significance of contrast enhancement?**

A. Enhancement suggests the presence of vascular tissue or communication with the collecting system. It is measured by the difference in Hounsfield units before and after contrast, and can point towards a malignant diagnosis (an approximate increase in enhancement of 20 Hounsfield units is considered to be significant).

Q. **How does the Bosniak classification affect clinical management?**

A. Type I cysts are benign and require no follow-up. Type II cysts require follow-up to look for change in size or the development of new features, as there is a 10–20% risk of malignant transformation. Surgical intervention should be considered for type III cysts, as 40–50% of these will be malignant. More than 90% of type IV cysts will be malignant, and nephrectomy should be considered.

Q. **What are type IIF renal cysts?**

A. Type IIF cysts have an increased number of hairline-thin septae with possible minimal enhancement or thickening of the septae or wall. These cysts definitely require close follow-up, as they have a greater malignant potential than conventional type II cysts.

Q. **What differential diagnosis would you consider for cystic renal lesions?**

A. Simple renal cysts, cystic renal-cell carcinoma, autosomal dominant polycystic kidney disease, multicystic dysplastic kidney, multilocular cyst, VHL syndrome.

Q. **What is the difference between autosomal dominant polycystic kidney disease, autosomal recessive polycystic kidney disease and acquired renal cystic disease?**

A. Autosomal dominant polycystic kidney disease (ADPKD) is an inherited condition, with an incidence ranging from 1 in 200 to 1 in 1000, leading to the development of multiple, expanding renal parenchymal cysts, 95% of which are bilateral, with symptoms presenting in the fourth decade leading to end-stage renal failure. ADPKD is responsible for 5–10% of all cases of end-stage renal failure. Diagnosis is normally by ultrasound scan as an incidental finding or with investigations for haematuria, flank pain or an abdominal mass. Treatment is expectant, with blood pressure control a priority.

Autosomal recessive polycystic kidney disease is distinct from ADPKD presenting in childhood, and has an incidence ranging from 1in 10 000 to 1 in 40 000. Diagnosis is often made *in utero* with the development of bilateral enlargement of renal parenchyma, which is replaced by radially orientated cysts. Oligohydramnios may occur and, if severe, termination is often considered in the second trimester.

Neonates have typical Potter's facies and a palpable mass. There is associated biliary dysgenesis leading to hepatic fibrosis. Management is supportive, including good blood pressure control, dialysis and consideration of transplantation. However, the prognosis is poor, particularly if pulmonary hypoplasia is present. Otherwise, with renal replacement therapy, approximately 50% of cases will survive childhood.

Acquired renal cystic disease (ARCD) was first described in the 1970s in patients with renal failure. It is now recognised as a feature of end-stage renal disease (ESRD) rather than a response to treatment. Uraemic toxins are implicated, and cyst regression after transplantation and recurrence after transplant failure are seen.

Patients may suffer pain and haematuria, which can require embolisation. A spectrum of renal adenoma to carcinoma is seen, with a 3 cm cut-off value usually considered for a malignant diagnosis. Most RCCs that develop in ESRD are associated with ARCD. Compared with the general population, RCC occurs on average 5 years earlier, has a 7:1 male predominance and is three to six times more common.

Q. How might a multicystic dysplastic kidney present?

A. Unilateral multicystic dysplastic kidney has an incidence of 1 in 2500 to 1 in 4000, and presents as an incidental finding or as an irregular flank mass. Bilateral disease is lethal, with an incidence of 1 in 25 000. Where inherited, it is an autosomal dominant disorder, although sporadic cases are more common.

Pathologically, an irregular collection of tense non-communicating cysts lined with cuboidal or flattened tubular epithelium and dysplastic renal parenchyma is seen. There is proximal ureteric atresia secondary to ureteric bud and metanephric mesenchymal defects.

Most unilateral cases are undetected at birth, and involution commonly occurs in early childhood, which may account for the recognised association with renal agenesis. Around 5–10% of cases have a contralateral pelvi-ureteric junction obstruction (PUJO), and even more have contralateral reflux.

Management is expectant. Rarely, nephrectomy will be performed for uncontrolled hypertension. There is a fourfold increased risk of malignancy (Wilm's tumour). However, prophylactic nephrectomy is not recommended.

Q. What do you understand by the term 'multilocular cyst' or 'cystic nephroma'?

A. This is a spectrum of multilocular cysts, seen in children and adults, which ranges from a benign multilocular cyst to a cystic Wilm's tumour or cystic renal-cell carcinoma.

Multilocular cysts tend to be bulky with thick capsules containing highly echogenic septae with loculi sometimes containing debris suggesting solid elements. Aspiration yields clear to yellow fluid.

Distribution is bimodal, with a 2:1 male predominance in those under 4 years of age, and an 8:1 female predominance in those over 30 years. Children present with an asymptomatic flank mass, whereas adults present with abdominal pain or haematuria.

Surgery is the treatment of choice in both children and adults. Nephron-sparing surgery should be considered.

Q. A 43-year-old woman has presented with frank haematuria without cardiovascular compromise. An initial ultrasound scan demonstrated a 4 cm, well-circumscribed, hyperechoic lesion with acoustic shadowing within the right kidney. How would you manage this patient?

A. I would arrange a pre- and post-contrast CT scan.

Q. CT reveals a fatty lesion of less than 10 Hounsfield units in the upper pole of the right kidney. What is the diagnosis and is this lesion associated with any inherited conditions?

A. The diagnosis is an angiomyolipoma (AML). Around 80% of AMLs are sporadic, with a 4:1 female predominance. These typically present in middle age, and 80% are right-sided, with a recognised growth rate of 5% per year.

The remainder are associated with tuberous sclerosis (TS), which has a 2:1 female predominance. These tumours tend to be smaller, bilateral and multicentric, with a mean age of presentation of 30 years, and a growth rate of 20% per year. TS is an autosomal dominant disorder characterised by mental retardation, epilepsy and adenoma sebaceum. There is incomplete penetrance, and 50% of patients with TS develop AMLs.

Q. **The haematuria settles and the patient has a normal contralateral kidney and no significant comorbidity. What would your management plan be?**

A. A diameter of 4 cm is recognised as the cut-off point at which an AML is more likely to become symptomatic. However, assuming that this was the patient's first episode of bleeding, I would discuss conservative management with ultrasound surveillance.

A significant increase in size or further haemorrhage would indicate the need for intervention. Selective embolisation of the lesion is an effective treatment in an acute or elective setting. Alternatively, nephron-sparing surgery dependent on the location of the tumour, or alternatively nephrectomy, should be considered.

Q. **What is an oncocytoma?**

A. This is a benign solid renal tumour, representing approximately 5% of solid renal masses, which has a 2:1 male predominance.

Q. **How do oncocytomas present?**

A. They are commonly asymptomatic, but can present with pain or haematuria.

Q. **Describe the clinical, radiological and pathological differences between an oncocytoma and a renal-cell cancer?**

A. Clinically it is not possible to differentiate between an oncocytoma and a renal-cell cancer. The age of presentation and male predominance are the same for the two conditions.

Radiologically it can be impossible to differentiate between the two, but a central stellate scar commonly seen on CT and MRI scan and a spoke-wheel pattern of feeding arteries on angiography/MRA can suggest an oncocytoma.

Macroscopically, oncocytomas are well-circumscribed, homogenous, tan-coloured lesions. Microscopically, uniform eosinophilic cells are seen packed with mitochondria originating from the intercalated cells of the collecting ducts, whereas RCC originates from the proximal tubules.

Cytogenetically, loss of the first and Y chromosomes, rearrangements of 11q13, and loss of heterozygosity on chromosome 14q are seen. Rarely, chromosome 3 abnormalities are seen. These genetic alterations are characteristic and distinct from RCC subtypes.

Absolute confirmation of the diagnosis of oncocytoma is histological. Therefore nephron-sparing surgery or radical nephrectomy are indicated in most cases. Once histological diagnosis has been confirmed, oncocytomas do not require follow-up, due to their benign nature.

Q. **Describe the role of renal biopsy in the management of oncocytoma?**

A. The limitations of biopsy are due to the difficulty in distinguishing between an oncocytoma and an eosinophilic variant of chromophobe renal-cell cancer. There is also a recognised coexistence of RCC and oncocytoma within the same lesion and at other locations within the kidney.

Q. **Describe two inherited or familial conditions associated with oncocytomas.**

A. Birt–Hogg–Dubé syndrome is an autosomal dominant, inherited condition due to a mutation on chromosome 17. Its features include fibrofolliculomas (neoplastic proliferation of the fibrous sheath of the hair follicle), pulmonary cysts, colonic lesions, oncocytomas and, rarely, malignant renal lesions.

Familial renal oncocytomatosis has been described with multi-centric, bilateral tumours, with an early age of onset seen, although the genetic basis for the condition is unknown.

REFERENCES

1. Mickisch GH *et al*. for the European Organisation for Research and Treatment of Cancer (EORTC) Genitourinary Group. Radical nephrectomy plus interferon-alfa-based immunotherapy compared with interferon-alfa alone in metastatic renal-cell carcinoma: a randomised trial. *Lancet* 2001; **358**: 966–70.

2. Flanigan RC *et al*. Nephrectomy followed by interferon alfa-2b compared with interferon alfa-2b alone for metastatic renal-cell cancer. *NEJM* 2001; **345**: 1655–9.

3. Flanigan RC *et al*. Cytoreductive nephrectomy in patients with metastatic renal cancer: a combined analysis. *J Urol* 2004; **171**: 1071–6.

4. Motzer RJ *et al*. Sunitinib versus interferon alfa in metastatic renal-cell carcinoma. *NEJM* 2007; **356**: 115–24.

5. Escudier B *et al*. Sorafenib in advanced clear-cell renal-cell carcinoma. *NEJM* 2007; **356**: 125–34.

6. Hudes G *et al*. Temsirolimus, interferon alfa, or both for advanced renal-cell carcinoma. *NEJM* 2007; **356**: 2271–81.

7. Motzer RJ *et al*. Efficacy of everolimus in advanced renal-cell carcinoma: a double-blind, randomised, placebo-controlled phase III trial. *Lancet* 2008; **372**: 449–56.

8. Escudier B *et al*. Bevacizumab plus interferon alfa-2a for treatment of metastatic renal-cell carcinoma: a randomised, double-blind phase III trial. *Lancet* 2007; **370**: 2103–11.

9. Motzer RJ *et al*. Survival and prognostic stratification of 670 patients with advanced renal-cell carcinoma. *J Clin Oncol* 1999; **17**: 2530–40.

FURTHER READING

Wein AJ, Kavoussi LR, Novick AC et al. (eds) *Campbell-Walsh Urology*, 9th edn. Philadelphia, PA: Saunders Elsevier; 2006.

Chapter 6
Paediatric urology

Aruna Abhyankar and Arash K Taghizadeh

FORESKIN: PHIMOSIS AND CIRCUMCISION

Q. **A 5-year-old patient is referred by his GP, who is concerned that the boy's foreskin does not yet retract and that he may require circumcision. What is phimosis?**

A. Phimosis is the inability to retract the prepuce. It is derived from the Greek word for 'muzzle.' It may be pathological or physiological. The term 'phimosis' does not indicate whether the condition is pathological or physiological, and therefore when it is used it is helpful to specify which applies.

Q. **Why is it not possible to retract the prepuce in a physiological non-retractile foreskin?**

A. The preputial opening is too narrow and there are adhesions between the prepuce and the glans, i.e. the epithelial lining of the inner preputial layer is fused with the epithelium covering the glans penis. Epithelial desquamation, spontaneous erections and penile growth eventually lead to the separation of these two layers of skin.

Q. **What is the cause of a pathological phimosis?**

A. Balanitis xerotica obliterans or BXO (also known as lichen sclerosis et atrophicus). This is a chronic skin condition with some evidence suggesting an autoimmune aetiology. BXO is rare in children, affecting less than 1% of boys (it is more commonly seen in middle-aged men). The process can affect the glans, foreskin and external urethral meatus, and occasionally the urethra. This may result in phimosis, difficulty in voiding and even, very rarely, retention. Examination often reveals a thickened, scarred, fissured prepuce with pale white patches and with no pouting/flowering upon retraction.

   It has been suggested, very controversially, that BXO may be associated with the later development of penile cancer in adults, at least 17 years after initial presentation.

Q. **How is a physiological non-retractile prepuce distinguished from a pathological phimosis?**

A. In a physiological phimosis, when an attempt is made to retract the foreskin by gently pulling it back, the inner mucosa of the foreskin pouts through the preputial opening, and appears rather like a carnation flower (*see* Figure 6.1). When a similar attempt is made in BXO, such pouting does not occur, and instead a scarred white ring appears around the preputial opening.

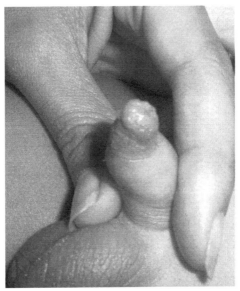

Figure 6.1 Physiological phimosis demonstrating 'flowering' of prepuce on retraction.

Q.   **How should pathological phimosis be managed?**
A.   By performing circumcision.

Q.   **How commonly are boys circumcised in the UK? How has this figure changed in the last 60 years?**
A.   Around 5.6% of boys are currently circumcised in the UK.[1] In 1949, Gairdner[2] estimated that there was a national incidence of 20%. The more startling finding reported in this paper was that between 1942 and 1947 about 16 boys a year were dying as a result of complications of circumcision.

Q.   **What is the natural history of physiological non-retractile foreskin?**
A.   Øster made 9545 serial observations on the state of the prepuce in a total of 1968 Danish schoolboys between 1957 and 1965.[3] Phimosis was present in 8% of 6- to 7-year-olds, 6% of 10- to 11-year-olds and 1% of 16- to 17-year-olds. Preputial adhesions were even more common, affecting 63% of 6- to 7-year-olds, 48% of 10- to 11-year-olds and 3% of 16- to 17-year-olds. The main conclusion to be drawn from his paper is that a non-retractile foreskin is a common observation in boys, and will usually correct itself.

   The current guidelines from the American Academy of Pediatrics (AAP), the British Association of Paediatric Surgery (BAPS) and the European Association of Urology (EAU) suggest that these patients with physiological phimosis can safely be managed conservatively with parental reassurance and advice on bathing and maintaining proper foreskin hygiene.

Q. **The boy's parents report that the foreskin 'balloons' when he voids. Should they be concerned?**

A. Ballooning of the foreskin is very common and is not in itself a cause for concern. However, it is worth being alert to the unusual possibility of buried penis megaprepuce. In this condition the parent will report that urine collects in the foreskin and that squeezing the foreskin then 'milks' urine out. When the penis is examined in a boy with buried penis megaprepuce, the outer preputial skin appears to meet directly with the skin of the abdominal wall dorsally, and the scrotum ventrally, and the penile shaft skin is deficient. Within the prepuce there are copious folds of inner preputial skin. A standard circumcision should be avoided in these boys. Surgical correction involves removing the inner preputial skin and excising the fibrotic tissue associated with it, and then re-applying the outer preputial skin to the shaft as a substitute for the penile shaft skin.

Q. **The boy's mother is worried because a family friend the same age as her son has had balanoposthitis. What is this?**

A. This is an acute condition characterised by redness and swelling of the foreskin, and associated with purulent discharge from the preputial opening. It is often associated with painful voiding. It may be related to separation of preputial adhesions. Frequently *E. coli* or *Proteus vulgaris* may be grown, although culture often proves sterile in up to 30% of cases. It is reasonable to treat these boys with analgesics and antibiotics. The condition is common, and because it is self-limiting it is not usually an indication for circumcision. However, if the episodes of balanoposthitis are recurrent, frequent and very bothersome, a circumcision may be warranted.

Q. **Are there any other clinical indications for circumcision?**

A. The commonest medical indications for circumcision are BXO and recurrent balanoposthitis. Circumcision may also be performed to reduce the boy's risk of developing urinary tract infection (UTI). However, the evidence for this is based on observational studies, which suggest that in otherwise healthy males, 111 boys would have to be circumcised in order to prevent one UTI. The number needed to treat improves to 11 in those with recurrent UTI and 4 in those with high-grade vesico-ureteric reflux (VUR). Although circumcision may be justified in the latter two groups, it would have to be part of a broader treatment plan to manage these conditions.

Q. **What are the main steps involved in performing a circumcision?**

A. In a suitably prepared and anesthetised child, lying supine on the operating table, the procedure can be summarised as follows.
- Retract the foreskin. This may require stretching of the preputial opening or a dorsal slit. This allows inspection of the urethral meatus, so that its appearance can be documented as normal (e.g. no evidence of hypospadias).
- Preputial adhesions are completely separated.
- The prepuce is excised.
- Haemostasis is achieved with a bipolar diathermy or absorbable ties.
- The skin is closed with sutures.

Q. **What risks specific to the operation should the parent be warned about?**

A. The incidence of post-operative complications following circumcision ranges from 0.034% to 7.4%. Complications may include the following:

- infection requiring antibiotics (2% of cases)
- post-operative bleeding requiring return to theatre (1–2%)
- dissatisfaction with the cosmetic result (4%)
- meatal stenosis (reported rates of 0–11%).

Other less common complications are inclusion cysts, abnormal rotation or chordee of the penis and, very rarely, formation of urethro-cutaneous fistula and partial penile amputation.

If circumcision is performed for BXO, the parents should be warned about the future small possibility of BXO affecting the glans, external meatus and/or urethra.

Q. **Are there alternatives to circumcision?**

A. In patients in whom the foreskin is slow to release, a short course of topical steroid, such as 0.1% Triamcinolone or Betnovate twice daily for 6–8 weeks, has been shown to accelerate the release of a physiological phimosis in up to 70–80% of boys. The use of topical steroids has been shown to have no significant side-effects or systemic toxicity.

Preputioplasty is a procedure in which a longitudinal preputial incision is closed transversely in order to widen the preputial opening. It is ineffective in BXO, and requires a motivated patient who will practise regular retraction of the foreskin post-operatively.

Q. **What are the contradictions to circumcision?**

A. Circumcision should be avoided in children with hypospadias, as the prepuce is often used in future surgical reconstruction. Buried penis is another contraindication. The procedure should also be avoided in those with an acute local infection. Other contraindications would include children with coexisting pathology (e.g. coagulopathy), in whom it would be unsafe to perform such an operation. However, where medical conditions coexist it would be prudent to carefully consider the parents' request for a cultural circumcision. The child may be at higher risk if the parents go ahead with the procedure in a more uncontrolled situation in the community.

HYOSPADIAS

Q. **You are asked to see a 6-month-old boy with hypospadias. What are the features of hypospadias?**

A. A ventrally situated urethral meatus, a hooded foreskin and ventral curvature, or chordee.

Q. **How might you categorise its severity?**

A. Typically hypospadias is described in terms of the situation of the urethral meatus. A distal hypospadias would have a meatus situated on the glans or at the corona, a moderate hypospadias would have a meatus on the distal or mid-penile shaft, and a proximal hypospadias would have a meatus sited on the proximal penile shaft, scrotum or perineum. However, this provides a very limited characterisation of the abnormality, and does not necessarily define which patients need which operation. The underlying problem in hypospadias is a failure of normal development of the ventral aspect of the penis. As well as a meatus that is too proximal, the urethral groove extending from the meatus to the end of the glans may be flattened, and the urethra, glans and corpora may be hypoplastic to a varying degree.

Q. **Is it worthwhile examining the testes at this age?**
A. Absent or impalpable testes raise the possibility of disorders of sexual differentiation, especially where both testes are impalpable. If there are impalpable testes (in conjunction with hypospadias), it may be worth checking the child's chromosomes (karyotype).

Q. **What are the principles of surgical repair?**
A. Correction of curvature, re-siting the urtehral meatus and dealing with the hooded foreskin. A very large number of operations have been described for the correction of hypospadias, and the ultimate choice of operation will depend on the surgeon's preference and expertise.

Correction of curvature is functionally probably the most important part of the operation. Often it is because the ventral skin is short and is corrected with de-gloving and redistribution of penile skin. In more severe cases it may be necessary to mobilise the urethra, to excise ventral fibrotic tissue (confusingly also called chordee), or even to perform a Nesbitt's procedure.

Re-siting the meatus will involve creating a new urethra extending from the original site to the tip of the glans. If there is adequate tissue, the existing urethral plate is used in a Snodgrass hypospadias repair. In the Snodgrass repair a longitudinal incision is made in the urethral plate. If the ventral tissues are insufficient to tubularise, then a two-stage repair is performed in which a free graft of preputial skin is applied to the ventral surface of the penis, and tubularised at the second operation when the graft has become fully established. The new tubularised urethra is protected with a vascular flap placed over it, usually of the Dartos layer.

The hooded foreskin may have been used as a source of Dartos layer, or taken to be used as a free graft, or redistributed to help to correct skin level curvature. In these cases the remainder will be excised to give the penis a circumcised appearance. Some surgeons may offer to reconstruct the foreskin to give the penis an uncircumcised appearance. However, this is unusual in the UK.

Most surgeons would manage their hypospadias repairs with catheter drainage and a dressing.

Q. **At what age would you attempt repair?**
A. Practice varies widely. My practice is to operate at about 1 year of age, which gives a balance between the size of the patient and how easy it will be to manage their catheter and dressing (which becomes more difficult between the ages of 2 and 3 years).

Q. **What are the potential long-term complications of hypospadias repair?**
A. These relate to the neo-urethra, and for a single-stage hypospadias repair, approximately 10% of patients will require re-operation for fistula, stenosis or dehiscence of the urethral repair.

DISORDERS OF SEXUAL DIFFERENTIATION

Q.   **You are asked to go to the neonatal ward where the staff are unable to elucidate whether a term newborn baby is a boy or a girl. What should be the broad principles of management of such a baby?**

A: This is a stressful situation for everyone concerned. Despite enormous pressure from the family, there should be no rush to assign gender, which may need to be done in a specialist unit with an appropriate multi-disciplinary team. This may involve tests which will take some time. The Registry Office makes provision for this, and this is one of the few situations in which full registration of the child may be delayed. It is wise to advise the parents not to give their child a first name until the sex of rearing has been formally decided upon.

One of the most commonly presenting causes of disorders of sexual differentiation is congenital adrenal hyperplasia (CAH) (which results in virilisation of the external genitalia in girls). Deficiency of the enzyme 21-hydroxylase accounts for 90% of cases of CAH. In this condition, two-thirds of children will be in a salt-losing state due to aldosterone deficiency. *This is a neonatal emergency.* Therefore one must immediately asses the state of hydration of the child and ensure that the serum electrolytes are being checked (if the child is in a salt-losing state, aggressive treatment with intravenous fluids, potassium-lowering agents, mineralocorticoid and glucocorticoid supplements will be necessary).

Examination of the baby will require an assessment of the genitals as well as searching for other abnormalities. This will include an assessment of whether gonads are palpable or present in the scrotum, the size and shape of the phallus, the appearance of the labia/scrotum and the number of openings present in the perineum. Complex investigation includes 17-hydroxyprogesterone levels, chromosomal analysis and pelvic imaging (initially pelvic ultrasound scan).

Ultimately, a child in whom there is ambiguity about the genitals will need management in a specialist centre with a full multi-disciplinary team that includes paediatric urology, endocrinology and psychology teams.

UNDESCENDED TESTIS

Q.   **What is the embryological basis of testicular differentiation and descent?**

A.   Until week 6 the gonads remain undifferentiated. Between weeks 6 and 7, under the influence of the SRY gene, the testes differentiate.

Testicular descent follows, and this occurs in two phases. The first phase is under the influence of Müllerian inhibiting substance, and occurs by 12 weeks, taking the testis down from the urogenital ridge to the internal inguinal opening. The second phase occurs between weeks 25 and 30 and is under the influence of testosterone, taking the testis from the inguinal canal down to the scrotum.

Q.   **You see a 3-month-old boy in clinic whose parents are concerned that he is missing a testis. Which aspects of the history are helpful?**

A.   Has the missing testis ever been present? This may give a clue about an undescended testis that was missed during the postnatal check, or a retractile testis that was present.

Are there any risk factors for undescended testis? For example, prematurity, low birth weight, neuromuscular disorders, family history (14% of boys with undescended testis have a family history).

Are there any concurrent medical conditions that may affect your potential decision to offer surgery?

Q. **What findings are helpful in examination?**

A. In addition to a full examination, looking at the baby's overall health and the existence of other abnormalities, the following should be specifically noted. Is the missing testis palpable? If so, what is its location? Can it be brought down without pain or tension to the fundus of the scrotum? The answers to these questions will distinguish between a retractile testis, an ectopic testis and an undescended testis.

If the testis is impalpable, is the contralateral testis normal or hypertrophic? Is the scrotum on the side of the missing testis hypoplastic? This would suggest that an impalpable testis might not be present.

An impalpable testis has important surgical implications (discussed below).

Q. **You see a 1-year-old child. One testis sits in the scrotum and the contralateral testis is not immediately visible. However, after you have calmed the child you are able to feel the other testis in the groin, and find that with gentle traction it comes down into the scrotum. What does this represent?**

A. This is a retractile testicle.

Q. **What is the difference between a retractile testis and a gliding testis?**

A. A retractile testis can be brought into the fundus of the scrotum, and when released it remains there. A gliding testis will only come down under tension and/or the traction required to pull it down causes pain. A retractile testis does not require surgery, whereas a gliding testis does.

Q. **The boy's parents are still worried about the retractile testis. What plan of management would you offer for their son?**

A. The testis is retractile because of an active cremasteric reflex. This would be expected to settle with time. There is a possibility that a *small* proportion of retractile testes may become 'ascending testes' at a later age, i.e. develop a position that is higher than the scrotum (requiring surgery). It would make sense to keep the boy under review until the testis is no longer retractile, or until it becomes obvious that it is an ascended testis.

Q. **The next 8-month-old boy you see in the clinic by coincidence has an inguinal testis on one side and a normal testis on the other side. The parents ask if this is a common problem.**

A. In premature boys the incidence of undescended testes is up to 30%.

In boys with a normal birth weight, the incidence of undescended testes at birth is about 3–4%. The incidence is considerably higher in low-birth-weight babies. By the age of 3 months this figure will have gone down to 1.5%, with little change in this figure by 1 year of age. However, it is interesting that the cumulative orchidopexy rate for boys is 3%.

(Note that in approximately 20% of boys the condition is bilateral.)

Q. Having assessed and examined this baby, how do you plan to manage him?

A. He has an undescended testis. Although some testes that are undescended at birth will continue to descend, it is unlikely that there is going to be very much more descent after the age of 3 months. It would be safe to conclude that this boy needed an orchidopexy.

Q. At what age would you perform this procedure?

A. Microscopic changes are seen in the testes of boys who have orchidopexy performed after the age of 2 years. However, early orchidopexy, with more delicate vas and testicular vessels, is technically challenging. A good compromise would be to aim to perform the inguinal orchidopexy at 1 year of age.

Q. The parents do not like the idea of an operation. Why should undescended testes be corrected?

A. They should be corrected for the following reasons:
- To preserve fertility – note that later paternity rates are 80–90% (a similar figure to that for the general population) if the patient has had unilateral inguinal orchidopexy before the age of 2 years, and 50% if the procedure was performed bilaterally. However, there is still some degree of subfertility in unilateral cases, with 11% failing to achieve paternity within 1 year, compared with only 5% of controls.
- Because of the increased risk of malignancy, which may be as much as 10 times the normal risk. Bringing the testis into the scrotum will most importantly allow the boy to perform testicular self-examination when he becomes at risk after puberty. There is now some evidence to suggest that orchidopexy may reduce the risk of germ-cell malignancy.
- For the purpose of cosmesis.
- Undescended testes are at higher risk of torsion.
- Orchidopexy would abolish the small risk of hernia arising from a patent processus vaginalis that is often present.

Q. What are the main steps involved in inguinal orchidopexy?

A. In a suitably prepared and anaesthetised child, lying supine on the operating table, the procedure can be summarised as follows.
- Examine the patient under anaesthesia to confirm the position of the testis.
- Make a skin crease incision.
- Open the external oblique to gain access to the inguinal canal.
- Identify the testis.
- Divide the gubernaculum, taking care not to injure a vas that may be looping below the testes.
- Separate the lateral bands that may be fixing the testis close to the inguinal canal.
- Carefully mobilise the vas and testicular vessels from the processus vaginalis.
- Once this is free, the processus may be transfixed and divided at the level of the internal inguinal ring.
- Mobilise the vas and vessels to gain length.
- Create a Dartos pouch in the scrotum and pass the testis into it without twisting the cord.
- Close the wounds.

Q. **What are the risks associated with inguinal orchidopexy for undescended testes?**

A. The risks are as follows:
- bleeding, infection and wound complications
- inability to bring down the testis to a satisfactory position
- later ascent of the testis – this is iatrogenic ascent, where scar around the cord holds it at a fixed length, so that the testis is pulled up as the boy grows
- an approximately 5% risk of injury to the testicular vessels or vas (injury to the former results in testicular atrophy).

Q. **You see a 15-month-old boy in clinic. He has a normal scrotal testis on one side. Despite your very best efforts with this cooperative infant, you are unable to palpate the other testis. What percentage of undescended testes are impalpable?**

A. Around 20% of undescended testes are impalpable (i.e. 80% are palpable). Of these impalpable testes, approximately 40% are intra-abdominal. In 30% the vas and vessels end blindly deep to the internal inguinal ring, in 20% the vas and vessels end blindly in the inguinal canal, and 10% have a testis within the inguinal canal which was not palpated on examination (ideally this examination should be performed under anaesthesia in cases of impalpable testes – see later).

Q. **Will imaging assist the location of the one impalpable testis in the child described above?**

A. It would be advantageous to identify the position of the testes before making any decisions. However, ultrasound scanning has a significant false-negative rate, and MRI is likely to require a general anaesthetic. Radiology will not help to decide whether this child needs an operation, and will not reliably help to plan the operation. Therefore there is no value in organising any imaging, and the patient should be taken to theatre for examination under anaesthesia, before deciding whether to proceed to inguinal orchidopexy/laparoscopy.

Q. **The above child with one impalpable testis therefore requires an operation. Can you explain to the parents what will be done?**

A. An impalpable testis means that treatment decisions will have to be taken in the operating theatre. An examination under anaesthesia is performed. If the testis is palpable when the child is relaxed and asleep, inguinal orchidopexy is performed. If the testis is impalpable under anaesthesia, an immediate laparoscopy is performed to look for an intra-abdominal testis. If an intra-abdominal testis is found, the first stage of a two-stage Fowler–Stephens procedure is performed. The testicular artery is divided, leaving the testis to survive on the artery of the vas (a branch of the inferior vesical artery). The second stage, which is performed 6 months later, involves mobilising the testis into the scrotum. This two-stage operation carries an approximately 20% risk of testicular loss.

If the vessels, *and especially the vas*, are blind ending or end in a poor nubbin of tissue, a diagnosis of vanishing testes is made. The nubbin of tissue should be removed. A possible explanation for this phenomenon is prior testicular torsion. For this reason it is worth considering performing an orchidopexy on the contralateral testis to prevent it from undergoing torsion, too.

If the testis has been impalpable, but vas and vessels are seen entering the internal inguinal ring, the subsequent decision is controversial. Some would argue that if a testis is found, it does not usually contain germ cells, so it is not at risk of malignancy, and therefore nothing further needs to be done. One would have to be confident about the examination findings in order to be certain that an ectopic testis or an inguinal testis in a more chubby boy had not been missed.

HYDROCELE AND PATENT PROCESSUS VAGINALIS (PPV)

Q. **A 9-month-old boy presents with unilateral scrotal swelling that is non-tender, fluctuant and trans-illuminable. What is the most likely diagnosis?**

A. Hydrocele.

Q. **What are the differential diagnoses and features of these conditions?**

A. These are as follows:
- Indirect inguinal hernia – this is an inguino-scrotal swelling, which is usually reducible (with a gurgle sound). One cannot get above a hernia. Contrary to statements in some textbooks, a hernia may trans-illuminate.
- Hydrocele of the cord/encysted hydrocele – this is fixed in the line of the cord. The testis is separate to it. Its origin relates to the processus vaginalis. It may be confused with a non-reducible hernia, but is non-tender, and one can get above it.
- Testicular tumour – these are rare in infancy and so are easily missed. They may be associated with a hydrocele. They cause a solid intra-testicular lump. It is therefore important to be able to palpate the underlying testis when a boy presents with an apparent hydrocele.

Q. **What is the usual cause of a hydrocele in an infant?**

A. A patent processus vaginalis.

Q. **How would you manage a hydrocele?**

A. Most will resolve by the age of 1 year and therefore require no surgery. If they persist as a problem beyond 2 years of age, they should be treated by ligation and division of the processus vaginalis, similar to a herniotomy.

ACUTE SCROTUM

Q. **You are called to A & E to assess a 2-year-old boy with acute scrotal swelling. When you examine him, you find redness and oedema of a hemi-scrotum, extending into his perineum and inguinal area. The testes are not tender. What is this likely to be?**

A. Idiopathic scrotal oedema.

Q. **How would you manage it?**

A. This condition is self-limiting. There is no association with any urinary pathology.

It can be treated with expectant observation and oral anti-inflammatory agents. Ampicillin is frequently prescribed as treatment, despite the fact that there is no proven infective aetiology.

Q. A & E are busy. They ask you to see a 12-year-old boy with a swollen painful left testis. On examination, you find a bluish tender lump at the upper pole of his testis. What might this be?

A. This represents torsion of the hydatid of the testis. The hydatid sits at the upper pole of the testis, and when twisted and infracted it can be seen as a bluish lump under the scrotal skin.

Q. How should it be managed?

A. *If there is any doubt about the diagnosis, the child should undergo a surgical exploration to exclude testicular torsion.* Expectant or medical management of this condition is sometimes suggested (with analgesics and anti-inflammatory medication). However, it would be important to be absolutely certain that there was no possibility of testicular torsion.

Q. What are the indications for ultrasound scan of an acutely painful scrotum?

A. Ultrasound is of no value in cases of acute scrotal pain of less than 48 hours' duration. It will not reliably diagnose or exclude torsion. Doppler flows may be present despite the testicle undergoing venous infarction. If the pain is of longer duration there may be value in obtaining a Doppler ultrasound scan, which may help to distinguish a necrotic testis from an infected one.

MUMPS ORCHITIS

Q. A GP calls you for advice about one of his patients, a 6-year-old boy who has mumps. The child's mother has done a search on the Internet and is concerned that the condition may affect his testes. What advice could you offer?

A. Mumps may be associated with orchitis. It is rare for mumps to affect the testes in *pre-pubertal* boys. In adolescents and adults, epididymo-orchitis may affect 15–30% of patients who have mumps (in general, 4–8 days after their parotitis). Following mumps orchitis, a reduced testicular size is seen in up to 50% of post-pubertal patients, with abnormalities of semen analysis in around 25% (the latter may be a result of pressure necrosis). Sterility is rare. The effect of mumps on endocrine function has been difficult to establish.

URINARY INCONTINENCE

Q. What is the aetiology of urinary incontinence in children?

A. More than 95% of cases are functional (i.e. not caused by disease, injury or congenital malformation) rather than organic in aetiology. Organic causes should be excluded in order to prevent irreversible deterioration in renal function. Organic causes can be either structural (e.g. ectopic ureter or epispadias) or neurogenic (e.g. spina bifida).

Q. What is functional incontinence?

A. Functional incontinence is incontinence not caused by disease, injury or congenital malformation. The main syndromes that comprise functional urinary incontinence include urge incontinence, voiding postponement, dysfunctional voiding, stress incontinence and giggle incontinence. Management of functional incontinence is dependent on aetiology, but usually includes behavioural measures (e.g. bladder retraining, timed and regular voiding, psychological support if necessary) and/or medication (e.g. anticholinergics for detrusor overactivity, antibiotics for infections, laxatives to relieve constipation).

Q. **What is voiding postponement?**

A. Voiding postponement occurs when children habitually postpone micturition, often until it is too late and urinary incontinence occurs as a result. This is much more common in girls. Eventually the detrusor may become hyporeflexic and sensation of fullness may decrease due to the misuse of the voluntary external sphincter, with voiding occurring only two or three times per day. Overflow and stress incontinence and recurrent urinary tract infections may occur in these advanced cases.

Q. **What is dysfunctional voiding?**

A. This is the tendency for intermittent or continuous sphincter contractions to occur during bladder emptying, commonly resulting in residual urine and possibly urinary tract infections.

Q. **A 7-year-old girl is referred to you because she suffers from urinary incontinence during the day and at night. What history would you elicit about her wetting?**

A. The history is the most important part of the evaluation of this girl, and will determine the basis of her management. It is important to elucidate the incidence, pattern and progression (if any) of the incontinence since birth, and to establish the type (e.g. urge, stress, continuous or giggle incontinence). Therefore the following points should be clarified:

- Is the condition primary or secondary? Has she had these symptoms since birth (primary) or have they developed after a period of being continent (secondary)?
- Primary incontinence refers to the occurrence of symptoms when there has never been a prolonged dry spell, whereas in secondary incontinence the child has previously been dry for at least 6 months. With primary incontinence it is more likely that a significant organic aetiology will be detected on investigation.
- The pattern of the incontinence. Is the incontinence associated with urgency? Is the incontinence continuous, which might be related to an ectopic ureter? If a girl has urinary incontinence shortly after voiding, this may indicate vaginal reflux. A specific entity is 'giggle incontinence' where the only provoking factor is laughing or giggling.
- Severity of the symptoms. How often does the incontinence occur? When it does occur, how severe is it? Does it just make her underwear damp, or is it so severe that she needs to change her clothes? Does she need incontinence pads?

Q. **What risk factors for incontinence would you inquire about in this child?**

A. - *Voiding frequency*. How often does the child void? This is better evaluated with a frequency–volume chart (see below). However, useful clues can be gleaned from what the child and her parents tell you. For example, 'She often holds on until the last minute' is useful to know. Similarly, the child will often give an indication of how often, if at all, they use the school toilets during the school day. This provides information about urinary frequency or withholding behaviour (voiding postponement).

- *Voiding behaviour.* 'Curtseying' or sitting with the heel of the foot pushed into the perineum to control sudden episodes of urge may indicate detrusor overactivity. Straining to void and poor stream would indicate bladder outlet obstruction. This is perhaps more important in a boy, where it may be a sign of meatal stenosis or more rarely posterior urethral valves.
- *Drinking habits.* Drinks that contain additives and particularly artificial colourings seem to be associated with voiding problems. One of the worst culprits is a particular proprietary blackcurrant drink. Stopping consumption of these drinks will often bring about a dramatic improvement in the child's frequency, urgency and wetting.
- *Constipation.* It is important to ask how frequently the child opens her bowels and whether she strains to pass hard stool. Again, correction of constipation will often improve urinary symptoms. Rarely, the coexistence of poor bowel function can be an indicator of a neuropathic aetiology.
- *Urinary tract infections.* These may be a cause of incontinence. It is worth asking about episodes of cystitis-like symptoms. Positive urine cultures may be significant, although this information should be interpreted in the context of the child's symptoms at the time, and exactly how the urine was collected.
- *Age at potty training.* A very young age at potty training seems to be associated with later wetting.
- *Antenatal history.* Congenital urological pathology may have been detected but not followed up.

Q. **What would you look for when you examine the child?**

A.
- *Abdomen.* A palpable bladder or palpable stool would be significant.
- *Genitals.* A split or bifid clitoris may be the only finding in epispadias, a rare condition where the sphincter mechanism will be severely deficient. Perineal excoriation may give an indication of severe wetting or vaginal reflux. In boys who have been circumcised, make sure that there is no meatal stenosis.
- *Spine.* Inspect and palpate the spine, looking for clues of spinal dysraphism such as pigmented or hairy lesions over the midline. Sacral agenesis is characterised by flattening of the buttocks. Abnormal gait or muscle wasting may indicate a neurological problem.
- *General health.* Does the child have other medical conditions that may contribute to poor bladder control?
- Perform a urine dipstick at the end of the examination.

Q. **The parents have very helpfully brought a frequency–volume chart with them. What instructions would you give to other parents so that they could fill out a frequency–volume chart?**

A. Two convenient days should be selected. On those days every time the child voids the urine is collected, and the volume and time of each void is recorded. Wetting episodes are also noted. Additional information that should be collected includes the time, volume and type of fluid intake.

Q. **What do you look at when you interpret a frequency–volume chart?**

A. The starting point is to determine the child's *expected bladder capacity (EBC)*. From the ages of 1 to 12 years this is calculated by adding 1 to the child's age and multiplying this by 30 to give the answer in millilitres (the formula is easier to remember if you work in Imperial units, when the bladder capacity in fluid ounces is simply age plus 1) (EBC in infants up to 1 year of age is weight in kilograms multiplied by 7). The frequency–volume chart will give you the child's *maximum voided volume (MVV)*, which should be 65–150% of EBC. Urinary frequency should not be less than four or more than eight times a day. The 24-hour urine output can also be calculated in addition to the total/type of fluid intake.

Q. **Is there any value in performing a renal ultrasound scan?**

A. This will provide information about bladder capacity. A post-void residual of more than 20 ml on repeated measurement is significant. A thickened bladder with upper tract dilation may reflect a neuropathic bladder. Renal abnormalities, such as a duplex kidney with an abnormal upper moiety, may indicate the presence of an ectopic ureter.

Q. **What other investigations may be performed to assess a child with incontinence?**

A. The most useful information is provided by the history and supplemented with a frequency–volume chart. In many units a clinical nurse specialist who spends time with the family and child, observing behaviour and wetting, recording voided volumes and measuring residuals will provide all of the further information that is needed. Other investigations are used in a very targeted way, when the clinical picture indicates that they may be required.

- *Flow rate measurements.* Just as in adult practice, repeated flow rate measurements are the most useful. If the square of the maximum flow rate is more than the voided volume, the flow rate is satisfactory. A normal flow pattern produces a bell-shaped curve. A flattened pattern may indicate bladder outlet obstruction, an interrupted pattern may indicate that the sphincter is closing, and a flow with discrete peaks may indicate abdominal straining.
- *Residual volume measurements.* These are easily performed using a dedicated ultrasound machine. When the child is not aware that they are voiding, detectors triggering alarms can be placed in their nappies, which will signal when voiding has occurred
- *Plain abdominal X-ray.* This is used to look for faecal loading or spinal dysraphism and sacral agenesis. However, a plain X-ray will only give an indication of how much fibre is in the large bowel, and is certainly not definitive in excluding spinal dysraphism.
- *MRI scan of the spine.* This should be performed if there is a concern that there has been an as yet undiagnosed abnormality of the spine giving rise to a neuropathic bladder.
- *Videocystometrogram (VCMG).* This test is performed under very limited and specific circumstances; most of the required information will have been gathered by the evaluation described above. VCMG is most commonly performed if:
  - it has not been possible to achieve a diagnosis by other means

– there has been no response to treatment
– there is a suspicion of a neuropathic bladder.

Catheter placement is often performed under anaesthesia, and the test is most sensitively performed in a dedicated paediatric setting.

NOCTURNAL ENURESIS

Q. **An 8-year-old boy attends the clinic with his mother. She is very concerned about the fact that he always wets the bed during the night, as she thinks he is too old to be doing this. You have taken a careful history about continence similar to the one above. The boy has no daytime urinary symptoms. What is this condition called?**

A. It is primary (i.e. it has always been present), monosymptomatic (i.e. there are no other urinary symptoms, such as urgency) enuresis (defined as 'intermittent incontinence while sleeping').

Q. **What is the prevalence of this condition?**

A. Around 5–10% of all 7-year-olds will have this condition. It is more common in boys than in girls. Around 2–3% of those who have this condition during childhood are still incontinent in their late teens.

Q. **If untreated, what is the natural history of this condition?**

A. If untreated, 15% of patients with this condition will get better every year.

Q. **Are there any explanations for monosymptomatic nocturnal enuresis?**

A. The normal circadian reduction in urine output during sleep is diminished in at least two-thirds of children with this condition.

Impaired bladder function has been described in children with the moniker of monosymptomatic nocturnal enuresis, with reduced functional bladder capacity, nocturnal and even daytime detrusor overactivity demonstrated in these individuals.

It is possible that these children have an abnormal arousal mechanism that prevents the sensation of a full bladder awakening them, as it would in other children. This is consistent with an observation made by many parents of children with this problem, who report that their children are very difficult to wake.

Q. **What management strategies could be offered?**

A. • *Behavioural strategies.* Encourage the establishment of a regular drinking and voiding pattern during the day. The child should reduce fluid intake in the evening, and void before going to bed. 'Lifting' is the practice of waking the child and taking them to the bathroom, typically at the time when their parents are going to bed.

• *Alarm.* An enuresis alarm in the bed is activated when the child wets the bed. This method can often take up to a couple of months to become effective. However, it is associated with the greatest long-term success, with benefit seen in up to two-thirds of children who use it, according to a recent Cochrane review.

• *Pharmacology.* Desmopressin will produce results quickly, but these are not sustained once treatment is stopped. Anti-muscarinics may be added as an adjunct to desmopressin. Tricyclic antidepressants have been used to treat this condition, but are more frequently associated with side-effects.

ANTENATALLY DETECTED HYDRONEPHROSIS: ASSESSMENT

Q. **You are called by a neonatal doctor who is concerned that a newborn has antenatally diagnosed hydronephrosis. Is there useful antenatal history that they can provide you with?**

A. The antenatal history is very useful in giving clues about the possible diagnosis and severity of the condition. It will be well recorded in the mother's notes, which are usually not available when the child is subsequently seen in clinic. The quality of antenatal scans is very high, so it would be a pity to lose sight of the information that they provide.

Antenatal scans will give information about the kidneys with regard to renal cysts, the presence and degree of hydronephrosis (objectively measured by the antero-posterior diameter of the renal pelvis), cortical thinning, and echo-genicity of the renal parenchyma. Dilated ureters should be noted. The bladder may be thick-walled, fail to empty, or never be seen (a sign of bladder exstrophy). Seeing a penis on ultrasound scan will indicate that the fetus is male. In posterior urethral valves (PUV) a dilated posterior urethra may be seen. Oligo- or anhydramnios suggests poor urine drainage and is an indicator of poor outcome.

Q. **The hydronephrosis affects only one kidney, and arrangements are made for the baby to be seen in your clinic at 6 weeks of age with an up-to-date ultrasound scan. It is often helpful to organise as much of the imaging as possible before they are seen. What would be your indications for a micturating cystourethrogram (MCUG) for this infant?**

A. It depends on what the ultrasound scans have suggested as the possible diagnosis:
- To look for vesico-ureteric reflux (VUR). The possibility of this is raised if dilated ureters have been seen on ultrasound. However, dilated ureters may also indicate vesico-ureteric junction (VUJ) obstruction or a mega-ureter.
- If there is a possibility of posterior urethral valves. This is suggested in a boy who has bilateral hydroureteronephrosis, a thick-walled or poorly emptying bladder, a visibly dilated posterior urethra, or who has had antenatal oligo- or anhydramnios. If the MCUG is being performed to look for PUV, it should be done postnatally before the child goes home.
- If there is concern about a neuropathic bladder. This is likely if there is an overt spinal abnormality, but it may be suggested by the possibility of a thick-walled bladder. Where there is a possibility of a neuropathic bladder and there is no overt cause, the spine may be imaged by ultrasound before the age of 3 months to look for spinal anomalies.
- A ureterocele with duplex kidney. It is helpful to know whether this might be obstructing the bladder outlet (as may occur in a large prolapsing uretero-cele), or whether there is coexisting vesico-ureteric reflux before the uretero-cele is treated.

Q. **The paediatric team have been very helpful. They bring you the ultrasound and MCUG images and wonder whether nuclear medicine or functional**

imaging would be useful before you see the child and the parents. They are more than happy to organise the test you request, but are not sure whether a dimercaptosucccinic acid (^{99m}Tc DMSA) or mercaptoacetyl-triglycine (^{99m}Tc MAG3) scan should be organised. How would you help them to decide?

A.
- The ^{99m}Tc MAG3 scan is a dynamic scan. It produces images like a video or cine film. The gamma radiation given off by the tracer can be quantitatively measured to provide information such as differential function, and washout curves. The images that are then supplied to the clinician are similar to a series of still photos taken from the cine film. ^{99m}Tc MAG3 scans are most useful in cases where there is a concern about upper tract obstruction (e.g. PUJ obstruction or VUJ obstruction). The investigation also provides an approximation of differential function.
- A ^{99m}Tc DMSA scan is a static scan and produces only a 'still image'. However, the detail and 'resolution' of the image of the kidney that is produced is much better than that of a ^{99m}Tc MAG3 scan. It will give a good measure of the differential function. It will also provide detail – for example, showing cortical defects seen in acute pyelonephritis or with cortical scarring (^{99m}Tc DMSA has a sensitivity of 90% and a specificity of 100% for detection of renal cortical scarring). It will provide good detail in duplex kidneys, showing the function of each moiety. A ^{99m}Tc DMSA scan is therefore most useful in cases where detailed information is required about the kidney and there is no concern about obstruction (e.g. in VUR).

Notes:

1. With regard to the MAG3 and DMSA nuclear medicine scans, a radio-isotope is bound to both of these carriers. The radio-isotope most commonly used is metastable technetium-99 (^{99m}Tc), which is extracted from a molybdenum-99 generator. The half-life of ^{99m}Tc is 6 hours.

2. Around 90% of ^{99m}Tc MAG3 is excreted in the urine by tubular secretion and 10% by glomerular filtration. Frusemide is given either 20 minutes after isotope injection (F+20) or 15 minutes before it (F–15). The maximal effect of frusemide occurs approximately 18 minutes after injection, and thus an F+20 renogram demonstrates obstruction late in the investigation and may give equivocal results in up to 15% of cases. The F–15 renogram results in maximal stress on the pelvi-ureteric junction (PUJ) (in terms of urine flow) earlier in the study, and reduces equivocal rates to around 7%. Therefore the F–15 renogram is the investigation of choice. The F+0 renogram is now also performed, and is acceptable in the majority of cases, but in complex cases an F–15 study will give the most reliable results.

A diuretic ^{99m}Tc MAG3 renogram has three phases:
- vascular phase (0–10 seconds), which reflects renal blood flow (a blush is obtained in kidney)
- extraction/parenchymal/uptake phase (10 seconds to 5 minutes), which reflects renal uptake or parenchymal function (i.e. renal parenchymal uptake and transit of radio-isotope)
- excretory phase (5 minutes onwards), which occurs with radio-isotope being excreted into the renal pelvis.

After injection of ^{99m}Tc MAG3, images are obtained approximately every 2 seconds for 60 seconds, and then every 10–60 seconds for 20–30 minutes. Post-void images are also taken, as a full bladder can affect drainage. In addition, in a child who is continent and cooperative, indirect ^{99m}Tc MAG3 cytography may be used in the diagnosis/follow-up of vesico-ureteric reflux (thus avoiding the need for a micturating cystogram, which is much more invasive and involves significantly more radiation exposure).

The diuretic response is proportional to the renal function, and therefore one should avoid this investigation or interpret the results with caution in those patients with a GFR of < 15 ml/minute.

The glomeruli and renal tubules take 6 weeks to mature after birth. Therefore isotope renograms should be avoided until this age.

One should be aware of and able to draw the diuresis renogram curves in the viva (sometimes known as O'Reilly's curves, as he pioneered diuresis renography). These are shown in Figure 6.2 (for F+20 renography):

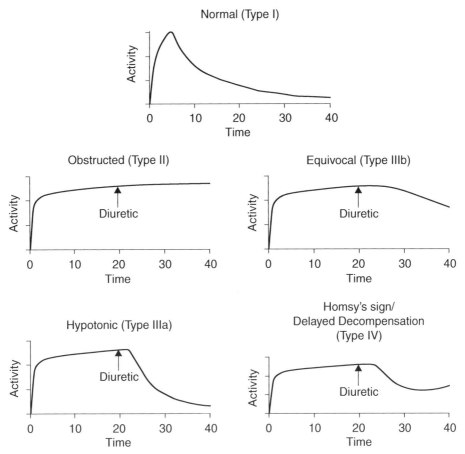

Figure 6.2 Diuresis renogram curves (for F+20 renography).

1. A type I curve shows normal renal uptake and drainage.
2. A type II curve demonstrates an obstructed pattern with no response to diuretic.
3. A type IIIa curve actually represents normal drainage (from a hypotonic renal pelvis). The curve rises initially but falls rapidly on injection of frusemide.

   A type IIIb curve is equivocal and rises initially, but neither falls rapidly nor continues to rise following injection of frusemide.
4. A type IV curve, which demonstrates Homsy's sign. The diuretic injection results in a transient response, which appears decompensated at higher urinary flow rates (within 15 minutes of frusemide injection). It is most likely to represent obstruction (although vesico-ureteric reflux can result in a similar appearance), i.e. intermittent hydronephrosis. Performing F–15 renography eliminates Homsy's sign and will confirm obstruction in these cases.

3. ^{99m}Tc DMSA is extracted from the peritubular extracellular fluid and deposited in the tubular cells. Static images following the administration of ^{99m}Tc DMSA are obtained 3–4 hours after injection (e.g. planar posterior, left and right posterior oblique, and coronal tomographic views).

POSTERIOR URETHRAL VALVES

Q. **Concern has been raised following an antenatal scan that a child on the neonatal unit may have posterior urethral valves. The neonatal junior doctor has been reassured by an ultrasound scan performed on the first day of life that looks nearly normal. What is your view of this recent scan result?**

A. In the first few days of life the child is often a little dry, and coupled with immature renal function, urine output is reduced. This would tend to result in a reduction in the degree of hydronephrosis, which could be falsely reassuring (the scan needs to be repeated after at least 1 week of age to obtain the correct diameter of the renal pelvis).

Q. **The baby's blood biochemistry has been checked on the first day of life. The neonatal doctors are anxious that the creatinine level is elevated at 320 μmol/l. Why should they be worried?**

A. In the uterus the fetus has been dialysed across the placenta. The baby's initial blood chemistry on the first day of life will reflect their mother's blood chemistry. In this case the blood test has detected the mother's poor renal function. It will take a week or so before the baby's blood test reflects their own renal function.

Q. **You go and review the child. The antenatal history for this boy includes severe bilateral hydro-ureteronephrosis, and thickened bladder wall. He has been seen to pass urine only with a poor and dribbling stream. What diagnosis are you concerned about?**

A. The most likely cause is posterior urethral valves. Hydro-ureteronephrosis may be seen in VUR or VUJ obstruction. A thickened bladder wall may be seen with a neuropathic bladder, or other more rare causes of bladder outlet obstruction.

Q. **The child is currently warm, well perfused and well hydrated. Outline the strategy for managing him during this admission.**

A. Management of posterior urethral valves requires specialist paediatric urology and nephrology input. The principles can be summarised as follows.

Treat possible bladder outlet obstruction with catheter drainage. A 6Fr feeding tube is suitable as a urethral catheter. Although a suprapubic catheter is advocated, it should be appreciated that these can be difficult to insert into the small, thick-walled bladder that is seen in posterior urethral valves.

Look for and treat post-obstructive diuresis. This will require intravenous fluid and should be done in conjunction with paediatric nephrologists. Fluid monitoring will include recording urine output, clinical examination, weighing the baby regularly and checking the serum biochemistry.

Start prophylactic antibiotics (e.g. trimethoprim).

Secure a diagnosis. Although a renal tract ultrasound scan is helpful, the diagnostic test is an MCUG. This should be covered with a short course of treatment with antibiotics.

Resect the valves. Once the baby is stable and well and their creatinine levels have reached a nadir value with catheter drainage, the urethral valves can be resected. This is done cystoscopically, under general anaesthesia.

The management of any renal impairment should be optimised by paediatric nephrologists before the baby goes home.

Q. **Before the baby goes home, the medical student on your firm asks you to explain to him the boy's MCUG (*see* Figure 6.3). How has the MCUG been done, and what features do the arrows point to?**

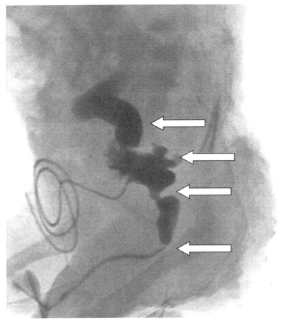

Figure 6.3 Micturating cystourethrogram (MCUG) in an infant with posterior urethral valves.

A.   The MCUG in Figure 6.3 has been done by passing contrast down a suprapubic catheter. From top to bottom, the arrows respectively point to:
- VUR into a very dilated ureter, but not entering the pelvicalyceal system on the image seen
- a very trabeculated bladder
- a hypertrophied bladder neck
- the narrowed junction between the dilated posterior urethra and the narrower anterior urethra. This is the site of the posterior urethral valves.

Q.   **What are the long-term outcomes for posterior urethral valves?**
A.   By 20 years of age 50% will have chronic renal disease, and a third will have end-stage renal disease. Bladder function is also frequently impaired. Potty training may be delayed, and up to 50% will have daytime and nocturnal incontinence at 5 years of age.

Q.   **What are the poor prognostic indicators for posterior urethral valves?**
A.   Rather intuitively, most of the factors which appear worse correlate with a worse outcome.
- Prenatal: earlier (< 24 weeks) detection, oligohydramnios, high levels of β2-microglobulin (> 13 mg/l) in the fetal urine
- Postnatal: presentation under 1 month of age, bilateral VUR 1 year of age: high nadir creatinine, reduced GFR 5 years of age: daytime incontinence and proteinuria 10 years of age: urodynamics showing poor compliance or myogenic failure.

PUJ OBSTRUCTION AND PYELOPLASTY

Q.   **In your clinic you see a 3-month-old infant. There was a severe unilateral hydronephrosis detected antenatally. The rest of the renal tract has appeared normal on all of the antenatal and postnatal scans. What is the most likely cause of the hydronephrosis?**
A.   Pelvi-ureteric junction (PUJ) obstruction.

Q.   **How does PUJ obstruction present in children?**
A.
- Most commonly with antenatal hydronephrosis.
- In older children, PUJ obstruction may present with loin pain. This pain may be exacerbated by drinking large volumes of fluid, where the subsequent diuresis exacerbates the stretching of the upper tract. This is referred to as Dietel's crisis.
- PUJ obstruction may be detected as an incidental finding during the investigation of other complaints.
- More rarely the child may present with a urinary tract infection, a mass or haematuria (a hydronephrotic kidney is more susceptible to trauma).

Q.   **What is the aetiology of PUJ obstruction in children?**
A.   Usually the PUJ junction is hypoplastic and aperistaltic in neonates.
   A significant proportion of older children, usually above the age of 7 years, who present with PUJ obstruction will have a lower pole anterior accessory vessel (artery) crossing the PUJ (these children usually present with intermittent

loin pain, which occurs after drinking large amounts of fluid; hydronephrosis is only present when patients are symptomatic).

Q. **What investigations are useful in children in whom you suspect PUJ obstruction?**

A. In children the two most useful tests are ultrasound scans and dynamic renography.

Ultrasound scans will provide information about the degree of hydronephrosis, the anterior–posterior renal pelvic diameter, the degree of calyceal dilation and whether there is renal cortical thinning. It will usefully exclude ureteric dilation and other renal tract abnormalities, in which case there is no indication for an MCUG. Dynamic renography will provide information about the differential function of the kidneys, and will also indicate how well the kidneys drain. IVU gives very little additional useful information, and is rarely performed in children.

Note:
If dynamic diuresis renography is equivocal, a Whitaker test can be performed, but this is done very rarely, especially in children. This investigation requires the placement of a nephrostomy tube in the affected kidney and a catheter in the bladder. With the patient prone, a mixture of contrast with saline is infused via the nephrostomy tube at a rate of 10 ml/minute. The pressure difference between the kidney and the bladder is measured. If it is less than 15 cmH_2O the system is not obstructed, and if it is greater than 22 cmH_2O the kidney is obstructed. Results in the range 15–22 cmH_2O are equivocal.

Q. **The mother has been told that her baby needs a ^{99m}Tc MAG3 scan. What does MAG3 stand for?**

A. Mercaptoacetyltriglycine. It is labelled with metastable technetium-99 (^{99m}Tc).

Q. **How is ^{99m}Tc MAG3 handled by the kidney?**

A. It undergoes both tubular and glomerular excretion. Dimercaptosuccinic acid (DMSA) binds only to the proximal renal tubules. Diethylenetriamine-pentacetic acid (DTPA) is only filtered by the glomeruli.

Q. **The mother wants to know how this test is performed. What would you tell her?**

A. The scan is performed in the nuclear medicine department.

Before the test begins, the mother should ensure that her child has had plenty to drink and is well hydrated. Intravenous access is obtained.

The tracer is then injected. Images are obtained using a gamma camera that records activity over the next 20 minutes or so. Final images are taken after the child has voided and/or undergone a change in position. Frusemide may be administered according to a locally agreed protocol. In children, in whom venous access is often not straightforward, the diuretic is often administered at the same time as the tracer.

Q. **The mother is very anxious about the dose of radiation. What advice will you give her?**

A. The radiation dose from a ^{99m}Tc MAG3 test is less than 0.4 mSv (millisieverts). For a DMSA scan it is approximately 1 mSV. The higher dose is easier to understand when one considers that ^{99m}Tc MAG3 is excreted by the kidney, whereas ^{99m}Tc DMSA binds to the renal tubule. In both cases the radiation dose is less than that for a plain abdominal X-ray.

Q. **Please interpret the MAG3 renogram shown in Figure 6.4.**

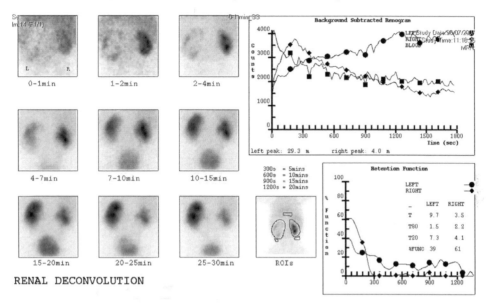

Figure 6.4 A ^{99m}Tc MAG3 renogram.

A. A series of images are shown taken at the intervals marked. 'ROI' indicates the regions of interest that have been drawn around the kidneys. The counts taken from these regions of interest provided the upper right-hand graph. The differential function is obtained by comparing the count from the two kidneys during the early part of the study before the trace has entered the collecting system. Inspection of the 1–2 minute images and the 2–4 minute images indicates that the left kidney has less function than the right one. This is born out by the measured differential of 39% annotated on the bottom right-hand graph. Tracer moves much more slowly through the left system than the right one, with significant tracer remaining in the left kidney at the end of the study. This is reflected in the curves in the top right-hand graph. It would have been advantageous to see how much more drains from the left kidney with voiding. There seems to be some bladder emptying between the 15–20 minute image and the 25–30 minute image, but the bladder has not emptied completely. It is not clear from the images whether diuretic has been administered.

Q. **What are your indications for pyeloplasty in PUJ obstruction?**
A. • Reduced function of the affected kidney. A differential function of less than 40% is significant.
   • Symptoms such as pain or urinary tract infection. Older children are able to articulate that they have pain. However, this is more difficult to establish

in infants, and when asked, it is unusual for the mothers of babies with PUJ obstruction to report that they think their child is experiencing pain.

- Deteriorating renal function (a decrease in differential function of more than 10% is significant) or increasing hydronephrosis on follow-up ultrasound scan.
- Concern that the function of the kidney will decline if it is left untreated. Based on the natural history studies by Dhillon,[4] gross hydronephrosis, with an anterior–posterior (AP) renal pelvis diameter of more than 50 mm, should be surgically treated. With a diameter in the range 20–50 mm the situation is not so clear cut, with an increasing proportion of patients requiring surgery with increased AP renal pelvic diameter, as shown in Table 6.1.

Table 6.1 Percentage of children who require surgery for increasing hydronephrosis in PUJ obstruction

AP renal pelvic diameter in transverse plane in PUJ obstruction (mm)*	Percentage of children requiring surgery
> 50	100
> 40	80
> 30	55
> 20	20
< 20	1–3

*Those infants with a persistent AP renal pelvic diameter of < 10 mm are discharged.

MULTICYSTIC DYSPLASTIC KIDNEY

Q. The paediatrician asks for your advice. He has taken over the care of a 13-month-old girl who had a renal anomaly detected antenatally. Ultrasound scan reveals a normal kidney on one side, but on the other side there is a 7-cm-long kidney composed of large cysts and no normal tissue. A DMSA scan has shown no function in the abnormal kidney. What is the most likely problem affecting this kidney?

A. Multicystic dysplastic kidney (MCDK).

Q. This is exactly what the paediatrician is concerned about. He would like to know how you would manage the child and your justification for the plan.

A. Usually these involute, in which case very little else needs to be done. However, if they persist at a significant size, management is more controversial. In theory there is a risk of malignancy with such kidneys, although in practice there have only been a few case reports in the world literature. A risk of hypertension is also cited as a concern, but again in practice this seems to be very unusual. It would be reasonable to offer a laparoscopic nephrectomy if there are other concerning features on radiology, such as the presence of a ureterocele or difficulty in distinguishing the MCDK from a severely hydronephrotic kidney. Some parents simply prefer to have the abnormal kidney removed rather than followed up.

DUPLEX KIDNEY

Q. Describe the embryology of a duplex kidney and the Meyer–Weigart law.

A. The ureteric bud originates from the lower mesonephric duct, grows cranially and meets the metanephros at 32 days. By reciprocal induction they generate a kidney. Urine production begins at 10 weeks. If an extra ureteric bud is generated it will also head to the metanephros and so develop into a second ureter and a duplex kidney will form. The ureteric bud that meets the more cranial metanephros will generate the upper moiety ureter. This ureteric bud will have arisen from a more caudal position on the mesonephric duct than the other ureteric bud. When this part of the mesonephric duct is subsumed into the developing bladder, the more caudal ureteric bud will maintain its lower position.

The resultant relationship with the upper moiety ureter inserting lower and more medially into the bladder is the Meyer–Weigart law (in contrast, the lower renal moiety ureter inserts higher and more laterally into the bladder).

Q. You see a 3-month-old girl in clinic with her parents. There was a confident prenatal diagnosis of a duplex kidney on one side. What is a duplex kidney and is it common?

A. A duplex kidney is a kidney with a double collecting system and two separate ureters that enter the bladder separately. It is said to occur in 1 in 125 births.

Q. Where does the ureter of the upper moiety insert relative to the lower moiety ureter?

A. The upper moiety ureter inserts inferiorly and more medially compared with the lower moiety ureter.

Q. What are the complications associated with a duplex kidney?

A. Complications are related to the insertion of the ureter into the bladder.

- The upper moiety ureter may insert into the bladder normally, or its insertion may be related to a ureterocele, or its insertion may be ectopic. A ureterocele is a swelling associated with the insertion of the ureter into the bladder. It is usually a cause of obstruction at the VUJ. A ureterocele may be complicated by infection, prolapse and bladder outlet obstruction. Ectopic ureter insertion in girls may be into the urethra or vagina, and if below the external sphincter it will cause continuous incontinence. The more ectopic the ureter, the more dysplastic the kidney it drains, and the more difficult it can be to detect radiologically. In boys the ectopic insertion may be into the prostate, ejaculatory duct or vas. *The insertion of the ectopic ureter is always above the external urethral sphincter in boys, so incontinence will not result.*
- The lower moiety ureter can insert normally or be associated with vesicoureteric reflux.

URINARY TRACT INFECTIONS (UTIS) IN CHILDREN

Q. How common are UTIs in children?

A. During childhood, UTIs occur in around 3–5% of girls and 1% of boys. The incidence of UTIs is higher in boys than in girls in the first year of life. Uncircumcised males under 1 year of age are more likely to be affected than circumcised males. Above 1 year of age, UTIs are more common in females.

Q. **A 9-month-old boy presents with pyrexia and vomiting. He is very unwell. What microbiology specimens would you want to have collected?**

A. A clean-catch urine sample is the most important specimen to collect. Blood cultures would also need to be taken.

Note:

In order to obtain a clean-catch urine sample, the urethral meatus should be clean, and if possible urine from the middle of the stream should be collected. For girls, cleaning involves separating the labia and cleaning the area. For circumcised boys, the glans of the penis should be cleaned. For uncircumcised boys the foreskin is gently retracted (where possible) prior to cleaning. After cleaning, the child voids, with the parent 'catching' the urine in a clean specimen container after the first few drops have been passed. In the case of those who can void on command, the child can void over the toilet and a clean-catch midstream voided urine specimen may be easily obtained. Although obtaining clean-catch samples can be time consuming and messy, this technique has a high sensitivity and specificity for diagnosing UTIs.

Q. **The urine of the infant described above shows more than 500 white blood cells, and CRP is 84. The boy responds to intravenous (IV) fluids and antibiotics. Is his infection typical?**

A. According to the 2007 NICE guidelines on the management of UTIs,[5] an atypical UTI is one in which any of the following apply:

- seriously ill
- poor urine flow
- abdominal or bladder mass
- raised creatinine levels
- septicaemia
- failure to respond to treatment with suitable antibiotics within 48 hours
- infection with non-*E.coli* organisms.

According to this definition this infant has an atypical urinary tract infection.

Q. **What imaging is helpful?**

A. An ultrasound scan of the renal tract.

Q. **The ultrasound scan shows a large, thick-walled bladder. On direct questioning the infant's mother admits that he has always had a rather 'dribbly' stream. What conditions are you concerned about?**

A. The possibilities are a bladder outlet obstruction (especially posterior urethral valves) or a neuropathic bladder.

Q. **Is any more renal tract imaging appropriate?**

A. According to the NICE guidelines,[5] a DMSA scan is the only other investigation required in a child between 6 months and 3 years of age with an atypical urinary infection. However, in those with a worrying history and an abnormal ultrasound scan, further investigations may also be appropriate. The diagnostic test for PUVs is an MCUG, which must include good views of the urethra during voiding.

The NICE guidelines on radiological imaging in children with UTIs are summarised in Table 6.2.

Table 6.2 Guidelines for imaging in paediatric UTI (adapted from NICE guidelines, 2007)

UTI	Age	USS in acute infection	USS in 6 weeks	DMSA in 4–6 months	MCUG*
Responds well to antibiotics in < 48 hours	< 6 months		Yes		
Responds well to antibiotics in < 48 hours	6 months to 3 years				
Responds well to antibiotics in < 48 hours	> 3 years				
Atypical UTI	< 6 months	Yes		Yes	Yes
Atypical UTI	6 months to 3 years	Yes		Yes	Consider
Atypical UTI	> 3 years	Yes			
Recurrent UTI	< 6 months	Yes		Yes	Yes
Recurrent UTI	6 months to 3 years		Yes	Yes	Consider
Recurrent UTI	> 3 years		Yes	Yes	

*Some centres may prefer MAG3 (mercaptoacetyltryglycine) renogram with indirect cystogram in cases with suspected vesico-ureteric reflux.

Q. A 7-month-old girl presents with pyelonephritis. She is admitted under the care of the paediatricians and responds well to antibiotics. She has an ultrasound scan before discharge which shows unilateral hydro-ureteronephrosis. What are the possible causes of unilateral hydro-ureteronephrosis?

A. An isolated hydro-ureteronephrosis raises the possibility of VUR, VUJ obstruction, or megaureter.

Q. An MCUG has been organised by the paediatric team. The child's mother would like to know a little more about the test before it is performed. What would you tell her?

A. The test carries a risk of provoking a further urinary tract infection, so it should be covered with a short course of treatment with antibiotics (e.g. trimethoprim).

The test is performed in the radiology department by the radiology doctors and will involve exposure to X-rays. The girl will be catheterised urethrally. Contrast material, which is a special dye that shows on X-ray, is then injected into the bladder and X-rays are taken. At the end of the test the catheter is taken out, and further X-rays are taken as the child urinates.

The aspect of the test that most parents – and patients – dislike is the catheterisation. Above the age of 1 year it becomes much more difficult to catheterise the child, as they will struggle more. An MCUG is not a test that should be requested lightly.

Q. The mother is very interested in what you say. The girl's aunt has also attended the consultation, but is not so convinced. The aunt, who is an adult, had pyelonephritis last year and objects that no one made all of this fuss about her infection. **Why is pyelonephritis in paediatrics taken so seriously?**

A. Investigation of pyelonephritis in the past has had a high yield for detecting problems, with up to 30% of children having a significant underlying renal tract anomaly.

Pyelonephritis in infants is important. During the acute episode it carries its own morbidity. In addition, following the acute episode, pyelonephritis may result in the following:

- *Scarring.* Young kidneys are susceptible to damage from the combination of intra-renal reflux and infection. It is unusual for scarring to result in renal impairment unless it is extensive and severe. The importance of scarring is that it carries a significant long-term risk of hypertension.
- *Recurrence.* Up to 20% of children with pyelonephritis will have a recurrence within 1 year.

Note:

There was a concern that a significant proportion of children with end-stage renal disease were thought to have this because of VUR with associated urinary tract infection. It is now thought that this may have been an overestimation, where children who had been born with poorly functioning dysplastic kidneys underwent extensive investigations, and some VUR was identified as the only cause. It is also being recognised that many children are being over-investigated with unpleasant tests. This is perhaps one of the motivations behind the current NICE guidelines on the investigation of UTI.

Q. **The MCUG is performed and the results are shown in Figure 6.5. Describe the findings.**

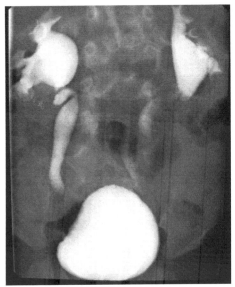

Figure 6.5 Micturating cystourethrogram (MCUG) in an infant girl.

A. Bilateral vesico-ureteric reflux with at least moderate ureteric and pelvi-calyceal dilatation.

Q. What functional imaging would be useful?

A. A DMSA scan would be very useful. Acutely during the infective episode it will show cortical defects and confirm a diagnosis if it is in doubt, although it is not often used for this indication. If performed 4–6 months after the pyelonephritis has been treated, it will show areas of permanent injury or scarring (in addition to providing relative renal function).

Q. Figure 6.6 is the patient's DMSA scan. What does it show?

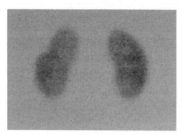

Figure 6.6 A DMSA scan in an infant girl.

A. There is a cortical defect in the mid to upper pole of the left kidney. Whether it is a scar depends on whether there has been a sufficient interval since the pyelonephritis – ideally at least 6 months.

Q. What is secondary reflux?

A. It occurs when the reflux is due to another clearly defined pathology (e.g. posterior urethral valves or neuropathic bladder). In secondary reflux, treatment is targeted at the underlying condition.

Q. What is the International Reflux Study Committee grading of primary VUR and the rates of spontaneous resolution?

A. This grading is based on the extent of retrograde filling and dilatation of the ureter, the renal pelvis and the calyces on an MCUG, and is shown in Table 6.3.

Table 6.3 International Reflux Study Committee grading of VUR

Grade of VUR	Characteristics	Rate of spontaneous resolution (%)
Grade 1	Reflux does not reach the renal pelvis; varying degrees of ureteral dilatation	90
Grade 2	Reflux reaches the renal pelvis; no dilatation of the collecting system; normal fornices	80
Grade 3	Mild or moderate dilatation of the ureter, with or without tortuosity; moderate dilatation of the collecting system; normal or minimally deformed fornices	50
Grade 4	Moderate dilatation of the ureter with or without tortuosity; moderate dilatation of the collecting system; blunt fornices, but impressions of the papillae still visible	20
Grade 5	Gross dilatation and tortuosity of the ureter; marked dilatation of the collecting system; papillary impressions no longer visible; intraparenchymal reflux	< 10

Q. **What are the broad management plans that could be offered for this girl's primary VUR?**

A. Medical or surgical management.

Q. **What are the differences in outcome between surgical and medical management?**

A. Several randomised controlled trials have compared ureteric re-implantation with conservative medical management. On all the most important outcome measures (frequency of UTIs, scarring and GFR) there was no difference between the two treatments, except for a lower incidence of febrile UTIs in the surgically treated group.

Q. **What are the important elements of conservative/medical management?**

A. • The most important aspect of this is educating the parents that if their child has a urinary tract infection, or unexplained pyrexia, she should be assessed and treated promptly. This means that urine should be sent for culture and sensitivity and then appropriate treatment with antibiotics should be started. Early treatment of urinary tract infection will reduce the likelihood of longer-term scarring.
- Maintain a good fluid intake.
- Maintain a regular bowel habit and avoid constipation.
- In an older child it is important that they are encouraged to void frequently. They should void during each break at school, and their parents should encourage them to void 3-hourly during the day when they are at home.
- Prophylactic antibiotics have been the mainstay of medical treatment for years. Only recently has their efficacy been assessed with randomised controlled trials, and the results proved disappointing for lower grades of reflux. Prophylactic antibiotics are continued until VUR resolves or is corrected.

Q. **What are the indications for surgical treatment?**

A. This is a controversial topic. The indications include:
- parental choice
- failure to comply with medical treatment
- breakthrough febrile urinary tract infections despite prophylactic antibiotics
- persistent reflux in girls over 5 years of age
- grade 4 and 5 reflux often requires surgical correction.

Q. **What surgical procedures are available?**

A. *Endoscopic surgery.* Cystoscopy is used to inject a bulking agent around the ureteric orifice. Subtrigonal injection (STING) of PTFE/Teflon has been much less widely used since it was discovered that Teflon can migrate to distant organs. The most commonly used agent is now dextranomer/hyaluronic acid copolymer (Deflux), and success rates of well over 80% have been quoted. Although it may require repeat treatments, its advantages are that it can be performed as a day-case procedure with minimal morbidity.

Open surgery. There are several methods of re-implanting the ureter.
- Intra-vesical re-implantation involves opening the bladder, mobilising the ureter and creating a sub-mucosal tunnel at least five times as long as the diameter of the ureter (Paquin's rule). The easiest is a Cohen cross-trigonal re-implantation (which has a success rate of more than 95%). The

Leadbetter–Politano procedure re-implants the ureter into a higher and more medial position in the bladder.

- The Lich–Gregoir procedure is an extra-vesical anti-reflux operation that involves burying the ureter in a tunnel of detrusor. The bladder mucosa is not opened in this procedure (and therefore a catheter is not necessary post-operatively).

Laparoscopic/vesicoscopic surgery. The previously described open operations are modified in the hands of adept laparoscopic surgeons.

Q. What is the definition of recurrent UTI?

A. Recurrent UTI is defined as, *over a period of 1 year or less*:
- three or more episodes of UTI with cystitis (lower urinary tract infection)
- two or more episodes of UTI with acute pyelonephritis (upper urinary tract infection)
- one episode of UTI with acute pyelonephritis plus one or more episodes of UTI with cystitis.

Q. You see a 7-year-old girl in your clinic with recurrent episodes of cystitis associated with positive urine cultures. What history will you take?

A. In the absence of pyrexial episodes her problems are a real nuisance to her rather than a threat to her health. A very similar assessment is made to that for the child with incontinence.
- *Symptoms that suggest significant predisposing pathology*: straining to void, poor stream, frank haematuria and neurological symptoms indicate that more detailed evaluation may be necessary.
- *Voiding history and frequency*: infrequent voiding is a common exacerbating factor; children do not like going to the bathroom to urinate, and the state of most school toilets is a further disincentive.
- *Fluid intake*: adequate fluid intake is necessary (with avoidance of fizzy and coloured drinks).
- *Bowel habit*: constipation will make episodes of cystitis more likely.

Q. You examine the girl's abdomen and find no masses, her perineum and genitals are unremarkable, and she has a normal spine. Is there anything else worth checking?

A. *Urine dipstick*: to check for leucocytes and nitrites (assessed in the context of whether she has current UTI symptoms), glucose and protein.

Q. Her voiding history is a little vague. How can you obtain more information about her voiding?

A. By means of a frequency–volume chart.

Q. Are any further investigations required?

A. A renal tract ultrasound scan is justifiable. It will show upper tract anomalies, bladder volume and residual urine volume.

Q. An ultrasound scan proves normal. What advice would you give to the parents on how to control the girl's frequent episodes of infection?

A. Set up a good voiding habit. She may need to be prompted to void 'by the clock' every 3 hours when she is awake. This also means voiding during each break at school. Treating constipation is often effective.

There is some (not particularly strong) evidence for consuming cranberry juice and bioactive yoghurt regularly. If, despite the above measures, the child continues to have problematic infections, it may be worth considering a course of prophylactic antibiotics. Trimethoprim and nitrofurantoin are excreted in the urine and are effective in this role, whereas ampicillin and cephalosporins affect the commensal bowel flora and therefore may not be so effective.

REFERENCES

1. Rickwood AM. Medical indications for circumcision. *BJU Int* 1999; **83 (Suppl. 1):** 45–51.
2. Gairdner D. The fate of the foreskin: a study of circumcision. *BMJ* 1949; **2:** 1433–7.
3. Oster J. Further fate of the foreskin. Incidence of preputial adhesions, phimosis, and smegma among Danish schoolboys. *Arch Dis Child* 1968; **43:** 200–3.
4. Dhillon HK. Prenatally diagnosed hydronephrosis: the Great Ormond Street experience. *Br J Urol* 1998; **81 (Suppl. 2):** 39–44.
5. National Institute for Health and Clinical Excellence. *Urinary Tract Infection in Children*. Clinical guideline 54. www.nice.org.uk (accessed May 2009).

FURTHER READING

Thomas DFM, Duffy PG and Rickwood AMK (eds) *Essentials of Paediatric Urology*, 2nd edn. New York: Informa Healthcare; 2008.

Chapter 7
Urological emergencies.
Part 1: Acute testicular pain, penile fracture and post-procedure emergencies

Iqbal S Shergill and Mark Emberton

ACUTE TESTICULAR PAIN

Q. A 15-year-old boy (*see* Figure 7.1) is referred to you with acute onset right testicular pain. What is the differential diagnosis?

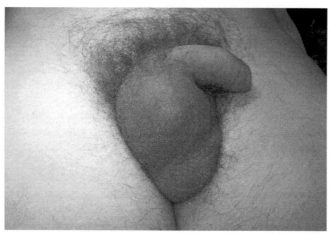

Figure 7.1 Image of a young boy presenting with acute-onset right testicular pain.

A. The differential diagnosis includes testicular torsion, epididymo-orchitis, testicular trauma, torted hydatid of Morgagni and mumps orchitis (and idiopathic scrotal oedema if the boy had been under 10 years of age).

Q. How would you assess this patient?

A. I would regard this as a urological emergency and would see the patient immediately myself, without delay. I would take a history, examine the patient, arrange further investigations (if required) and institute a management plan as appropriate.

Q. What features would be suggestive of testicular torsion?

A. Testicular torsion is a clinical diagnosis. However, even with a high index of suspicion, the definitive diagnosis can only be made at emergency surgical exploration.

The clinical features of testicular torsion are as follows.

History
- Pain is of acute onset.
- Mainly testicular pain.
- Occasionally radiating to groin, abdomen or thigh.
- History of previous testicular pain (intermittent torsion) may be common.

Examination
- Acutely tender and swollen testicle.
- Horizontal lie (bell-clapper deformity).
- High-riding testis in scrotum (*see* Figure 7.1).
- Absent cremasteric reflex.
- Mild fever and erythema of the scrotal skin (late signs).

Investigations
- Urinalysis is usually normal.
- Doppler ultrasound scan (only in equivocal cases) may show poor or absent blood flow.

Q. When does torsion typically occur and what is the difference between intra-vaginal and extra-vaginal torsion?

A. Testicular torsion can occur at any age, but commonly the incidence has a bimodal distribution,[1] with the main peak around puberty (12–18 years) and a smaller peak in the first year of life (*see* Figure 7.2).

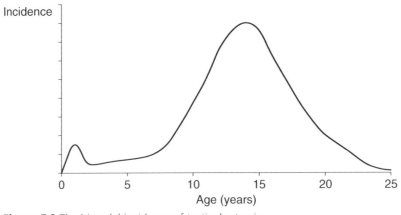

Figure 7.2 The bimodal incidence of testicular torsion.

Intravaginal torsion is the most common form of testicular torsion seen in adolescents and adults, and is due to a congenital high investment of the tunica vaginalis on the cord, resulting in a horizontally lying testis, and produces the so-called 'bell-clapper' deformity. This anomaly allows the testis and cord to rotate more readily than a normal testis. The bell-clapper deformity is often bilateral, with a significant risk of torsion to the contralateral testis.

Extravaginal torsion is most commonly seen in the first year of life. It can occur both pre- and postnatally. The attachment between the tunica vaginalis and the scrotum is loose, i.e. there is incomplete fixation of the gubernaculum to the scrotal wall, resulting in the entire testis and tunica vaginalis twisting in a vertical axis on the spermatic cord.

Q. **Are there any investigations that can diagnose testicular torsion in certain patients?**

A. Testicular torsion is a clinical diagnosis and the gold standard management for suspected testicular torsion is urgent surgical exploration of the scrotum.

However, in cases where clinical features are equivocal and urgent scrotal exploration is not indicated on clinical grounds, colour Doppler ultrasound scan may be used to aid diagnosis. Poor arterial blood flow signal in the testicular artery suggests a diagnosis of torsion. This technique is operator-dependent, with studies demonstrating 85–90% sensitivity and 75–95% specificity. Radionuclide imaging has been proposed to be of high sensitivity (87–98%) and specificity (100%). However, it is time-consuming and as yet has no place in the clinical assessment of an acute scrotum. The most important point to bear in mind is that the use of radiological investigations must not unnecessarily delay definitive surgical treatment.

Q. **If you think that the patient has testicular torsion, how quickly should you perform the operation?**

A. Salvage rates are directly correlated with the number of hours after the onset of pain (as shown in Figure 7.3). Therefore, in my practice, I perform urgent scrotal exploration immediately.

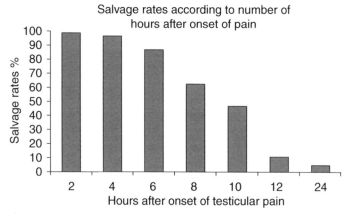

Figure 7.3 Salvage rate according to number of hours after onset of pain.

Q. **The patient appears to have a clinical diagnosis of testicular torsion. What are the key features in the pre-operative consent for emergency scrotal exploration?**

A. The informed consent for emergency scrotal exploration would involve a description of the procedure, discussion of alternative treatments and an explanation of potential complications. The following points would need to be raised:[2]

- Bilateral testicular fixation (orchidopexy) in cases of torsion, where testis is viable.
- Orchidectomy in cases of torsion, where testis is not viable, with orchidopexy of the contralateral testicle.
- No fixation in cases where no torsion is found.
- If orchidopexy is performed, non-absorbable sutures may be palpable.
- Risk of haematoma, which may require subsequent surgical exploration.
- Risk of wound infection or subsequent orchitis.
- Long-term risks of testicular atrophy.
- No guarantee of fertility.
- Small risk of future testicular torsion, despite fixation.

Q. **What incision do you use? Describe your technique of fixation.**

A. At scrotal exploration, although various skin incisions can be employed, including transverse, bilateral, vertical and oblique, I use the midline incision through the median raphe.

The layers of the scrotum (skin, Dartos, external spermatic fascia, cremasteric fascia, internal spermatic fascia and tunica vaginalis) are divided. The affected testis is delivered and inspected. Testicular torsion occurs inwards and towards the midline, and in a case of torsion the testis is initially untwisted. The testis is then wrapped in a warm saline-soaked swab and the anaesthetist supplies 100% oxygen via an endotracheal tube.

If the testis is viable, I perform an orchidopexy using the three-point fixation technique. The testis is fixed medially, laterally and infero-anteriorly to the scrotal wall using non-absorbable sutures (typically 3/0 or 4/0 prolene). If the viability of the testis is questionable, I make a small stab incision through the tunica albuginea to assess for evidence of viability through signs of bleeding. If the testicle is not salvageable, I perform an orchidectomy.

In cases of confirmed testicular torsion, I explore the contralateral testis through the same incision, and perform a prophylactic three-point orchidopexy, to prevent future torsion on that side. This is supported by reports of contralateral torsion following unilateral orchidopexy and a 40% incidence of anatomical abnormalities predisposing to torsion in the contralateral testis. If an appendix testis is found at operation, I remove it to prevent future torsion of appendix testis mimicking testicular torsion.

Additional procedures have been proposed, namely eversion of the tunica vaginalis at the time of surgical exploration to prevent future re-torsion, as well as the use of a sub-Dartos pouch.

In cases where no torsion is found, I do not perform orchidopexy, due to the potential complications of needle trauma (including breach of the blood–testis barrier). The testis should be replaced intact. In addition, in such a case scenario, I do not perform contralateral exploration.

Q. **Are you aware of any potential complications of testicular torsion?**

A. Misdiagnosis, especially as an epididymo-orchitis, is the commonest problem. If a patient shows no improvement despite 48–72 hours of antibiotic therapy, the diagnosis of testicular torsion (dead testis) should be considered. An infarcted testis that is left in the scrotum may result in abscess or sinus formation. The potential long-term complication of this event is the formation of antisperm antibodies, causing infertility in the contralateral testis. Other long-term complications include future torsion in a testis that has undergone previous inadequate prophylactic fixation. In cases where orchidectomy is performed, a testicular prosthesis insertion may be considered, in the future, to improve cosmetic outcome and psychological recovery. In my practice, I do not insert the prosthesis at the time of emergency exploration, through the scrotal route, due to the significant risk of erosion.

MANAGEMENT OF COMPLICATIONS OF TURP

Q. **A fit 75-year-old man presents for TURP. Pre-operative assessment revealed good effort tolerance, no symptoms of cardiac failure, and all investigations were normal. He undergoes spinal anaesthetic after a pre-load of 500 ml of saline, and is given oxygen via a Hudson mask. Surgery begins after the block has been confirmed at T8 level. At 60 minutes into the procedure, the patient complains of nausea and is given ondansetron. His heart rate is 106 beats/minute and his blood pressure is normal. Then, 15 minutes later, he becomes anxious, pulls off the oxygen mask and tries to get off the operating table. What is the probable diagnosis and how does it occur?**

A. I would strongly suspect that the diagnosis is transurethral resection (TUR) syndrome.

TUR syndrome is a multifactorial syndrome, which arises from absorption of large volumes of irrigation fluid (1.5% glycine), typically during TURP. Although it is commonly thought to be solely due to dilutional hyponatraemia, fluid overload and the effects of glycine toxicity contribute significantly to the pathophysiology of this condition.

Q. **What is the incidence of TUR syndrome?**

A. Classic studies quote an incidence of 0.5–2.0% following TURP.[3,4] Recent contemporary studies suggest an even lower incidence, based on technological improvements. Interestingly, TUR syndrome may also be associated with transurethral resection of bladder tumour (TURBT) and percutaneous nephrolithotomy (PCNL).

Q. **What concentration of glycine is used in resection, and what is its osmolality?**

A. Typically, 1.5% glycine is used. It is an inhibitory amino acid, and a non-electrolyte solution, with an osmolality of 200 mosmol/l. Therefore it is hypotonic with respect to plasma.

Q. **How is glycine handled in the body?**

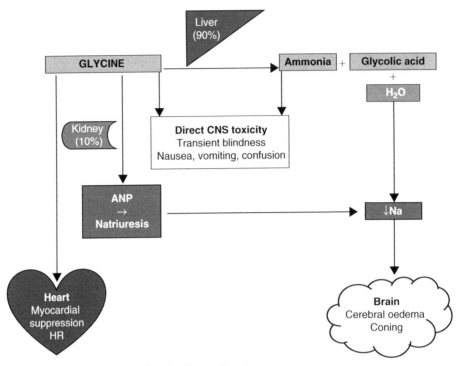

Figure 7.4 The handling and toxic effects of glycine.

A.   Figure 7.4 shows the handling and toxic effects of glycine. Absorption of 1.5% glycine solution occurs directly (and thus immediately) into the peri-prostatic venous plexus, as well as indirectly (resulting in delayed absorption) from the peri-vesical and retroperitoneal spaces. In a typical TURP, fluid absorption occurs at a rate of approximately 20 ml/minute. Therefore during a 60-minute resection one would anticipate that 1.2 litres of glycine solution would be absorbed. This amount of absorbed hypotonic fluid is relatively easily dealt with in a normal individual, with 90% of glycine being metabolised to ammonia, glycolic acid and water by the liver, and the remaining 10% being metabolised by the kidney.

Q.   Can you explain the symptoms of TUR syndrome?
A.   TUR syndrome is a multifactorial syndrome that is caused by absorption of large volumes of 1.5% glycine solution, resulting in dilutional hyponatraemia, fluid overload and the effects of glycine toxicity. Knowledge of these three factors allows an understanding of the clinical symptoms of TUR syndrome (see Figure 7.4).

   The dilutional hyponatremia results in an osmotic shift of water from plasma into the brain. The symptoms are generally dependent on sodium concentration, resulting in cerebral herniation and death if left untreated (*see* Table 7.1).

Table 7.1 Symptoms associated with dilutional hyponatraemia

Sodium concentration (mmol/l)	Symptoms
130–135	Asymptomatic
120–130	Restlessness
	Confusion
115–120	Nausea
< 115	Seizures
	Coma

Furthermore, glycine induces an osmotic diuresis, which results in absolute losses of sodium from the body, and this can be further exacerbated by the release of atrial natriuretic peptide, which promotes natriuresis (*see* Figure 7.4).

With fluid overload, the patient initially develops hypertension, shortness of breath, chest pain and cyanosis, due to resultant pulmonary oedema and cardiac failure. Later clinical features include bradycardia and a marked decrease in systolic arterial pressure.

Glycine is an inhibitory neurotransmitter in the retina, present at a concentration of 400 mmol/l in humans. An excess amount slows down the transmission of impulses from the retina to the cerebral cortex, with prolongation of visual evoked potentials and deterioration of vision occurring after absorption of as little as a few hundred millilitres of glycine. Thus, clinically, if the patient is under spinal anaesthesia, they may report seeing flashing lights. Prickling sensations and facial warmth are also early signs of glycine absorption. At higher concentrations, glycine results in bradycardia due to direct and indirect cardiotoxic effects. Late clinical features include hypotension and coma.

Q. **How would you manage TUR syndrome?**
A. For convenience I divide the management of TUR syndrome into prevention, detection and definitive treatment.

Prevention

Initially, I diagnose and treat any pre-existing hyponatraemia, before considering the patient for TURP. Secondly, I identify putative risk factors for TUR syndrome. In the American Urological Association (AUA) National Cooperative Study of immediate and post-operative complications in almost 4000 patients from 13 institutions, Mebust *et al.*[3] identified significant differences in TUR syndrome when time of resection and size of gland were assessed. Among patients with a resection time of > 90 minutes, the incidence of TUR syndrome was 2.0%, compared with 0.7% when there was a shorter resection time ($P < 0.01$).[3] Similarly, a statistically significant difference was noted in patients with glands weighing > 45 g (incidence 1.5%) as opposed to those weighing < 45 g (incidence 0.8%).[3] At first glance it would therefore seem logical to suggest that standard TURP should be avoided if the operative time will exceed 90 minutes or if the prostate gland weighs more than 45 g. However, in my practice, and in contemporary practice in the UK, an operative time of 60 minutes is usually standard, and open prostatectomy is only usually performed for glands that weigh over 100 g.

Other potential risk factors, such as height of irrigation fluid and intravesical pressure, racial origin and age have also been suggested, but the evidence for these is less robust. Despite this, in my practice, I use the Iglesias continuous-flow resectoscope, avoid aggressive resection near the capsule, and try to complete the TURP as soon as the capsule is breached. In addition, if a prolonged procedure is inevitable, I request the anaesthetist to administer furosemide prophylactically, to offload the excess fluid that may be absorbed. More recently, other preventive strategies have included the use of bipolar or laser resection with normal saline irrigation, as well as the use of 5% glucose as an irrigation solution in a randomised, prospective trial.

Detection

I aim to perform TURP with the patient awake, under spinal anaesthesia, as several of the clinical factors described above will become apparent if TUR syndrome develops. However, with general anaesthetic, hypertension due to fluid overload may be the only early warning sign, often detected by the anaesthetist. Arrhythmias, hypotension and decreased oxygen saturation are usually late features. Although it is not universally used, I am aware that 1% ethanol in the irrigant can be a useful strategy for detection, as it allows breath alcohol levels to be checked by a breathalyser, thus enabling an estimate of the volume of excess fluid that has been absorbed. The addition of weighing machines to the ordinary operating table has also been reported as technique for measuring fluid overload.

Treatment

In mild cases of established TUR syndrome, supportive management together with a period of watchful waiting is often sufficient. In my practice, the serum sodium concentration and electrolytes are checked, but the result is not awaited prior to commencing medical treatment in the form of the loop diuretic furosemide (this drug results in relative loss of more water than sodium, thus decreasing fluid overload and also increasing serum sodium levels). Typically, a dose of 40 mg is given intravenously. More diuretic may be warranted depending on the serum sodium levels, as slower absorption from the retroperitoneal or perivesical space occurs (an alternative to furosemide that is given by many is mannitol). Concurrently, I ensure that I quickly control any haemorrhage and finish the operation as soon as possible. In addition, I think it is essential to have early input from the intensive-care team in all cases of TUR syndrome.

Severe cases occur due to lack of recognition or inadequate early treatment of mild cases. In these cases it is vital that the HDU/ITU team are called early. Using this multi-disciplinary approach, a central line and invasive arterial monitoring are usually used, and the patient is transferred to the HDU/ITU when stable. Clearly in extreme cases the patient may need to be intubated and ventilated. Furthermore, the intensive-care environment is useful for the small minority of patients who have a dangerously low serum sodium level, which requires correction with hypertonic saline solution. A correction of 1 mmol/litre per hour is recommended to avoid the devastating complication of rapid correction of hyponatraemia resulting in central pontine myelinolysis.

Typically, no specific treatment of hyperglycinaemia/hyperammonaemia is required, as patients usually recover within 12–24 hours with general supportive care. Furthermore, depending on the blood loss, blood transfusion may also be required.

Q. **A 65-year-old man with recurrent acute urinary retention undergoes TURP. His prostate volume was 70 ml, and during the procedure it was noted that the prostate was extremely vascular. A large perforation of the surgical capsule was made on the left side, but otherwise the procedure was performed uneventfully. Post-operatively, in the recovery room, you are called because the catheter is draining dark red urine and the patient is pale, drowsy and looking unwell. His heart rate is noted to be 120 beats/minute and his blood pressure is 80/55 mmHg. How would you manage this patient?**

A. I would regard this as a urological emergency and see the patient immediately, myself, without delay, as I suspect that he may have uncontrolled haemorrhage after TURP.

Normally around 2–5% of patients require blood transfusion after TURP, and although venous ooze usually settles with conservative management, arterial bleeding may be present and necessitate early return to theatre. Importantly, several manoeuvres described below often need to be performed in quick succession or simultaneously, and early help should be enlisted from the HDU/ITU team.

Initially, using basic principles of advanced trauma life support (ATLS), I would resuscitate this patient, with the close involvement of my HDU/ITU anaesthetist colleagues. I would administer 100% high-flow oxygen and give good analgesia. In addition, I would draw blood to check the full blood count (Hb), clotting, U&E (creatinine), and cross-match 4 units of blood.

Urologically, I would first check to see whether the catheter is blocked and that the irrigation is running adequately. If clot retention is present, I would immediately perform a bladder washout, to remove all clots. If this did not improve the situation, or clot retention was not present, I would inflate the catheter balloon to 50 ml and maintain in-line traction with the irrigation running on maximum flow. There is no recognised time limit for traction on the catheter, although clearly the longer this is applied (in some cases many hours), the higher the risk of future contracture due to bladder neck ischaemia. I usually apply traction for 20–30 minutes and release for 5 minutes. Traction can then be reapplied at a later stage if further bleeding occurs.

In the mean time, I would give a blood transfusion and correct any clotting abnormalities, as required. If the traction does not stabilise the situation and if there is ongoing bleeding, persistent hypotension, persistent clot retention or an excessive blood transfusion requirement, the patient requires urgent return to theatre, which I would organise.

In theatre, initially, clot evacuation, endoscopic washout and careful diathermy to bleeding points are performed. In my practice I perform a thorough washout with a resectoscope (26Fr or 28Fr) and Ellick evacuator, using the diathermy loop to dislodge any organised clot (without current). Use of a bladder syringe attached to the end of the resectoscope can aid the evacuation of clot that is resistant to washout with the Ellick evacuator. If arterial bleeding is present, it can be difficult to detect in the presence of hypotension. Careful observation with low-pressure irrigation can sometimes be helpful.

If there is ongoing bleeding despite this, the patient requires open surgical exploration and packing of the prostatic fossa.

Alternatively, if appropriate facilities are available, super-selective internal iliac artery embolisation may be performed. This procedure can be done under local anaesthesia and may be a safer option in frail elderly patients.

Q. **How do you perform open surgical exploration of the prostatic fossa?**

A. In my practice, I perform a Pfannenstiel incision and the bladder is opened to pack the prostatic fossa (around the urethral catheter) with swabs through a transvesical approach. The packs are left in place for 48 hours to tamponade any bleeding points, and are subsequently removed in theatre, with the definitive closure of the anterior abdominal wall.

SEPSIS FOLLOWING TRUS BIOPSY

Q. **A fit and healthy 65-year-old man has transrectal ultrasound-guided prostate biopsy (TRUS-Bx) for a raised PSA. He had been given prophylactic 120 mg gentamicin (IV) and 500 mg metronidazole (PR), and subsequently started a 5-day course of 500 mg bd ciprofloxacin (PO). The urology clinical nurse specialist is contacted 36 hours later by the patient's wife, as he has developed severe flu-like symptoms. What advice would you give the urology clinical nurse specialist?**

A. I would regard this as a urological emergency and advise the urology clinical nurse specialist that I will contact the patient immediately, myself, without delay, advising him to attend A&E urgently, where I would arrange to see him personally. I would strongly suspect that this patient has developed sepsis following TRUS-Bx.

Q. **What is systemic inflammatory response syndrome (SIRS)?**

A. It is the response of the body to a variety of infectious (e.g. sepsis) or non-infectious (e.g. burns, pancreatitis) stimuli. Two of the criteria listed in Table 7.2 are required.

Table 7.2 Criteria for diagnosis of systemic inflammatory response syndrome

Temperature	> 38°C or < 36°C
Heart rate	> 90 beats/min
Respiratory rate	> 20 breaths/min
	or
	p_aCO_2 < 32 mmHg (< 4.3 kPa)
	or
	need for mechanical ventilation
White cell count	> 12 000 cells/mm³ or < 4000 cells/mm³ or > 10% immature (band) forms

Q. **How do you define sepsis, severe sepsis, septic shock and refractory septic shock?**

A. The definitions are stated in Table 7.3.

Table 7.3 Definitions of sepsis, severe sepsis, septic shock and refractory septic shock

Term	Definition
Sepsis	Proven infection causing SIRS
Severe sepsis	Sepsis associated with organ dysfunction, hypoperfusion or hypotension. Hypoperfusion and perfusion abnormalities may include, but are not limited to, lactic acidosis, oliguria or an acute alteration of mental status
Septic shock	Sepsis with hypotension despite fluid resuscitation, together with the presence of perfusion abnormalities that may include, but are not limited to, lactic acidosis, oliguria or an acute alteration in mental status
Refractory septic shock	Septic shock lasting > 1 hour, that is resistant to fluid resuscitation or pharmacological intervention

Q. **How would you initially manage this patient?**

A. I would regard this as a urological emergency and see the patient myself, without delay. On arrival, I would resuscitate him using the basic principles of ALS/ATLS. I would administer 100% high-flow oxygen, insert two large-bore venflons, taking blood for full blood count, U&E, CRP and blood cultures. In addition, a midstream urine specimen (MSU) would be sent for microscopy, culture and sensitivity (MCS). I would catheterise the patient in order to monitor urine output. Aggressive intravenous fluid resuscitation would be initiated. I would then administer high-dose intravenous antibiotics, initially giving gentamicin (3–5 mg/kg), metronidazole and a third-generation cephalosporin. I would also contact my HDU/ITU anaesthetist colleagues and involve them early on in the multi-disciplinary management of this patient, as I am conscious of the high morbidity and mortality risk associated with this condition. If the patient is very unwell, he may need invasive monitoring or pharmacological support in the HDU/ITU setting.

Q. **What are the organisms most commonly involved?**

A. The most likely organisms would include Gram-negative and anaerobic organisms, such as *E.coli*, *Klebsiella*, *Pseudomonas*, enterococci and *Bacteroides*.

PENILE FRACTURE

Q. **A 34-year-old man presents with acute penile pain and swelling following sexual intercourse. He says that he heard a 'snapping' sound during coitus and there was immediate detumescence. What is the likely diagnosis?**

A. Penile fracture.

Q. **Anatomically, what actually becomes 'fractured' in this condition?**

A. A penile fracture involves rupture of the tunica albuginea and the enclosed corpus cavernosum. However, it may also extend into the urethra in 10% of cases. During erection, the thickness of the tunica albuginea typically decreases from 2 mm to 0.25 mm, predisposing the penis to injury, either from bending or direct forces.

Q. **How do you diagnose this condition?**

A. *It is actually a clinical diagnosis based on history and examination findings.*

However, I am aware of a number of recent advances in diagnostic investigations:

- MRI is the most accurate pre-operative investigation, and can detect even small tears in the tunica albuginea. Unfortunately, it has the limitations of high cost and limited availability in the emergency setting, where most cases of penile fracture present.
- Penile ultrasound scan may be used as an adjunct, as it is non-invasive and easily available. However, it may be difficult to interpret in the presence of oedema and haematoma, and is currently only used in trial settings.
- Cavernosography is no longer used, as it is an invasive procedure and has potential side-effects, including reaction to contrast, priapism, and the risk of corporal fibrosis due to extravasated contrast material.

Q.   How would you exclude a urethral injury?

A.   Clinical features that suggest urethral injury include blood at the urethral meatus, haematuria and an inability to pass urine following the injury. A retrograde urethrogram should be performed if urethral injury cannot be excluded.

Q.   What is the management of penile fracture?

A.   I would regard penile fracture as a urological emergency and see the patient myself, without delay. Early surgical exploration and repair of the tunica albuginea is considered to be the treatment of choice. Conservative treatment is associated with a high incidence of penile fibrosis and erectile dysfunction.

Q.   Outline the principles of surgical repair.

A.   Standard surgical exploration involves a degloving circumferential incision of the penile skin. This approach provides easy exposure of both corpora and spongiosum. Once the haematoma has been evacuated and the defect in the tunica albuginea has been identified, the defect should be repaired using interrupted non-absorbable sutures. The laceration in the tunica albuginea is usually sutured transversely, and an artificial erection is then induced to ensure that the penis is straight. Other incisions that have been described include a direct incision over the presumed site of fracture.

REFERENCES

1.   Li CY, Zaman F and Minhas S. Testicular torsion and acute testicular pain. In: Shergill IS, Arya M, Patel HR and Gill IS (eds) *Urological Emergencies in Hospital Medicine*. London: Quay Books; 2007. pp. 1–9.
2.   British Association of Urological Surgeons. www.baus.org.uk/information_links/procedure_specific_consent_forms.phtml (accessed 31 October 2009)
3.   Mebust WK *et al.* Transurethral prostatectomy: immediate and postoperative complications. A cooperative study of 13 participating institutions evaluating 3,885 patients. *J Urol* 1989; **141:** 243–7.
4.   Pickard R *et al.* The management of men with acute urinary retention. *Br J Urol* 1998; **81:** 712–20.

FURTHER READING

Rob J, Bahl K, Shergill IS and Fowlis GA. TUR syndrome. *Urology News* 2008; **13:** 12–14.

Chapter 8

Urological emergencies. Part 2: Genitourinary trauma and urethral stricture

Davendra M Sharma, Deendyal P Sharma and Manit Arya

RENAL TRAUMA

Q. A 26-year-old motorcyclist, travelling at 20 mph, has collided with a car. The motorcyclist was thrown from his bike. You are called to A&E because he complains of left flank pain. His pulse is 90 beats/minute, blood pressure is 120/80 mmHg, respiratory rate is 16 breaths/minute and oxygen saturation is 99%. How would you assess this patient?

A. As with all trauma cases, advanced trauma life support (ATLS) principles should be strictly followed. It is important to adopt a multi-disciplinary approach, consulting with emergency, orthopaedic, general surgical and any other specialty doctors if necessary (standard answer to trauma question).

Traumatic injuries remain an important cause of mortality and morbidity in the civilian population. Trauma may be generally classified as due to blunt or penetrating injury. Blunt trauma, which is much more common in the UK, may result in significant genitourinary injury. Urologists are expected to understand the principles of trauma management and safely manage these patients.

Q. Your colleagues have 'cleared' this patient of other major injuries. What specific information would you like to have in order to assess him urologically?

A. I would take a focused history and relevant examination (standard answer). It is important to elucidate the following points from the history:
- the mechanism of injury
- whether there is any previous urological or renal history
- whether the patient has noticed any blood in the urine.

Q. What examination findings are important?

A. The following findings are important:
- the extent and location of any bruising and tenderness

159

- haematuria (macroscopic in adults or dipstick/macroscopic in children), particularly in the first sample obtained following the accident. *Microscopic analysis (at least 5 red blood cells per high-power field) is more reliable in assessing the extent of haemorrhage than dipstick testing*
- blood pressure – it is important to ascertain whether there has been a significant drop in blood pressure (i.e. systolic < 90 mmHg at any time since the accident.

Q. **This patient has dipstick haematuria. What would you do?**

A. If the patient has had a measured (even single) drop in his systolic blood pressure (< 90 mmHg), an urgent contrast spiral CT scan should be arranged. If no significant drop in blood pressure has been recorded, the patient should be admitted for analgesia, 24 hours of observation and repeat full blood count.

Q. **In a stable adult patient with dipstick haematuria, are there any factors that would lower your threshold for imaging, and why?**

A. Yes. If the mechanism of injury is that of a rapid deceleration injury or a fall from a significant height, imaging is recommended. These patients may have a pelvi-ureteric junction (PUJ) disruption or vascular injury which may not result in haematuria or a fall in blood pressure. In fact haematuria (micro- and macroscopic) may be absent in up to 40% of renal injuries and 25% of pedicle injuries.

Q. **What are the indications for imaging (spiral CT with contrast) in a stable patient following renal trauma as suggested by the European Association of Urology (EAU)?**

A.
- Penetrating trauma.
- Deceleration injuries (or any other 'significant' mechanism of injury, e.g. fall from a considerable height).
- Blunt trauma in adults associated with a systolic blood pressure < 90 mmHg at any time following the injury.
- Blunt trauma in adults associated with frank haematuria. Thus blunt trauma associated with dipstick/microscopic haematuria in adults is not an indication for imaging so long as it is not a deceleration injury and the patient's blood pressure has remained stable.
- Blunt trauma in children associated with dipstick/microscopic or frank haematuria. In children, a lower threshold for imaging (ideally spiral CT with contrast) is required as hypotension is a late manifestation of hypovolaemia.

Q. **What are the objectives of radiographic imaging in renal trauma? Which modality best delivers these objectives?**

A. The objectives of radiographic imaging are as follows:
- to accurately stage the injury
- to document contralateral renal function
- to recognise pre-existing renal pathology
- to identify injuries to other organs.

A contrast spiral CT scan is superior to all other forms of imaging in trauma. As well as fulfilling the above objectives, it is quick and now familiar to most surgeons. Ultrasound resolution is inferior to CT, but it may be useful in the follow-up of renal injury.

Q. How is the CT scan performed and why?

A. Spiral CT scan with contrast:

- arterial and/or portal venous phase – demonstrates vascular and parenchymal injury as well as haematoma
- delayed images (10–20 minutes) – demonstrates PUJ or collecting system injury. May be omitted if, on the early-phase scan, the kidneys are normal, and there is no perinephric, retroperitoneal, pelvic or perivesical fluid present.

Q. What do Figures 8.1 and 8.2 show? How would you stage the injury and what are the different grades? What are the essential components of the staging system?

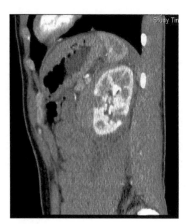
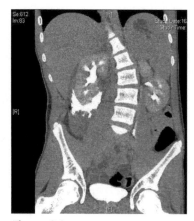

Figure 8.1   **Figure 8.2**

A. Figure 8.1 shows a sagittal contrast CT scan demonstrating grade III renal trauma. Figure 8.2 shows a coronal contrast CT scan demonstrating grade IV renal trauma.

The AAST (American Association for the Surgery of Trauma) grading system is based primarily on the CT findings (*see* Table 8.1). The essential components describe the presence of a renal haematoma, and injury to the renal parenchyma, the collecting system or the vasculature.

Table 8.1 The American Association for the Surgery of Trauma (AAST) renal trauma severity scale

Grade (AAST)	Type of injury	Description of injury
I	Contusion	Microscopic or gross haematuria, urological studies normal
	Haematoma	Subcapsular, not expanding, with no parenchymal laceration
II	Haematoma	Non-expanding perirenal haematoma confined to renal retroperitoneum
	Laceration	< 1 cm parenchymal depth of renal cortex with no urinary extravasation
III	Laceration	> 1 cm parenchymal depth of renal cortex with no urinary extravasation

continued

Table 8.1 *continued*

IV	Laceration	Parenchymal laceration extending through kidney into collecting system
	Vascular	Segmental renal artery or vein injury with contained haematoma
V	Laceration	Completely shattered kidney
	Vascular	Avulsion of renal hilum which devascularises kidney

Q. **What proportion of renal trauma is due to blunt trauma?**

A. In the UK the majority (over 95%) of injuries are due to blunt trauma. In South Africa and territories affected by violent conflict, the incidence of penetrating trauma is much higher.

Q. **You are called to theatre later that night by the on-call trauma team. Another blunt trauma patient was taken to the emergency theatre as he was not able to maintain his blood pressure despite fluid boluses. No imaging was performed prior to laparotomy, which reveals normal viscera and no intraperitoneal blood. However, there is a large left retroperitoneal haematoma. What is your next step?**

A. Arrange a one-shot on-table intravenous urogram (IVU).

Q. **Why would you do a one-shot IVU and how would this be performed?**

A. Most importantly, it shows whether there are two functioning kidneys. Delayed contrast excretion or extravasation may also be detected. A normal film may obviate the need for renal exploration.

A one-shot IVU depends on a rapid bolus administration of 2 ml/kg contrast (e.g. Omnipaque). A single portable plain abdominal X-ray is performed at 10 minutes. Fluoroscopy (C-arm) results in poor images and should be avoided.

Q. **What are the absolute indications for exploring the kidney in trauma?**

A. These are as follows:
- persistent life-threatening blood loss that is believed to stem from renal injury
- renal pedicle avulsion (grade V injury) which is suspected clinically, by imaging or by the observation of an expanding pulsatile retroperitoneal haematoma at laparotomy
- penetrating renal trauma (most cases).

Q. **What are the principles of exploration of a kidney in trauma?**

A. These can be summarised as follows.
- Make a midline generous laparotomy incision from sternum to pubis.
- Lift the small bowel out of the peritoneal cavity in order to expose the retroperitoneum.
- Incise the peritoneum over the aorta above the inferior mesenteric artery and dissect alongside it superiorly up to the left renal vein (if a large perirenal haematoma obscures the site for this incision, make the incision medial to the inferior mesenteric vein). The left and right renal arteries are then easily identified. Vessel loops can then be placed around the renal artery and vein, thus establishing early vascular control.
- The colon can now be reflected, thus exposing the kidney (or haematoma).

- If nephrectomy is avoided, renal tissue is preserved by controlling bleeding and debriding all non-viable tissue.

Q. **How would you deal with a non-expanding, non-pulsatile haematoma at laparotomy?**

A. If imaging (either pre- or intra-operative) is normal or this is a single functioning kidney, the haematoma can be left alone. This is because exploration increases the probability of loss of the kidney because of bleeding, which can be controlled only by nephrectomy.

If imaging (either pre- or intra-operative) of the injured kidney is abnormal but the contralateral kidney is normal, one can evacuate the haematoma and repair the renal injury.

Q. **What proportion of patients with blunt trauma to the kidneys require surgical internvention?**

A. Less than 5%.

Q. **What is the role of angioembolisation?**

A. Selective renal artery angioembolisation is increasingly being used to successfully manage stable patients with haemorrhage following blunt or penetrating trauma.

Q. **What are the potential complications of conservatively managed renal trauma and how are they managed?**

A. Early complications:
- secondary haemorrhage requiring radiological or surgical intervention
- urinary extravasation leading to urinoma (or if superimposed infection, leading to perinephric abscess formation). Radiological drainage with or without internal stenting may be necessary
- infection (e.g. perinephric abscess or systemic sepsis)
- vascular complications, including arterio-venous fistula (AVF) or pseudoaneurysm formation.

Late complications:
- hypertension – re-evaluate to look for renal artery thrombosis, subcapsular haematoma, extensive fibrosis (Page kidney is hypertension due to scar formation) or AVF
- renal insufficiency – a follow-up DMSA scan is necessary to look for significant functional loss
- calculus formation and chronic pyelonephritis.

It is recommended that higher-grade renal injuries (grades IV and V) are imaged by CT 48–72 hours after injury to look for complications such as secondary haemorrhage or urinoma formation.

Q. **How are renovascular injuries managed?**

A. - *Arterial injuries.* Irreversible damage ensues after 2–6 hours, so most kidneys will not function following arterial injury. Reconstruction should be attempted in solitary kidneys, bilateral renal injury or in cases that are diagnosed very quickly. Incomplete injury (e.g. intimal flaps) can be managed conservatively. Segmental arterial injuries are managed with angioembolisation.

Endovascular techniques are also described for main artery and branch injuries, and may play a primary role in future. Hypertension develops in a small subset of patients with major arterial injury. Elective nephrectomy may be necessary in these cases.

- *Venous injuries.* These are rare and difficult to identify. Avulsion from the inferior vena cava (IVC) following blunt trauma requires urgent laparotomy, IVC repair and nephrectomy. The left renal vein may be tied, leaving the kidney to drain from the gonadal and adrenal veins. Penetrating injuries should be repaired.

Q.   **What does the image in Figure 8.3 show?**

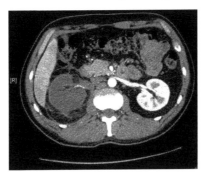

Figure 8.3

A.   Figure 8.3 is a contrast CT scan (arterial phase) showing right arterial injury with absence of a right nephrogram.

Q.   **Figure 8.4 is an investigation of the above patient 3 months later. What does this demonstrate?**

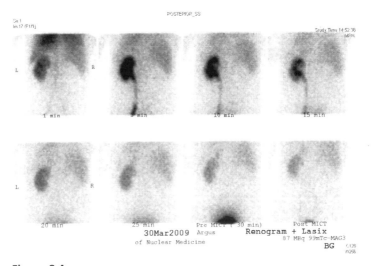

Figure 8.4

A.   Figure 8.4 is a ^{99Tm}MAG3 renogram showing absence of right renal function.

URETERIC INJURY

Q. You are called by the gynaecology specialist registrar on call. She is concerned about a patient who had an abdominal hysterectomy 2 days ago. The patient is unwell and complaining of left flank pain, and a urological injury is suspected by the gynaecology team. What would you do initially?

A. One must regard this as a urological emergency and review the patient without delay. Bear in mind that, potentially, a urological complication of gynaecological surgery may have occurred, and thus may have future medico-legal implications. On arrival, carefully review all the medical notes, especially the operation note, and speak personally to the gynaecological surgeon who performed the procedure, to establish the following:

- the indication for surgery (cancer vs. benign aetiology)
- any difficulties encountered at the time of surgery (e.g. prolonged procedure, untoward bleeding, presence of adhesions)
- past medical history, for endometriosis, previous abdominal surgery and previous radiotherapy treatment.

Then take a focused history, perform a physical examination and carry out any necessary investigations.

Q. What features of the history and examination would you be interested in?

A. First, characterise the pain (type, location, etc.) and note any previous urological history and the patient's comorbidity.

An abdominal examination is necessary to look for scars, full bladder and loin tenderness/mass. Perform a vaginal palpation (PV), with a chaperone present, if the patient can bear it (to look for a vesico-vaginal fistula).

The presence of pyrexia and tachycardia should be noted, as should the patient's blood pressure. If a drain is present, what is it draining and how much? Is a catheter present? If so, what colour is the urine and what is the quantity of urine output?

Q. Assessment reveals a stable but pyrexial patient with left loin tenderness and excess clear fluid from the drain. What investigations are necessary?

A.
- Blood tests – full blood count, U&Es, CRP and G&S.
- Urine dipstick and MSU for culture (or CSU if a catheter is present).
- Drain fluid – send for biochemical analysis (particularly urea and creatinine – creatinine levels > 300 µmol/l will be urine if serum creatinine level is normal).
- Urgent IVU – to identify the injury and look for *another* injury. CT-urogram, if available urgently, is an alternative. A retrograde ureteropyelogram is very sensitive for detecting ureteric injury, but may be difficult to arrange in an acute setting (an ultrasound scan, showing hydronephrosis, has often already been performed, but is an inadequate investigation in this scenario).

If a urological injury is suspected, the patient should be transferred immediately to a urology ward.

Q. What potential injuries may have occurred?

A. Ureteric (unilateral or bilateral) or bladder injuries, or a combination of both.

Q.   What does Figure 8.5 show?

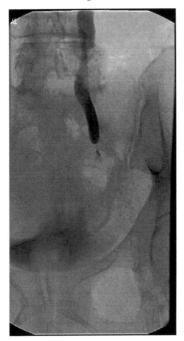

Figure 8.5

A.   Figure 8.5 is an antegrade nephrostogram demonstrating a left ureteric stricture as a result of iatrogenic injury following gynaecological surgery.

Q.   What are the management options? Are you aware of any staging systems for ureteric injury?

A.   Management depends on the stage, location and timing of the injury, and the patient's general condition (see Tables 8.2 and 8.3).

Ideally, this patient should be taken back to theatre as soon as possible for cystoscopy (to exclude associated bladder injury), bilateral retrograde studies (to exclude injury to the contralateral ureter), an attempt at retrograde stenting or alternatively formal repair or reconstruction if necessary.

Traditionally, it has been suggested that if ureteric injury was diagnosed within a few days, then if open repair/reconstruction is needed this should ideally be performed immediately. However, if the injury was discovered after approximately 7–14 days, then if open repair/reconstruction is necessary, this should be delayed for at least 3 months (as this is generally thought to be the time of maximal oedema and inflammation). Currently, it is believed that an earlier repair can still give good results, and that the time of diagnosis of the ureteric trauma is not so important as it was formerly thought to be.

Delayed repair is certainly essential if the patient is unwell or there are any contraindications for re-operation (e.g. infected urinoma at the site of injury). In these cases, nephrostomy drainage should be arranged. A careful attempt at antegrade stenting can be tried in expert centres (*see* Figure 8.6).

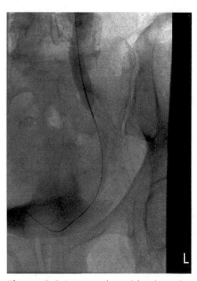

Figure 8.6 Antegrade guidewire prior to stenting across iatrogenic ureteric stricture.

Table 8.2 Staging system and management options for ureteric injury

Grade of ureteric injury (AAST)	Injury	Management
I	Haematoma only	Conservative with or without stent
II	Laceration < 50% of circumference	Stent with or without suturing (applicable to cases of open surgical exploration)
III	Laceration > 50% of circumference	Stent with or without suturing (applicable to cases of open surgical exploration) Ureteroureterostomy plus stent
IV	Complete tear < 2 cm of devascularisation	Ureteric reconstruction
V	Complete tear > 2 cm of devascularisation	Ureteric reconstruction

Table 8.3 Options for ureteric reconstruction

Location of injury	Reconstructive option
Upper ureter	Ureteroureterostomy Ureterocalycostomy Transureteroureterostomy
Mid ureter	Ureteroureterostomy Boari flap Transureteroureterostomy
Lower ureter	Ureteroureterostomy Direct reimplantation Psoas hitch Boari flap
Complete injury (e.g. avulsion)	Ileal interposition Renal autotransplantation

Q. What basic principles govern ureteric reconstruction?
A. The basic principles are as follows:
- mobilisation of the ureter, preserving the adventitia
- debridement of non-viable tissue
- spatulation
- tension-free mucosa-to-mucosa anastomosis with fine absorbable sutures (5/0 or 6/0)
- an internal ureteric stent and separate drain placed near the site of anastomosis.

Omental interposition to separate the repair from associated intra-abdominal injuries or suture lines is recommended.
   A bladder catheter should be inserted to limit stent reflux.

Q. How would you manage the patient post-operatively?
A. Remove the bladder catheter 2 days post-operatively. The drain can also be removed on day 2 if output is minimal. The ureteric stent is removed at 6 weeks. A dynamic renogram and IVU are arranged at 3 months (or earlier if the patient has worrying symptoms).

Q. How do missed ureteric injuries present?
A. Missed ureteric injuries are relatively common. They may present with ureteric obstruction (stricturing), urinoma, abscess formation, or fistulation. Ureteric obstruction can result in nephron loss, stones, infection and pain.

Q. What is the likely outcome of ureteric injuries?
A. The outcome of ureteric reconstruction is usually favourable if the principles outlined above are adhered to. Ureteric reflux may result from reconstruction, but this is not considered to be an important problem in the adult patient.

Q. What is the role of the interventional radiologist in ureteric injury and reconstruction?
A. The interventional radiologist has several key roles:
- relieving renal obstruction by percutaneous nephrostomy
- performing nephrosto-ureterograms, which are essential for planning definitive management
- antegrade stenting with or without retrograde assistance ('rendezvous procedure') may be definitive in partial or short ureteric defects, although this requires careful follow-up to look for ureteric stricturing
- balloon dilatation of ureteric strictures, which may be successful in 50% of cases.

Q. What is the role of ureteroscopy in managing ureteric strictures?
A. Short ureteric strictures can be managed by incision with or without balloon dilatation and stenting. Success rates of around 75% have been quoted. Endoscopic treatment of strictures of 2 cm or more has high failure rates. Longer-term stents are being evaluated and may become established as an option in the future in carefully selected patients.

Q. Is there a role for laparoscopy in ureteric reconstruction?
A. Yes. Experienced laparoscopists have successfully reconstructed ureteric injuries, and this may in future be the surgical approach of choice.

BLADDER TRAUMA

Q. A 36-year-old man presents to A&E with acute lower abdominal pain. He was punched in the abdomen after having consumed several pints of beer. He is stable but has been referred to you because of pain and difficulty voiding. What findings make you suspicious of urological injury?

A. The classic triad of lower abdominal pain, inability to void, and frank haematuria with a history of direct trauma to a full bladder suggest a bladder perforation.

(Note that in spinal cord injury/spina bifida patients who have augmented bladders, spontaneous bladder rupture can occur without significant pain. The presenting features may be those of sepsis or vague symptoms of non-specific illness.)

Q. What are the common causes of bladder injury?

A. Pelvic fractures, blunt or penetrating trauma to a distended bladder, and iatrogenic causes (associated with lower abdominal, pelvic and endoscopic surgery).

Q. What percentage of pelvic fractures are associated with a bladder injury?

A. Approximately 5–6%. However, around 80% of bladder injuries are due to pelvic fractures.

Q. How would you assess this patient?

A. As with all trauma cases, ATLS principles should guide management. It is important to adopt a multi-disciplinary approach, and to consult with emergency and general surgical colleagues if necessary.

Q. What specific investigation would you request?

A. In a stable patient, I would request a stress (retrograde) cystogram.

Q. Is there any other investigation that could be requested which might yield more information?

A. Yes, a CT stress (retrograde) cystogram.

Q. How is a stress (retrograde) cystogram performed?

A. In the absence of urethral trauma, the bladder is catheterised and filled to capacity by gravity with diluted (50:50) water-soluble contrast. At least 400 ml must be infused in adults in order to distend the bladder and adequately diagnose a perforation (otherwise blood clot or small bowel/omentum may fill the perforation and prevent extravasation of contrast). AP and post-drainage films are obtained. The post-drainage films are particularly important for diagnosing a posterior bladder perforation, which may be obscured by a bladder filled with contrast.

Q. Why not perform an IVU and wait for the cystographic phase?

A. The bladder is a low-pressure, highly compliant organ. Intravesical pressure has to be raised by adequate bladder distension (at least 400 ml in adults), otherwise the injury may easily be missed

Q. What classification do you use for bladder injuries?

A.
- Bladder contusion.
- Intraperitoneal rupture (30–40%).
- Extraperitoneal rupture (50–60%).
- Combined intra- and extraperitoneal ruptures (5–10%).

169

Q. What does the CT retrograde cystogram in Figure 8.7 show and how would you manage it?

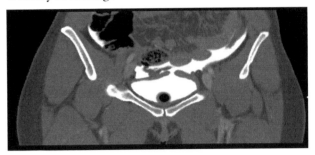

Figure 8.7

A. Figure 8.7 is a CT retrograde cystogram showing an intraperitoneal bladder perforation.

Contrast is seen leaking into the peritoneal cavity (note that in *extraperitoneal* bladder perforation contrast only extravasates into the surrounding perivesical space).

The patient should be resuscitated and treated with broad-spectrum antibiotics. *Intraperitoneal perforations require surgical repair.* Therefore a lower midline laparotomy is performed to inspect the viscera and close the bladder rupture with absorbable sutures. A urethral catheter (with or without a suprapubic catheter) and intra-abdominal drain should be placed.

Q. How would you manage extraperitoneal ruptures?

A. *In general, extraperitoneal ruptures do not require surgical repair.* They are managed with a urethral catheter on free drainage for 10–14 days and antibiotics. A stress (retrograde) cystogram is then performed to ensure that healing has occurred.

Q. Are there any indications to proceed with surgical repair in extraperitoneal ruptures?

A. Yes. They include the following:
- failure of the catheter to drain (e.g. due to clot obstruction)
- persistent extravasation
- bladder neck injury
- patients undergoing internal fixation for pelvic fracture or laparotomy for other viscus repair (e.g. bowel, rectum, vagina) can have concurrent bladder repair
- a bone spike puncturing the bladder on imaging.

Q. What complications may be seen after missed bladder perforation injury?

A. Intraperitoneal urinary extravasation can result in urinary ascites, peritonitis, ileus and systemic sepsis.

Injuries involving the bladder neck can result in incontinence or stricture. Recto/colovesical fistulae and vesicovaginal fistulae may also occur.

Q. How would you manage a penetrating injury to the bladder?

A. By means of operative exploration, closure, bladder drainage and treatment with antibiotics. Careful attention should be paid to the posterior bladder wall, the ureters and neighbouring viscera.

URETHRAL TRAUMA

Q. **What constitutes the anterior urethra and posterior urethra and how are they most commonly injured?**

A.
- *Anterior urethra* (bulbar and penile and navicular). Straddle/fall-astride injury is the most common mechanism of trauma, which usually results in bulbar urethral damage. Penile fracture, which obviously affects the penile urethra, is another cause.
- *Posterior uretha* (prostatic and membranous). Pelvic fracture (due to road traffic accidents or falling from a height) is the cause of injury in virtually all cases (of blunt trauma). The injury occurs due to the shearing effects of bone disruption. Thus the prostate, which is attached to the puboprostatic ligaments, moves in one direction and the membranous urethra, which is fixed to the urogenital diaphragm, moves in another.

Q. **What is the AAST classification of urethral injuries?**

A. The AAST classification is shown in Table 8.4.

Table 8.4 The American Association for the Surgery of Trauma (AAST) urethral trauma severity scale

Group	Type	Description
1	Contusion	Blood at the urethral meatus; normal urethrogram
2	Stretch injury	Elongation of the urethra without extravasation on urethrography
3	Partial disruption	Extravasation of contrast at injury site with contrast visualised in the bladder
4	Complete disruption	Extravasation of contrast at injury site without visualisation in the bladder; < 2 cm urethral separation
5	Complete disruption	Complete transection with > 2 cm urethral separation, or extension into the prostate or vagina

Q. **How can you explain the 'butterfly' pattern of perineal bruising, following urethral injury?**

A. In order to explain this one must understand the fascial layers of the scrotum and anterior abdominal wall.

In the anterior abdominal wall the subcutaneous fatty layer is known as Camper's fascia. Scarpa's fascia lies deep to this, and is attached to the coracoclavicular ligaments superiorly. Inferiorly, it fuses with the deep fascia of the thigh (fascia lata) 1 cm below the inguinal ligament. Medially, Scarpa's fascia is continuous with Colles' fascia in the perineum. Colles' fascia attaches to the posterior edge of the urogenital diaphragm and perineal body and the inferior ischiopubic rami. Colles' fascia is continuous with the dartos fascia of the penis and scrotum.

In the penis, Buck's fascia lies beneath the dartos fascia (which, as already mentioned, is continuous with Colles' fascia). Buck's fascia is attached distally to the base of the glans (coronal sulcus) and laterally to the pubic rami, ischial spines and tuberosities.

If the anterior urethra has ruptured but Buck's fascia is intact (e.g. as may occur in a penile fracture), urine and haematoma are confined in a sleeve-like or tubular configuration along the length of the penis.

However, if Buck's fascia is breached or ruptured or the bulbar urethra is injured (e.g. as may occur in a straddle injury to the bulbar urethra), blood and urine extravasation are limited by the attachments of Colles' fascia. That is, their spread is limited by the fusions of Colles' fascia to the ischiopubic rami laterally and to the posterior edge of the urogenital diaphragm and perineal body posteriorly. The subsequent bruising is therefore butterfly shaped. Bruising and urine can also travel up the anterior abdominal wall beneath Scarpa's fascia to the clavicles (coracoclavicular ligaments), but extravasation will not extend down the leg or into the buttock.

A posterior urethral injury will only be associated with a butterfly distribution of bruising if the pelvic fracture has resulted in urethral disruption with the tear extending below the urogenital diaphragm into the bulbar urethra.

Q. A 40-year-old farmer is brought into A&E after being run over by a tractor. He is resuscitated by the trauma team and is now stable. He has a pelvic fracture. What urological injuries could this patient have and how might they present?

A.
- Bladder injury characterised by suprapubic pain, inability to void, and frank haematuria.
- Urethral injury characterised by blood at the external meatus (present in 37–93% of patients with posterior urethral injury and at least 75% of those with anterior urethral injury), pain or inability to void, and palpable bladder (the latter two suggest urethral disruption).

Q. How would you assess the patient?

A. As with all trauma cases, ATLS principles should guide management. It is important to adopt a multi-disciplinary approach, consulting with emergency, orthopaedic and general surgical colleagues if necessary. The patient should be questioned about previous urological problems.

Positive examination findings include the following:
- blood at the penile meatus
- bruising in the perineum
- distended bladder on palpation
- digital rectal examination may demonstrate a pelvic haematoma (soft and boggy swelling) or blood on the glove (the latter suggests a rectal injury, which is associated with 5% of cases of pelvic fracture). The classically described 'high-riding prostate' (which occurs as a result of prostate–membranous urethral disruption with the subsequent haematoma pushing up the prostate) can be difficult to feel due to the associated pelvic haematoma.

Q. The above patient with a pelvic fracture has blood at the meatus, perineal bruising and a large pelvic haematoma on rectal examination. There is no blood on the glove after digital rectal examination. What is the likely diagnosis?

A. This is typical of a posterior urethral distraction injury (pelvic fracture urethral distraction defect – PFUDD), which usually occurs between the prostatic and membranous urethra. As mentioned earlier, the injury occurs as a result of the severe shearing effects of bone disruption. Thus the prostate, which is attached to the puboprostatic ligaments, moves in one direction and the membranous urethra, which is fixed to the urogenital diaphragm, moves in another.

Q. **How commonly are pelvic fractures associated with urethral injury?**

A. Around 3–25% of pelvic fractures are associated with urethral injury. The incidence of double injuries involving the urethra and bladder is 10–20%.

Q. **What investigation would you perform?**

A. Immediate retrograde urethrogram.

Note:

In an unstable patient, one careful attempt can be made to pass a urethral catheter. If there is any resistance, a suprapubic catheter is inserted (either via ultrasound guidance or via a formal open approach) and a retrograde urethrogram is performed later. *It is extremely unlikely that gentle passage of a urethral catheter would convert a partial injury into a complete injury.*

Q. **How is the urethrogram performed?**

A. • The patient should be positioned in a 30% oblique position with the bottom leg flexed at the hip and knee (if this is not possible due to pain or the patient's condition, a supine position with AP views is acceptable, although one must ensure that extravasation from the bulbar urethra is not masked, as in the AP views the bulbar urethra is superimposed upon itself).

• A 12F catheter is placed in the fossa navicularis and the balloon is inflated with 2 ml of water to create a seal that prevents leakage of contrast.

• A total of 20–30 ml of full-strength water-soluble contrast is injected slowly into the urethra using fluoroscopic guidance. If fluoroscopy is not available, a series of plain X-rays using 10-ml aliquots each time will provide sufficient information.

Q. **How would you treat a partial urethral injury?**

A. Partial urethral injuries can be managed with a suprapubic catheter (SPC) or urethral catheter for 4 weeks. If an SPC is *in situ*, voiding cystourethrography is then performed. If there is no contrast extravasation or stricturing, the SPC can be safely removed and normal voiding can be re-established.

If a urethral catheter is *in situ*, a urethrogram can be performed via a 6 Fr nasogastric (NG) tube that is inserted alongside the urethral catheter. Contrast can then be passed down the NG tube to exclude extravasation (*one uses the same method to perform a retrograde urethrogram following urethroplasty when the urethral catheter is* in situ).

Q. **What does the antegrade urethrogram shown in Figure 8.8 demonstrate?**

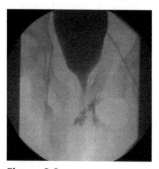

Figure 8.8

A. Figure 8.8 shows an antegrade urethrogram demonstrating complete disruption of the posterior urethra with extravasation of contrast due to a pelvic fracture urethral distraction injury. This occurs in 65% of urethral injuries. Partial injuries account for the remaining 35%.

Q. **How would you manage the above patient initially?**

A. I would manage them with suprapubic catheter drainage of the bladder to minimise urinary extravasation, and treatment with broad-spectrum antibiotics.

Q. **What difficulties might be anticipated when performing the suprapubic puncture?**

A. The bladder may not be palpable. The pelvic haematoma can cause significant distortion of the anatomy and difficulty in identifying the normal tissue planes. Therefore one must never insert an SPC blindly in this situation. Ultrasound can be used to guide the puncture, otherwise open cystotomy is recommended.

Q. **On inserting the SPC into the bladder via ultrasound guidance, the urine is found to be bloodstained. What do you suspect and how will you manage this?**

A. I would suspect a combined urethral and bladder injury. A cystogram should be performed via the SPC, and the bladder injury should be dealt with accordingly.

Q. **What is the next step in the management of the PFUDD following an antegrade urethrogram?**

A. A more detailed urethrogram – the so-called up-and-downogram (i.e. simultaneous retrograde and antegrade urethrogram) – is performed to assess the site, severity and length of the urethral defect.

Definitive reconstruction is performed between 3 and 6 months post injury (deferred treatment).

Q. **Why wait prior to the reconstruction?**

A. There are two reasons for this:
- to allow the patient to recover from major trauma
- to allow the pelvic haematoma and any urinary extravasation to resolve. This reduces the length of the defect, and allows the tissue planes to return to normal.

Q. **What operation is used to re-establish urethral continuity (following the above PFUDD) and what steps can be used to bridge the urethral defect?**

A Bulbo-prostatic anastomotic urethroplasty (BPA) via a perineal approach is used. It is sometimes necessary to use a combined abdominal and perineal approach.

The steps used to deal with the defect include bulbar urethral mobilisation and, if necessary, midline separation of the corporal bodies, inferior pubectomy, and supracorporal urethral rerouting. Defects up to 7cm can be dealt with using these manoeuvres in sequence.

Q. **What are the approximate success rates for deferred treatment and how is the outcome of urethral reconstruction following pelvic fracture judged?**

A. The success rate of deferred BPA approaches 95%. The outcome is judged by observing restricture rates (< 10%), incontinence (5%) and erectile dysfunction (ED) (20%).

Q. **Is there a role for 'early' urethral realignment following PFUDD?**

A. Early realignment is performed either by open or endoscopic surgery. Immediate open repair is associated with a high incidence of strictures (70%), incontinence (20%) and erectile dysfunction (44%).

Although the incidence of incontinence and erectile dysfunction is reported to be less with endoscopic realignment, there are high restricture rates requiring multiple follow-up procedures.

Therefore, due to the relatively poor outcomes of early realignment, deferred repair is preferred in specialist centres in the UK.

The only indications for early realignment are concomitant bladder neck or rectal injury. These injuries require immediate open exploration and repair. Bladder neck injury combined with PFUDD will result in incontinence in most cases, so repair is essential. Early realignment is recommended in these cases.

Q. **How are fall-astride injuries managed?**

A. The principles are similar to those for the management of PFUDDs. However, the injury differs in that it is due to a crushing force on the bulbar (anterior) urethra which results in an obliterative stricture and loss of normal urethral length. Deferred treatment is again recommended, with initial suprapubic diversion to minimise extravasation, antibiotics to minimise infection and abscess formation, and time to allow bruising and haematoma to resolve. After 3 months, stricture excision and primary anastomosis can be performed.

GENITAL TRAUMA

Q. **A 21-year-old university student is kicked in the groin during an intercollegiate football match. He is brought to hospital because he has a swollen painful scrotum. He is otherwise well. How would you assess this patient and what injuries may be have sustained?**

A. A focused history and examination should be undertaken. It is important to rule out the possibility of other major injuries prior to concentrating on the genitalia. The possible injuries include scrotal bruising with localised haematoma formation, haematocele, and testicular, epididymal and spermatic cord injury (including torsion).

Q. **How may testicular injuries be classified?**

A. Tunica albuginea disruption (testicular rupture) or contained intratesticular haematoma.

Q. **Is there any role for imaging?**

A. Yes. It is often difficult to perform an adequate physical examination in the presence of bruising, swelling, haematoma and pain. Scrotal utrasound is the imaging method of choice for detecting intrascrotal injury, the primary goal being to assess the integrity (intact tunica albuginea) and vascularity of the testis. It has a specificity of 75% and a sensitivity of 64% in detecting testis rupture (although the sensitivity may be higher in more experienced hands). A combination of clinical and ultrasound findings will guide management.

Q. **What may be seen on an ultrasound scan of an injured testis?**

A. Disruption of the tunica albuginea may be detected. However, more commonly the diagnosis is made by a combination of findings, including a haematocele, a contour abnormality of the testis and heterogeneous echotexture of the testis (the latter suggests associated parenchymal bleeding).

Q. **What does the intra-operative scrotal image in Figure 8.9 show?**

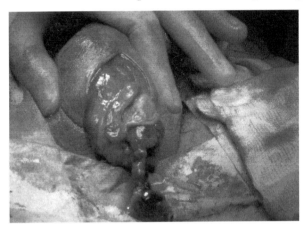

Figure 8.9

A. Figure 8.9 shows a testicular rupture.

Q. **How would you manage this patient?**
A. This patient should be counselled for urgent scrotal exploration. Extruded or necrotic seminiferous tubules should be debrided and the tunica albuginea should be closed with fine (4/0) absorbable sutures. A small drain may be left to drain dependently and the patient treated with broad-spectrum antibiotics for 7 days. For reproductive, endocrine and psychological reasons, every effort should be made to preserve the testis, but in the presence of gross injury, orchidectomy should be performed.

Q. **Is there a role for delayed (> 48 hours) scrotal exploration?**
A. Studies have shown that testicular salvage after blunt trauma decreased from 80% to 30% if exploration was delayed by more than 3 days.

Q. **How would you manage a haematocele?**
A. Prompt drainage is recommended for large haematoceles to prevent infection, testicular ischaemia and prolonged pain. Scrotal haematomas, bruising and smaller haematoceles can be treated conservatively with ice, rest and elevation.

URETHRAL STRICTURE

Q. **Describe the blood supply to the urethra.**
A. The blood supply to the urethra is derived from the internal pudendal branch of the internal iliac artery. It enters the perineum via the pudendal canal (Alcock's canal) and terminates in the common penile artery which provides three branches that supply the structures of the penis. The urethra receives a generous blood supply from the bulbourethral and dorsal penile branches which arborise in the glans penis.

Q. A previously well 24-year-old man is referred to you with a history of slow urinary stream. He has recently been treated for a urinary tract infection, but is otherwise well. What is the most likely cause of this patient's problems?

A. A urethral stricture. The differential diagnosis includes bladder neck obstruction, neuropathic bladder and late presentation of posterior urethral valves.

Q. What is the aetiology of urethral strictures?

A.
- Posterior urethral strictures (prostatic and membranous urethra) are due to a fibrotic process that narrows the lumen, and most commonly these are due to trauma such as a PFUDD or surgery (e.g. radical prostatectomy, TURP, cryotherapy, laser use).
- Anterior urethral strictures (bulbar, penile and navicular urethra) are a result of scar formation in the spongy erectile tissue of the corpus spongiosum. This scarring may be subsequent to any of the following:
  - inflammatory processes (gonococcal urethritis, BXO)
  - trauma due to direct blow or straddle/fall-astride injury (usually affects bulbar urethra)
  - iatrogenic causes (traumatic catheterisation, instrumentation, post-hypospadias repair/urethral surgery)
  - idiopathic/congenital causes. These may be the result of a previous straddle injury, which may have gone unnoticed. However, there is a distinct group of young men in whom strictures occur between the proximal and middle thirds of the urethra, which contain a high content of smooth muscle on biopsy and are termed 'congenital' (they form between the point of fusion of the urethra from its two different embryological origins).

Q. What would you look for on examination?

A. In patients with urethral strictures, there are often no external signs of the disease process. However, it is important to inspect for BXO, meatal stricturing, hypospadias and evidence of prior surgery. Palpation may reveal spongiofibrosis adjacent to the stricture.

Q. What does the flow curve in Figure 8.10 show? What other investigations are important?

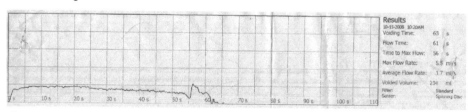

Figure 8.10

A. Figure 8.10 shows a prolonged slow flow typical of a urethral stricture. This is typically termed a 'plateau'-shaped trace with little change in flow rate.
Further investigations would include the following:
- flexible urethroscopy – direct inspection of the urethral lumen is probably the commonest first-line investigation in the UK

- urethrography – ascending and descending studies. In specialist centres, urethrography is performed instead of urethroscopy, as it provides the most detailed information about the urethra. A diagnosis and management plan can be formulated and the patient counselled appropriately.

In addition, ultrasound scan may show a thickened bladder wall and residual urine. If hydro-ureteronephrosis is present, estimation of renal function should be performed.

Urinanalysis will exclude concurrent urinary tract infection.

Q. **What does the antegrade urethrogram in Figure 8.11 show?**

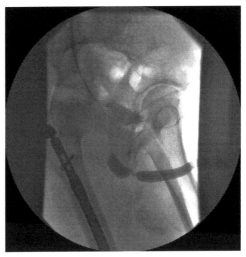

Figure 8.11

A. Figure 8.11 is an antegrade urethrogram that demonstrates a short narrowing of the bulbar urethra consistent with a stricture. Ascending, descending and dynamic images should be reviewed.

Q. **How would you manage this patient and why?**
A. I would counsel this patient for an optical urethrotomy. The alternative is a urethral dilatation or a combination of urethrotomy and dilatation. There is no advantage in terms of outcome, but the optical urethrotomy is performed under direct vision so may be considered safer. Approximately 50% of urethral strictures require no further treatment following optical urethrotomy urethral dilatation. These are typically short (< 1.5 cm), located in the bulbar urethra, associated with minimal spongiofibrosis, and have had no previous interventions.

A urethral catheter should be left *in situ* for 3 days following an optical urethrotomy, and the patient should be taught intermittent self-catheterisation/ dilatation, which should be continued for 6 months (this reduces restricturing rates).

Q. **How would you manage a patient whose short bulbar stricture recurs following an optical urethrotomy?**
A. If the patient is fit for anaesthesia, and the stricture is < 2 cm in length, I would counsel them for an anastomotic bulbar urethroplasty, which is curative in

approximately 90% of cases at 10-year follow-up. Any anastomotic repair must be spatulated, tension-free and 'stented' (catheterised in this case).

Note:

The alternative option is palliative (if the patient considers this preferable) repeat urethral dilatation/optical urethrotomy followed by long-term self-dilatation. Older age should not be considered a contraindication to urethroplasty.

Q. **What are the indications for anastomotic urethroplasty?**

A. This procedure is used in two situations:
- for short strictures of the bulbar urethra (not more than 2 cm in length)
- for a pelvic fracture-related injury of the membranous urethra or bulbo-membranous junction. This is not so much a stricture as a distraction defect with no continuity of the urethra and obliteration of the lumen by fibrous tissue, which separates the ends of the urethra.

Note:

The membranous urethral strictures following TURP, sometimes known as 'sphincter strictures' because they are due to fibrosis within the external sphincter mechanism, are best treated by urethral dilatation in order to avoid incontinence.

Q. **Which manoeuvres can be used to bridge the defect during anastomotic urethroplasty (in order to bring the two ends of the urethra together) if bulbar urethral mobilisation alone is not adequate?**

A. If the elasticity of the urethra and mobilisation are not sufficient to bridge the defect, the principle is to straighten out the natural curve of the bulbar urethra so that its course from the penoscrotal junction to the prostatic apex is a straight line (rather than a semi-circle). The following manoeuvres are used to do this:
- separation of the crura at the base of the penis
- wedge pubectomy of the inferior pubic arch
- re-routing of the urethra around the shaft of the penis.

Defects up to 7 cm can be bridged using these steps in sequence.

Q. **What specific complications can occur after bulbar anastomotic urethroplasty?**

A. Bleeding, wound infection, post-micturition dribbling (due to division of the bulbospongiosus muscle) and stricture recurrence.

Q. **What operative options are available for longer bulbar strictures?**

A. *Substitution urethroplasty* is used for bulbar strictures that are too long for anastomotic repair and in strictures of the penile urethra where anastomotic urethroplasty is not advised due to buckling on erection. A dorsal stricturotomy with placement of a dorsal patch (Barbagli procedure) is the preferred procedure (complete excision of the stricture with circumferential repair is only performed if the affected section of urethra definitely needs to be completely excised, e.g. BXO strictures or anterior strictures related to previous hypospadias repair, in which the tissue is totally scarred). A dorsal patch is preferred, as it is well supported by the cavernosal bodies and thus out-pouching does not occur. The current dorsal patch of choice is a buccal mucosal graft.

Other options include an augmented anastomotic urethroplasty, which is not commonly performed, and a perineal urethrostomy, which is generally used only when reconstructive surgery fails.

Q. **For complex strictures, such as those related to radiotherapy, should one use a graft?**

A. No. In the presence of diseased tissue (e.g. following radiotherapy), grafts will not take. Thus any tissue transfer needs to have its own blood supply, and a genital skin flap is used pedicled on the vascular dartos layer of the penis.

Q. **What are the success rates of anastomotic and substitution urethroplasty?**

A. Anastomotic urethroplasty is associated with an approximately 90% success rate at 10 years. Substitution urethroplasty success rates are worse, with 85% patency rates at 1–3 years and deteriorating at 3–5% per year so that by 10–15 years approximately 50% of patients have developed recurrent strictures.

Q. **What options are available for the management of penile urethral strictures?**

A. The management of penile strictures is complex. Aetiology, length, location and the condition of the surrounding tissues are important. *Urethral dilatation or optical urethrotomy will inevitably fail in penile strictures, and anastomotic urethroplasty should not be performed for penile strictures as this will result in unacceptable penile deformity on erection.* More proximal simple penile urethral strictures (i.e. those not caused by BXO or failed hypospadias repair) can be managed with a stricturotomy and penile skin flap (Orandi flap). Distal strictures, which are usually related to previous hypospadias repair or BXO, can be managed with excision of the affected segment followed by a circumferential repair involving a two-stage urethroplasty using buccal mucosal graft (for BXO, genital skin cannot be used as the disease will recur in this tissue).

Q. **Why has buccal mucosa become the graft of choice?**

A. There are several reasons for this, including the following:
- its ready availability in sufficient quantities
- its minimal morbidity to the donor site
- its toughness, and the fact that it is easy to handle
- it behaves like a full-thickness graft, so there is little or no contraction and a rich sub-dermal plexus (much more vascular than skin), and thus the graft takes well
- it is accustomed to a wet environment
- it appears to have antibacterial properties
- it is resistant to skin diseases.

Q **What specific donor site complications can occur after harvesting of a buccal mucosal graft?**

A. Discomfort, bleeding, donor site infection, injury to the parotid duct (Stenson's duct), numbness in the oral cavity, persistent difficulty with mouth opening, and change in salivary function.

FURTHER READING

Andrich DE *et al*. Urethral strictures and their surgical treatment. *BJU Int* 2000; **86:** 571–80.

Lynch D *et al*. *Guidelines on Urological Trauma. European Association of Urology Guidelines 2008*; www.uroweb.org/fileadmin/tx_eauguidelines/UroTrauma.pdf (accessed 31 October 2009)

McAninch JW (ed.) Genitourinary trauma. *Urol Clin North Am* 2006; **33:** 1–132.

Santucci RA *et al*. Evaluation and management of renal injuries: consensus statement of the renal trauma subcommittee. *BJU Int* 2004; **93:** 937–54.

Shergill IS, Arya M, Patel HR and Gill IS (eds) *Urological Emergencies in Hospital Medicine*. London: Quay Books; 2007.

Chapter 9
Urinary tract infections

Vibhash Mishra and Jas Kalsi

DEFINITIONS

Q. **What is the definition of a urinary tract infection?**

A. Urinary tract infection (UTI) is the inflammatory response of urothelium to microorganism invasion (commonly bacterial), usually associated with bacteriuria and pyuria.

Q. **What is the definition of bacteriuria?**

A. Bacteriuria is the presence of bacteria in urine.

Q. **What is the definition of pyuria?**

A. Pyuria is the presence of white blood cells (WBCs) in urine.

Q. **What is the definition of sterile pyuria and what is the differential diagnosis?**

A. Sterile pyuria is pyuria without bacteriuria. Possible causes include tuberculosis, carcinoma *in situ* of the bladder, schistosomiasis, urinary tract stones, partly treated UTI and other inflammatory bladder conditions (interstitial cystitis or leucoplakia).

Q. **What is the definition of cystitis?**

A. Cystitis is a clinical syndrome consisting of dysuria, frequency and urgency with or without suprapubic pain.

Q. **What is the definition of acute and chronic pyelonephritis?**

A. Acute pyelonephritis is a syndrome consisting of chills, fever, flank pain, bacteriuria and pyuria. Chronic pyelonephritis is a radiological diagnosis describing a scarred, shrunken kidney, which may or may not have resulted from recurrent infections.

Q. **What is the definition of an isolated UTI?**

A. An isolated UTI is one that occurs at least 6 months after the previous UTI.

Q. **What is the definition of recurrent UTI?**

A. Recurrent UTI is an episode of UTI after documented, successful resolution of an earlier episode, and occurring at a frequency of at least twice in the last 6 months, or three times in the last 12 months. Recurrent UTI can be sub-classified as 'persistent' or 'reinfection':

- Persistence refers to recurrent UTI caused by the same organisms. It indicates a possible focus of infection in the urinary tract, such as stones (commonly struvite), chronic prostatitis, bladder diverticulum, urethral diverticulum or colo-vesical fistula.
- Reinfection refers to recurrent episodes of UTI caused by different organisms. It usually indicates an increased susceptibility to UTI (including genetic susceptibility), and is associated with poor hygiene, sexual intercourse, and post menopause. *More than 95% of all recurrent UTIs in female patients are due to reinfection.*

Q. **What is the definition of unresolved infection?**

A. An unresolved infection is one that has not responded to treatment. Possible causes include natural or acquired bacterial resistance to antimicrobial therapy, development of resistance in a previously susceptible organism, simultaneous infection with multiple organisms, rapid reinfection, an overwhelming size of bacterial inoculum, or antimicrobial level below the minimum inhibitory concentration.

Q. **What is the definition of a complicated UTI?**

A. A complicated UTI indicates infection in the presence of a structurally or functionally abnormal urinary tract, or UTI in the presence of underlying disease which is known to increase the risk of acquiring infection, or failing therapy.

Factors that suggest complicated UTI include male gender, the elderly, pregnancy, indwelling catheter/stent, recent urinary tract instrumentation, immunosuppression, diabetes, symptoms that have persisted for > 7 days at presentation, hospital-acquired infection, recent use of antimicrobial drugs, and functional or anatomical abnormality of the urinary tract.[1]

Q. **What is the definition of an uncomplicated UTI?**

A. An uncomplicated UTI indicates infection in the presence of a structurally or functionally normal urinary tract, or UTI in the absence of any underlying disease that increases the risk of acquiring infection, or failing therapy.

RECURRENT UTIS

Q. **A 45-year-old woman has been referred by her GP with a history of recurrent UTIs. How will you approach this case?**

A. I would first take a thorough history, in which I would try to establish whether this is a case of an isolated or recurrent UTI, cystitis or pyelonephritis, and whether there are any features which indicate that this is a complicated infection. I would also want to exclude symptoms that may be attributable to a sexually transmitted infection, such as itching, vaginal discharge or any symptoms in the woman's partner. I would make sure that all of the MSU results from the GP are available so that it is possible to ascertain which organism caused the infection or whether there is a non-infective process (e.g. interstitial cystitis, stones, CIS). The MSU results would also allow me to differentiate reinfection from persistence, and to ascertain the number of confirmed UTIs in one year.

I would then ask about the patient's past medical history (diabetes, stones, constipation, neurological illness or previous UTIs as a child). This would help to differentiate between a complicated and uncomplicated UTI. It is important to establish whether there is a family history of UTIs (UTIs associated with ABO blood group antigen non-secretors, Lewis non-secretor or P blood group secretors). The pregnancy status of the patient should always be established, and whether she is on an oral contraceptive pill (as there may be possible interactions with antibiotics).

Q. What will you look for on clinical examination?

A. On physical examination (with a chaperone present), I would aim to identify any underlying anatomical predisposing factors such as a palpable kidney or a palpable bladder, and whether there is any loin tenderness. On vaginal examination (PV) (again with a chaperone present) I would ascertain the state of tissue oestrogenisation, the presence or absence of genital prolapse and/or urethral diverticulum. I would also perform a focused neurological examination.

Q. Which investigations will you request in this case?

A. In general I would request a urine dipstick test followed by an MSU for urine microscopy and culture and sensitivity (C&S), an X-ray of the kidneys, ureters and bladder (KUB), and a renal tract ultrasound scan with a post-void residual measurement (PVR).

Q. What findings on urinalysis suggest the presence of an infection?

A. The presence of blood, leucocytes and nitrites. I would also note the urinary pH.

Q. Can you explain how urinary dipstick analysis works?

A.

Blood

The chromogen indicator on the dipstick, orthotolidine, is a peroxidase substrate. When haemoglobin, which contains peroxidase activity, comes into contact with orthotolidine, an oxidation reaction takes place resulting in a colour change (to a blue colour) of the indicator. False-positives (oxidising agents) can result from exercise, dehydration, menstrual blood, povidone iodine and hypochlorite solutions (bleach). False-negatives (reducing agents) can be due to vitamin C, gentisic acid and poorly mixed urine. Dipstick-positive but microscopy-negative results indicate dilute urine (low specific gravity).

Leucocytes

Neutrophils (present in infected urine) produce the enzyme leucocyte esterase. This enzyme causes hydrolysis of an indoxyl carbonic acid ester (the substrate on the dipstick) to indoxyl, which in turn oxidises a diazonium salt chromogen on the dipstick to produce the colour change. False-positive results are caused by contamination by vaginal discharge and the presence of formalin. False-negative results may be caused by high specific gravity of urine, dehydration, glycosuria, the presence of urobilinogen, ingestion of large amounts of vitamin C, and also if the test is read too soon (within < 2 minutes) or the sample has been left standing for too long (due to lysis of WBCs).

However, not all patients with bacteria in their urine (bacteriuria) have significant pyuria. The sensitivity of this dipstick test for the detection of infection is 70–95%, which means that 5–30% of patients with an infection will have a dipstick result that is negative for leucocyte esterase.

Nitrites

Most Gram-negative bacteria, which are the commonest uropathogens, convert nitrates (present in urine) to nitrites (not normally present in urine). Nitrites then react with the aromatic amine reagent on the dipstick to form a diazonium salt. The diazonium salt then interacts with hydroxybenzoquinolone to form a pink-coloured azo dye (Griess reaction). It usually takes 4 hours for the Griess reaction to occur. False-positive results occur due to contamination. False-negative results include non-nitrite-converting bacteria (Gram-positive organisms and *Pseudomonas*), urine present in the bladder for < 4 hours, absent dietary nitrates, ascorbic acid and dilute urine (low specific gravity).

The sensitivity of nitrite dipstick detection is 35–85%, whereas the specificity is 92–100%. This means that if the nitrite test is positive the patient is likely to have a UTI, but a negative test often occurs even though an infection is present. The combination of the nitrite test with leucocyte esterase with a positive result on either is more specific but less sensitive than either test alone (sensitivity of 75–84% and specificity of 82–98%).

Q. **Why is the urinary pH important?**

A. The average urinary pH ranges from 5.5 to 6.5. A consistently alkaline pH (> 7.5) in the presence of a UTI suggests the possibility of stones. Certain organisms (*Proteus, Klebsiella, Staphylococcus, Pseudomonas, Providencia, Serratia*) produce the enzyme urease, which catalyses the hydrolysis of urea to carbon dioxide and ammonia. Ammonia raises the pH of urine, causing precipitation of magnesium ammonium phosphate to form staghorn stones.

Q. **How would you ask a patient to take a urine sample which is to be sent for microscopy and culture?**

A. In the case of female patients, I would ask for a midstream urine (MSU) sample to be collected by asking them to spread the labia, wash and cleanse the periurethral area with a moist gauze from back to front, void the first 100–150 ml of urine in the toilet and then place a wide-mouthed sterile container to collect the next 10–15 ml.

In the case of circumcised men, no special preparation is required. For uncircumcised men, I would ask them to retract their foreskin, wash their glans penis with soap and rinse it with water, keep the foreskin retracted and then collect 10–15 ml of midstream urine as described previously.

The collected sample should be cultured within a couple of hours. If that is not possible, it should be refrigerated immediately and then cultured within 24 hours.

For microscopy, sediment is obtained by centrifuging 5–10 ml of the sample for 5 minutes at 2000 rpm, and this is then examined for the presence of bacteria and white blood cells.

For culture, 0.1 ml of urine is delivered on to each half of a split-agar plate which contains blood agar on one half for Gram-positive organisms and eosin-methylene blue (EMB) on the other half for Gram-negative organisms. The number of colonies is then estimated after an overnight incubation.

Q. **How is Gram staining performed?**

A. Gram staining is performed in the following manner. The bacterial smear is stained on a slide with crystal violet for 1–2 minutes. This is then poured off and Gram's iodine is added for 1–2 minutes. After this time, the iodine is poured off and the stain is then decolourised by washing the slide with acetone for 2–3 seconds. The slide is washed with water and safranin counterstain is added for 2 minutes. Finally, the slide is washed with water and dried.

Q. **What is the basis of the Gram stain?**
A. The cell wall of Gram-positive bacteria retains the purple colour of crystal violet, whereas that of Gram-negative bacteria does not, and only takes up the pink safranin counterstain.

Q. **What is the microbiological definition of significant bacteriuria?**
A. Kass was the first person to introduce the concept of quantitative microbiology in the diagnosis of urinary infections. In the context of pyelonephritis in pregnant women, he proposed 10^5 cfu/ml of urine (pure growth) as a cut-off value for significant bacteriuria.[2] This remained an essential criterion for the diagnosis of UTI for many years. However, it is now known that 20–40% of women with symptomatic UTIs present with bacterial counts of 10^2–10^4 cfu/ml of urine (pure growth).[3] The following bacterial counts are currently considered to be significant in the relevant groups of patients (all pure growth):1
- $\geq 10^3$ cfu/ml of MSU in acute uncomplicated cystitis in women
- $\geq 10^4$ cfu/ml of MSU in acute uncomplicated pyelonephritis in women
- $\geq 10^4$ cfu/ml of straight catheter urine sample in a complicated UTI in women
- $\geq 10^4$ cfu/ml of MSU in men (all UTIs in men are considered to be complicated)
- $\geq 10^5$ cfu/ml of MSU in a complicated UTI in women.

Q. **Despite your investigations, no cause for the infections has been identified. Can you please explain to the patient why she is having recurrent urinary tract infections?**
A. I would explain to the patient that in the absence of an identifiable cause, recurrent UTIs are a function of the individual's susceptibility, the virulence of the organism and the host defence mechanisms.

Q. **What is meant by susceptibility to infections?**
A. Studies have demonstrated that women who have recurrent UTIs may be inherently more susceptible due to their increased epithelial-cell receptivity for uropathogens. Pathogenic bacteria adhere more readily to the vaginal, urethral and buccal epithelial cells of susceptible women, due to the presence of an increased number of receptor sites. This trait (of increased susceptibility to UTI) is associated with the HLA-A3 phenotype, Lewis blood group status Le(a-b-) and Le(a+b-), P blood group secretors and ABO blood group antigen non-secretors.

Q. **What is pathogenicity?**
A. It is defined as the ability of an organism to cause disease.

Q. **What is virulence?**
A. It is the degree of pathogenicity.

Q. **What are bacterial virulence factors?**
A. They are the characteristics of uropathogens that allow them to colonise and flourish within the host. They can be divided into factors which are directed against external agents and those that are directed against the host.

Factors that are directed against external agents (e.g. antimicrobial resistance) can either be inherited chromosomally (e.g. the intrinsic resistance of *Proteus* to nitrofurantoin), acquired chromosomally (mutations) or extra-chromosomally mediated (via plasmids).

Factors that are directed against the host include:

- toxin production (e.g. haemolysin)
- enzyme production (e.g. urease)
- production of antihumoral substances (e.g. IgA inactivating protein by gonorrhoea and *Proteus*)
- general mechanisms (e.g. penetration of host by schistosoma spine, phage variation by organisms to change from a fimbriated to a non-fimbriated form to evade phagocytosis)
- adherence mechanisms – bacterial adherence to vaginal and urothelial epithelium is a prerequisite for the initiation of a UTI. To facilitate this process, certain uropathogens express a number of antigenically and functionally active proteins called adhesins on their cell surface. These adhesins may take the form of fimbriae or pili, or may be afimbrial. The most well-known afimbrial adhesin is the Dr adhesin, which is associated with UTIs in children and pregnant women. The most well described pili, found on *E. coli*, are as follows:
  - Type 1 – associated with *E. coli* causing cystitis; also known as mannose-sensitive pili, as the haemagglutination of guinea pig erythrocytes mediated by these pili is inhibited by mannose
  - P pili – associated with strains of *E. coli* causing pyelonephritis; also called mannose-resistant pili, as the haemagglutination reaction is not inhibited by mannose
  - S pili – associated with both bladder and kidney infection.

Q. **What are the normal host defence mechanisms against UTIs?**

A. A number of host defence mechanisms exist to reduce the incidence of and propensity to acquire and develop urinary tract infections. These defences normally work in parallel and include the following:

- the normal commensal flora of the vaginal introitus and periurethral area (e.g. lactobacilli reduce the ability of uropathogens to colonise by lowering the vaginal pH as a result of converting glycogen to lactic acid)
- the normal antegrade flow of urine
- the vaginal environment related to oestrogen and cervical IgA
- the physical and chemical characteristics of urine (osmolality, pH, urea and organic acid concentration)
- the normal exfoliation of urothelial cells
- Tamm–Horsfall protein (secreted by cells of the ascending limb of the loop of Henle) – binds the type 1 pili of *E. coli* and thus prevents adherence
- the presence of an intact GAG layer.

Q. **Are you aware of any risk factors for the development of recurrent UTIs?**

A. There are certain factors which increase the propensity to develop recurrent urinary tract infections. These may be divided into general and specific factors.

The general factors are applicable to all patient groups and include the following:

- factors that reduce the normal antegrade flow of urine, such as bladder out-flow obstruction, low fluid intake and a neurogenic bladder
- factors that promote bacterial colonisation, such as sexual intercourse, the use of spermicides and vaginal oestrogen depletion
- factors that facilitate the retrograde ascent of pathogens, such as female gender, the presence of an indwelling catheter, urinary/faecal incontinence and incomplete bladder emptying with ischaemia of the bladder wall
- factors that reduce the ability of the immune system to fight infection, such as diabetes mellitus, steroid use or HIV-positive status.

Certain specific factors are applicable to female patients of different age groups. These include:

- premenopausal women:
  - recent sexual debut
  - previous UTIs
  - age at first UTI
  - maternal history of UTI
- pregnant women:
  - UTI in non-pregnant state
  - asymptomatic bacteriuria
  - length of gravidity (maximum between weeks 9 and 17)
- menopausal women:
  - genital prolapse
  - incontinence
  - large post-void residue.

Q. **What are opportunistic infections?**

A. They are infections caused by non-pathogens (e.g. commensals) due to weakened host defence mechanisms.

Q. **You have found no cause for infections in this woman. How will you manage her?**

A. As the investigations have revealed no reversible factors, it is unfortunately not possible to ensure that her recurrent urinary tract infections will not re-occur. I would explain to the patient that the aims of management in her case would be first to control her symptoms and secondly to reduce the frequency of infections. Therefore I would first give her the following general advice:

- to ensure that she has a high fluid intake
- to make sure that she voids before and after sexual intercourse
- to avoid using detergents in her bath
- to avoid using spermicidal contraceptives, as spermicides promote colonisation by pathogens by destroying the commensal bacterial flora
- to try to keep her urine acidic if possible
- to consider applying lactobacilli topically to the vaginal area (in the form of live yoghurt)
- to apply topical oestrogen to the vagina (if there is evidence of vaginal atrophy) in order to eliminate pathogenic colonisation by restoring a normal vaginal environment and recolonisation with lactobacilli

- to aim to have a regular daily intake of cranberry juice or cranberry tablets. It is known that the active ingredient, which consists of proanthocyanidins, blocks bacterial adherence to urothelium and reduces the frequency of infections by up to 12–20%.

More specifically, I would then counsel the patient about the potential use of antimicrobial therapy. Three regimes are available depending upon the frequency of UTIs, the relationship between UTIs and intercourse, and the acceptability of the regime to the patient.

- Intermittent self-start therapy usually involves a three-day course of a quinolone, trimethoprim or nitrofurantoin at full therapeutic dose. This may be initiated by the patient upon the onset of symptoms. The patient is asked to take an MSU sample before starting treatment and to keep it in the fridge. If treatment with the antibiotics is successful, the MSU sample does not necessarily need to be cultured. However, if the symptoms do not resolve, the sample can be used to assess bacterial sensitivities. The literature suggests that three-day courses are superior to single-dose therapy, and equivalent to longer courses, with fewer side-effects.[4] However, seven-day courses are recommended for men and for women with symptoms that have persisted for ≥ 1 week or with complicating factors.
- Post-intercourse prophylaxis consists of a single dose of a quinolone, trimethoprim, cephalexin or nitrofurantoin which is taken immediately after intercourse if UTIs are closely related to sexual activity.[5]
- Low-dose long-term antibiotic prophylaxis works by eliminating the introital and enteric reservoirs of pathogenic bacteria, and does not appear to cause reinfections with resistant organisms. It is prescribed in the form of one tablet of trimethoprim (100 mg), cephalexin (250 mg), nitrofurantoin (50 mg) or a quinolone (e.g. ciprofloxacin 250 mg) every night for 6–12 months.[6] In general, breakthrough infections should be treated with therapeutic courses of a different antibiotic that is chosen on the basis of sensitivities (if available), and prophylaxis should be resumed after treatment. Recurrences may be reduced by up to 95%. However, prophylaxis does not alter the long-term baseline infection rate, and around 60% of women start to develop infections again a few months after stopping the regime.[1]

Q. **You find out that the patient is now pregnant. How common are UTIs in pregnancy?**

A. Urinary infections are not uncommon in pregnancy. Around 4–7% of pregnant women have asymptomatic bacteriuria (the same percentage as that in the normal population). However, of these, 20–40% will develop pyelonephritis during pregnancy (usually in the third trimester). Therefore pregnancy is one condition in which asymptomatic bacteriuria should be treated.

Q. **Which antibiotics may be used safely in pregnancy and what other precautions are required?**

A. The antibiotics that are safe to use during pregnancy are penicillins and cephalosporins. Nitrofurantoin may be used in the first and second trimesters only. The following antibiotics should be avoided during pregnancy:

- tetracyclines – all trimesters
- quinolones – all trimesters
- trimethoprim – first trimester
- aminoglycosides – second and third trimesters
- chloramphenicol – third trimester
- sulphonamide – third trimester
- nitrofurantoin – third trimester.

It is very important that once the treatment has been completed a negative urinary culture is performed to confirm eradication of the bacteria. This is in contrast to simple uncomplicated UTIs, where this is not necessary.

Q. How would you treat recurrent UTIs in pregnancy?

A. In cases of recurrent UTIs in pregnancy, a low dose of cephalexin, 125–250 mg daily, is usually safe and effective.

Q. Can you describe the mode of action and side-effects of the common antibiotics?

A. The mode of action and the side-effects of the commonest antibiotics are listed in Table 9.1.

Table 9.1 The mode of action and side-effects of the antibiotics most commonly used in the treatment of UTIs

Agent	Action	Mode of action	Common side-effects and cautions	Relevance in pregnancy
Penicillins	Bactericidal	Interference with bacterial cell wall synthesis	Hypersensitivity, diarrhoea	Safe
Cephalosporins	Bactericidal	Interference with bacterial cell wall synthesis	Hypersensitivity, diarrhoea	Safe
Macrolides (erythromycin, etc.)	Bacteriostatic	Inhibition of ribosomal protein synthesis		Safe
Quinolones (ciprofloxacin, etc.)	Bacteriostatic	Prevention of DNA replication by inhibition of DNA gyrase	Tendon damage (higher risk when given with steroids), diarrhoea, contraindicated in epileptics, interaction with warfarin	Unsafe
Tetracyclines	Bacteriostatic	Inhibition of ribosomal protein synthesis	Hepatotoxicity, deposition in growing bones and teeth	Unsafe
Trimethoprim	Bacteriostatic	Prevention of DNA replication by inhibition of dihydrofolate reductase		Unsafe in first trimester

continued

Aminoglycosides (gentamicin)	Bactericidal	Inhibition of ribosomal protein synthesis	Nephrotoxicity, ototoxicity, impairs neuromuscular transmission, caution in elderly and renal impairment	Unsafe in second and third trimesters
Nitrofurantoin	Bactericidal	Damages bacterial DNA by inhibiting multiple enzyme systems	Acute and chronic lung toxicity, hepatotoxicity, allergic reactions, inadequate urine concentration at GFR < 50	Unsafe in third trimester

Q. **How would you administer therapeutic doses of gentamicin?**

A. I use gentamicin at a single daily dose of 3–7 mg/kg body weight based on the Hartford protocol so long as there are no contraindications. The advantages of this regime include convenience for the patient and staff, the need to check levels less frequently, and the lower risk of nephrotoxicity, as too many peak serum levels are avoided and a more steady level is achieved. The treatment outcome is better, as the ratio of peak serum concentration to minimum inhibitory concentration is higher. Subsequent interval adjustments are made by using a single concentration in serum, and hospitals use their own protocols for monitoring of once-daily therapy.

An example of one such protocol is as follows:

* Give the first dose when indicated.
* Give the second and subsequent doses at 17.00 hours the next day.
* Check gentamicin levels after the third dose at 12.00 hours.
* Give the next dose based on the levels:
  - < 1 mg/l – give the same dose
  - 1–2 mg/l – reduce the dose by 25% and re-check the levels before giving the next dose
  - 2 mg/l – omit that day's dose, and re-check the levels next day.

URINARY TRACT TUBERCULOSIS

Q. **A 53-year-old Bangladeshi woman has been referred to you with a few months' history of frequency, nocturia and malaise. Urine cultures initiated by the GP have been negative. How would you investigate this patient?**

A. I would first take a general and focused urological history. Given the ethnic background of the patient, the chronicity of the symptoms and the associated malaise, I am concerned that there may be an underlying history of urinary tuberculosis (TB). However, recurrent UTIs, stones and interstitial cystitis should be considered in the differential diagnosis.

I would specifically ask about previous exposure to TB, loss of appetite, fever, night sweats, loin pain, haematuria and suprapubic pain. I would then ask about a past history of pulmonary TB and renal stones. I would want to exclude any underlying conditions that might result in an immunocompromised state, such as diabetes mellitus, steroid use and HIV status.

In the examination, I would specifically record the patient's temperature and the presence or absence of any lymphadenopathy. A general examination of the chest and abdomen is mandatory, as well as a specific examination of the genitalia. I would then perform a dipstick urinalysis and send the urine off for formal microscopy and culture and sensitivity (C&S) if required. I would also request baseline blood tests (including full blood count, U&Es, ESR and LFTs). I would then ask for radiological tests, including a chest X-ray, a plain X-ray of the kidneys, ureters and bladder (KUB), and then a renal tract ultrasound scan with a formal post-void residual.

Q. **The dipstick urinalysis shows blood and WBCs, but no nitrites. What would be your next step in the investigation process?**

A. I would send the urine for cytology and arrange for three early-morning urine (EMU) samples to be sent for acid-fast staining and TB culture.

Q. **Why would you send three samples and why would the samples need to be obtained in the early morning?**

A. The organism that causes TB is excreted only intermittently in the urine, and therefore sending multiple samples of urine that has been standing in the bladder overnight gives the best chance of obtaining a positive yield.

Q. **How are early-morning urine samples processed? Why is the Gram stain not used?**

A. The smear made of the urine sample is stained using the Ziehl–Neelsen stain to look for acid-fast bacilli, and the specimen is also cultured using Lowenstein–Jensen culture medium. The causative organism of TB, *Mycobacterium tuberculosis* (an obligate aerobic rod, which is not suitable for Gram staining due to the high lipid content of the cell wall), is a slow-growing organism, and cultures may take 6–8 weeks to grow.

Q. **How is acid-fast staining performed? What is the basis behind this stain?**

A. Acid-fast staining may be performed in the following way. First, a fixed smear of the bacteria is covered on a slide with a piece of blotting paper. This is then stained with carbol fuchsin for 2 minutes. The blotting paper is then removed and the stain is decolourised with a mixture of HCl and ethanol for 10–15 seconds and rinsed. The stain is then restained with crystal violet for 1 minute and rinsed again.

When viewed under oil immersion, acid-fast cells appear pink, whereas non-acid-fast cells appear purple.

Q. **Are there any other investigations that can be used to potentially confirm the presence of TB?**

A. Yes. A molecular biological technique known as polymerase chain reaction (PCR), which uses pooled urine samples to amplify *M. tuberculosis* species-specific DNA by *in-vitro* enzymatic replication, is also available.

Q. **Does the tuberculin test have a role in the diagnosis of urinary TB?**

A. This is a skin test that consists of an intradermal injection of a purified protein derivative of *M. tuberculosis*. A positive result suggests exposure to TB, although not necessarily an active infection. The importance of the test is that in a patient with suspected TB, a positive tuberculin test is consistent with the diagnosis, and a negative test excludes it.

Q. **How is TB acquired?**

A. Primary TB is usually acquired in childhood by inhalation of infected droplets resulting in deposition of bacilli in the lungs. In immunocompetent individuals, this primary infection is self-limiting or subclinical. Clinical features may later develop as post-primary manifestations at times of reduced immunity. The spread of infection from the lungs to the urinary system is haematogenous and starts in the kidney, from where it spreads by direct extension to the ureters and bladder. In the genital tract, the primary site of involvement by haematogenous spread is the epididymis in males and the fallopian tubes in females, from where it may spread by direct extension to adjacent organs such as the testes, prostate and uterus.

Q. **What are the pathological manifestations of urinary TB?**

A. The pathognomonic lesion of TB is a caseating granuloma, which consists of Langhans' giant cells surrounded by lymphocytes and fibroblasts. The healing of these lesions results in fibrosis and calcification. This is the reason for the scarring, calcification and parenchymal destruction and distortion that are seen with healed TB. The kidney classically becomes small, shrunken and distorted, and in extreme cases this results in 'autonephrectomy.' The calyceal necks as well as the ureters may develop strictures, most commonly in the region of the vesico-ureteric junction (VUJ). There may be distortion of ureteric orifices (the so-called 'golf-hole' appearance), leading to reflux (VUR). In the bladder, active lesions show bullous oedema, ulceration and haemorrhage. Chronic lesions in the bladder may have a discrete stellate appearance, or the whole bladder may become small and fibrotic (thimble bladder).

Q. **What is the investigation in Figure 9.1 and what does it demonstrate?**

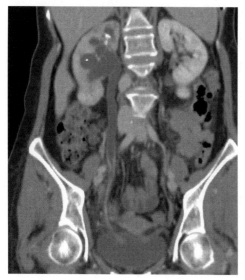

Figure 9.1

A. Figure 9.1 is a coronal reconstruction of a post-contrast CT scan of the abdomen showing right renal upper pole cortical atrophy, linear calcification in the upper pole calyx with infundibular stenosis, lower pole hydronephrosis and a dilated proximal ureter with a long distal ureteric stricture.

Q. What is the radiological investigation of choice?

A. I would ideally request a CT urogram or an IVU to assess the anatomy, the presence of calcification, parenchymal destruction or areas of narrowing.

Q. How would you manage this patient?

A. In my experience, genito-urinary TB is still rare and hence management may be complicated. Thus I believe the patient is best managed in a multi-disciplinary team setting involving shared care between urologists, microbiologists and respiratory physicians. The mainstay of management is usually medical treatment with multi-drug antituberculous therapy with isoniazid (INH), rifampicin, ethambutol and pyrazinamide for 2 months followed by INH and rifampicin for a further 4 months.

Q. Why is TB treated with three or four drugs?

A. Multi-drug anti-TB regimens are used to achieve prompt bacterial eradication, to decrease the duration of therapy and to decrease the likelihood of development of drug-resistant organisms.

Q. Can you describe the names, dosages and common side-effects of anti-tuberculous drugs?

A. The names, dosages and common side-effects of anti-tuberculous drugs are listed in Table 9.2.

Table 9.2 Names, dosages and common side-effects of anti-TB medication

Drug	Dose	Common side-effects
Isoniazid (INH)	5 mg/kg body weight	Hepatotoxicity, peripheral neuropathy (prevented by adding vitamin B6 10–25 mg daily)
Rifampicin	10 mg/kg body weight	Hepatotoxicity, orange discoloration of urine
Pyrazinamide	20 mg/kg body weight	Hepatotoxicity, arthralgia
Ethambutol	20 mg/kg body weight	Retrobulbar neuritis, reduced visual acuity, altered colour vision with reduced red–green discrimination

Q. Is there a role for the use of steroids in the management of urinary TB?

A. Steroids are indicated in cases of ureteric stricture that do not respond to anti-tuberculous therapy alone in 4–6 weeks on serial IVU or CT urogram.

Q. What are the radiological manifestations of genito-urinary TB?

A. Radiologically the following may be seen: small shrunken kidneys, calyceal distortion, infundibular stenosis, cavitation, calcification, ureteric dilatation proximal to a VUJ stricture, multiple ureteric strictures or a contracted and calcified bladder. Pelvic calcification may be present secondary to calcification of vas, seminal vesicle or prostate.

PYELONEPHRITIS

Q. A 47-year-old man is brought to A&E with high fever and severe right loin pain. How would you manage this case?

A. This is a urological emergency and I would see the patient myself, in A&E, without delay. On arrival, I would resuscitate him using basic principles of advanced life support. I would administer 100% high-flow oxygen, insert two large-bore venflons, taking blood for full blood count, U&Es, CRP, clotting and blood cultures. In addition, I would ensure that he is catheterised and a catheter specimen of urine (or a prior MSU) is sent for urine dipstick and subsequent microscopy and C&S. The patient should be provided with adequate analgesia.

I would then take a general and focused urological history asking specifically for a history of dysuria, haematuria, recent urological intervention or a past history of stones. I would also ask questions relating to a non-urological cause (gastrointestinal or respiratory symptoms). It is important to establish the patient's immune status (i.e. diabetes, steroid use, HIV status).

Upon examination, I would record the patient's mental state, pulse, blood pressure, temperature, respiration and oxygen saturation. A full and thorough examination is then required to look for a septic focus, including examination of the chest, abdomen, loins and genitalia, and a rectal examination (for prostatic tenderness).

After ensuring that he is appropriately resuscitated with IV fluids, I would commence the patient on broad-spectrum IV antibiotics. In my practice, I initially give gentamicin (3–7 mg/kg) together with a second-generation cephalosporin. Subsequent antibiotic treatment is reviewed according to culture results, microbiology advice and the clinical situation. Clearly, such a patient would be admitted for inpatient parenteral antibiotic treatment and observation. In my practice, I seek the early assistance of the microbiologist and, if necessary, HDU/ITU anaesthetist colleagues, to help in the multi-disciplinary management of these patients.

Q. What is systemic inflammatory response syndrome (SIRS)?

A. It is a response to a variety of infectious (sepsis) or non-infectious (burns, pancreatitis) stimuli. Two of the criteria listed in Table 9.3 are required.

Table 9.3 Criteria for diagnosis of systemic inflammatory response syndrome

Body temperature	> 38°C
	or
	< 36°C
Heart rate	> 90 beats/min
Respiratory rate	> 20 breaths/min
	or
	$paCO_2$ < 32 mmHg (< 4.3 kPa)
	or
	need for mechanical ventilation
White cell count	> 12 000 cells/mm³ or < 4000 cells/mm³ or > 10% immature (band) forms

Q. What is the definition of sepsis?

A. Sepsis is defined as proven infection causing SIRS.

Q. What is the definition of severe sepsis?

A. Severe sepsis is defined as sepsis with evidence of organ dysfunction (e.g. confusion, lactic acidosis, oliguria).

Q. What is the definition of septic shock?

A. Septic shock is defined as sepsis-induced hypotension (systolic blood pressure < 90 mmHg) that persists despite adequate fluid resuscitation.

Q. What is the definition of refractory septic shock?

A. Refractory septic shock is defined as septic shock that lasts for > 1 hour and does not respond to fluid administration or pharmacological intervention.

Q. What is your understanding of the pathogenesis of sepsis?

A. The major pathogenesis of sepsis is secondary to the presence of endotoxins released by Gram-negative bacteria in the circulation. This in turn results in a cascade of events resulting in release of mediators such as TNFα, interleukins (IL-2, IL-6, IL-8) from target cells (e.g. neutrophils, macrophages, lymphocytes and plasma cells), and activation of the kinin system, complement system and fibrinolytic system. These events result in widespread microvascular injury, tissue ischaemia and clinical manifestations of sepsis.

Q. Unfortunately, despite your initial management, the patient's blood pressure is falling. What would you do now?

A. I would acknowledge that this patient is very unwell. In order to manage this patient effectively, further treatment should take place in an ITU setting and would include consideration of vasopressors, inotropes, steroids and recombinant human activated protein C. Once the patient is more haemodynamically stable, radiological investigations should be organised to identify the source of sepsis, and steps should be taken to eradicate it.

Q. What imaging would you like to arrange?

A. I would initially request an ultrasound scan of the renal tract.

Q. Ultrasound scanning shows strong focal echoes in the right renal parenchyma without acoustic shadowing. What would you do now?

A. This is not diagnostic, although hydronephrosis (infected obstructed kidney) has been excluded, I would therefore organise a CT scan of the abdomen with contrast, provided that there are no contraindications (e.g. renal failure).

Q. The CT scan is shown in Figure 9.2. Can you describe this? What is the likely diagnosis?

A. Figure 9.2 is an unenhanced axial CT scan of the abdomen showing air-fluid levels and debris in the right renal pelvis suggestive of an emphysematous pyelonephritis (EPN).

Q. What is EPN?

A. It is an acute necrotising parenchymal and perirenal infection caused by gas-forming organisms. It commonly occurs in diabetics. Other associated conditions include urinary tract obstruction, stones and impaired immunity.

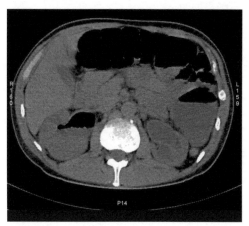

Figure 9.2

Q. **What is this condition commonly caused by?**

A. The organisms that are most commonly isolated include *E. coli* and *Klebsiella*. However, EPN may also be associated with *Proteus*, *Pseudomonas* and *Streptococcus infection*.

Q. **What is the pathogenesis of EPN?**

A. Unfortunately, this is a poorly understood process. The possible mechanisms that lead to accumulation of gas include a mixed acid fermentation of glucose by bacteria and an overwhelming local inflammation, coupled with slow transport of the end products due to diabetic microangiopathy. The analysis of accumulated gas has shown to include nitrogen, hydrogen, carbon dioxide and oxygen.

Q. **Are you aware of any different types of EPN and what is the significance of this?**

A. EPN may be classified on the basis of the CT appearance into type I and type II. Type I is classically characterised by gross parenchymal destruction with either absence of fluid collection or presence of streaky or mottled gas radiating from the medulla to the cortex. Type II EPN is associated with a confined, bubbly or loculated intra-renal gas pattern, and the presence of renal or perirenal fluid or gas within the collecting system. The differentiation is important because type I EPN is associated with a higher mortality rate, of up to 60%, compared with around 20% for type II.

Q. **Four days after treatment in the ITU, the patient is still not better. What can you do next?**

A. In this patient, the CT does not show any evidence of obstruction or a large perirenal fluid collection. Therefore the next step would be a nephrectomy. The functional status of the contralateral kidney will determine the involvement of nephrologists. In the presence of obstruction or perirenal fluid collection, percutaneous drainage may stabilise the patient, allowing complete urological work-up and deferred nephrectomy.

Q. **Figure 9.3 shows a CT scan from a different patient whose symptoms have not resolved with conservative treatment. What does it demonstrate?**

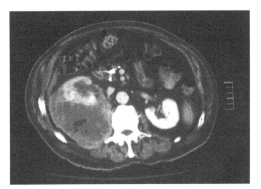

Figure 9.3

A. This is an axial CT scan with contrast of the abdomen showing a large right-sided collection in and around the kidney. The collection distorts and enlarges the renal contour, infiltrates peri-nephric fat and extends into the psoas muscle. The normal renal collecting system fat has been obliterated by the process. This is highly indicative of a perinephric abscess.

Q. What is your management plan?

A. Surgical drainage, or nephrectomy if the kidney is non-functioning or severely infected, is the classic treatment. However, more recently renal ultrasound and CT have made percutaneous aspiration and drainage of small perirenal collections possible. In this case, I would consider percutaneous drainage to be contra-indicated because it is a large abscess cavity which is likely to be filled with thick, purulent fluid. Moreover, percutaneous drainage might be more appropriate if this was a single kidney or single functioning kidney.

Q. How would you differentiate a case of acute pyelonephritis clinically from a perinephric abscess?

A. The literature suggests that most patients with uncomplicated pyelonephritis are symptomatic for less than 5 days before hospitalisation, whereas most of those with perinephric abscesses are symptomatic for longer than 5 days. Moreover, patients with acute pyelonephritis do not usually remain febrile for longer than 4 days once appropriate antimicrobial agents have been started. In contrast, patients with a perinephric abscess often have fevers for on average 7 days. Therefore a perinephric abscess should be suspected in patients with abdominal pain or a flank mass with a persistent fever after 4 days of antimicrobial therapy.

Q. What causes a perinephric abscess?

A. The most common causes of a perinephric abscess are secondary to the rupture of an acute cortical abscess into the perinephric space or from haematogenous spread from other sites of infection (e.g. skin). When patients develop an obstructed infected kidney (pyonephrosis) secondary to an obstructing stone, they are at high risk of developing a perinephric abscess if the obstruction is not relieved at an early stage. This is especially true in patients with immunosuppression and diabetes mellitus (30% of patients). Rarer causes include secondary infection of a perirenal haematoma or infection from nearby structures (bowel perforation, Crohn's disease, osteomyelitis from the thoracolumbar spine).

Q. Figure 9.4 shows a CT scan from a different patient with a history of fever, rigors and right flank pain. Can you describe the findings and suggest the likely diagnosis?

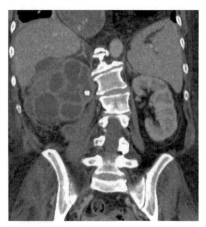

Figure 9.4

A. Figure 9.4 is a coronal reconstruction of an unenhanced CT scan of the abdomen showing an expanded non-enhancing right kidney invading into the surrounding tissues, and a stone within it suggesting a xanthogranulomatous pyelonephritis (XGP).

Q. What is XGP?
A. It is a severe chronic renal infection that results in diffuse parenchymal destruction and an enlarged non-functioning kidney usually associated with calculi.

Q. What are the organisms most commonly associated with XGP?
A. This condition is most commonly associated with infection with either *E. coli* or *Proteus* species. However, *Pseudomonas* and *Klebsiella* infection is also frequently demonstrated.

Q. What is the pathology?
A. Under the microscope, the pathology seen in cases of XGP is described as diffuse infiltration of inflammatory cells (e.g. lymphocytes, giant cells and plasma cells) within the kidney. The characteristic finding is the presence of xanthoma cells, which are lipid-laden foamy macrophages.

Q. What is the usual course of events in this condition?
A. If the patient is systemically unwell, they are usually admitted to the HDU/ITU and require intensive treatment for sepsis. On subsequent imaging, the distinction from cancer may be difficult and a nephrectomy is usually performed. If nuclear medicine function scans such as DMSA are performed, these often demonstrate that the kidney is associated with very poor or no function. Moreover, the formal diagnosis is often delayed until the post-operative histology is available.

Q. How would you perform a nephrectomy in this patient?
A. Performing a nephrectomy in a patient with XGP is usually technically very challenging, as there is generally extension of the inflammatory process into the

retroperitoneum. Furthermore, the inflammation results in tissue planes becoming very stuck and difficult to dissect. As a result, I believe that an open nephrectomy is more suitable than a laparoscopic approach, as there is a high risk of injury to the blood vessels, bowel and other neighbouring organs due to the difficult tissue planes.

CHRONIC PROSTATITIS

Q. **A 52-year-old man is referred with recurrent UTIs. What questions are important in the history?**

A. It is known that recurrent UTIs are very uncommon in male patients. Therefore in the history I would ask specifically about the presence of any lower urinary tract symptoms (LUTS), particularly a reduced or prolonged flow and a feeling of incomplete emptying, in order to exclude a urethral stricture or a large post-void residue. I would also enquire about a past or present history of renal stone disease. Other important questions in the history include the possible presence of pneumaturia, a previous history of diverticular disease, recurrent diarrhoea, or rectal bleeding which may indicate the possibility of a colo-vesical fistula. I would also ask about the presence of dysuria, storage type LUTS symptoms, perineal/suprapubic discomfort and ejaculatory problems. These may indicate underlying chronic prostatitis. In general, recurrent UTIs can be due to either reinfection or bacterial persistence. As reinfections are very uncommon in men, it is important to try to elicit symptoms which may suggest a persistent focus of infection.

Q. **The patient has been experiencing frequency, urgency, dysuria, perineal discomfort and painful ejaculation intermittently for several years. What do you think this suggests?**

A. On the basis of these symptoms, the most likely diagnosis at this stage would be chronic prostatitis. However, the latter is quite often a diagnosis of exclusion, so it is important to exclude other conditions.

Q. **What is chronic prostatitis?**

A. It is a clinical syndrome characterised by pain in the perineum, pelvis, suprapubic area or external genitalia, with a variable degree of voiding and /or ejaculatory disturbance. However, it is important to note that in chronic prostatitis there may not be either inflammation or an exclusively prostatic origin.

Q. **What would you want to do next for this patient?**

A. I would want to obtain more information from the history about the duration of his symptoms, what his most troublesome symptoms are, and how severely these symptoms are impairing his quality of life. Furthermore, I would like to find out whether he has previously had any medical or surgical treatments for the condition. To be able to effectively measure the severity of the condition and the possible effect of any treatments, I would use the NIH-CPSI questionnaire as a baseline.

After obtaining all of the necessary information in the history, I would then perform a focused physical examination of the kidneys, suprapubic region, external genitalia and prostate. This would be followed up by some basic investigations in the form of dipstick urinalysis, MSU for microscopy and C&S, X-ray of the kidneys, ureters and bladder (KUB), renal ultrasound scan, flow rates and PVR.

Q. **What is NIH-CPSI?**

A. NIH-CPSI stands for National Institutes of Health – Chronic Prostatitis Symptom Index. It is a validated questionnaire that was initially produced by the NIH/NIDDK (National Institute of Diabetes and Digestive and Kidney Diseases) Workshop on Chronic Prostatitis. It is recommended for use both in clinical practice and in research. It is a nine-item questionnaire with three main domains (pain, urinary symptoms and quality of life). It is used to establish the patient's baseline bother score which can be used to assess the need for any treatment. It can also be used to stratify patients on the basis of their predominant symptoms, and to monitor the response to treatment.[7]

Q. **How would you establish the diagnosis of chronic prostatitis?**

A. In general, chronic prostatitis is a diagnosis of exclusion and therefore it is important to exclude conditions such as BPH, urethral stricture or UTI, which may cause similar symptoms. After excluding these conditions, chronic prostatitis is diagnosed on the basis of symptoms and localisation of organisms and/or leucocytes in segmented urogenital specimens. The gold standard is the four-glass test described by Meares and Stamey, which involves microscopy and culture of urine and expressed prostatic secretion (EPS).[8]

Q. **How would you perform the four-glass test?**

A. In my practice, I perform this test in a standardised manner as follows:
1. I ask whether and confirm that the patient has drunk 400 ml of water 30 minutes before the test.
2. I make sure that four sterile specimen containers are marked VB_1, VB_2, EPS and VB_3 and that their lids are removed.
3. The glans penis is exposed and the foreskin is kept retracted throughout the test.
4. I cleanse the glans penis with a soap solution and then remove the soap with sterile gauze.
5. I make sure that the first 10–15 ml of urine are collected in the container marked VB_1.
6. I then ask the patient to pass the next 100–200 ml of urine into the toilet, and then collect the subsequent 10–15 ml in the container marked VB_2.
7. I then ask the patient to bend forward holding the container marked EPS near their urethral meatus.
8. I then massage the prostate until a few drops of prostatic secretion are collected in the EPS container.
9. Immediately after the prostatic massage, I ask the patient to again urinate and collect the first 10–15 ml of urine in the container marked VB_3.

Q. **How are the results of the four-glass test interpreted?**

A. I ensure that all four specimens are sent off for formal microscopy and culture. A positive VB_1 or VB_2 indicates urethritis and cystitis, respectively. A diagnosis of chronic prostatitis is made in the presence of organism(s) and/or leucocytes in the EPS or VB_3 specimen.

Q. Are you aware of any alternative methods of diagnosis to the four-glass test?

A. An alternative method is the pre- and post-massage test (PPMT) proposed by Nickel. It is a less tedious, time-consuming and expensive, but equally effective, modification of the four-glass test. This test involves microscopy and culture of a pre- and post-prostatic massage urine sample, with a positive post-massage sample indicating the possibility of chronic prostatitis.

Q. The four-glass test in this patient shows leucocytes in EPS, but no organisms. What does this result mean?

A. This result is consistent with a diagnosis of type IIIA prostatitis.

Q. What types of prostatitis are you aware of?

A. The contemporary classification of prostatitis is the NIH classification (1995), which divides prostatitis into the following categories:
- type I – acute bacterial prostatitis (acute bacterial infection)
- type II – chronic bacterial prostatitis (recurrent bacterial infection)
- type III – chronic non-bacterial prostatitis/chronic pelvic pain syndrome (CPPS) (no demonstrable infection)
  - Type IIIA – inflammatory (WBCs in semen/EPS/post-prostatic massage urine)
  - Type IIIB – non-inflammatory (no WBCs in semen/EPS/post-prostatic massage urine)
- type IV – asymptomatic inflammatory prostatitis.

Q. How is prostatitis caused?

A. The aetiology of prostatitis is poorly understood. It is likely that there are multiple factors operating not only in different patients, but also within an individual patient. The proposed aetiological factors include infection, chemical irritation, dysfunctional high-pressure voiding, intraductal reflux, neuromuscular disturbances and altered immunity. Many experts believe that there is a link between chronic prostatitis and interstitial cystitis. Even when the triggering factors are not known, the resultant inflammatory process causes tissue oedema and intraprostatic pressure, leading to local hypoxia and varied mediator-induced tissue damage. It is proposed that this in turn leads to altered neurotransmission in sensory nerve fibres, resulting in pain and other symptoms associated with the condition.

Q. How would you manage this patient?

A. I would manage this patient according to his predominant symptoms and their impact on his quality of life. It is imperative to have a long, frank discussion with the patient to reassure him about the benign nature of the condition and provide an explanation about the lack of unequivocal evidence in favour of any treatment. The goal should be symptom control rather than eradication, and the management should be multi-modal, of an appropriate duration and incremental in nature.

    The cornerstones of management are antibiotics, anti-inflammatories and alpha-blockers. I would start the patient on a combination of antibiotics and an NSAID, and if there was an improvement within 2 weeks, I would continue these agents for 6 weeks.

Q. **Which antibiotics are particularly suitable for chronic prostatitis and why?**

A. I regularly use either quinolones, tetracyclines, azithromycin, trimethoprim or amoxycillin. Quinolones and tetracyclines are particularly useful as they show good penetration and bioavailability into the prostate with oral as well as parenteral administration, and are likely to be effective against the usual pathogens.

Q. **Is there any evidence that using antibiotics in a patient when there is no evidence of infection is helpful?**

A. There is a lack of strong evidence that antibiotics are of any benefit. The treatment strategies used in the management of this condition are based on expert opinion panels. It is generally believed that even in culture-negative cases, there may be an underlying sub-clinical infection with *Chlamydia*, *Ureaplasma* or other fastidious organisms. Thus a trial of an agent such as a tetracycline seems sensible.

Q. **There is no response to these agents within 2 weeks. What would you do next?**

A. I would continue the NSAID for a total of 6 weeks and also consider adding in an alpha-blocker, which I would advise the patient to take for at least 3 months.

Q. **Unfortunately, the symptoms are only partly relieved. Are you aware of any other options?**

A. The NSAID can be replaced with a muscle relaxant such as diazepam or baclofen, or a tricyclic antidepressant, and I would counsel the patient with regard to considering regular prostatic massage on a bi- or tri-weekly basis for 6 to 12 weeks, depending on the response.

Q. **How is prostatic massage believed to work?**

A. The benefits of prostatic massage are believed to be derived from a combination of several factors, including expression of inspissated prostatic secretions, relief of pelvic muscle spasm, physical disruption of any protective biofilm (see below), and improved circulation and thus penetration of antibiotics.

Q. **In your clinical experience, do you believe that it works?**

A. In my experience, the results of prostatic massage are variable. Unfortunately, the benefit has not been shown in the setting of a randomised controlled trial, but there are case studies and anecdotal reports that suggest some symptomatic relief in a quarter to a third of patients.

Q. **What is a biofilm?**

A. A biofilm is a complex aggregation of organisms on a solid substrate, protected by an extracellular mucopolysaccharide matrix in an aqueous environment.

EPIDIDYMO-ORCHITIS

Q. **You have been called to A&E to review a 30-year-old man who is presenting with a few hours' history of pain in the scrotum. What is important in the history?**

A. I would see this patient without delay as this is a urological emergency. The main differential diagnoses in this situation are trauma, testicular torsion and epididymo-orchitis. I would ask about a history of trauma, similar self-limiting episodes in the past, mode of onset, exact duration of symptoms and any other associated symptoms such as fever, dysuria, urethral discharge and urinary symptoms. I would also take a thorough past sexual history, including any recent unprotected casual sexual contact.

Q. The patient is sexually active and has no long-term lower urinary tract symptoms. The pain started yesterday with some chills and dysuria. What is important in the examination of this patient?

A. The history is consistent with epididymo-orchitis. I would perform a general survey to exclude features of sepsis such as high-grade fever, tachycardia, tachy-pnoea and mental confusion, and then proceed to a local examination of the genitalia to elicit signs of inflammation and exclude a missed torsion and abscess formation.

Q. How would you distinguish between torsion and epididymo-orchitis?

A. It is sometimes difficult to distinguish between epididymo-orchitis and torsion clinically, and I have a low threshold for exploring the patient unless there are obvious features to suggest an infection. The history of a sudden onset of pain and an absence of urinary symptoms tends to suggest a torsion. Similarly, the demonstration of redness and raised local temperature, at least early in the course of the illness, is more likely in epididymo-orchitis. A urethral discharge is suggestive of epididymo-orchitis. In early torsion, actual twists in the spermatic cord may be palpable, and elevation of the affected side of the scrotum relieves the pain in epididymo-orchitis, but aggravates it in torsion. However, if there is any doubt, one must surgically explore the patient.

Q. Elevation of the affected side of the scrotum relieves the pain. What is this finding called and how reliable is it?

A. It is called Prehn's sign. It is not particularly reliable, and I would not base my decision to surgically explore the patient or otherwise solely on this finding.

Q. The history and examination do indeed point towards epididymo-orchitis. What is the likely cause in this patient?

A. The likely cause is a sexually acquired chlamydial or gonococcal infection, either singly or in combination. Gonococcal infection is more common in homosexual men.

Q. How would you manage the patient?

A. I would investigate him with urinalysis, urine culture, and Gram staining and culture of any urethral discharge. I would also send off baseline blood tests, including an full blood count, U&Es and CRP. I would then manage him with bed rest, scrotal support, analgesics and antibiotics.

Q. What might you see on Gram staining of the urethral discharge in gonococcal infection?

A. Gram-negative intracellular diplococci.

Q. On investigation, how may chlamydial infection be diagnosed in the absence of a urethral discharge?

A. Detection of DNA of *Chlamydia trachomatis* is now possible by performing polymerase chain reaction on a first-void urine sample.

Q. **Which antibiotic would you use?**

A. I usually treat epididymo-orchitis in a young man with ciprofloxacin (500 mg twice daily) and doxycycline (100 mg twice daily) for at least 2 weeks.

Doxycycline covers chlamydial infection and ciprofloxacin covers gonococcal infection.

However, it should be noted that there is increasing resistance of gonococcal infection to ciprofloxacin, penicillins and tetracyclines. Thus current first-line treatment in those with a confirmed infection with *Neisseria gonorrhoeae* is an immediate dose of oral cefixime 400 mg.

(In addition, if chlamydial or gonococcal infection is diagnosed, sexual contacts must be traced and treated.)

Q. **Unfortunately, this patient is allergic to doxycycline. What antibiotic can you give him as an alternative for chlamydial infection?**

A. As he is allergic to doxycycline, I would use an immediate dose of 1 g of azithromycin instead.

Q. **If this man was 67 instead of 30 years of age, would your approach be any different?**

A. Yes, in that age group the most likely cause of epididymo-orchitis is an ascending urinary tract infection as a result of bladder outflow obstruction, and the likely organism is *E. coli* (i.e. Gram-negative enteric organisms are the commonest cause of epididymo-orchitis in this age group). I would therefore treat him with a course of ciprofloxacin without doxycycline. I would ask specifically about any preceding lower urinary tract symptoms and their impact on the patient's quality of life. After the infection had settled I would investigate his lower urinary tract with uroflowmetry and post-void residual ultrasound scanning of the bladder. I could then address any abnormalities that might be seen, and therefore attempt to prevent any recurrence of the infection.

Q. **Four days after the initiation of treatment, the patient is not getting better, and in fact the pain is getting worse. What would you do?**

A. I would check the patient's compliance with medication, chase the culture result and modify the antibiotic regime if indicated. I would also arrange a scrotal ultrasound scan to exclude an abscess.

Q. **What does the ultrasound scan in Figure 9.5 show?**

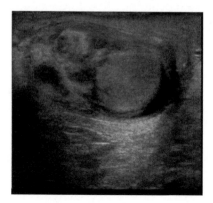

Figure 9.5

A. The ultrasound scan in Figure 9.5 demonstrates a small hydrocele surrounding a relatively normal-looking testis and a thick expanded epididymal head with fluid levels suggestive of an epididymal abscess.

Q. What would you do now?

A. I would advise the patient that the infection has unfortunately got worse and has now developed into an abscess. After appropriate counselling and obtaining consent, I would arrange for the patient to undergo incision and drainage of the abscess under a general anaesthetic. It is important to explain to the patient that, despite the drainage, the infective process may continue or may indeed require an orchidectomy at the time of drainage if there is severe infection that has spread into the testicle itself. It may also be necessary to leave the wound open with or without a drain.

ACKNOWLEDGEMENTS

We are very grateful to Dr Clare Allen (Consultant Radiologist, University College London Hospitals) for providing the radiology images to complement this chapter.

REFERENCES

1. Grabe M *et al*. EAU Guidelines on Urological Infections 2009. www.uroweb.org/fileadmin/tx_eauguidelines/2009/Full/Urological_Infections.pdf (accessed 31 October 2009).

2. Kass EH. Bacteriuria and pyelonephritis of pregnancy. *Arch Intern Med* 1960; **105:** 194–8.

3. Stamm WE *et al*. Management of urinary tract infections in adults. *NEJM* 1993; **329:** 1328–34.

4. Warren JW *et al*. Guidelines for antimicrobial treatment of uncomplicated acute bacterial cystitis and acute pyelonephritis in women. Infectious Diseases Society of America (IDSA). *Clin Infect Dis* 1999; **29:** 745–58.

5. Melekos MD *et al*. Post-intercourse versus daily ciprofloxacin prophylaxis for recurrent urinary tract infections in premenopausal women. *J Urol* 1997; **157:** 935–9.

6. Harding GK *et al*. Long-term antimicrobial prophylaxis for recurrent urinary tract infection in women. *Rev Infect Dis* 1982; **4:** 438–43.

7. Litwin MS *et al*. The National Institutes of Health chronic prostatitis symptom index: development and validation of a new outcome measure. Chronic Prostatitis Collaborative Research Network. *J Urol* 1999; **162:** 369–75.

8. Meares EM *et al*. Bacteriologic localization patterns in bacterial prostatitis and urethritis. *Invest Urol* 1968; **5:** 492–518.

Chapter 10
Urinary tract stones

Mark Rochester and Oliver Wiseman

STAGHORN STONES

Q. A 44-year-old woman presents with a 6-month history of recurrent urinary tract infections and occasional left loin ache. A recent midstream urine culture grew *Proteus mirabilis* 10^5 cfu/ml with > 200 leucocytes. Her GP has requested an ultrasound scan of the renal tract and a plain KUB (kidneys, ureters and bladder) X-ray. What does the KUB X-ray in Figure 10.1 show?

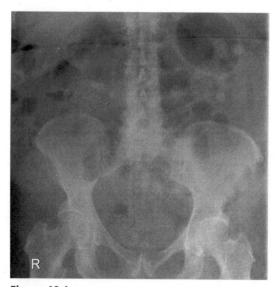

Figure 10.1

A. This shows a large left staghorn calculus and upper-third right ureteric calculus.

Q. **What further investigations are required?**
A. This woman should have urine sent for culture and sensitivity in the first instance, and blood for full blood count, U&Es, calcium and urate and a urine spot test for

cystine. Imaging to define the stone burden and calyceal anatomy, and also split renal function is then required prior to planning definitive treatment.

Q. **Which imaging modalities would you use and why?**

A. The choice of imaging to determine burden and anatomy varies among endourologists, but the two options are CT or IVU. The advantages of each type of study are discussed elsewhere in this chapter.

The function of the affected kidney is determined by renography, typically a ^{99m}Tc DMSA (^{99m}Tc dimercaptosuccinic acid) renogram. DMSA is a protein that is actively extracted and bound by functioning renal tubules, with very little filtered. It is the drug of choice for high-quality cortical imaging. The standard dose is 100 MBq. Images are taken 2–3 hours later with a gamma camera, or after a longer interval in the presence of renal failure. Posterior and posterior oblique views are taken.

Q. **Should the left staghorn renal calculus be treated or left alone? Justify your answer.**

A. The case for a more aggressive approach to staghorn calculi was outlined in a paper by Blandy and Singh.[1] This paper was presented in three parts.

Part 1

The first part of the paper was a post-mortem study. The authors retrospectively studied 8996 consecutive post-mortems. Only 9 staghorns were discovered, of which 5 had caused severe symptoms and were thought to have contributed to the death of the patients. The authors concluded that 'the notion of an incidentally discovered silent staghorn is false.'

Part 2

The second part of the paper concerned the conservatively managed staghorn calculus. A total of 60 staghorns were identified retrospectively over the period 1955–75, in patients from whom stones were not removed, of whom 20 had early nephrectomy. Of 40 patients observed, 16 went on to develop pyonephrosis and had drainage problems and difficult nephrectomies with a high mortality. Overall, 17 of 60 patients (28%) died during follow-up (mostly from renal failure). All of the others were said to have had pain and infection.

Part 3

The final section of the paper described a case study of surgical removal of staghorn calculi. A total of 152 staghorns were found in 125 patients in this retrospective study. The authors described stone 'clearance' in 80%, and 'dust' only remaining in a further 5%. The mortality rate was 7% during follow-up.

The authors concluded that there is no such clinical entity as a 'silent staghorn', based on the post-mortem study. Furthermore, they stated that long-term survival is better in those treated surgically (mortality rate of 7%) than in those managed conservatively (mortality rate of 28%).

Critical analysis of this paper allows the following points to be raised. It is a simple message which has been supported by subsequent data. Reliable data concerning the fate of residual fragments are presented. However, it could be criticised for its retrospective design, and no statistical analysis was performed. Case selection error is likely, and the autopsy data may be incomplete. For example, 5 symptomatic staghorns are referred to in Part 1, but 24 deaths are cited in Parts 2 and 3. Furthermore, almost 50% of the staghorns found in the autopsy study were asymptomatic, which possibly does not support the authors' first conclusion. Complications of surgery were probably underestimated due to the retrospective design of the study, and the method of assessment of renal function is not described.

Further guidance on the management of staghorn calculi has been provided by Teichman et al.,[2] who analysed retrospectively 177 consecutive staghorn calculus patients to determine the risk factors for ultimate renal deterioration and renal-cause-specific death. Over a mean follow-up period of 7.7 years, the overall rate of renal deterioration was 28%. This was associated more frequently with solitary kidneys (77% vs. 21%), previous stone disease (39% vs. 14%), hypertension, complete staghorn calculi and neurogenic bladder, as well as patients who refused treatment (100% vs. 28%). With regard to mortality, no patient with complete clearance of fragments died of renal-related causes, compared with 3% of those without clearance of fragments and 67% of those who refused treatment, which compares favourably with the earlier findings of Blandy and Singh.

Q. **The patient opts for PCNL. What are the indications and contraindications for this procedure?**

A.

Indications
- Stone size:
  - stones > 3 cm in diameter
  - renal pelvis stones > 2 cm in diameter
  - lower pole stones > 1 cm in diameter
  - staghorn stones.
- Obstruction:
  - the presence of an anatomical abnormality that will prevent stone fragments from passing spontaneously, especially where ESWL is usually contraindicated.
- Anatomical considerations:
  - abnormal renal anatomy such as horseshoe kidney or calyceal diverticular stones
  - abnormal patient anatomy such as kyphoscoliosis or obesity preventing ESWL.
- Failed ESWL/ureteroscopy (URS).
- Stones associated with a foreign body.
- Patient choice or desire for one treatment only.

Contraindications
- Absolute:
  - uncorrected bleeding disorder
  - pregnancy

- sepsis
- poor kidney function (e.g. < 15%), where nephrectomy would be indicated
- need for coincidental open procedure.
- Relative:
  - horseshoe or ectopic kidney, where the risk of bowel injury risk is high
  - medical problems (e.g. patient at high risk for anaesthesia)
  - anterior calyceal diverticulum.

Q. **Describe how you would take informed consent for this procedure.**

A. Informed consent must include a discussion of the alternative treatment options available, as described above, the intended benefit of the proposed procedure, and the potential complications, which are listed below with approximate percentages in brackets.

Complications related to access

- Bleeding:
  - requiring transfusion (11%)
  - requiring embolisation (1%)
  - requiring nephrectomy (rare).
- Perforation of adjacent organs (bowel < 1%, pneumothorax 0–5%).
- Access failure (5%).

Complications related to stone removal

- Infection (bacteriuria, 77%; sepsis, 0.25–1.5%).
- TUR syndrome.
- Irrigant extravasation (30%).
- Renal pelvis injury.
- Residual stones (> 10%).

Others

- Pleural effusion (10%).
- Hypertension and fibrosis (late).
- Mortality (0.3%).

Q. **In this case, what is this stone likely to consist of?**

A. It is most likely to be a struvite stone, named after the nineteenth-century Russian diplomat Baron von Struve. Such stones are also referred to as triple-phosphate stones (calcium, ammonium and magnesium phosphate), infection stones or urease stones. The following conditions must coexist for crystallisation of struvite:

- alkaline urinary pH (> 7.2)
- the presence of ammonia in the urine
- the driving force is urinary tract infection with urease-producing bacteria.
- Urease-producing bacteria hydrolyse urea to ammonia molecules and carbon dioxide (*see* Figure 10.2).

High urinary pH with high ammonia concentration, abundant phosphate and magnesium lead to crystallisation of magnesium, calcium and ammonium phosphate and the subsequent formation of large branched staghorn stones.

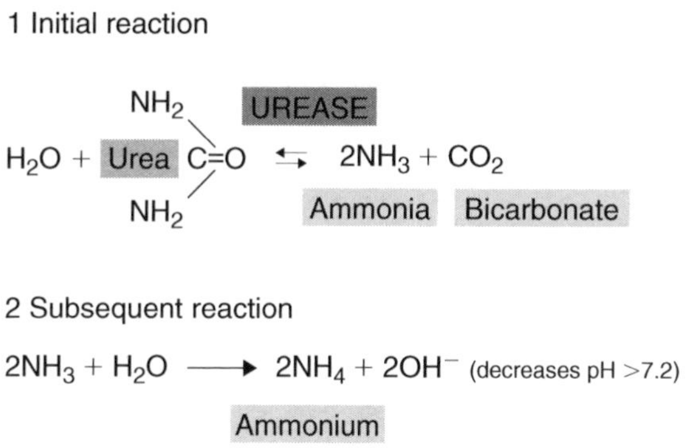

1 Initial reaction

$$H_2O + \underset{NH_2}{\underset{|}{Urea}}\ \underset{NH_2}{\overset{NH_2}{\overset{|}{C}}}{=}O \quad \overset{\text{UREASE}}{\rightleftarrows} \quad 2NH_3 + CO_2$$

Ammonia   Bicarbonate

2 Subsequent reaction

$$2NH_3 + H_2O \longrightarrow 2NH_4 + 2OH^- \text{ (decreases pH >7.2)}$$

Ammonium

Figure 10.2 Urease-producing bacteria hydrolyse urea to ammonia and carbon dioxide.

Q. **Which bacteria produce urease?**

A. • Gram-positive organisms:
  – *Proteus mirabilis*
  – *Providencia*
  – *Klebsiella*
  – *Pseudomonas.*
 • Gram-negative organisms:
  – *Staphylococcus.*
 • Mycoplasma:
  – *Ureaplasma urealyticum.*

LOWER POLE STONES

Q. **A 51-year-old man is referred to the one-stop haematuria clinic with occasional left loin ache and microscopic haematuria. He is otherwise well and takes no regular medication. Examination is unremarkable. His GP has requested a plain abdominal film. What does the KUB X-ray in Figure 10.3 show?**

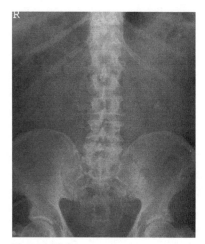

Figure 10.3

A. The X-ray in this figure shows a 1.2 cm left lower pole calculus.

Q. **He asks you what treatment options are available for the stone in the left kidney. What is the success rate of ESWL?**

A. The available treatment options for this patient include ESWL, PCNL or flexible URS.

Lingeman et al.[3] reported the results of a meta-analysis which showed that the overall stone-free rate for ESWL when applied to lower pole stones (LPS) was 59%, whereas ESWL for upper and middle pole calyces had a stone-free rate of up to 90%.

Stratified by stone size, LPS fare worse than other sites. The meta-analysis showed the following stone-free rates for LPS (using ESWL):
- up to 10 mm: 74%
- 11–20 mm: 56%
- over 20 mm: 33%.

Q. **Are there any factors that predict outcome with ESWL?**

A. Clearance after ESWL may be influenced by lower pole collecting system anatomy. Sampaio et al. first described the spatial anatomy of the lower pole as a possible factor in stone passage.[4]

Three anatomical features were described:
- the angle between the lower pole infundibulum and renal pelvis
- the diameter of the lower pole infundibulum
- the spatial distribution of the calyces.

However, different studies have addressed the calculation of predictive angles in different ways, making direct comparison of results problematic.

Keeley et al.[5] measured the lower pole infundibulopelvic (LIP) angle as the angle created by the lower border of the pelvis with the medial border of the lower pole infundibulum. A total of 116 patients underwent ESWL for LPS. The LIP angle was the only factor to achieve significance in predicting stone-free status.

Elbahnasy et al.[6] published a retrospective study of 159 patients undergoing ESWL, PCNL and URS for LPS. These authors used an alternative method for measuring the angle between two lines, namely the central point of the renal pelvis to the central point of the proximal ureter, to determine the ureteropelvic axis and the central axis of the lower pole infundibulum. In this study, all patients with three favourable factors (LIP > 70 degrees, infundibular length < 3 cm, and width > 5 mm) became stone-free. Conversely, among the patients with a combination of three unfavourable factors, only 16% became stone-free. However, these data must be interpreted with caution, as the results obtained from other studies have provided conflicting evidence.

It is intuitive that an obtuse versus an acute angle in LPS is important in fragment clearance after ESWL, but further prospective randomised studies are required to clearly determine the role of intrarenal anatomy.

Q. **Is there anything else which can be done to improve the efficiency of stone clearance after ESWL for LPS?**

A. Pace et al.[7] described percussion, diuresis and inversion (PDI) to enhance stone-free rates. Three months after ESWL, 69 patients with residual lower calyceal fragments < 4 mm were randomised to either mechanical percussion and inversion or observation for 1 month. They were treated with a mechanical chest percussor applied to the flank while inverted to greater than 60 degrees after receiving 20 mg of furosemide. A total of 35 patients underwent PDI and 34 underwent observation. In the observation group 28 patients subsequently received mechanical percussion and inversion after completing the observation period. Stone-free rates were 40% for the PDI group compared with 3% for the observation group.

Q. **Are there any studies that have compared ESWL, URS and PCNL for LPS?**

A. ESWL was compared with PCNL in the 'Lower Pole I' study, which was published in 2001.[8] This was a prospective, randomised, multi-centre trial that compared PCNL and ESWL for LPS smaller than 30 mm. A total of 128 patients were randomised to undergo PCNL (n = 60) and ESWL (n = 68). Overall 3-month stone-free rates were 95% for PCNL and 37% for ESWL. The direct comparison of stone-free rates, stratified by stone size, is shown in Table 10.1.

Table 10.1 Direct comparison of stone-free rates, stratified by stone size

	Overall	< 10 mm	11–20 mm	21–30 mm
ESWL	37%	63%	23%	14%
PCNL	95%	100%	93%	86%

Retreatment and ancillary rates in the ESWL and PCNL groups were 31% and 11%, respectively. The overall morbidity of both procedures was thought to be low.

Reported complication rates were 12% and 23% for ESWL and PCNL, respectively. Cost analysis has revealed that PCNL and ESWL were equally effective for stones less than 10 mm in diameter, and PCNL was more cost-effective for larger stones. The authors suggested that PCNL should be regarded as the primary approach for LPS larger than 10 mm. The drawback of this study is that URS was not considered.

This issue was addressed in the subsequent 'Lower Pole II' study.[9] A total of 78 patients with isolated lower pole stones 1 cm or less in diameter were randomised to ESWL or URS. The operative time was significantly shorter for ESWL than for URS. Intraoperative complications occurred in 1 ESWL case (unable to target stone) and in 7 URS cases (failed access in 5 patients and perforation in 2 patients). This study did not show a statistically significant difference in stone-free rates between ESWL and URS for LPS, even though URS was 15% better. However, with continuing improvements in ureteroscopic technology and a larger number of study participants, a different outcome might be achieved if such a study were to be repeated.

URS could be proposed as the primary approach or as a less morbid treatment modality for patients with LPS who failed ESWL, rather than proceeding to PCNL. The success rate (including 'insignificant' residual fragments) of URS for LPS is relatively high, with an average of 86% for LPS larger than 20 mm in diameter.

Anatomy of the lower pole may affect the results of URS for LPS, in a similar manner to ESWL, as an acute angle may prevent passage of the laser fibre to the stone by limiting flexion.

ESWL is the preferred initial approach for most patients with LPS smaller than 1 cm, as it is a less invasive approach, and does not require general anaesthesia. Patients who failed ESWL, and patients known to have stones resistant to ESWL, should be treated with PCNL or URS when they have considered the risks and benefits after an informed discussion with their urologist.

In contrast to the results for URS and ESWL, PCNL outcomes are independent of stone size and renal anatomy.

Q. **Should a JJ stent be placed before considering ESWL in this patient?**

A. Indications for stenting include the following:

- obstructed infected systems
- new-onset renal insufficiency.

In the past, stents were placed to allow passive dilatation of the ureter, facilitating future endoscopic evaluation and treatment. Newer smaller ureteroscopes have reduced complication rates and the need for stenting for this reason.

Stents should be considered in patients with larger stones (> 2 cm), as the rate of steinstrasse after ESWL increases with stone burden (1–4% in general vs. 10% for stones > 2 cm).

CALYCEAL DIVERTICULAR STONES

Q. **Figure 10.4 shows the KUB X-ray of a 36-year-old man. He complains of intermittent left loin pain and has microscopic haematuria. How would you treat this stone initially?**

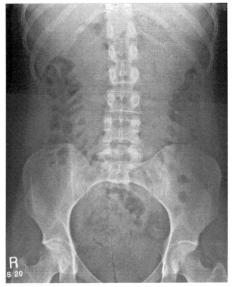

Figure 10.4 There is a 4–5 mm radiopacity in the left kidney, which is likely to be a stone.

A. The initial management of a stone of this size would be with ESWL. There is a 70% probability that stone clearance would be achieved, if it is in anatomically normal calyx.

Q. **This stone has been treated with two sessions of ESWL. Although it appeared to have partially fragmented, the fragments did not clear. What is the most likely reason for this?**

A. The most likely reason is that this stone lies within a calyceal diverticulum. Another possibility is that the stone is too hard to be fragmented with ESWL, and this might indicate that it is a calcium oxalate monohydrate stone.

Q. **What is a calyceal diverticulum, and how would you manage this stone?**

A. Calyceal diverticula are non-secretory urothelial-lined compartments that are in communication with the renal collecting system, although the point of communication is often only very narrow. While it is reasonable to manage asymptomatic diverticular stones conservatively, those that are causing pain, infection or bleeding should be treated.

   ESWL can be used to treat calyceal diverticular stones, but due to poor drainage of the fragments, the stone-free rates are low (often only 20–30%), and are not comparable with the results of PCNL, where stone-free rates are around 90%. Ureteroscopy can also be used, often with laser incision of the diverticular neck initially, allowing stone-free rates of up to 70% to be achieved.

   However, as well as clearance of the stone, obliteration of the diverticulum should be attempted. This is not possible with ESWL, and success at ureteroscopy is low. However, PCNL provides excellent access for this, and obliteration rates of up to 80% are observed. Finally, laparoscopic approaches to calyceal diverticular stones have been reported with good success.

HORSESHOE KIDNEY STONES

Q. **This 46-year-old man presented with left loin pain. What do you see in the CT slice shown in Figure 10.5?**

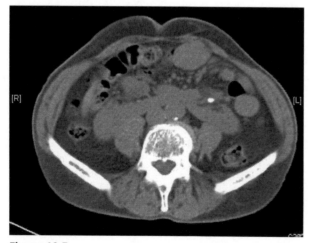

Figure 10.5

A. Figure 10.5 shows an unenhanced axial CT slice in which there is a 7 mm stone in the left renal pelvis of a horseshoe kidney.

Q. **What is the prevalence of horseshoe kidney, and how does it arise embryologically?**

A. The prevalence is approximately 1 in 400. This congenital anomaly is due to abnormal medial fusion of the metanephric blastema causing failure of ascent and rotation of the kidneys. Ascent is arrested by the inferior mesenteric artery.

Q. **What do you know about the anatomical differences between a horseshoe kidney and a normal kidney?**

A. The fused horseshoe kidney lies in a more caudal position compared with normal kidneys and, because of incomplete rotation, the renal pelvis is anterior to all of the calyces. The ureter is usually inserted high and lateral on to the renal pelvis. In a horseshoe kidney, the calyces point posteriorly with the lower pole calyces pointing caudally and medially. In a normal kidney, all of the calyces are located lateral to the renal pelvis and point laterally.

Q. **How would you manage this patient, and what problems might arise with the various management options?**

A. *ESWL* would be a reasonable first-line treatment option for this patient. Problems which might arise include difficulties with stone localisation with ultrasound, due to the medial location of the kidney and the fact that intervening bowel gas may further impair visualisation. Fluoroscopy may be difficult because of overlying bony landmarks. Even if there is good visualisation and fragmentation, dilatation of the collecting system, relative urinary stasis and the relatively high insertion of the ureter on the renal pelvis all impair the drainage of fragments. However, with good patient positioning, for a stone of this size there is a significant chance that ESWL would leave the patient stone-free.

Ureteroscopy is a viable treatment option for small symptomatic stones that have not responded to ESWL. Because of the tortuous path of the ureter and the complicated intra-renal anatomy, a flexible instrument will be needed, but if used with an access sheath to allow for continuous irrigation and the ability to remove small fragments, high stone-free rates are achievable, although not as high as in those obtained in patients with normal kidneys.

PCNL should be used for large stones (> 2 cm) and for stones where ureteroscopy or ESWL has failed. Because of the anterior location of the kidney, the track may be long, and the usual point of access is the upper pole posterior calyx. This means that in order to reach the lower pole calyces or PUJ, a flexible instrument will probably be required. The track is usually more medial than in normal kidneys, with a higher risk of retrorenal colon, but a lower likelihood of pulmonary injury. High stone-free rates of over 70% are achievable.

URETERIC STONES

Q. **A 29-year-old man presents to the emergency department with a 72-hour history of right loin pain, radiating to the groin. He is otherwise well. Examination shows that he is writhing in pain and is difficult to assess, but observations are stable and he is not pyrexial. Full blood count and U&E**

are both normal, and urine dipstick is positive for blood. What is your next step and why?

A. This patient should be given non-steroidal anti-inflammatory drugs (NSAIDs), unless these are contraindicated, in order to relieve his pain.

A Cochrane review of the management of pain in acute renal colic was published in 2005.[10] Randomised controlled trials (RCTs) comparing any opioid with any NSAID, regardless of dose or route of administration, were included. A total of 20 trials from nine countries with a total of 1613 participants were identified. Both NSAIDs and opioids led to clinically significant reductions in patient-reported pain scores. Due to unexplained heterogeneity these results could not be pooled, although 10 of 13 studies reported lower pain scores in patients who received NSAIDs. Patients who were treated with NSAIDs were significantly less likely to require rescue medication. The majority of the trials showed a higher incidence of adverse events in patients who were treated with opioids.[10]

Q. What is the imaging test of choice and why?
A. IVU and non-contrast CT have advantages and disadvantages as investigations for ureteric colic. These are outlined in Table 10.2.

Table 10.2 The advantages and disadvantages of IVU and non-contrast CT as investigations for ureteric colic

Advantages of IVU	Disadvantages of IVU	Advantages of non-contrast CT	Disadvantages of non-contrast CT
Lower radiation dose (2.5 mSv)	Time consuming	Rapid	Higher radiation dose (4.7 mSv) (particular problem in recurrent stone formers)
Images are familiar and easier to read	Other diagnoses cannot be established	Other diagnoses can be established	Images may be unfamiliar (may be difficult to distinguish phleboliths and lower ureteric stones)
Easier to arrange in emergency	Requires IV contrast (allergic reaction, toxicity in certain patients)	No IV contrast required	May be difficult to arrange in emergency
Better 'functional' information, especially in obstructed systems	Low sensitivity (60–80%)	Excellent sensitivity (95–98%) and specificity (96–100%)	Signs may be subtle, especially in obstructed systems
	Cannot always accurately measure stone size and site	Can accurately measure stone size and site	
	Can only see 90% of stones	All stones seen (except indinavir)	

Q. What is the radiation risk associated with CT and IVU?
A. Table 10.3 shows the relative radiation exposure associated with various radiological investigations.

Table 10.3 Relative radiation exposure associated with various radiological investigations of urinary tract stones

Diagnostic procedure	Typical effective dose (mSv)	Chest X-ray equivalent for effective dose	Time for equivalent dose from natural background radiation
Chest X-ray (PA)	0.02	1	2.4 days
Skull X-ray	0.07	4	8.5 days
Lumbar spine	1.3	65	158 days
IVU	2.5	125	304 days
Barium swallow	3.0	150	1.0 year
CT of KUB (non-contrast)	4.7	250	1.6 years
CT of abdomen with contrast	10.0	500	3.3 years

With regard to the associated increased risk of cancer related to such exposure, the US Food and Drug Administration has stated that the natural incidence of fatal cancer is 1 in 5. A 10 mSv dose increases this risk by 1 in 2000. Therefore an IVU of 1.5–3.0 mSv increases the risk by 1 in 10 000, whereas a CT of KUB of 4.5–5 mSv increases the risk by 1 in 4000.

Q. **How sensitive are these tests?**

A. It is accepted that the sensitivity of CT for urinary tract calculi is higher than that of IVU, with various publications suggesting that it is in the region of 95–99%, compared with 60–95% for IVU (*see* Table 10.4). Niall *et al.*[11] studied 40 patients, all of whom had CT, IVU and plain KUB. The gold standard was considered to be spontaneous passage or surgical removal of the stone.

Table 10.4 The sensitivity and specificity of various investigations[11]

	CT of KUB	IVU	Plain KUB
Sensitivity (%)	100	64	54
Specificity (%)	92	92	67
Time (minutes)	4	63	–
Alternative diagnoses	17	1	–

Q. **Are you aware of any UK studies that have examined the role of non-contrast CT in ureteric colic?**

A. One study which is often quoted as reflecting the practicalities of imaging in the UK is that of Greenwell *et al.*[12] Over a period of 1 year, patients with acute loin pain suggestive of renal colic were assessed by examination, urine analysis and unenhanced spiral CT. They were excluded if they were thought to have an infected obstructed kidney. At that time CT was available from 8.30am to 9.00pm. After hours, patients were managed symptomatically until the next day.

Definitive diagnosis was based on documented stone passage or visualisation/stone removal on retrograde studies. A total of 116 patients were studied, of whom 63 patients had calculi identified on CT, with 2 false-positive results (phleboliths) and 1 false-negative result. Seven patients (6%) had an alternative diagnosis, including RCC (*n* = 2), ureteric TCC (*n* = 1), PUJ obstruction (*n* = 1), ovarian cyst ($n = 2$) and diverticulitis ($n = 1$). The effective radiation dose was 4.7 mSv for CT and 1.5 mSv for IVU.

The authors concluded that CT allowed rapid, contrast-medium-free, anatomically accurate diagnosis of obstructing ureteric stones (with a sensitivity of 98% and specificity of 97%). They qualified this by stating that there was no information on the degree of obstruction (as there was no visualisation of delay in excretion of contrast) and no information on the urothelium (filling defects).

Reporting of CTs caused a mean delay of 9 hours in diagnosis. The authors did not advocate CT as a replacement for IVU at that time.

As urologists have become more familiar with reading CT scans, and imaging availability has increased, these concerns have diminished, and in many departments CT has replaced IVU as the investigation of choice for ureteric colic.

Q. **This patient had an IVU (*see* Figures 10.6a, 10.6b and 10.6c). What does it show?**

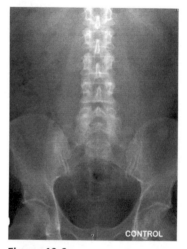

Figure 10.6a

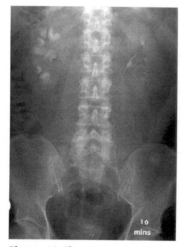

Figure 10.6b

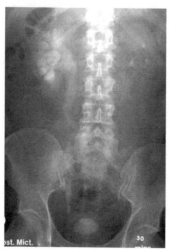

Figure 10.66

A. These are serial films from an IVU showing an 8–9 mm obstructing distal right ureteric calculus that is causing significant hydronephrosis and hydroureter.

Q. **How would you perform an elective IVU?**

A. First, I review the indication, as I have to clinically justify and authorise the procedure. Secondly, I review any contraindications, such as pregnancy and risk factors for contrast reaction (see below). Then, for an elective IVU in my practice, the patient would be given an information leaflet about bowel preparation. They are asked to switch to a low-fibre diet and 2 Senna tablets, 2 days prior to the IVU study. In addition, although they are asked to be well hydrated, no food is advised 6 hours prior to the procedure, to reduce bowel gas and decrease the potential risk of contrast-induced vomiting. Just before the start of the IVU, I make sure that I am prepared for a potential adverse reaction, with the resuscitation trolley and emergency medication readily available. The elective IVU study is then performed as follows:

- KUB X-ray (to include the upper borders of both kidneys and the lower border of the bladder)
- administration of contrast (Omnipaque 1 ml/kg depending on the protocol), after first warning the patient that they may experience a warm feeling in their arm and a metallic taste in their mouth
- immediate nephrogram
- 5-minute film (will normally see a pyelogram, but looking for abnormalities such as delayed dense nephrogram in obstruction, calyceal distortion, calyceal clubbing, irregularities of the calyces or any filling defects)
- tomograms (at 1-cm intervals – a series of three, especially in haematuria, is used to exclude an unexpected mass, and allows excellent visualisation of the renal contours, as shadows that obscure the kidneys are blurred)
- 10-minute film (with compression and release, as partial obstruction of the ureters allows distension and a better view of the ureters and the PC system; this can be done with the patient in a prone position. Contraindications to compression include obstruction, AAA, COPD and recent abdominal surgery)
- 20-minute film (full length for haematuria or stones)
- post-micturition study (allows assessment of upper tract drainage, stones in the distal ureter, bladder outflow obstruction, bladder diverticuli and mucosal lesions of the bladder)
- delayed films as necessary.

Q. **How would you perform an emergency IVU?**

A. Having reviewed the indication, to justify and authorise the procedure, I would exclude any contraindications, such as pregnancy and risk factors for contrast reaction (see below). Just before the start of the IVU, I would make sure that I am prepared for a potential adverse reaction, with the resuscitation trolley and emergency medication readily available. The emergency IVU study is then performed as follows:

- KUB X-ray (to include the upper borders of both kidneys and the lower border of the bladder)
- administration of contrast (Omnipaque 1 ml/kg), after first warning the

patient that they may experience a warm feeling in their arm and a metallic taste in their mouth)
- 20-minute film with the patient in a supine position
- post-micturition study
- delayed films as necessary.

Q. **What are the signs of obstruction on an IVU?**
A. Delayed dense nephrogram, clubbing of calyces, dilated renal pelvis/ureter and delayed excretion of contrast and extravasation of contrast.

Q. **What are the signs of obstruction on CT?**
A. Hydronephrosis, increased renal size (nephromegaly), unilateral perinephric stranding, periureteric stranding and ureteric wall oedema/soft tissue cuff/ring around stone (rim sign).

Q. **What are the adverse effects of intravenous contrast media?**
A. The Royal College of Radiologists (RCR) guidelines outline the risks of adverse effects (see Table 10.5).

Table 10.5 The risks of adverse effects of contrast media

	Ionic high osmolar media	Non-ionic low osmolar media
Non life-threatening reaction	1–2%	0.2–0.4%
Life-threatening reaction	0.2%	0.04%
Mortality	1 in 100 000	1 in 100 000
Late reaction		6%

However, this mortality rate may be an overestimate. Wysowski and Nourjah, investigators from the Division of Drug Risk Evaluation of the US Food and Drug Administration, looked at the risk of death between 1999 and 2001 using death certificate information, and quoted a rate of 1.1–1.2 per million, most often due to renal failure or allergic reaction.[13]

Adverse effects include the following:
- dose-related problems:
  - nausea and vomiting
  - cardiac arrhythmia
  - renal failure
  - pulmonary oedema
- idiosyncratic dose-unrelated anaphylactoid reactions:
  - urticaria
  - pruritus
  - facial and laryngeal oedema
  - bronchospasm
  - respiratory collapse
  - circulatory collapse.

Delayed adverse effects include the following:
- erythematous rashes
- fever, chills and flu-like symptoms
- joint pain

- headache fatigue
- abdominal pain
- diarrhoea.

Q. **A patient starts to become tachypneoic 15 seconds into an IVU, and is complaining of shortness of breath. How would you manage him?**

A. I would regard this a urological emergency, as he has most probably developed an idiosynchratic reaction/anaphylaxis. I would immediately call for the cardiac resuscitation team. In the mean time, I would resuscitate the patient according to the principles of advanced life support, securing the airway and intubating if necessary. I would then administer 100% oxygen by face mask at a rate of 15 litres/minute. I would check the pulse and blood pressure, and I would insert two large-bore venflons into each antecubital fossa and give intravenous fluids, elevating the patient's legs if he is hypotensive. I would then give adrenaline 0.5 mg intramuscular injection (1:1000 = 0.5 ml). This would be repeated again every 5 minutes depending on the patient's pulse and blood pressure. In addition, I would give intravenous chlorpheniramine 10 mg, and intravenous hydrocortisone 200 mg. If there was no improvement in the patient's clinical state, I would urgently transfer him to the HDU/ITU, in collaboration with my anaesthetist colleagues.

Note: This type of reaction simulates anaphylactic reaction, but is not mediated by antibodies and therefore is correctly termed an *anaphylactoid* reaction.

Q. **What are the risk factors for this type of reaction?**

A. The risk factors include past history of reaction, asthma, multiple allergies/atopy and severe allergy requiring therapy.

Q. **Two days after an IVU, the patient's creatinine levels double. What do you think has happened and are there any risk factors for this condition?**

A. The patient appears to have developed a chemotoxic reaction, which is defined as an increase of 25% or > 44 μmol/l in serum creatinine concentration during the first 3 days after an intravenous contrast study, in the absence of an alternative explanation. Risk factors for chemotoxic reaction include renal insufficiency, elevated baseline creatinine levels, dehydration, diabetes, age > 70 years, nephrotoxic drugs, congestive cardiac failure, myeloma and repeated administration of contrast at intervals of < 48 hours.

Q. **If this patient has type 2 diabetes mellitus and takes metformin, what important considerations are there?**

A. The main concern would be the potential precipitation of lactic acidosis, with accumulation of metformin, which is exclusively excreted via the kidneys. According to the EAU guidelines, in this patient the metformin should be withheld for 48 hours after the IVU, and only restarted if the serum creatinine concentration remains normal. In patients on metformin who require an IVU and who have impaired renal function, the metformin should be discontinued for the 48 hours prior to the study. Clearly, alternative investigations (e.g. CT KUB) should be considered. If the unfortunate situation arises in which a patient who is taking metformin with reduced renal function has an IVU performed, the patient should be kept well hydrated and metformin withheld. Regular measurements of creatinine, pH and lactate should be performed, and medical/ITU consultation undertaken as required. Interestingly, metformin in diabetic patients with renal impairment is in fact not recommended, and a discussion with the endocrine team should be arranged to consider changing the medication.

Note: The Royal College of Radiologists (RCR) of England has provided slightly different guidelines for use of intravascular contrast in patients on metformin. If serum creatinine levels are normal and less than 100 ml of low osmolar contrast media are to be used, no special precautions are needed. If serum creatinine levels are normal and more than 100 ml are to be used, metformin should be withheld for 48 hours after the procedure. If the serum creatinine levels are abnormal, first reassess the need for the procedure. If it is deemed necessary, withhold metformin for 48 hours before the procedure and at least 48 hours afterwards, checking renal function again before re-starting.

Q. Should patients with asthma be managed differently?

A. Patients with asthma are at a 6-fold increased risk of severe contrast reaction with low osmolar contrast media (LOCM) and at a 10-fold increased risk with high osmolar contrast media (HOCM). The current advice of the RCR is to defer the investigation and optimise the medical treatment if it is non-urgent, if the patient is wheezy or if they report poor control. Non-contrast alternatives should be considered, but if it is deemed to be necessary, use LOCM, arrange close medical supervision, leave the IV cannula in place for 30 minutes and have the emergency drugs box available. Prophylactic steroids are not used.

Q. A 22-year-old man would like to try conservative management in the first instance for a 5 mm distal ureteric stone. He is also aware that certain medications will help the stone to pass. However, his friends have also had stones treated with ESWL and URS. What evidence is there for the optimum management of ureteric calculi?

A. The evidence is based on the joint EAU/AUA Guideline for the Management of Ureteral Calculi, which was published in 2007.[14,15] In summary, these guidelines address a number of issues.

First, this meta-analysis concluded that the median probability of spontaneous passage of ureteric stones < 5 mm in diameter is 68%, compared with 47% for stones of diameter 5–10 mm.

Secondly, medical expulsive therapy (MET) was considered efficacious and can be recommended, specifically in patients with ureteric stones < 10 mm in diameter, whose symptoms are controlled, who are not septic and who have adequate renal reserve. With regard to specific medical treatment, 29% more patients receiving alpha-blocker therapy passed their stones than did controls, a difference which was statistically significant. In contrast, only 9% of patients who were receiving nifedipine passed their stones, as compared with controls. This difference was not statistically significant. In conclusion, alpha-blockers facilitate stone passage, whereas the effect of nifedipine is only marginal.

Finally, with regard to intervention, and the stone-free (clearance) rates of ureteric stones when treated with ESWL or with URS, the guidelines addressed proximal, mid and distal stones separately. The overall stone-free data and the breakdown for stones < 10 mm and > 10 mm in diameter are presented in Table 10.6.

Table 10.6 The overall stone-free data, and the breakdown for stones < 10 mm and > 10 mm in diameter, according to joint EAU and AUA guidelines

		ESWL (%)	URS (%)
Proximal	Overall	82	81
	< 10 mm	90	80
	> 10 mm	68	79
Middle	Overall	73	86
	< 10 mm	84	91
	> 10 mm	76	78
Distal	Overall	74	94
	< 10 mm	86	97
	> 10 mm	74	93

Briefly, for proximal ureteric stones, it appears that ESWL may be superior for stones < 10 mm in diameter, but that URS is better for stones > 10 mm. In patients with distal ureteric stones, URS is considered to be superior irrespective of size. Finally, for patients with mid-ureteric stones, the treatments are generally considered to be equivalent. Importantly, it should be understood that the data from the guidelines have been based on the 'index patient', designed to reflect the typical individual with a ureteric stone. The definition of an index patient is a non-pregnant adult with a unilateral non-cystine/non-uric acid radiopaque ureteral stone without renal calculi requiring therapy, whose contralateral kidney functions normally and whose medical condition, body habitus and anatomy allow any one of the treatment options to be undertaken.

Q. **While under observation, this patient develops a temperature of 39° C. What is your further management?**

A. An infected obstructed system is a urological emergency and must be drained expeditiously after initial resuscitation of the patient and administration of intravenous antibiotics according to local microbiology department guidelines.

The question of whether to use nephrostomy tube drainage or to pass a retrograde JJ stent under anaesthesia cystoscopically has been addressed in two studies. Pearle *et al.*[16] compared the efficacy of percutaneous nephrostomy with retrograde ureteral catheterisation for renal drainage in cases of obstruction and infection associated with ureteral calculi. A total of 42 patients presenting with obstructing ureteral calculi and clinical signs of infection were randomised to nephrostomy or stenting. There was no significant difference in the time to treatment between the two groups. Procedural and fluoroscopy times were significantly shorter in the retrograde ureteral catheterisation group. One treatment failure occurred in the percutaneous nephrostomy group, which was successfully salvaged with retrograde ureteral catheterisation. Time to normal temperature was 2.3 days in the percutaneous nephrostomy group and 2.6 days in the retrograde ureteral catheterisation group. The authors concluded that stenting and percutaneous nephrostomy both effectively relieved obstruction and infection due to ureteral calculi. Neither modality demonstrated superiority in promoting more rapid recovery after drainage. The decision as to which mode of drainage to use may be based on logistical factors, surgeon preference and stone characteristics.

In a similar study, Mokhmalji *et al.*[17] observed that patients randomised to nephrostomy tube drainage required antibiotics for a shorter time after drainage, and that this mode of drainage appeared to be superior to stent insertion, especially in those with a high temperature, male patients and juveniles. In addition, stent insertion was unsuccessful in 20% of cases, compared with an 100% success rate with percutaneous nephrostomy.

Q. **What are the advantages and disadvantages of JJ stents and nephrostomy tubes?**

A. These are listed in Table 10.7.

Table 10.7 Advantages and disadvantages of stents and nephrostomies

Advantages of stent	Disadvantages of stent	Advantages of nephrostomy	Disadvantages of nephrostomy
Resources and availability – there is no need for a radiologist, as the urologist can perform the procedure	Renal pelvis pressure still remains elevated	Rapid and maintained decrease in renal pelvis pressure is achieved	Resources and availability – a radiologist is needed
No risk of injury to adjacent organs	Usually has to be performed under general anaesthetic, which may be risky, particularly in a sick or unwell patient	Can be performed under local anaesthetic/ sedation, so a general anaesthetic is not required	Risk of injury to adjacent organs
A nephrostomy bag is not needed	Risk of ureteric manipulation and resulting bacteraemia/ ureteric injury	Avoids the need for ureteric manipulation and risk of bacteraemia/ ureteric injury	A nephrostomy bag is needed
Better 'functional' information, especially in obstructed systems	Failure rate (due to impacted stone)	Low failure rate	Signs may be subtle, especially in obstructed systems
	Cannot monitor urine output from kidney	Can monitor urine output from kidney	
	No access available for subsequent tract, if required	Access available for subsequent tract, if required	

Q. **Describe how you would obtain informed consent for ureteroscopy.**

A. Informed consent must include a discussion of the alternative treatment options available (as described above), the intended benefit of the proposed procedure, and the potential complications, which are listed below (with approximate percentages), based on complications of 3000 semi-rigid ureteroscopies performed by Geavlete et al.[18]

Intraoperative complications (3.5%)

Mucosal injury or abrasion	1.5%
False passage	1.0%
Ureteric perforation	0.6%
Extraureteric stone migration	0.2%
Ureteral avulsions	0.1%
Bleeding	0.1%

Early complications (10%)

Fever or sepsis	1.0%
Persistent haematuria	2.0%
Renal colic	2.0%
Transient VUR	4.5%

Late complications

Ureteric stricture	0.5%
Persistent VUR	Rare

Intra-operative incidents

Stone migration	4.2%
Inability to access calculi	3.7%
Trapped stone extractors	0.7%
Equipment damage	0.7%
JJ stent malpositioning	0.7%
Migrated JJ stent	0.66%

Q. **When would you insert a stent following ureteroscopy?**

A. A JJ stent is often inserted in the following circumstances:
- ureteric perforation during the procedure
- stone fragments greater than 2 mm in diameter remaining in the ureter
- if treating an impacted stone (usually the ureter is very oedematous at the site of impaction)
- prolonged manipulation within the ureter, particularly the upper one-third.

METABOLIC STONES

Q. **A 26-year-old man comes to see you after having experienced a second episode of renal colic. He has passed his stone and presents it to you. He is currently symptom-free. There is no family history of renal stones. What might the stone be made of?**

A. The majority of stones have more than one constituent, but the main constituents of stones with their relative percentages are as follows:
- calcium oxalate   70–80%
- struvite (magnesium ammonium phosphate)   10%

- uric acid   8–10%
- cystine   1–2%
- calcium phosphate   1%.

Q. **What are the two different forms of calcium oxalate stone, and how are such stones believed to form?**

A. Calcium oxalate stones occur in two different forms – calcium oxalate monohydrate (whewellite) and calcium oxalate dihydrate (weddellite). The former are much more difficult to break than the latter.

Calcium oxalate stones are believed to develop as a result of a number of factors. There is an imbalance between promoters of stone formation, which are increased, and inhibitors of stone formation, which are decreased. Thus a decreased urinary volume, decreased urinary pH, and decreased urinary citrate, magnesium and glycosaminoglycan levels, with increased urinary uric acid, oxalate and calcium levels, are all risk factors for urinary supersaturation with calcium oxalate. The more supersaturated the urine is, the higher the risk of stone formation. If the saturation is below the *solubility product*, a stone will not form. However, once the saturation increase above this level, crystal growth will occur, and crystals will aggregate, but *de-novo* nucleation is very slow. An increase in the level of inhibitors in the urine at this level may prevent stone formation. However, as the saturation of calcium oxalate in the urine increases above the *formation product*, nucleation can occur and inhibitors are not effective.

Q. **What investigations does this patient require?**

A. There is debate as to how stone formers should be evaluated metabolically. One way to approach this is to determine the patient's risk of developing a further stone, so that resources are directed to where they are likely to have the most benefit.

Thus first-time stone formers who are at lower risk of developing a further stone can undergo an abbreviated work-up, whereas higher-risk patients should have a more thorough work-up.

The following are risk factors for recurrent stone formation, which necessitate a thorough metabolic work-up:
- children
- white patients with a positive family history
- black patients
- patients with chronic diarrhoea or malabsorptive states
- history of gout
- osteoporosis
- nephrocalcinosis
- recurrent UTIs
- pathological skeletal fractures
- patients with stones composed of uric acid, cystine or struvite.

An abbreviated work-up consists of the following:
- bloods: U&Es (renal function, hypokalaemia in distal renal tubular acidosis), urate (hyperuricaemia in patients with uric acid stones), serum calcium and serum phosphate (hypercalcaemia and hypophosphataemia in patients with hyperparathyroidism)

- urine: MSU (C&S and microscopy of the sediment to look for crystals), spot cystine, urinary pH (high in infection stones, < 5.5 in patients with uric acid stones)
- stone: analysis of the stone.

An extensive work-up consists of all of the above, plus:
- 24-hour urine collections: the standard in the UK is for patients to provide two 24-hour urine collections, one in a bottle with hydrochloric acid (looking for 24-hour calcium, oxalate, phosphate, citrate and magnesium) and one plain bottle (looking for 24-hour uric acid and electrolytes and pH); 24-hour urine volume is also measured
- a dietary diary is useful for helping to address with the patient any changes that need to be made. Furthermore, some urologists would advocate the collection of a 24-hour urine sample after 3 days on a standardised diet. This allows comparison of the results with a patient's normal diet, to see which abnormalities are attributable to the diet. The standardised diet consists of avoidance of meats, as well as sodium restriction, oxalate restriction and moderate calcium restriction.

Q. **How would you explain to your patient how to perform a 24-hour urine collection?**

A. It is important to obtain a complete 24-hour collection of urine, and to ensure that the patient understands how to perform such a collection. Many will not really understand what you tell them in the clinic, and thus it is imperative to give them some written information to take home with them to read.

On the day that the patient decides that they are going to do their collection, they should wake up in the morning and immediately void into the toilet and note the time (i.e. discard first void on the day of starting the collection). Every time they pass urine for the next 24 hours, including the first void of the following day (which should be at the same time as the void into the toilet at the start of the collection), this should be collected in the bucket/collection bottle. The urine should then be kept in a cool place until it is analysed, ideally as soon as possible after the collection is complete.

Q. **What is different about the metabolic management of patients with uric acid stones?**

A. Uric acid stones are only formed in acid urine. Diet may be especially important in patients with uric acid stones, as a diet rich in purines and proteins with a high consumption of alcohol increases uric acid excretion and lowers urinary pH. Over 20% of patients who have gout will develop uric acid stones, due to hyperuricosuria.

Uric acid stones are the only type of stone that can be dissolved by medical agents. This can be successful in the majority of patients. Oral chemolysis is carried out by alkalinising the urine, preferably using potassium citrate. The dosage of agent should be determined by the pH response in the urine. In patients who have high rates of uric acid excretion, prescription of allopurinol should be considered. Finally, as with all stone formers, diuresis should be promoted by increasing fluid intake.

Q. **Tell me what you know about cystinuria.**

A. Cystine stones are caused by an autosomally recessive inherited inborn error of metabolism, such that the proximal tubular reabsorption of the dibasic amino acids **c**ystine, **o**rnithine, **l**ysine and **a**rginine (COLA) is decreased. However, of these four, cystine is the only poorly soluble amino acid, and thus these patients form only cystine stones.

Cystine stones account for about 1% of adult renal tract stones. The peak incidence of stone formation is in the second and third decades of life, but these patients develop recurrent stones, which typically have a 'ground-glass' appearance. The crystals are hexagonal.

Diagnosis is made on the basis of stone examination, microscopy of urinary sediment or measurement of urinary cystine levels. The cyanide-nitroprusside test (Brand's test) is a spot test to detect cystinuria, but in patients with a suspected diagnosis a 24-hour collection is performed, which will determine whether the patient is homozygous or heterozygous.

Medical care of these patients consists of advice to drink copious amounts of fluid, aiming for 4 or more litres of fluid intake a day. Alkalinisation of the urine to a high pH increases the solubility of cystine, and further medical treatment includes the use of complexing agents to bind with cystine to form soluble compounds. Such agents include D-penicillamine and alpha-mercaptopropionylglycine (Thiola). Finally, captopril can be used. This is a first-generation ACE inhibitor which has been shown to form a complex with cystine that is 200 times more soluble.

Surgical care of these patients is similar to that for patients with other types of stone, except that it should be noted that cystine stones are more resistant to ESWL than many other stone types.

Q. **How does Brand's test work? What levels of cystine in the urine would indicate that the patient was homozygous?**

A. The cyanide–nitroprusside test is a rapid, simple and qualitative way to determine cystine concentration. Cyanide converts cystine to cysteine. Nitroprusside then binds, causing a purple hue within 2–10 minutes. The test detects cystine levels higher than 75 mg/l. False-positive test results occur in some individuals with homocystinuria or acetonuria, and in people who are taking sulfa drugs, ampicillin or N-acetylcysteine. The normal excretion rate is 40–80 mg/day. Heterozygotes excrete 200–400 mg/day, whereas homozygotes usually excrete >600 mg/day.

Q. **What are the principles of treatment of patients with cystine stones?**

A. The main considerations are that these patients are young, will tend to have recurrent stone episodes and therefore may require multiple interventions. As such, prevention is vitally important, bearing in mind the significant risk of poor compliance.

- *Diet.* As cystine is produced from the essential amino acid methionine, attempts are made to reduce foods that contain high levels of methionine, such as red meat, fish and poultry.
- *High fluid input.* Ideally this should be more than 3–4 litres/day, as it is known that 250 mg cystine will dissolve in 1 litre of fluid.

- *Alkalinisation.* This is achieved using potassium citrate, sodium bicarbonate (NaHCO$_3$) or in some cases acetazolamide, which is a carbonic anhydrase inhibitor and thus increases HCO$_3$ excretion.
- *Oral chelators.* These drugs combine with cystine to form a soluble complex, thus preventing stone formation and possibly even dissolving existing cystine stones. They include D-penicillamine, alpha-mercaptopropionylglycine and captopril.

Q. **How would you make a clinical diagnosis of renal tubular acidosis?**

A. Patients with RTA are unable to acidify their urine, and thus the pH of the urine never goes below 5.8. Confirmation of the diagnosis requires an ammonium chloride loading test. In addition, there is a decrease in blood pH, lowered plasma bicarbonate and raised serum chloride levels. Urinary calcium and phosphate levels are raised.

Q. **Why do you obtain these findings with RTA?**

A. RTA results from impaired secretion of H$^+$ ions in the renal tubules, with too few H$^+$ ions available for adequate bicarbonate reabsorption in exchange for acid ions. Instead, chloride ions are reabsorbed and a hyperchloraemic metabolic acidosis develops, which in turn leads to resorption of apatite from bone and thus increased serum calcium levels. Hypercalciuria follows, with recurrent stone formation and often nephrocalcinosis. Only distal RTA is of importance in stone formers.

REFERENCES

1. Blandy JP *et al.* The case for a more aggressive approach to staghorn stones. *J Urol* 1976; **115**: 505–6.
2. Teichman JM *et al.* Long-term renal fate and prognosis after staghorn calculus management. *J Urol* 1995; **153**: 1403–7.
3. Lingeman JE *et al.* Management of lower pole nephrolithiasis: a critical analysis. *J Urol* 1994; **151**: 663–7.
4. Sampaio FJ *et al.* Inferior pole collecting system anatomy: its probable role in extracorporeal shock-wave lithotripsy. *J Urol* 1992; **147**: 322–4.
5. Keeley FX Jr *et al.* Clearance of lower-pole stones following shock-wave lithotripsy: effect of the infundibulopelvic angle. *Eur Urol* 1999; **36**: 371–5.
6. Elbahnasy AM *et al.* Lower caliceal stone clearance after shock-wave lithotripsy or ureteroscopy: the impact of lower pole radiographic anatomy. *J Urol* 1998; **159**: 676–82.
7. Pace KT *et al.* Mechanical percussion, inversion and diuresis for residual lower pole fragments after shock-wave lithotripsy: a prospective, single-blind, randomized controlled trial. *J Urol* 2001; **166**: 2065–71.
8. Albala DM *et al.* Lower pole I: a prospective randomized trial of extracorporeal shock wave lithotripsy and percutaneous nephrostolithotomy for lower pole nephrolithiasis – initial results. *J Urol* 2001; **166**: 2072–80.
9. Pearle MS *et al.* Prospective, randomized trial comparing shock wave lithotripsy and ureteroscopy for lower pole caliceal calculi 1 cm or less. *J Urol* 2005; **173**: 2005–9.

10. Holdgate A *et al.* Nonsteroidal anti-inflammatory drugs (NSAIDs) versus opioids for acute renal colic. *Cochrane Database Syst Rev* 2005; **2:** CD004137.

11. Niall O *et al.* A comparison of non-contrast computerized tomography with excretory urography in the assessment of acute flank pain. *J Urol* 1999; **161:** 534–7.

12. Greenwell TJ *et al.* One year's clinical experience with unenhanced spiral computed tomography for the assessment of acute loin pain suggestive of renal colic. *BJU Int* 2000; **85:** 632–6.

13. Wysowski DK *et al.* Deaths attributed to X-ray contrast media on U.S. death certificates. *Am J Roentgenol* 2006; **186:** 613–15.

14. Preminger GM *et al.* American Urological Association Education and Research, Inc; European Association of Urology. 2007 Guideline for the management of ureteral calculi. *Eur Urol* 2007; **52:** 1610–31.

15. Preminger GM. EAU/AUA Nephrolithiasis Guideline Panel. 2007 Guideline for the management of ureteral calculi. *J Urol* 2007; **178:** 2418–34.

16. Pearle MS *et al.* Optimal method of urgent decompression of the collecting system for obstruction and infection due to ureteral calculi. *J Urol* 1998; **160:** 1260–4.

17. Mokhmalji H *et al.* Percutaneous nephrostomy versus ureteral stents for diversion of hydronephrosis caused by stones: a prospective, randomized clinical trial. *J Urol* 2001; **165:** 1088–92.

18. Geavlete P *et al.* Complications of 2735 retrograde semi-rigid ureteroscopy procedures: a single-center experience. *J Endourol* 2006; **20:** 179–85.

Chapter 11
Female urology and neurourology

Rizwan Hamid, Vinay Kalsi and Julian Shah

OVERACTIVE BLADDER

Q. **A 35-year-old woman presents with urinary frequency, urgency, urgency incontinence and nocturia. How would you approach this patient's problem?**

A. I would review her in my dedicated bladder dysfunction clinic. I would like to elucidate the following points from her history:
- When did the symptoms first appear?
- Are there any exacerbating factors?
- Are there any associated obstructive symptoms or proven urinary infections?
- How many (if any) pads does she have to wear throughout the day?
- Is this problem affecting her quality of life?
- Is there any history of neurological disease?
- Has she had any previous pelvic operations?
- Is she a smoker?
- Does she drink excessive amounts of caffeinated beverages?
- What medication is she taking?

Q. **What initial tests would you perform?**

A. I would request the following:
- urine dipstick and culture
- flow rate and estimation of post-void residual urine volume
- a bladder diary
- if there is suprapubic pain or dipstick haematuria, I would organise urine cytology and a flexible cystoscopy.

(Note that if an elderly woman presents with these symptoms, I would perform urine cytology and a flexible cystoscopy initially, in order to exclude bladder pathology, e.g. bladder stone, carcinoma *in situ* or overt bladder cancer.)

Q. **What is the difference between a bladder diary and a frequency–volume chart?**

A. A bladder diary records the type and volume of fluid intake, incontinence episodes and the number of pads used, together with a recorded chart of urinary frequency and voided urine volume (i.e. functional bladder capacity). A frequency–volume chart records only the volume of fluid intake, urinary frequency and incontinence episodes.

Q. **What do you understand by the term overactive bladder (OAB)?**

A. The International Continence Society (ICS) defines overactive bladder as symptoms of urgency with or without urge incontinence, usually associated with urinary frequency and nocturia in the absence of local pathology and significant endocrine factors.

ICS definitions relating to urinary incontinence are listed in Table 11.1.

Table 11.1 Definitions of terminology relating to overactive bladder and urinary incontinence

Overactive bladder syndrome	A symptom syndrome of urgency with or without incontinence, usually accompanied by urinary frequency and nocturia, in the absence of pathological (e.g. UTI, stones, bladder tumour) and metabolic factors (e.g. diabetes)
Urgency	A sudden and compelling desire to pass urine, which cannot be deferred
Urge urinary incontinence	Involuntary leakage of urine accompanied by or immediately preceded by urgency. It usually represents a severe form of overactive bladder syndrome
Stress urinary incontinence	Involuntary leakage of urine on effort or exertion, or on coughing or sneezing
Mixed urinary incontinence	Involuntary leakage of urine associated with urgency and also with exertion, effort, sneezing and coughing

Q. **What is the difference between overactive bladder (OAB) and idiopathic detrusor overactivity (IDO)?**

A. OAB is a *symptomatic diagnosis*, whereas IDO is *urodynamic evidence* of involuntary detrusor contraction(s) which may be spontaneous or provoked (in the absence of any other pathology, OAB is assumed to be the result of IDO).

Q. **How frequent is 'frequent'?**

A. According to the ICS, more than 8 voids during the daytime is frequent.

Q. **What is the differential diagnosis for this patient's symptoms?**

A. This can be divided into the following:
- Urological:
  - UTI
  - detrusor overactivity
  - urethral syndrome
  - urethral diverticulum
  - interstitial cystitis
  - bladder cancer
  - large residual volume.
- Gynaecological:
  - cystocele
  - pelvic mass.
- Genital:
  - vulvo-vaginitis

- urethritis
- urethral caruncle
- atrophy.
- Medical:
  - upper motor neuron lesion
  - diabetes mellitus.
- General:
  - excessive fluid/caffeine intake
  - anxiety
  - pregnancy.

Q. **What are the treatment options for this patient if she has an overactive bladder?**

A. The stepwise 'ladder' of management is as follows:
- Lifestyle changes (i.e. decreasing intake of caffeinated drinks, stopping smoking, losing weight if obese).
- Bladder re-training and pelvic floor muscle exercises (both have been shown to be effective in OAB).
- Pharmacotherapy (efficacy is 50–75%).
- Intravesical injection of botulinum toxin A (efficacy is 36–89%, mean efficacy is 70%, up to a mean time of 6 months).
- Neuromodulation (50% cure rate, 25% significant improvement of symptoms, 25% failure rate).
- Clam (augmentation) cystoplasty (50% cure rate, 25% significant improvement of symptoms, 25% failure rate).
- Urinary diversion is an option if all else fails in very severe cases.

Note: The first three options in the above list may be tried in the absence of urodynamic investigation. However, prior to any invasive procedure, urodynamic confirmation of the diagnosis of IDO (leading to OAB) should be sought.

Q. **What do you understand by bladder re-training and pelvic floor muscle training (PFMT)?**

A. Bladder re-training works on the principle that the central control can be re-learned in the same way as it was learned in infancy. This is done by setting a target time for using the toilet, before which the patient should not void. Once this has been achieved, the time is increased. The patient has to maintain a normal fluid intake.

PFMT was originally described by Kegel. The purpose is to strengthen and rehabilitate the pelvic floor, by increasing the urethral resistance and improving the tone of the pelvic floor muscles. It is performed by long slow contractions and short sharp pull-ups at regular intervals. Generally, several sets consisting of 8–10 contractions of each are performed every day.

Q. **What is the efficacy of anticholinergic drugs?**

A. It ranges from 50% to 75%. They help to reduce urgency and incontinence episodes as well as reducing the frequency of micturition. The voided volume is also increased.

Q. How do anticholinergic drugs work?

A. Anticholinergics are competitive muscarinic receptor antagonists and have a high binding affinity for the cholinergic muscarinic receptors that mediate contraction of the urinary bladder (and enhance salivation). The majority of muscarinic receptors expressed in the detrusor muscle are M2. However, *M3 muscarinic receptors are the functionally important ones in the detrusor muscle*. Anticholinergics in general have a low affinity for other neurotransmitter receptors and other possible targets such as calcium channels. Selective anticholinergics result in selective blockade of M2 or M3 muscarinic receptors, with the particular advantage that they do not affect brain M1 receptors, and thus have a better side-effect profile than non-selective agents.

Anticholinergics exert a significant effect on the lower urinary tract by reducing spontaneous detrusor muscle activity during the filling phase, decreasing detrusor pressure (and increasing the residual urine).

Q. Which anticholinergic drugs do you know?

A. See Table 11.2.

Table 11.2 Different anticholinergic drugs and their properties

Trade name/ generic name	Dose (mg)	Frequency	Receptor subtype selectivity	Active metabolite	Elimination half-life of drug (hours)
Pro-Banthine/ propantheline	15	Three times daily	Non-selective	No	< 2
Detrusitol/ tolterodine tartrate	2	Twice daily	Non-selective	Yes	2.4
Detrusitol XL/ tolterodine tartrate	4	Once daily	Non-selective	Yes	8.4
Regurin/trospium chloride	20	Twice daily	Non-selective	No	20
Ditropan/oxybutynin chloride	2.5–5	Twice daily to four times daily	Non-selective	Yes	2.3
Lyrinel XL/ oxybutynin chloride XL	5–30	Once daily	Non-selective	Yes	13.2
Detrunorm/ propiverine hydrochloride	15	Once daily to four times daily	Non-selective	Yes	4.1
Emselex/darifenacin	7.5–15	Once daily	Selective muscarinic M3 receptor antagonist	Yes	3.1
Vesicare/solifenacin	5–10	Once daily	Selective muscarinic M2 and M3 receptor antagonist	Yes	40–68

Q **What are the side-effects of anticholinergic drugs?**

A. Common side-effects of muscarinic-receptor blockade include a dry mouth, dyspepsia, constipation, blurred vision and drowsiness. Serious side-effects include anaphylaxis, drowsiness and cognitive and memory impairment (particularly in the elderly), dementia, and cardiac arrhythmias due to prolongation of the QT interval. Selective M3 agents are least likely to cause side-effects.

Q. **What are the contraindications to anticholinergics?**

A. Contraindications include the following:
- myasthenia gravis
- narrow-angle glaucoma, uncontrolled
- significant bladder outflow obstruction or urinary retention
- severe/active ulcerative colitis
- toxic megacolon
- gastrointestinal obstruction or intestinal atony
- hypersensitivity to the agent.

Q. **What is the next step if anticholinergics fail?**

A. The next step would be to perform a urodynamic study (CMG), as further treatment options involve invasive therapies.

Q. **How would you perform a cystometrogram (CMG)?**

A. This is performed in a dedicated room with specialised urodynamic equipment, or in the radiology department where fluoroscopy facilities are available. The test takes around 40–60 minutes, and the aim is to duplicate the patient's symptoms. An initial urine dipstick test is performed in order to exclude possible UTI. A flow test may then be performed and subsequently, after verbal consent has been obtained, a 6–8 French biluminal catheter is inserted into the bladder after cleaning the external urethral meatus and anaesthetising the urethra. This records the intravesical pressure. Using a biluminal catheter avoids the need for two separate urethral catheters. The bladder is drained of urine and this initial volume is recorded. A 6–8 F single lumen catheter is placed into the rectum and secured. This records the intra-abdominal pressure (intravesical pressure minus intra-abdominal pressure = true detrusor pressure). The lines are then connected to the urodynamic transducers and all lines are flushed through with saline, thereby excluding all air bubbles from both the tubing and the transducer chambers. All systems are zeroed at atmospheric pressure, and for the external transducers the reference point is the level of the superior edge of the pubis symphysis. An initial cough ensures good subtraction. Contrast medium or saline (in a non-video study) at room temperature is then instilled via a peristaltic pump. Medium and fast fill (50–100 ml/min) is often used. However, slower fill rates (10–30 ml/min) approaching the physiological range are mandatory when assessing a neuropathic bladder. During the study, notes are made of the initial bladder residual volume, the bladder volume at the time of the patient's first sensation of filling, the final tolerated bladder volume and the final residual volume. The study is initially performed with the patient in the supine position, and the radiographic table is gradually tilted when the patient experiences the sensation of bladder filling. During bladder filling the patient is asked to consciously suppress bladder contraction, and filling is discontinued at maximum tolerated capacity. Quality control is obtained by asking the patient to cough at regular intervals (usually every minute during the study and at the end of the study). In units where a tipping table is not available, the study can be performed with the patient in the sitting or standing position. The patient is asked to stand at the end of the study to assess whether there is postural detrusor instability.

Q. **What would you look for during the filling phase of a CMG?**

A. During the filling phase I would note the following:
- evidence of detrusor overactivity (non-provoked or provoked)
- evidence of stress urinary incontinence (e.g. on coughing)
- bladder compliance (see case study on neurourology below)
- maximum bladder capacity.

Q. **What are the different traces shown in Figure 11.1?**

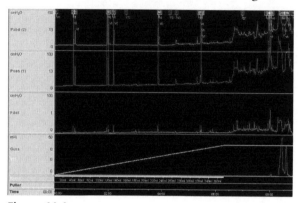

Figure 11.1

A. Figure 11.1 basically demonstrates four traces. These show the intra-abdominal (Pabd) and intravesical (Pves) pressures, the subtracted pressure, i.e. detrusor pressure (Pdet = Pabd – Pves), and the flow trace (Qura). A filling trace is also seen (Vin – lowest trace). For quality-control purposes a cough is seen approximately every minute. Ideally there should be a cough every minute (this ensures consistently good subtraction).

Q. **What has happened in Figure 11.2?**

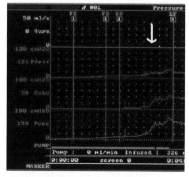

Figure 11.2

A. Figure 11.2 is a CMG trace showing the filling phase only. The arrow shows the point when the patient stood up.

Q. **What has happened in Figure 11.3?**

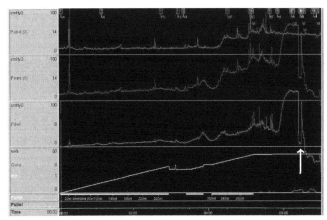

Figure 11.3

A. In Figure 11.3 there is a sharp decrease in Pdet and Pves (arrowed) due to the Pves (bladder) catheter falling out (the adjacent short peak is the result of the catheter passing out through the external sphincter).

Q. **Figure 11.4 is the filling phase of a CMG. What does it demonstrate?**

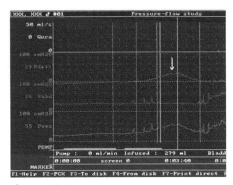

Figure 11.4

A. Figure 11.4 shows idiopathic detrusor overactivity (arrowed) during the filling phase of a CMG (urgency symptoms in patient are present).

Q. **What type of botulinum toxin is normally used in urology?**

A. Botulinum toxin is a neurotoxin derived from *Clostridium botulinum*. There are seven serotypes of botulinum toxin, each with different antigenic profiles and biochemical actions. However, they all have a similar pharmacological effect. Botulinum toxin type A (BoNT/A) and B (BoNT/B) have been developed for clinical use. BoNT/A, although as yet unlicensed, is used for urological indications. The available formulations of BoNT/A are Botox (Allergan, USA), Dysport

(Ipsen, UK), and Xeomin (Merz, Germany). Each formulation of BoNT/A has its own dosing regimen which is not interchangeable. Botox is most commonly used, followed by Dysport (the former is five times more potent than the latter).

Q. **How does botulinum toxin work and how would you give the injections?**

A. Botulinum toxin type A (BoNT/A) temporarily blocks the presynaptic vesicular release of acetylcholine (ACh) at the neuromuscular junction of the parasympathetic nerves supplying the detrusor. This results in a temporary paralysis of the detrusor muscle. BoNT/A prevents the exocytosis of ACh by cleaving SNAP-25 from the SNARE proteins (complex proteins which when intact form the core of the neuroexocytosis machinery). It is on this premise that intradetrusor injections of BoNT/A were introduced to treat intractable bladder symptoms of detrusor overactivity, and this is the basis of the decrease in detrusor pressures and phasic contractions in both idiopathic and neuropathic bladders. However, patients also report a significant decrease in urgency, and therefore it is postulated that botulinum toxin also modulates the sensory pathways. This is thought to work by its action on P2X receptors.

Administration of intradetrusor BoNT/A injections has been described under local, regional or general anaesthetic using a flexible or rigid cystoscope. For idiopathic detrusor overactivity, typically 200 units of Botox (diluted in 20 ml of normal saline) or 750–1000 units of Dysport have been used. There is no standard injection technique. However, intradetrusor injections, as opposed to submucosal injections, with sparing of the trigone are favoured. Again there is no consensus on the number of injection sites and the dilution of the toxin, but generally 20 sites are injected and the volume per injection is usually 0.5–1 ml.

Q. **What are the efficacy and potential side-effects of intravesical injection of botulinum toxin?**

A. The efficacy for idiopathic detrusor overactivity (IDO) is in the range 36–89% (mean 70%). The effects last from 4 to 10 months (mean 6 months) (note that botulinum toxin is much more effective in neurogenic detrusor overactivity).

The local side-effects include pain, UTI (< 5%), bleeding (< 5%), no benefit, requirement for further injections, and requirement for temporary self-catheterisation (very variable, but may be necessary in approximately 10–15% of cases). The generalised side-effects include flu-like symptoms, dry mouth and malaise.

Q. **Are you aware of any long-term effects of repeated injections or of loss of efficacy of botulinum toxin after repeated injections?**

A. No significant bladder fibrosis has been reported on histological examination after repeated injections. Furthermore, seven repeat injections have not demonstrated any decrease in efficacy of Botox.

Q. **What is the basis of sacral neuromodulation (SNM)?**

A. The precise mechanism of action has yet to be ascertained. SNM is used in the treatment of intractable detrusor overactivity and also in women with urinary retention due to a primary disorder of sphincter relaxation (Fowler's syndrome). It is thought that the continuous use of mild electrical activity to stimulate the sacral afferents (mainly S3) to the bladder and pelvic floor modulates local neural reflexes and inhibits bladder contraction. In addition, there is evidence to suggest that signals from higher brain centres involved in the control of micturition are also affected, thus explaining its use in the above-mentioned conditions.

Q. How is SNM delivered?

A. This is a minimally invasive procedure that can be performed under general or local anaesthesia. In general a two-stage technique is used, as it has been shown that the two-stage method improves the efficacy from 50% to 75% for refractory idiopathic detrusor overactivity. Initially a test implant (stimulation wire) is inserted into the S3 foramina. This is attached to a temporary pulse-generator device that the patient wears externally. The patient goes home and keeps a symptoms diary for 2 weeks and this is compared with the pre-operative evaluation. A greater than 50% benefit in symptoms entitles the patient to have the second stage, i.e. a permanent electrode fitted into the S3 foramen with the pulse generator being implanted in a pouch superficial to the posterior superior iliac crest.

Q. What are the efficacy, side-effects and complications of SNM?

A. SNM is thought to be effective in 60–75% of cases of idiopathic detrusor overactivity (efficacy rates are higher in women for Fowler's syndrome). If the procedure proves to be efficacious, the beneficial effects should be long term. However, the battery life of the latest implants is about 7 years, after which the unit will require revising. Previously the main complication was migration of the lead, but this problem has decreased since the introduction of a tined (barbed) lead. Occasionally the patient complains of pain at the site of implantation of the pulse generator or in the lower limb. The explantation rate is 10%, and this is mainly due to infection or lack of sustained efficacy.

Q. What is a clam augmentation cystoplasty and how does it work?

A. The principle is to bivalve the bladder coronally (like a clam) and patch the defect with a piece of bowel, generally ileum (enterocystoplasty) (*see* Figure 11.5). This impairs bladder contraction, lowers the detrusor pressure and increases the capacity of the bladder. It decreases the amplitude of contractions by preventing sustained detrusor contractions.

Figure 11.5 Bladder bivalved coronally and ileal augmentation being performed.

Q. **What are the contraindications to clam augmentation cystoplasty?**

A. These include the following:

- severe inflammatory bowel disease (i.e. Crohn's disease)
- previous pelvic radiotherapy
- a critically short bowel
- unwillingness or inability (due to poor hand function) of the patient to perform self-catheterisation
- significant renal impairment (which results in inability to compensate for hyperchloraemic metabolic acidosis)
- significant hepatic impairment (which results in inability to metabolise ammonia).

Q. **What are the potential complications of clam augmentation cystoplasty (enterocystoplasty)?**

A. These include the following:

Major early complications

- Mortality: 0–2.5% (especially in neurogenic patients due to bladder rupture).
- Myocardial infarction: 0–2.5%.
- Thromboembolic events: 1–7%.
- Re-operation for post-operative bleeding: 0–3%.
- Wound infection with or without dehiscence: 5–6.5%.
- Small bowel obstruction due to adhesions: 3–5.5%.
- Fistula: 0.4–30%.

Long-term complications

1. *The need for post-operative intermittent catheterisation*: the rate is around 50–60% in idiopathic patients. This generally increases over time.
2. *Stones*: the reported rate is highly variable (0–53%), but is generally thought to be around 15%. Stones are more common if there has been an associated Mitrofanoff procedure.
3. *Troublesome mucus production*: the average daily mucus production from the incorporated bowel segment is 35–40 g. This does not decrease over time, and can lead to infections, stone formation and blockages. Bladder washouts with acetylcysteine might be required to dissolve excess mucus.
4. *Bacteriuria and UTI*: almost 100% of patients will have asymptomatic bacteriuria. The incidence of clinically significant UTI is around 4–43%.
5. *Biochemical abnormalities*: the presence of permeable bowel in the urinary tract leads to reabsorption of ammonium chloride and excretion of bicarbonate, resulting in acid–base imbalance. Ammonium chloride (NH_4Cl), which is readily reabsorbed, dissociates into ammonia (NH_3) and hydrochloric acid (HCl), and the HCl in solution in turn dissociates into H^+ and Cl^-, thereby resulting in hyperchloraemic acidosis. However, this is clinically significant in only a few cases (15%), and in these the treatment is administration of bicarbonate. The above biochemical changes explain why augmentation cystoplasty is contraindicated in liver and significant renal failure. In these patients the ammonia cannot be metabolised by the damaged liver and the acidosis cannot be corrected by the failing kidneys.

Note: The incidence of this biochemical abnormality in patients with an ileal conduit is much lower, since the conduit is exactly that – a conduit for urine, and not a reservoir, unlike the augmented bladder. Thus the urine in a conduit does not remain in it for long enough for the above-mentioned exchange (i.e. absorption of NH_4Cl) to take place.

6. *Renal function deterioration*: this can occur in 0–15% of cases. It is more marked in patients who have a creatinine clearance of less than 15 ml/min (corrected for surface area) pre-operatively. However, it has been reported that renal function has actually improved in 4% of cases.

7. *Perforation*: spontaneous perforation is a rare complication (< 1%) but carries a mortality of 25%, mainly due to delay in diagnosis.

8. *Malignancy*: there is an increased incidence of cancer in augmented bladders. However, there is a long latent period (> 10 years). This is associated with chronic inflammation, urinary stasis and recurrent UTIs. The tumours are generally adenocarcinomas and in the region of the anastomosis. The mechanism seems to be related to bacteriuria. This leads to reduction of urinary nitrates to nitrites by colonic bacteria. The nitrites react with urinary amines to form N-nitrosamines, which are implicated in carcinogenesis.

9. *Bowel changes*: these usually result in diarrhoea. This symptom is troublesome in up to 30% of cases. In addition, there can be a decrease in absorption of vitamin B_{12} and folic acid, leading to neurological complications (vitamin B_{12} deficiency may also be due to loss of absorptive terminal ileum).

10. *Reduced growth potential and increased incidence of fractures in growing children*: the hydrogen ions (from the acidosis) are buffered in exchange for calcium, causing demineralisation of bone (this calcium is subsequently lost in the urine). The acidosis in growing children, if present, should be treated with sodium bicarbonate.

Q. **How would you follow up a patient with clam augmentation cystoplasty?**

A. Once stable, the patient would be seen on a yearly basis with ultrasound scan of kidneys and a KUB. The biochemical analysis includes evaluation of kidney and liver function and estimation of serum chloride, bicarbonate, vitamin B_{12} and folic acid levels. The patient is advised to contact the department urgently if they develop recurrent UTIs, haematuria, significant weight loss or severe lethargy. They will undergo yearly surveillance cystoscopies from 10 years after operation.

STRESS URINARY INCONTINENCE

Q. **What is the ICS definition of stress urinary incontinence (SUI)?**

A. Stress urinary incontinence is the involuntary leakage of urine on cough, straining, or exertion and effort. The prevalence is 12–52%. Of all incontinence cases, approximately 50% have SUI, 11% have urge urinary incontinence and 36% have mixed urinary incontinence. SUI is troublesome in 20% of patients with this problem.

Q. **A 52-year-old fit woman presents with worsening complaints of urinary leakage when coughing and lifting heavy items. How would you assess her?**

A. I would see this patient in a specialist clinic, with my continence nurse specialist present, and with the following completed prior to the patient being seen:
- validated symptom questionnaire – I use the ICIQ-SF as recommended by the EAU
- a representative bladder diary (frequency/volume chart) over a period of 3 days
- MSU result
- PVR result.

I would then take a detailed history. In the history I would establish the type of incontinence (stress, urge or mixed), the severity of incontinence (ICIQ-SF outcome, and how many pads used, of what type, and how wet they were), effect on quality of life, treatments (surgical and non-surgical) that have already been tried, the desire for further treatment, and the patient's expectations. I would also enquire about associated voiding and bowel dysfunction (frequency, urgency, nocturia, dysuria, incomplete emptying, suprapubic pain, haematuria, UTIs, constipation and faecal leakage). A detailed gynaecological and obstetric history would be elicited, including, pregnancies (vaginal or Caesarian section), menopausal status (including previous history of hysterectomy), use of HRT, oral contraceptives and whether there was any dyspareunia, vaginal irritation or dryness. Past medical history of diabetes, neurological disease and previous pelvic cancer surgery or radiotherapy would be established. Finally, I would enquire about drug history (diuretics, anticholinergics) and whether the patient is a smoker.

Q. **The patient has had three normal vaginal deliveries in the past and has not had a hysterectomy or any other abdominal or pelvic surgery. She does not complain of urinary infections or any other urinary symptoms. What would you look for on examination?**

A. I would obtain verbal consent and examine her in the presence of a chaperone. I would perform a general examination first, as this might have a bearing on subsequent management, looking specifically for obesity (BMI). Then, with the patient in the supine position, I would perform an abdominal examination looking for a palpable bladder. I would then perform a pelvic examination with the patient in the supine and left lateral position with the aid of a Sims speculum. On inspection, I would look at the tissue state of the introitus (well oestrogenised or atrophic). I would then ask the patient to cough or perform a Valsalva manoeuvre to elicit the sign of stress incontinence. If positive, I would then gently place my index and middle fingers on either side of the bladder neck and ask her to cough again. If there is no leakage, the test is positive (Marshall's test). This would imply that good support of the bladder neck may correct incontinence. Although not used in my practice, depending upon the presence of descent of the bladder neck, a Q-tip test can be performed. This involves introducing a lubricated cotton-tipped applicator into the urethra. An angle of > 30 degrees on straining signifies considerable hypermobility of the urethra. A Sims speculum would then be introduced and an evaluation for cystocele and rectocele would be performed. The presence of anterior wall prolapse can then be demonstrated in the left lateral position. Finally, I would check perineal sensation and assess anal tone to evaluate the patient for any neurological abnormality. If the latter is present, a lower limb neurological examination would also be performed.

Q. **Clinical examination revealed no significant abnormalities. What investigations would you want to perform?**

A. Initially, I would want to perform a dipstick urine test to rule out infection and dipstick-positive haematuria. If UTI was present, this would be treated and the patient would be re-assessed. I would also perform a flow rate and estimation of post-void residual volume, as well as reviewing a representative bladder diary with the patient. Pad tests can be used to objectively confirm incontinence. Further investigations depend on causative factors in the history. Specifically, if neurological features are present, a renal ultrasound scan and creatinine measurement are requested.

Q. **How would you perform a pad test?**

A. The test can be performed over 1 hour (short-term test) or over a 24-hour period (long-term test). In a 1-hour test, the patient is required to drink 500 ml of fluid (non-saline based) and then to perform a set series of exercises over the next hour. The 24-hour test is a more physiological test in which the patient is encouraged to perform the kind of normal daily activity that would cause her to leak urine. A weight gain of up to approximately 1.4 g for the 1-hour pad test and up to 8 g during the 24-hour pad test is considered normal (note that an increase in weight of the pad(s) of 1 g is considered to be equivalent to 1 ml of urine).

Q. **What are the indications for urodynamics?**

A. According to the NICE guidelines, indications for urodynamics include the following:
- previous surgery for stress incontinence or anterior compartment prolapse
- clinical suspicion of detrusor overactivity
- symptoms suggestive of voiding dysfunction
- unclear clinical diagnosis prior to surgery
- the presence of neurological clinical features.

However, in my practice, I perform urodynamics in all patients prior to surgery, for several reasons. First, there is evidence that 11–16% of patients with a history of stress incontinence also have detrusor overactivity on urodynamic testing and, conversely, 22% of patients with a history of overactive bladder symptoms have demonstrable stress incontinence on urodynamic testing.

Q. **What are the indications for video-urodynamics?**

A. In my practice, it is used in those patients with previous failed surgery, those with neurological features and in children. Furthermore, I am aware that in specialist centres, VCMG is used more widely than in my practice, because of its perceived advantages, such as allowing better evaluation of bladder neck descent and urethra, as well as quantifying anterior wall prolapse more accurately.

Q. **How would you describe a urodynamic trace?**

A. I use a systematic method to describe the trace as follows:
- Establish which line is which on the trace (especially as the trace colours may be different to what you are used to normally)
  - Pves
  - Pabd
  - Pdet

- volume infused
- uroflow rate.
- Quality control:
  Are the baseline pressures correct?
  - supine 5–20 cmH$_2$O
  - sitting 15–40 cmH$_2$O
  - standing 30–50 cmH$_2$O
  - subtracted Pdet 0–6 cmH$_2$O.
  Coughing – does it lead to good subtraction and a biphasic waveform in Pdet?
  Are there any artefacts that need to be looked at?
- Filling phase:
  - first desire
  - normal desire
  - strong desire.
  Cystometric capacity
  Is there any detrusor overactivity?
  Is there any stress incontinence?
  Is quality control still OK? (see above)
- Standing:
  Do the pressures increase on standing?
  Is quality control still OK? (see above)
- Provocative manoeuvres:
  Which ones have been used?
  What are the effects of these?
  Is quality control still OK? (see above)
- Voiding phase:
  - Pdet
  - Pdet at Qmax
  - Qmax
  - volume coided.
  Is quality control still OK? (see above)

Q. **Do you know of any theories for the development of SUI?**

A. The first theory, which was proposed by Kelly, Bonney and Enhorning, is known as urethral position theory. It suggested that the urethra should remain above the pelvic floor so that the pressure from the abdomen could be equally transmitted to the urethra, closing it.

Intrinsic sphincter deficiency (ISD) theory was proposed by McGuire in the 1970s. It proposed that the abnormality was due to the weakness of the sphincter itself. McGuire introduced the concept of Valsalva leak point pressure (VLPP) and maximum urethral pressure (MUP). It was suggested that patients with a VLPP of < 60 cmH$_2$O had ISD, whereas those with a VLPP of > 90 cmH$_2$O had an anatomical cause of SUI. Patients with a VLPP in the range 60–90 cmH$_2$O had a combination of the two problems.

Hammock theory was suggested by Delancey in 1994. He described the urethra as resting on a supportive layer of endopelvic fascia and anterior vaginal wall. This was reinforced by the lateral attachments of this fascia with the arcus tendineus.

Integral theory was proposed by Petros and Ulmsten. They suggested that laxity of the anterior vaginal wall and pubo-urethral ligaments causes hyper-mobility of the bladder neck and dissipation of urethral pressure, resulting in urinary incontinence.

Recently, a trampoline theory has been proposed which incorporates all of the above theories. This is applied to the female pelvis as acting as the outer ring, the fabric is the pelvic musculature and the ligaments are the springs. According to this theory, SUI is a multifactorial problem and all of the above are compromised to some extent in its aetiology.

Q. **In this 52-year-old woman, a diagnosis of stress incontinence is made. What treatment options are available?**

A. The following options are available.

Non-surgical treatments

- Lifestyle changes:
  - weight loss
  - cessation of smoking
  - modification of high or low fluid intake.
- Supervised pelvic floor exercises.
- Bladder re-training.
- Oestrogen therapy if there is evidence of atrophy.
- Oral medical therapy in rare cases.

Surgical treatments

- Occlusive:
  - bulking agents
  - compressive (artificial urinary sphincter).
- Supportive:
  - suburethral sling
  - colposuspension.

Q. **The patient wants to know more about the medical therapy and especially how it works. What information would you give her?**

A. The only agent for which there are published data is duloxetine (Yentreve), which is a combined norepinephrine and serotonin reuptake inhibitor at the spinal cord level (Onuf's nucleus). It increases the activity of the pudendal nerve and increases the urethral muscle tone. Its efficacy is about 20–40%. However, it is limited by its side-effects, and discontinuation rates are very high. The main adverse effects are nausea, dizziness, dry mouth, constipation, insomnia, somno-lence and asthenia. Duloxetine is not recommended as a first-line treatment for women with predominant SUI, although it may be offered as second-line ther-apy for women who prefer pharmacological therapy to surgery or who are not suitable for surgical treatment. In clinical practice, if duloxetine is prescribed, the patient should be counselled very carefully about its adverse effects.

Q. **What are the indications for bulking agents?**

A. The main indications are symptomatic patients who are high risk for major sur-gery, elderly patients, patients with a history of multiple failed procedures, and patient preference. I would offer bulking agents to patients with mild to moderate SUI on the understanding that although this is a minimally invasive technique, the success rate is only 50–70% and the effects are not long-lasting. I would also mention that more than one injection might be required to achieve continence.

Q. What types of bulking agents are you aware of?

A. I know of Contigen (bovine collagen), Durasphere (carbon beads), Zuidex (cross-linked dextranomer), Macroplastique (silicone) and Coaptite (calcium hydroxyl-apatite). I use Macroplastique because it is permanent and there is no significant risk of migration, due to the size of the particles.

Q. What materials are mid-urethral slings made of?

A.
- Autologous:
  – rectus fascia
  – fascia lata.
- Synthetic:
  – prolene (polypropylene)
  – dacron (mersilene).
- Non-synthetic.

Q. What is the efficacy of mid-urethral TVT slings?

A. After TVT, 90% of women were still objectively cured according to a study in which 11-year prospective follow-up data were available.[1] Similar data have been reported at 5- and 7-year follow-up.[2]

Q. What are the complications associated with mid-urethral TVT slings?

A. These include the following:
- Complications at insertion:
  – bladder perforation (0–12%)
  – significant haemorrhage (1.9%)
  – major vascular injury (< 1%)
  – urethral laceration
  – bowel injury
  – neural injury.
- Material-related complications:
  – erosion (< 1%)
  – UTI (4–17%).
- Post-operative symptoms:
  – post-operative voiding dysfunction (30%)
  – *de-novo* urgency (3–9%)
  – urinary retention (2.5–5%).

Q. How is erosion treated?

A. The tape has to be removed if there is a urethral or vaginal erosion. The urethral defect can be buttressed with a Martius fat pad if there is a significant defect. A rectus fascial sling can be inserted later on if the patient is incontinent. The bladder perforation is more difficult to treat. It is difficult to endoscopically remove the tape from inside the bladder. Laser can be used with some success, although it may require more than one sitting to remove the tape. If there is considerable erosion, a cystotomy is required.

Q. How does TVT compare with other pubo-vaginal slings?

A. In a recent systematic review and meta-analysis of five randomised controlled trials comparing TVT and other pubo-vaginal slings, a comparable cure rate between the two procedures was found.[3]

Q. How does TVT compare with TOT?

A. The effectiveness and complications associated with TOT were assessed in a recent systematic review of five randomised controlled trials that compared TVTO with TVT, and six randomised controlled trials that compared TOT with TVT.[4] Both techniques had similar efficacy with regard to subjective cure. However, the risk of bladder perforation (odds ratio = 0.12) and voiding difficulties (odds ratio = 0.55) with TOT was lower, whereas groin and thigh pain (odds ratio = 8.28), vaginal injuries or erosion of mesh (odds ratio = 1.96) were significantly more common after tape insertion by the transobturator route.

Long-term follow-up data on TOT are limited.

Q. How does TVT compare with Burch colposuspension?

A. A recent systematic review and meta-analysis of nine randomised controlled trials comparing TVT and Burch colposuspension, in which 1170 patients were followed up for 3–24 months, concluded that TVT had a significantly higher efficacy in terms of overall cure rate than Burch colposuspension.[3]

This was true for any definition of cure, namely according to the presence of negative stress test (odds ratio = 0.38) and according to the presence of negative pad test (odds ratio = 0.59). Complication rates were similar after the two procedures, with the exclusion of bladder perforation, which was more common after TVT, and reoperation rate, which was significantly higher after Burch colposuspension.

In summary, TVT appears to be significantly more effective than and followed by similar complication rates to Burch colposuspension.

Q. When would you offer colposuspension and what is its efficacy?

A. I would recommend this to patients with *significant* urethral hypermobility (TVT/TOT in these cases is likely to fail, with the patient re-presenting with SUI in the future). Also, this procedure has the longest follow-up and the cure rate at > 10 years is 69%.

Q. What are the main complications after Burch colposuspension?

- Immediate complications:
  - retropubic space haemorrhage (transfusion risk is approximately 0.5%)
  - bladder trauma (2–3%).
- Long-term complications:
  - enterocele or rectocele (up to 20%)
  - dyspareunia (4%)
  - voiding dysfunction (up to 30%, and need for CISC 0.5%)
  - *de-novo* urgency (5–15%)
  - recurrent bacterial cystitis (1–2%).

Q. What are the causes of failure of anti-incontinence surgery?

A. These include the following:
- anatomical failure due to technical reasons

- functional failures due to poor tissue support
- inappropriate patient selection
- failure due to post-operative complications.

BLADDER PAIN SYNDROME/INTERSTITIAL CYSTITIS

Q. **A 27-year-old woman presents with frequency and urgency associated with severe suprapubic pain. She also complains of cystitis-like symptoms and UTIs requiring repeated courses of antibiotics over the last 3 years. She has seen multiple specialists, including pain consultants, without much benefit. She appears to be very distressed by her symptoms and thinks that she has got bladder pain syndrome/interstitial cystitis. How would you make this diagnosis?**

A. Bladder pain syndrome/interstitial cystitis is defined as 'the complaint of suprapubic pain related to bladder filling, accompanied by other symptoms such as increased daytime and night-time frequency, in the absence of proven urinary infection or other obvious pathology.' It is distinctly possible that this patient has a diagnosis of bladder pain syndrome/interstitial cystitis, but I am aware that this is a diagnosis which is made by exclusion. Therefore I would perform a very detailed history, including ICSI score, and a careful clinical examination. I would then perform investigations such as a 3-day frequency–volume diary, MSU, cystometrogram and cystodistension and biopsy. These patients require a very considerate approach, and will have to be given a considerable amount of time, especially during the first consultation.

Q. **What is the NIDDK Workshop research definition?**

A. These criteria were devised in 1987–88 and were developed for scientific studies. It appears that only one-third of the patients who were thought by experts to have bladder pain syndrome/interstitial cystitis fulfilled these strict criteria.

Automatic inclusions
- Hunner's ulcer.

Positive factors
- Pain on bladder filling that is relieved by emptying.
- Pain (suprapubic, pelvic, urethral, vaginal or perineal).
- Glomerulations on endoscopy.
- Decreased compliance on cystometrogram.

Automatic exclusions
- < 18 years old.
- Benign or malignant bladder tumours.
- Radiation cystitis.
- Tuberculous cystitis.
- Bacterial cystitis.
- Vaginitis.
- Cyclophosphamide cystitis.
- Symptomatic urethral diverticulum.

- Uterine, cervical, vaginal or urethral cancer.
- Active herpes.
- Bladder or lower ureteral calculi.
- Waking frequency less than five times in 12 hours.
- Nocturia less than twice.
- Symptoms relieved by antibiotics, urinary antiseptics or urinary analgesics.
- Duration < 12 months.
- Involuntary bladder contractions (urodynamics).
- Capacity > 400 ml, absence of sensory urgency.

Q. What are the types of bladder pain syndrome/interstitial cystitis according to the European Society for the Study of Interstitial Cystitis (ESSIC)?

A. They are classified on the basis of cystoscopic hydrodistension and biopsy. The hydrodistension is classified as normal, glomerulations or Hunner's ulcer (denoted by 1, 2 or 3, respectively). The biopsy is classified as normal, inconclusive or positive (denoted by A, B or C, respectively). Therefore a normal result is classified as 1A whereas the presence of a Hunner's ulcer and positive biopsy is denoted by 3C.

Q. What is Hunner's ulcer?

A: This is not a true ulcer but an inflammatory lesion which presents as a deep rupture through the mucosa and submucosa on hydrodistension. It appears as a reddened area with small vessels radiating to the centre, and it oozes blood like a waterfall after distension.

Q. What do you know about the pathogenesis of bladder pain syndrome/interstitial cystitis?

A. This is a multifactorial syndrome, and none of the causes implicated in the aetiology have definitely been proved. These include:
- urinary infections – initially recurrent UTIs were thought to be the starting point, but this is now in doubt
- mast cells – these are reported to be both a pathological mechanism and a pathognomonic marker
- epithelial permeability – an abnormality in the glycosaminoglycan (GAG) layer leads to passage of urine causing inflammation
- neurogenic mechanisms – neurogenic inflammation can lead to abnormal sensory nerve activity with release of neuropeptides
- autoimmunity – there is no clear evidence that this is the triggering factor for interstitial cystitis
- others causes – stress
- female preponderance (10:1) – hence the role of hormones.

Q. How would you tell this patient about her treatment?

A. I would explain to the patient that there is no cure for this condition. However, the symptoms could be controlled with a variety of treatments, and it may be that we will have to try many different treatment options before the symptoms can be maintained on one. Importantly, the patient should be made aware that there will be exacerbations and remissions over the long term. I would also tell her that 50% of patients achieve temporary remission without any treatment.

Q. **What are the treatment options for this patient?**

A. The treatment options are as follows:

- support – psychological support, IC support group
- avoidance of triggers – drugs, chilli diet, bubble bath, caffeine, etc.
- hydrodistension under anaesthesia – this is done for 1–2 minutes at 80 cmH$_2$O
- medical therapy – amitriptyline 75 mg daily (effects are seen in 1–7 days)
- cimetidine 400 mg twice daily
- hydroxyzine 25 mg at night
- dothiapine 75 mg daily
- diclofenac 75 mg twice daily
- pregabalin/gabalin 100–300 mg daily (can be increased to three times daily)
- sodium pentosanpolysulphate (heparin analogue; 3–6% is secreted in the urine) – a 3- to 6-month trial is needed
- intravesical therapy:
  - dimethyl sulphoxide (DMSO) – 50 ml of 50% instilled for 15 minutes, repeated after 2–4 weeks (response rate is 50–80%)
  - pentosan polysulphate (Elmiron) – works as an exogenous GAG layer (response rate is 16–32%)
  - hyaluronic acid – weekly instillations (response rate is 70%)
  - chondroitin sulphate – weekly for 6 weeks, then monthly for 16 weeks (response rate is 60%)
- nerve stimulation:
  - transcutaneous nerve stimulation (TENS) (response rate is 26%)
  - acupuncture
  - sacral nerve stimulation (SNS) – an option, but it has not been widely tried
- surgery:
  - transurethral resection of Hunner's ulcer
  - transurethral resection by laser of Hunner's ulcer
  - denervation procedures
  - supratrigonal cystectomy
  - substitution cystoplasty with or without Mitrofanoff
  - urinary diversion by conduit and cystourethrectomy.

NEUROUROLOGY

Q. **Please describe the motor innervation to the lower urinary tract.**

A. The LUT receives innervation from both the parasympathetic and the sympathetic branches of the autonomic nervous system. The parasympathetic preganglionic fibres are located in S2–4 spinal segments, and these synapse with postganglionic cell bodies lying within the detrusor muscle. These parasympathetic nerves provide cholinergic excitatory input to bladder smooth muscle, resulting in detrusor contraction. However, parasympathetic innervation of the outflow tract exerts an inhibitory effect, resulting in relaxation of the bladder neck and urethra.

The sympathetic cell bodies are located in spinal segments T10–12 and L1–2. The preganglionic fibres synapse with postganglionic fibres in the hypogastric plexus. The predominant effect of the sympathetic innervation is inhibition of the parasympathetic pathways, thus providing an inhibitory control on detrusor contraction. In addition, sympathetic innervation results in contraction of the outflow tract (in males by stimulating contraction of the pre-prostatic sphincter, and in females there is some, albeit relatively sparse, sympathetic innervation to the bladder neck).

The somatic nerve supply to the pelvic floor musculature and the external urethral rhabdosphincter originates from S2–4, and is conveyed peripherally via the pudendal nerves. The cell bodies of the axons that innervate the external urethral rhabdosphincter lie in a distinct, medially placed motor nucleus at the same spinal level, called Onuf's nucleus.

Q. **What is the sensory innervation of the bladder?**

A. Sensory nerves have been identified in the suburothelial layer as well as in the detrusor muscle. This suburothelial plexus is particularly prominent at the bladder neck and is relatively sparse at the dome of the bladder.

Sensations of bladder fullness are conveyed to the spinal cord in the pelvic and hypogastric nerves. The afferent components of these nerves contain myelinated (A) and unmyelinated (C) axons. The A fibres respond to passive distension and active contraction, and thus convey information about bladder filling. The C-fibres respond primarily to noxious stimuli such as chemical irritation of the urothelium or cooling. The cell bodies of both of these classes of axons are located in the dorsal root ganglia (DRG) at the level of S2–S3 and T11–L2 spinal segments. Bladder afferent activity enters the spinal cord through the dorsal horn and ascends rostrally to higher brain centres involved in bladder control, i.e. the pontine micturition centre and then on to the cerebral cortex.

Afferent fibres originating from the trigone and urethra run in the hypogastric and pudendal nerves, respectively.

Q. **Please describe the micturition cycle.**

A. The micturition cycle consists of filling and voiding phases.
- During the filling phase, the intravesical pressure is kept low by the phenomenon of receptive relaxation. The extent to which a change in volume occurs in relation to a change in pressure is known as bladder compliance (i.e. compliance = change in volume/change in pressure). Factors that contribute to bladder compliance include the vesicoelastic properties of the bladder and also the ability of detrusor smooth muscle cells to increase in length without a significant increase in tension. During bladder filling, afferent activity from stretch receptors passes to the pons and cerebral cortex. If voiding is not to be initiated, activity within the external urethral rhabdosphincter is increased. In addition, central inhibition decreases parasympathetic activity to the detrusor. Detrusor contraction is prevented by the 'gating mechanism'. This is the inhibitory influence of interneurons via the symapathetics to prevent the transmission of afferent activity. This prevents the transmission of activity from preganglionic to postganglionic parasympathetic efferent neurons.
- When appropriate, voiding is initiated. The voiding phase begins with relaxation of the external urethral sphincter, followed by contraction of the detrusor muscle. Micturition is coordinated by Barrington's nucleus in the pons.

The afferents from the bladder travel via parasympathetic nerves to the peri-aqueductal grey matter (PAG) in the pons. The PAG and cerebral cortical areas decide whether it is appropriate to void. If it is, the pontine micturition centre relays impulses that result in external sphincter relaxation, and urine enters the posterior urethra. It also sends direct signals to the detrusor parasympathetics to initiate contraction. If this coordination is lost, as in a suprasacral type of spinal cord injury (SCI), the patient develops detrusor sphincter dyssynergia (i.e. uncoordinated contraction of the detrusor and external sphincter).

Q. **What are the main urological characteristics of suprapontine, suprasacral and conus (S1–S5)/cauda equina/peripheral nerve (lower motor neuron) lesions?**

A. • *Suprapontine lesions (e.g. CVA, Parkinson's disease).* In these lesions, micturition reflexes are intact. Following a CVA, voiding at inappropriate times occurs (although voiding itself is normal) in addition to detrusor overactivity (the latter also occurs in Parkinson's disease). These are 'safe' low-pressure bladders.

• *Suprasacral spinal cord injuries/lesions (i.e. lesions between the pons and spinal cord segment L5).* These are characterised by neurogenic detrusor overactivity (NDO), detrusor sphincter dyssynergia (DSD, i.e. synchronous contraction of the detrusor and external urethral sphincter) and low-compliance bladders. In lesions above T6, autonomic dysreflexia may be a significant problem (see below). Unlike suprapontine and conus/cauda equine/peripheral nerve lower motor lesions, suprasacral injuries can result in 'unsafe' high-pressure bladders, as upper tract damage can result (due to DSD and low compliance).

• *Conus (S1–S5)/cauda equina peripheral nerve lesions.* These lead to a lower motor neuron-type injury, and are characterised by an acontractile (areflexic) bladder with urethal sphincter weakness (leading to stress incontinence) (possible low compliance may also occur). The bladders tend to be 'safe' low-pressure bladders.

Q. **What is detrusor sphincter dyssynergia?**

A. It is defined as involuntary contraction of the urethral and/or periurethral striated muscle simultaneously with a detrusor contraction. This is usually specific to a suprasacral neurological disorder.

Q. **How would you define urodynamic stress incontinence?**

A. This is observed during filling cystometry, and it is defined as the involuntary leakage of urine during increased abdominal pressure, in the absence of a detrusor contraction.

Q. **What do you know about detrusor leak point pressure (DLPP) and abdominal leak point pressure (ALPP)?**

A. • *The term DLPP must only be used in relation to patients with a neurological disorder/ injury, i.e. those with a neuropathic bladder.* DLPP is the lowest detrusor pressure at which urine leakage occurs in the absence of either a detrusor contraction or increased abdominal pressure. McGuire observed, in spina bifida patients, that if the DLPP is greater than 40 cmH$_2$O there is a significant risk of damage to the upper tracts.[5]

- The ALPP (also called the Valsalva leak point pressure) is terminology used in relation to stress incontinence in *non-neuropathic female patients*. It is the intravesical pressure at which urine leakage occurs due to increased abdominal pressure in the absence of a detrusor contraction. If the ALPP is < 60 cmH$_2$O, stress incontinence is likely to be due to intrinsic sphincter deficiency. If the ALPP is > 90 cmH$_2$O, stress incontinence is likely to be due to urethral hypermobility. An ALPP in the range 60–90 cmH$_2$O is an equivocal result. If the ALPP is > 150 cmH$_2$O, the urethra is unlikely to be the cause of urinary incontinence.

Q. **A 28-year-old man sustained a T5 spinal cord injury (SCI) a year ago. He can walk and has been emptying his bladder by strain voiding, and he complains of recurrent UTIs and urinary leakages. What type of injury does he have?**

A. He has sustained a suprasacral type of injury and is likely to have NDO, poorly sustained bladder contractions, DSD, low bladder compliance and reflex bladder voiding. As the lesion is above T6, he may also suffer from autonomic dysreflexia (see below).

Q. **What is the most important investigation in this patient, which will help you in management?**

A. A video-urodynamic study.

Q. **What are your indications for urodynamics in general?**

A. These include the following:
- patients with persistent LUTs after appropriate therapy
- patients with previous failed incontinence surgery*
- patients with mixed urinary symptoms with or without incontinence
- any patient with suspected neurological disease and urinary symptoms*
- any patient in whom potential therapy may be hazardous
- children with complex voiding dysfunction.*

*A video-urodynamic study (VCMG – synchronous cystography and cystometry recordings) is more appropriate than a CMG in these cases, as it allows a combined evaluation of the anatomy and function of the lower urinary tract.

Q. **What do Figures 11.6a and 11.6b show?**

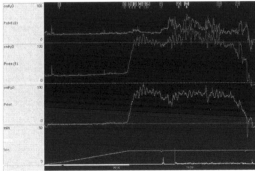

Figure 11.6a

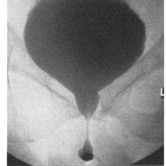

Figure 11.6b

A. Figure 11.6a demonstrates a classical DSD trace with a saw-toothed appearance on the Pdet line (also sustained detrusor contraction lasting for more than 5 minutes, with Pdet pressures of 80–90 cmH$_2$O).

Figure 11.6b shows cystography performed during a VCMG investigation. It demonstrates hold-up of contrast at the level of the external urethral sphincter, typical of DSD.

Q. **How would you treat this patient?**

A. The aim is to achieve low-pressure storage and complete bladder emptying without incontinence.

I would be guided by the urodynamics result, but assuming that this patient with T6 SCI has NDO and DSD, I would start him on anticholinergic medication and institute a programme of clean intermittent self-catheterisation (CISC). He would be closely monitored and would undergo ultrasound scan of the kidneys and repeat urodynamics in 3 to 6 months' time to ensure that the bladder pressures have come down. Assuming that there are no problems (i.e. UTIs or problems with CISC), the patient would be reviewed on an annual basis.

Q. **The above patient returns and states that he does not like performing CISC and wants to know about the other options that are available. Could you explain these to him?**

A. Apart from CISC and the Crede manoeuvre (which he was practising), the other options include the following:
- behavioural and timed voiding – not suitable for this patient
- intradetrusor botulinum toxin injections – unsuitable for this patient as he would have to continue to perform CISC
- an indwelling catheter (suprabubic or urethral) – not a good option for this patient as he is very young and mobile
- urethral stents or external sphincterotomy (with a subsequent Convene sheath) – both of these treat DSD (the urethral stent is placed across the external urethral sphincter, thus holding it open), but the patient will be completely incontinent afterwards. Therefore, as he is young and mobile, these are not good options for him
- augmentation cystoplasty (see section on overactive bladder above) with or without a Mitrofanoff – however, following this procedure the patient will almost certainly need to perform CISC
- sacral anterior nerve root stimulator (SARS) with dorsal rhizotomy – not suitable for this patient as he is walking and has an incomplete SCI. This is an option for wheelchair-bound patients with a complete spinal cord injury.

Q. **What are the advantages and disadvantages of a SARS (this is currently combined with a sacral dorsal rhizotomy)?**

A. The benefits include the following:
- abolition of reflex bladder
- increased bladder capacity
- abolition of autonomic dysreflexia
- improved bowel management.

However, the disadvantages are:
- stress incontinence
- loss of reflex erections
- loss of reflex ejaculation
- loss of reflex defaecation.

Q. What are the complications of long-term catheters?

A. These include the following
- recurrent UTIs
- blockages
- need for regular changes
- stones
- risk of cancer.

Q. What are the complications of urethral stents to treat DSD in this case?

A. This patient will be completely incontinent (as the urethral stents are placed across the external urethral sphincter to hold it open) and will have to wear a sheath, with risk of detachment. The urethral stents can dislodge, block or become encrusted. They are generally reserved for immobile patients, as is external sphincterotomy, which is irreversible.

Q. What is the success rate of botulinum toxin injections in NDO?

A. The success rate is 70–90%, with effects lasting an average of 9 months.

Q. What is autonomic dysreflexia (AD)?

A. This is a medical emergency. It occurs only in patients with an SCI above T6 level. It is a result of sudden disordered sympathetic activity due to a specific stimulus below the level of SCI. If left untreated, cerebrovascular accidents (CVA), convulsions and death may ensue.

Q. What are the causes of AD?

A. It is triggered by noxious afferent stimulation below the level of SCI. Stimulation of the genitourinary tract is the commonest cause of AD. This includes bladder distension, urological interventions (e.g. catheterisation, urodynamics, cystoscopy), UTI and urinary calculi. Non-urological causes include constipation, pressure sores, fractures, ingrowing toenails, and distal skin infections.

Q. What is the mechanism of AD?

A. There is sympathetic overactivity of the distal autonomous cord (i.e. *below* the level of SCI), leading to vasoconstriction of territory supplied by sympathetics in the distal autonomous cord with compensatory vasodilation of normally innervated sympathetic territory (i.e. *above* the level of SCI).

Q. What are the symptoms and signs of AD?

A. They include the following:
- severe headache
- profuse sweating (above the level of the injury)
- flushing (above the level of the injury)
- significant hypertension
- in advanced untreated cases, convulsions, intracranial bleeds, hypertensive encephalopathy and ultimately death.

Q. **What is the treatment of AD?**
A. This is a life-threatening condition. Management includes the following:
- prompt recognition of the condition
- remove the precipitating cause (e.g. drain the bladder, evacuate the bowels, examine the toes and nails)
- sit the patient up (this induces a relative orthostatic hypotension)
- administer sublingual GTN spray *or*
- sublingual captopril/nifedipine *or*
- IV labetalol/phentolamine.

Q. **How would you manage a patient with a conus (S1–S5) spinal cord injury?**
A. He has a generally safe bladder (see above) and the management options include the following:
- behavioural and timed voiding
- emptying by straining if the bladder has good capacity
- CISC if there is incomplete voiding or the patient complains of UTIs.

If the patient complains of (stress) urinary incontinence, the management options are as follows:
- sheaths
- bulking agents
- tapes/slings
- artificial urinary sphincter (AUS).

Q. **What does Figure 11.7 show?**

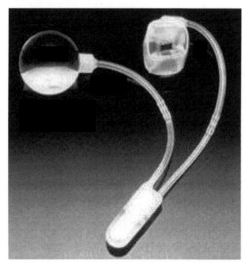

Figure 11.7

A. It shows an artificial urinary sphincter (AMS 800).

Q. **How many components does an AUS have?**
A. It has three components, namely a urethral cuff, a scrotal/labial control pump and a reservoir (which is usually implanted in the preperitoneal retropubic space).

Q. **What is the success rate of the AUS?**

A. The AUS (AMS 800) enables more than 75% of patients to be completely continent and more than 90% to be socially dry. Satisfactory long-term continence is present in approximately 61% of patients 10–15 years after implantation. However, success rates are lower in SCI patients, especially if they are wheelchair-bound.

Q. **What are the complications of AUS?**

A. They include the following:

- infection
- cuff erosion
- urethral atrophy (in up to 33–39% of cases; it has been reported to be the commonest cause of surgical revision)
- persistent leakage
- mechanical failure
- upper urinary tract damage (particularly in children with neuropathic bladders).

REFERENCES

1. Nilsson CG *et al.* Eleven years prospective follow-up of the tension-free vaginal tape procedure for treatment of stress urinary incontinence. *Int Urogynecol J Pelvic Floor Dysfunct* 2008; **19**: 1043–7.
2. Liapis A *et al.* Long-term efficacy of tension-free vaginal tape in the management of stress urinary incontinence in women: efficacy at 5- and 7-year follow-up. *Int Urogynecol J Pelvic Floor Dysfunct* 2008; **19**: 1509–12.
3. Novara G *et al.* Tension-free midurethral slings in the treatment of female stress urinary incontinence: a systematic review and meta-analysis of randomised controlled trials of effectiveness. *Eur Urol* 2007; **52**: 663–78.
4. Latthe PM *et al.* Transobturator and retropubic tape procedures in stress urinary incontinence: a systematic review and meta-analysis of effectiveness and complications. *Br J Obstet Gynaecol* 2007; **114**: 522–31.
5. McGuire EJ *et al.* Prognostic value of urodynamic testing in myelodysplastic patients. *J Urol* 1981; **126**: 205.

FURTHER READING

Arya M, Shergill IS, Silhi N *et al. Essential Urology in General Practice*. London: Quay Books; 2009.

Wein AJ, Kavoussi LR, Novick AC *et al.* (eds) *Campbell-Walsh Urology*, 9th edn. Philadelphia, PA: Saunders Elsevier; 2006.

Chapter 12
Benign prostatic hyperplasia

William J McAllister

ANATOMY, EMBRYOLOGY AND PATHOPHYSIOLOGY

Q. **What is the embryological basis of prostate development?**

A. The prostate develops between weeks 10 and 16 of gestation from epithelial buds which branch out from the posterior aspect of the urogenital sinus to invade the mesenchyme.

Stromal–epithelial interaction is important through the production of dihydrotestosterone by epithelial cells acting on mesenchymal androgen receptors.

Q. **What is the blood supply to the prostate?**

A. The arterial blood supply is from the branches of the inferior vesical artery. This provides the prostatic artery which divides into urethral and capsular groups of arteries. From the urethral group arise Flock's and Badenoch's arteries (both of which supply the transition zone). Flock's arteries approach the bladder neck at 1 and 11 o'clock and Badenoch's arteries approach it at 5 and 7 o'clock. The capsular branches of the prostatic artery run with the cavernosal nerves.

The venous drainage is via the periprostatic venous plexus. This also receives the deep dorsal vein of the penis and numerous vesical veins. The periprostatic venous plexus eventually drains into the internal iliac vein.

Q. **Describe the lymph drainage from the prostate.**

A. The lymph drainage is mainly to the obturator nodes and then the internal iliac chain.

Q. **Can you describe and draw the zonal anatomy of the prostate?**

A. The zonal anatomy is described using McNeal's zones (*see* Figure 12.1).
These zones can be summarised as follows:
- transition zone (comprises 10% of the glandular tissue of the prostate – site of origin of benign prostatic hyperplasia)
- central zone (comprises 25% of the glandular tissue of the prostate)
- peripheral zone (comprises 65% of the glandular tissue of the prostate)
- anterior fibromuscular stroma.

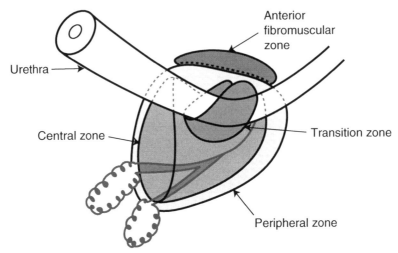

Figure 12.1 McNeal's zones of the prostate.

LUTS

Q. **A 67-year-old man is referred to you by his GP with 'mild prostatism.' What is 'prostatism'?**

A   Prostatism is an outdated term for lower urinary tract symptoms (LUTS) due to benign prostatic enlargement (BPE).

Q. **What are LUTS?**

A. Lower urinary tract symptoms (LUTS) is a non-specific term for symptoms which may be attributable to lower urinary tract dysfunction. There are two main groups of LUTS – storage LUTS (previously called irritative symptoms) and voiding LUTS (previously called obstructive symptoms).

Q. **What is BPH?**

A. BPH is benign prostatic hyperplasia which is the term given to a histological basis for a diagnosis of benign prostate enlargement (BPE) leading to bladder outflow obstruction (BOO) that results in LUTS.[1]

Q. **What is BOO?**

A. BOO is bladder outflow obstruction which refers to urodynamically proven obstruction to passage of urine.

Q. **What is BPE?**

A. BPE is the clinical finding of an enlarged prostate due to the histological process of BPH.

Q. **What is BPO?**

A. BPO is benign prostatic obstruction which refers to BOO caused by BPE.

Q. **How would you assess the patient in your clinic?**

A. I would take a history, examine the patient and arrange further investigation.

Q. **What features would you seek to elicit in your history?**
A. • Symptoms:
  – duration
  – extent
  – impact/troublesome nature.
 • Lifestyle:
  – fluid intake
  – adjustments that have already been tried by the patient.
 • Drugs:
  – possible trial of medication in primary care, and outcome
  – drugs with sympathomimetic and anticholinergic effects.
 • Past medical history:
  – urethral injury/instrumentation
  – pelvic surgery
  – neurological disorders.

Q. **Are you aware of any standardised instruments for the measurement of LUTS in male patients?**
A. There have been a number of different questionnaires which have been used in the study of symptomatic BPE. These questionnaires include the IPSS, AUA, DAN and Bristol male LUTS. The IPSS questionnaire, derived from the AUA questionnaire,[2] is the most commonly used instrument and has been shown to be valid, reliable and reproducible.

Q. **Can you describe the AUA/IPSS questionnaire?**
A. The IPSS consists of 7 questions based on the extent of symptoms and a single quality-of-life question to assess how troublesome the symptoms are to the patient (*see* Table 12.1). On the basis of the answers to the individual questions a total score is obtained which can be used to divide patients into three categories. The IPSS scores seven questions on a scale from 0 to 5. Mild LUTS is defined as a score of 0–7, moderate LUTS as a score of 8–19, and severe LUTS as a score of 20–35. The quality of life question is scored from 0–6.

Table 12.1 The IPSS questionnaire

Over the past month, how often have you:	Not at all	Less than 1 time in 5	Less than half the time	About half the time	More than half the time	Almost always
1. had a sensation of not emptying your bladder completely after you finished urinating?	0	1	2	3	4	5
2. had to urinate again less than two hours after you finished urinating?	0	1	2	3	4	5
3. stopped and started again several times when you urinated?	0	1	2	3	4	5
4. found it difficult to postpone urination?	0	1	2	3	4	5

continued

Table 12.1 *continued*

	None	Once	Twice	3 times	4 times	5 times or more
5. had a weak urinary stream?	0	1	2	3	4	5
6. had to push or strain to begin urination?	0	1	2	3	4	5
7. Over the past month, how many times did you most typically get up to urinate from the time you went to bed at night until the time you got up in the morning?	0	1	2	3	4	5

Supplementary question: quality of life due to urinary symptoms.
If you were to spend the rest of your life with your urinary condition the way it is now, how would you feel about that?

0. Delighted
1. Pleased
2. Mostly satisfied
3. Mixed – about equally satisfied and dissatisfied
4. Mostly dissatisfied
5. Unhappy
6. Terrible

Q. What would you look for on examination?

A.

Specific features

- Palpable bladder.
- Enlarged (ballotable) kidneys.
- Prostate – size, consistency, presence of nodules.
  Note: assess anal tone and sensation during digital rectal examination.

General features

- Renal failure (e.g. fluid overload, signs of uraemia).
- Neurological disorders (e.g. tremor, gait disturbance).

Q. Your history indicates that the patient has an IPSS of 14, with no other relevant medical conditions. Clinical examination confirms a moderately enlarged benign prostate with no other significant findings. How would you investigate the patient?

A. I would arrange the following tests:

- frequency–volume chart
- urinalysis
- serum creatinine
- PSA (after counselling)
- uroflowmetry
- ultrasound measurement of post-void residual urine.

Q. Would you perform a renal ultrasound scan?

A. No. A renal ultrasound scan would only be indicated in the following situations:

- impaired renal function

- loin pain
- haematuria
- renal enlargement/mass on clinical exam.

Q. **Would you perform a cystoscopy on this patient?**
A. No, but it may be useful if there is a history of haematuria, equivocal flow rates or previous urological surgery.

Q. **Is transrectal ultrasound indicated in the investigation of this patient?**
A. No. It would be indicated if there was an elevated PSA or an abnormal DRE, and it is useful in surgical treatment planning (i.e. TURP or Millin's prostatectomy – latter if transrectal ultrasound volume is > 100 ml).

Q. **Which patients should be considered for urodynamics evaluation before surgical intervention?**
A. The EAU guidelines (2008) recommend urodynamics in the following patients:
- equivocal flow rates, e.g. voided volume (VV) < 150 ml, Qmax > 10 ml/s
- age < 50 years or > 80 years
- previous unsuccessful treatment for BPH
- neurological disease.

Q. **What would you tell the patient in preparation for a flow rate?**
A. The patient will need to attend for 2–3 hours. I tell them to wait until they have a comfortably full bladder before performing the test (they are usually asked to attend having drunk 500–1000 ml of fluid). Drinks are provided so that the patient can continue to drink while providing two or three flow rates when bladder volumes are at least 150 ml. When they pass urine into the flow meter they should avoid compressing the penis, as this may lead to squeeze artefact. Similarly, they should not allow the urinary stream to wander around the funnel, as this may also lead to abnormal recordings. I tell them that they should aim to pass at least 150 ml, and if it is less than this than I ask them to repeat it. If it is persistently difficult to obtain an adequate voided volume, I ask them whether the flow is representative. If I have any doubts about the veracity of the recordings, I arrange for pressure-flow urodynamics.

Q. **What factors affect the flow rate?**
A. Flow rates are affected by the following:
- age
- gender
- voided volume (VV) (should be > 150 ml and < 500 ml)
- bladder outflow obstruction/hypocontractility.

Q. **What are the normal age-specific flow rates (Qmax) in male patients?**
A. Normal age-specific flow rates (Qmax) in males are as follows:
- < 40 years: > 21 ml/s
- 40–60 years: > 18 ml/s
- > 60 years: > 13 ml/s.
  Note: Age-specific flow rates (Qmax) in females are as follows:
- < 50 years: > 25 ml/s
- > 50 years: 18 ml/s.

Q. **What factors do you analyse when interpreting the flow tracing?**
A. • Voided volume – adequate, i.e. > 150 ml
   • Overdistention – VV > 500 ml
   • Maximum flow:
      – normal > 15 ml/s
      – suggestive of obstruction if < 10 ml/s
   • Overall pattern:
      – box-like curve (plateau curve) suggestive of stricture (for trace see Chapter 8)
      – hyperflow suggestive of overactive bladder
      – prolonged time to Qmax suggestive of BPH
      – intermittent bursts of flow suggestive of DSD (for trace see Chapter 11).

Q. **What is the significance of a reduced urinary flow rate?**
A. A reduced Qmax is usually taken to be evidence of bladder outflow obstruction (BOO). Around 90% of men with a flow rate of less than 10 ml/s will be obstructed on pressure-flow urodynamic criteria. The remaining 10% will have reduced detrusor contractility (low-pressure, low-flow situation). Similarly, 75% of men with a flow rate of more than 15 ml/s will not have BOO. The remainder of men with a good flow rate may have high-pressure, high-flow situations where flow is maintained at the expense of increased detrusor work. (As an approximate guide, there is a 90% probability of obstruction with a Qmax of < 10 ml/s, a 60% probability of obstruction with a Qmax in the range 10–15 ml/s, and a 30% probability of obstruction with a Qmax of > 15 ml/s).

In the clinical setting, a reduced flow rate is a risk factor for acute urinary retention[3] and symptomatic progression.[4]

Q. **If the principal significance of a reduced Qmax is that it indicates the likelihood of BOO, then what is the significance of BOO?**
A. The main significance of BOO is that it underpins the rationale behind disobstructing operations (e.g. TURP) in men with BPH. It allows more accurate prediction of symptomatic outcome after surgical intervention. Studies suggest that men with BOO who undergo TURP have a 90% chance of symptomatic improvement, as compared with men without BOO, who have a 60% chance of benefit.[5]

Q. **How can you accurately measure BOO?**
A. BOO is a urodynamic diagnosis. It represents a high-pressure, low-flow situation. It can only be defined by the simultaneous measurement of detrusor pressure and urinary flow. There are a number of different ways of categorising the presence or absence of obstruction.

Q. **Can you draw the ICS nomogram?**
A. The ICS nomogram (*see* Figure 12.2) categorises patients as obstructed, equivocal or unobstructed. The Abrams–Griffith number (Bladder Outlet Obstruction Index) gives a single numerical value through the following equation:

Pdet Qmax – 2 × Qmax = Abrams–Griffith number.

Values of > 40 are indicative of obstruction, values of < 20 represent unobstructed voiding, and values in the range 20–40 are equivocal.

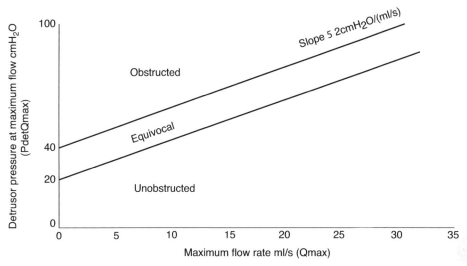

Current ICS method for definition of obstruction in patients with BPH

The Abrams-Griffith number (Bladder Outlet Obstruction Index) gives a single numeric value through the equation PdetQmax –2 x Qmax = Abrams-Griffith number. Values over 40 are indicative of obstruction, values less than 20 represent unobstructed voiding with values between 20 and 40 being equivocal.

Figure 12.2 The ICS nomogram.

Q. How would you describe the relationship between BOO and LUTS? Can you draw the diagram to illustrate this?

A. Hald's rings depict the relationship between BOO, BPH and LUTS (*see* Figure 12.3).

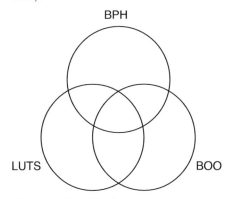

Figure 12.3 Hald's rings.

Q. What is BPH?

A. Benign prostatic hyperplasia (BPH) properly describes the histological basis of a diagnosis of benign prostatic enlargement (BPE) resulting in bladder outflow obstruction (BOO) that gives rise to lower urinary tract symptoms (LUTS).

265

Q. **Your patient in clinic asks why he has developed BPH. What can you tell him about the aetiology of this condition?**

A. We do not understand exactly what the causative agent or agents are in BPH. The following factors are important:

- age
- androgens
- race
- diet
- growth factors.

Q. **How common is BPH?**

A. The exact prevalence of BPH varies according to the definition used.

Data from post-mortem studies show that histological evidence of BPH can be detected from the age of 30 years, and the prevalence increases to 88% of 80-year–olds.[6]

Studies which define BPH on the basis of presence of symptoms alone give a higher prevalence than those studies which include reduced urinary flow rates or demonstrable prostatic enlargement. The Olmsted County study[4] showed a prevalence of moderate to severe urinary symptoms in 13% of men aged 40–49 years, rising to 28% of men over the age of 70 years. A UK study which defined BPH as the presence of an enlarged prostate (> 20 g) with symptoms or reduced urinary flow (Qmax < 15 ml/s) gives a BPH prevalence of 138 in 1000 members of the population aged 40–49 years (13.8%), rising to 430 in 1000 men aged 60–69 years (43%).[7]

Q. **Your patient asks what will happen if he does not have any treatment. Using the information that you already know about the patient, what can you tell him about the likely course of his condition? What other information would you ask for to try to predict the outcome in his particular case?**

A. Information on the natural history of BPH can be obtained from two main sources, namely cross-sectional studies of community-dwelling men and the placebo arms of drug trials.

The Olmsted County study measured the prevalence of symptoms of BPH in men aged 40–80 years. An average AUA symptom score deterioration of 0.18/year was observed across the study, with the fastest rate of deterioration observed in the 60–69 years age group. It seems reasonable to conclude that there is a gradual increase in urinary symptoms with age, but that the overall extent of these increases in the population is small.

Some risk factors have been identified which can help to predict disease progression in individual patients. Factors which have been shown to be associated with an increased likelihood of disease progression include age, symptom severity, reduced urinary flow rate and prostate size (*see* Table 12.2). The above patient in clinic has moderate symptoms, a reduced urinary flow rate and moderate prostate enlargement, which would all increase the likelihood of progression, but he is under 70 years old, which would reduce the overall likelihood of deterioration.

Data from placebo arms of large drug trials have shown that PSA is an independent marker of disease progression. I would therefore ask the patient to have a PSA test performed in order to try to refine his risk further. A PSA level of 1.4 ng/ml or higher indicates an increased risk of disease progression.

Other potential markers of disease progression include failure to respond to medical therapy,[8] symptom deterioration while on treatment, increasing residual urine volume,[9] and the presence of inflammation on prostate biopsies.[10]

Table 12.2 The important risk factors with regard to disease progression, and their associated hazard ratio (HR)

Risk factor	Risk of treatment
Moderate to severe symptoms	HR 5.3
Enlarged prostate (volume > 30 cm³)	HR 2.3
Reduced flow rate (Qmax < 12 m/s)	HR 2.7

MEDICAL TREATMENT

Q. **A 72-year-old man presents to your outpatient clinic with an IPSS of 18, a PSA of 1.9 and a reduced maximum urinary flow rate of 9 ml/s. Discuss this man's options for non-surgical treatment.**

A. His options are as follows:
- watchful waiting
- lifestyle changes
- phytotherapy
- medical therapy:
  - monotherapy
  - combination therapy.

For many men, the reason for seeking medical attention is a fear about cancer. On the basis of his PSA, and assuming that DRE is unremarkable, it is reasonable to reassure him that there are no signs of prostate cancer. If he has minimal inconvenience from his symptoms, no active intervention may be required. I would reassure him that the risk of a significant deterioration in his symptoms or an episode of acute urinary retention is low, based on data from the placebo arms of randomised controlled trials.

Lifestyle changes may have a beneficial effect on some categories of LUTS, especially storage LUTS.[11] Advice to maintain a reasonable fluid intake, avoid excess caffeine and restrict fluids before going to bed may help with symptoms of frequency, urgency and nocturia. Double voiding and urethral milking may help to reduce the sensation of incomplete bladder emptying and reduce post-micturition dribble.

Phytotherapy is an increasingly popular therapeutic option in the UK. Plant extracts (e.g. saw palmetto, rye pollen extract, *Pygeum africanuum* and beta-sitosterols) may have some benefit in alleviating symptoms and improving urinary flow.

Pharmacological treatment can be with alpha-adrenergic antagonists, 5-alpha-reductase inhibitors or a combination of the two. There is a large body of evidence from randomised controlled trials to support the efficacy of both of these groups of drugs.

Monotherapy with alpha-blockers is recommended for all men with uncomplicated LUTS. Meta-analysis of alpha-blocker trials has shown a reduction in symptoms of 30–40% and an improvement in flow rates of 16–25%. These effects appear to be durable.

Finasteride appears to be less effective than alpha-blockers when used as a single agent. The principal advantage of 5-alpha-reductase inhibitors is their ability to prevent disease progression. Data from the PLESS[12] study show a reduction in both the need for TURP (55%) and the incidence of acute urinary retention (57%) over 4 years. Similar data are available for dutasteride, which blocks both type 1 and type 2 5-alpha-reductase.[13]

Initial trials of combination therapy failed to demonstrate any advantage of combination treatment over monotherapy.[14] However, the publication of the MTOPS trial[15] and 2-year results from the CombAT study[16] has demonstrated a significant symptomatic benefit from combination therapy. BAUS guidelines for the management of men with LUTS suggest combination treatment for those with troublesome LUTS, prostatic obstruction and risk factors for progression.[17]

The above patient has a number of risk factors for disease progression, but we do not know how troublesome his LUTS are. If he has troublesome LUTS, combination treatment would be the best way to alleviate his symptoms and reduce his likelihood of BPH-related adverse events.

SURGICAL TREATMENT

Q. **A fit 64-year-old man is reviewed in your clinic with severe LUTS which have not responded to medical therapy. Investigations confirm benign prostatic obstruction. He is bothered by his LUTS and wants further treatment. What would you offer him?**

A. I would offer him a transurethral resection of the prostate (TURP).

Q. **What would you tell him about the likely symptomatic outcome of this operation?**

A. I would advise him that he has a 90% chance of symptom improvement, given that he has bladder outlet obstruction. I would also counsel him that voiding symptoms tend to improve much more quickly after a TURP than storage symptoms of frequency, urgency and nocturia.

Q. **What other groups of patients may benefit from TURP?**

A. In addition to men with troublesome LUTS who have failed a trial of medical management, the EAU gives the following indications for TURP:

- refractory urinary retention
- recurrent urinary retention
- recurrent haematuria that is refractory to medical treatment with 5-alpha-reductase inhibitors
- renal insufficiency
- bladder stones
- recurrent urinary tract infections as a result of BPH resulting in BOO
- increased post-void residual volume (exact value not defined).

TURP is also indicated in those with chronic high-pressure urinary retention.

Q. What complications would you warn this patient about?

A. I would use the BAUS procedure specific consent form for TURP. Potential complications include the following:

Early complications
- Anaesthesia related, ischaemic event, DVT.
- Blood transfusion in 1–2% of cases (on average 10 ml of blood loss per gram of tissue resected).
- Urinary sepsis in up to 3% of cases.
- Systemic sepsis in up to 1.5% of cases.
- TUR syndrome:
  - risk is 0.8% if < 45 g of tissue is resected and 1.5% if > 45 g of tissue is resected
  - risk is 0.8% if resection time is < 90 minutes and 2% if resection time is > 90 minutes.
- There is a risk of mortality of approximately 0.3% (within 30 days of operation).

Late complications
- Urinary incontinence in less than 1% of cases.
- Retrograde ejaculation in 80–100% of cases.
- Erectile dysfunction is reported in approximately 10% of cases.
- Bladder neck stenosis/urethral stricture in 3–5% of cases.
- The need to re-do TURP – there is cumulative risk of 2% per year of needing re-do surgery (thus 10% of cases at 5 years and 16% at 8 years require TURP to be performed again).

Q. How would you perform a TURP?

A. I would take an adequately prepared and consented patient to theatre, and after the patient has been anaesthetised, I would perform the following steps:
- Place the patient in the Lloyd Davis position.
- Clean and drape them with TUR drape allowing rectal examination to be performed to assess the size of the prostate.
- Perform initial cysto-urethroscopy to exclude other abnormalities of the lower urinary tract.
- Perform a urethral dilatation or Otis urethrotomy if either urethra is tight or using a 28Fr resectoscope.
- Insert the resectoscope and begin by resecting the median lobe down to the circular fibres of the bladder neck.
- Resect each lateral lobe in turn by resecting a channel down to the capsule at 10 or 2 o'clock and then dislocating the lateral lobe to allow efficient resection.
- If < 10 g is resected, perform additional TUIP.
- Remove prostate chips using an Ellik bladder evacuator.
- Achieve haemostasis with a rollerball.
- Check that all chips have been removed, that the ureteric orifices are visible and undamaged, and that no flaps have been created which might cause obstruction.

- Insert a three-way urethral catheter using an introducer.
- Assess catheter drainage and degree of haematuria before the endoscopic equipment is removed.
- Perform abdominal palpation to exclude extravasation.

Q. **What is TUR syndrome?**

A. TUR syndrome is the absorption of irrigating fluid during the procedure. The risk of this is 2% in some large studies. 1.5% glycine solution is the most commonly used irrigating fluid in the UK. This fluid is hypotonic with respect to plasma, and therefore absorption of irrigating fluid can lead to dilutional hyponatraemia and fluid overload. The clinical manifestations of this may include tachycardia, bradycardia, other cardiac dysrhythmias, hypotension, headache and convulsions. Glycine itself can be metabolised in the GABA pathway to produce a neurotransmitter that causes opisthotonus and cerebral irritation (see the chapter on urological emergencies for a more detailed discussion of TUR syndrome).

Q. **What steps can you take to reduce the likelihood of TUR syndrome?**

A. I would keep the height of the irrigating fluid above the patient to the minimum consistent with good vision. I would also avoid prolonged resection, particularly if there is evidence of capsular perforation or venous haemorrhage. I routinely use a continuous-flow resectoscope and examine the patient's abdomen at the end of the operation for any sign of extravasation.

Q. **How would you treat TUR syndrome?**

A. If evidence of TUR syndrome occurred during the procedure, I would act swiftly to obtain haemostasis and bring the operation to a close. I would place a 24Fr three-way catheter in the bladder and consider traction if there has been venous perforation or in the presence of persistent bleeding. I would ensure that irrigation is kept to an absolute minimum using normal saline solution. I would examine the abdomen for signs of extravasation. I would ask the anaesthetist to send bloods, including full blood count, U&E and clotting studies, and to give a 40 mg dose of intravenous furosemide. Any dysrhythmias should be treated in accordance with cardiac guidelines, and the patient should be carefully monitored post-operatively in an ITU facility. The serum sodium concentration should be restored slowly through the judicious use of fluid restriction, diuretics and, rarely, hypertonic saline (see Chapter 7 for a more detailed discussion of TUR syndrome).

Q. **You are called to recovery to see the patient on whom you have just performed a TURP. The nurses are concerned by the extent of the haematuria and inform you that the catheter keeps clotting off. What actions would you take?**

A. I would assess the patient to ensure that they are cardiovascularly stable and resuscitate as necessary.

I would examine the patient's abdomen to see if the bladder is distended. I would then perform a bladder washout with normal saline, also ensuring that the irrigation channel is patent. I would endeavour to wash out any clots and recommence bladder irrigation.

If this failed to control the haematuria, I would deflate the catheter balloon, push the catheter further into the bladder and then insert 50 ml of water into the catheter balloon and apply traction by strapping the catheter to the patient's thigh. I would reassess the patient's cardiovascular status and the degree of haematuria.

If faced with ongoing haematuria, I would contact the consultant in charge of the patient with a view to returning to theatre. I would ensure that blood was cross-matched and explain to the patient the need to return to theatre to control bleeding. Assuming that the patient's condition allowed, I would take written consent. In theatre, I would re-insert the resectoscope and perform an Ellik bladder washout. I would then conduct a thorough inspection of the prostatic bed to look for obvious sources of bleeding. The commonest sites of bleeding are from arteries at the bladder neck or from venous perforation. I would attempt to control bleeding with the rollerball, accepting that this is usually more successful in arterial bleeding. In the presence of significant venous perforation I would re-insert a catheter, over-inflate the balloon and apply traction for 10 minutes by the clock. If none of these measures controlled the bleeding, I would make a lower midline incision, open the bladder between stay sutures, inspect the cavity for bleeding points, diathermise or under-run bleeding vessels as appropriate, and ultimately pack the prostatic cavity if none of the above-mentioned steps had worked (see also the chapter on urological emergencies).

Q. What other conventional operations have been used for the treatment of BPH?

A. Transvesical prostatectomy was commonly used at the beginning of the twentieth century, and is still practised in many developing countries. It can still be indicated if there are large bladder calculi or other bladder abnormalities (e.g. large diverticulae which require simultaneous treatment). Millin's retropubic prostatectomy is the preferred operation if open surgery is indicated, as it allows better haemostasis and visualisation of the prostatic cavity.

Open prostatectomy is no longer commonly performed in the UK, but is indicated with large prostate size (> 100 g) or difficulty in positioning the patient due to hip contractures. Cancerous prostates or small fibrous glands in which there is no surgical plane in which to conduct the enucleation should not be treated by a Millin's prostatectomy. In general, the risks of open prostatectomy are greater than those of TURP, particularly with regard to bleeding, blood transfusion, incontinence, bladder neck contracture and thromboembolic complications (although the need to re-do procedures is decreased).

Small prostate glands (< 30 ml) may be treated by transurethral incision of the prostate (TUIP) with good symptomatic results and reduced complications.

Q. What would you do if you found a stone in the bladder on initial cystoscopy?

A. It would depend on the size of the stone and the size of the prostate.

If the stone is small and the prostate is of a reasonable size, I would perform a cystolitholapaxy and proceed to TUIP or TURP at the same sitting according to the size of the prostate.

If the stone is larger but can still be managed endoscopically, I would deal with the stone and perform a TURP at a later date.

If the stone is too large to be dealt with endoscopically, open surgery will be necessary. Traditionally this would be an indication for a transvesical prostatectomy and open stone removal. If the stone has been found on pre-operative assessment and the possible need for open surgery with its attendant complications has been discussed with the patient, I would proceed with the operation. If the stone is an unexpected finding, each individual surgeon must decide whether they feel that they have obtained the patient's informed consent to proceed with open surgery and be prepared to justify that decision – in court if necessary!

Q. **What other procedures are currently used in the UK as alternatives to conventional TURP?**

A. There are two principal types of procedure which are offered as alternatives to TURP, namely those which utilise modifications of conventional electrosurgery, and those which use alternative energy sources (e.g. lasers).

Transurethral electrovaporisation of the prostate is a technique that employs a modified electrode which produces vaporisation of tissue with a zone of underlying coagulation to improve haemostasis. It has been shown in randomised controlled trials to produce equivalent outcomes to TURP, with reduced bleeding complications.[18]

Bipolar electroresection of the prostate is inherently safer than conventional monopolar surgery, as the patient does not form part of the electrical circuit. It allows the use of normal saline as an irrigating fluid, which minimises the risk of TUR syndrome. Clinical results have been variable.[19]

Laser prostatectomy has been used in the treatment of symptomatic BPH since the early 1990s, and has evolved through a number of different techniques. The most common types of laser used are the holmium (Ho:YAG) and KTP (KTP:YAG) lasers.

There are three different techniques utilised with the holmium laser, namely ablation (HoLAP), resection (HoLRP) and enucleation (HoLEP). Ablation uses the vaporising ability of the laser to create a cavity by repeated passage of the laser over the surface of the prostate. Resection involves the removal of pieces of tissue using the cutting action of a bare laser fibre. HoLEP is the endoscopic equivalent of an open prostatectomy in which the plane between the adenoma and prostatic capsule is developed to dissect the lobes of the prostate out before they are then morcellated to allow extraction. There is evidence from randomised controlled trials of HoLRP[20] and HoLEP[21] that they produce symptomatic outcomes which are at least equivalent to, if not better than, conventional TURP. The main drawbacks of HoLEP are the expense of the laser, the perceived difficulty of learning the procedure, and the inherent risks of bladder damage during the morcellation process.

KTP lasers have been in use for over a decade, but have gradually increased in power with a corresponding increase in vaporisation efficiency. The technique is similar to that of HoLAP. They have been shown in randomised controlled trials[22] to produce equivalent symptomatic outcomes to TURP, but with reduced bleeding and shorter hospital stays. Day-case prostate surgery is now a realistic proposition, and at the author's institute over 80% of men who undergo this procedure are discharged on the same day.

The general concern about many of the alternatives to TURP is the completeness of tissue removal and the lack of robust long-term efficacy data. Time will tell whether the longer-term effectiveness of these techniques is indeed equivalent or superior to standard TURP.

ACUTE URINARY RETENTION

Q. **A 65-year-old man is referred to you by his GP with moderate LUTS. He is primarily concerned that he may develop a 'complete stoppage'. How would you assess and counsel him?**

A. There are a number of risk factors which have been identified for acute urinary retention (AUR) both in community-based observational studies and in randomised controlled trials of drug treatment for BPH. These include age, reduced flow rate, prostate volume, PSA and a previous episode of urinary retention (*see* Table 12.3).

Table 12.3 The important risk factors with regard to acute urinary retention and their respective relative risk

Risk factor	AUR relative risk
IPSS > 7	3.2
Qmax < 12 ml/s	3.9
Prostate volume > 30 ml	3.0
PSA > 1.4	2.0
Age > 70 vs. 40–49 years	10–11

Q. **A 78-year-old man presents to A&E with a painfully distended bladder and an inability to pass urine. How would you manage this patient?**

A. I would take a concise history, examine the patient and then insert a urinary catheter. Having relieved his discomfort I would then arrange further investigations, including urinalysis, full blood count, U&E and ultrasound scan.

Q. **Your investigations reveal a serum creatinine concentration of 427 µmol/l, and the ultrasound scan demonstrates bilateral hydronephrosis. What is your further management of this patient?**

A. I would arrange for the patient to be admitted. I would ask the nurses to record hourly monitoring of pulse, blood pressure and urine output. I would ask to be informed if the patient produces more than 200 ml of urine per hour for 2 consecutive hours. I would ensure that his admission weight is recorded and request daily weighing to monitor for gross fluid shifts.

If there is evidence of post-obstructive diuresis, I would give replacement intravenous *normal saline* equivalent to 90% of the patient's previous hour's urine output (the amount of fluid replacement is variable – some would only replace 50% of the previous hour's urine output). I would recheck the serum U&E to ensure that the creatinine level is falling and that potassium levels remain within range. I would expect to continue intravenous fluid support for 24–48 hours.

Q. **What is the mechanism behind post-obstructive diuresis?**

A. There is both a physiological and pathological component to the diuresis.

A physiological diuresis occurs because of the accumulation of fluid, electrolytes and waste products during the preceding period of renal failure. Relief of obstruction allows elimination of excess amounts of these substances to occur.

Pathological diuresis occurs because of a number of factors which lead to tubular dysfunction and inappropriate salt and water handling by the kidney. These include the following:

- defective generation of medullary solute gradient secondary to:
  - decreased re-absorption of NaCl by the thick ascending limb of the loop of Henle
  - decreased reabsorption of urea by the collecting tubule
- inability to maintain medullary solute gradient secondary to:
  - increased medullary blood flow (solute washout)
- increased endogenous production of ANP (plus other natriuretic peptides)
- poor response of collecting duct to ADH.

Q. **Draw a graph to show the recovery of glomerular filtration rate (GFR) following the relief of obstruction.**

A. This is illustrated in Figure 12.4. As the GFR continues to recover for up to 3 months, plasma creatinine levels will continue to decrease over this period.

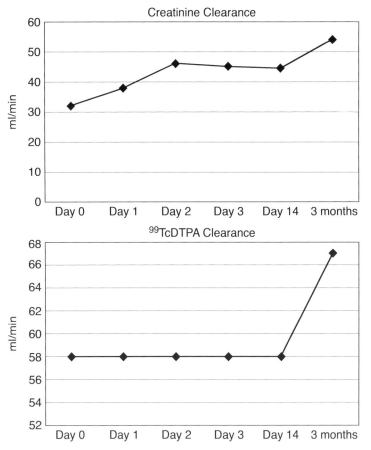

Figure 12.4 Changes in creatinine clearance and ^{99m}Tc DTPA clearance following relief of obstruction. Both are estimates of glomerular filtration rate.

Q. If creatinine clearance and ^{99m}Tc DTPA clearance are both indicators of glomerular filtration rate, why does creatinine clearance improve more quickly?

A. Creatinine is excreted by the tubules of the kidney as well as through glomerular filtration. Following relief of bilateral ureteric obstruction in this case tubular function recovers in the first 14 days, but full recovery of glomerular function may take up to 3 months. The return of tubular function increases creatinine clearance and allows serum creatinine levels to fall, but this does not reflect a real change in GFR.

Note: Creatinine clearance estimates the GFR and can be measured over 12–24 hours by the formula UV/P, where U is the urinary concentration of creatinine, V is the volume of urine produced over a timed interval, and P is the plasma concentration of creatinine. About 80% of creatinine clearance is due to GFR and 20% is due to renal tubular secretion. Thus creatinine clearance is an over-estimate of actual GFR (this becomes important in very poor renal function, when tubular secretion may be responsible for a relatively greater proportion of the creatinine clearance).

Q. What is your definitive management of the patient?

A. This is a case of high-pressure urinary obstruction, and therefore definitive management would be a TURP performed after at least 2 weeks of catheterisation.

REFERENCES

1. Abrams P. New words for old: lower urinary tract symptoms for 'prostatism.' *BMJ* 1994; **308:** 929–30.
2. Barry MJ *et al.* The American Urological Association symptom index for benign prostatic hyperplasia. The Measurement Committee of the American Urological Association. *J Urol* 1992; **148:** 1549–57.
3. Jacobsen SJ *et al.* Natural history of prostatism: risk factors for acute urinary retention. *J Urol* 1997; **158:** 481–7.
4. Jacobsen SJ *et al.* Natural history of prostatism: longitudinal changes in voiding symptoms in community-dwelling men. *J Urol* 1996; **155:** 595–600.
5. Abrams PH *et al.* The results of prostatectomy: a symptomatic and urodynamic analysis of 152 patients. *J Urol* 1979; **121:** 640–2.
6. Berry SJ *et al.* The development of human benign prostatic hyperplasia with age. *J Urol* 1984; **132:** 474–9.
7. Garraway WM *et al.* High prevalence of benign prostatic hypertrophy in the community. *Lancet* 1991; **338:** 469–71.
8. Emberton M *et al.* Response to daily 10 mg alfuzosin predicts acute urinary retention and benign prostatic hyperplasia-related surgery in men with lower urinary tract symptoms. *J Urol* 2006; **176:** 1051–6.
9. Emberton M. Definition of at-risk patients: dynamic variables. *BJU Int* 2006; **97 (Suppl. 2):** 12–15.
10. Mishra VC *et al.* Does intraprostatic inflammation have a role in the pathogenesis and progression of benign prostatic hyperplasia? *BJU Int* 2007; **100:** 327–31.
11. Brown CT *et al.* Self-management for men with lower urinary tract symptoms: randomised controlled trial. *BMJ* 2007; **334:** 25.

12. Roehrborn CG *et al*. Serum prostate-specific antigen concentration is a powerful predictor of acute urinary retention and need for surgery in men with clinical benign prostatic hyperplasia. PLESS Study Group. *Urology* 1999; **53:** 473–80.

13. Roehrborn CG *et al*. Efficacy and tolerability of the dual 5-alpha-reductase inhibitor, dutasteride, in the treatment of benign prostatic hyperplasia in African-American men. *Prostate Cancer Prostatic Dis* 2006; **9:** 432–8.

14. Lepor H *et al*. The efficacy of terazosin, finasteride, or both in benign prostatic hyperplasia. Veterans Affairs Cooperative Studies Benign Prostatic Hyperplasia Study Group. *NEJM* 1996; **335:** 533–9.

15. McConnell JD *et al*. The long-term effect of doxazosin, finasteride, and combination therapy on the clinical progression of benign prostatic hyperplasia. *NEJM* 2003; **349:** 2387–98.

16. Roehrborn CG *et al*. The effects of dutasteride, tamsulosin and combination therapy on lower urinary tract symptoms in men with benign prostatic hyperplasia and prostatic enlargement: 2-year results from the CombAT study. *J Urol* 2008; **179:** 616–21.

17. Speakman MJ *et al*. Guideline for the primary care management of male lower urinary tract symptoms. *BJU Int* 2004; **93:** 985–90.

18. McAllister WJ *et al*. Transurethral electrovaporization of the prostate: is it any better than conventional transurethral resection of the prostate? *BJU Int* 2003; **91:** 211–14.

19. Dunsmuir WD *et al*. Gyrus bipolar electrovaporization vs transurethral resection of the prostate: a randomized prospective single-blind trial with 1 y follow-up. *Prostate Cancer Prostatic Dis* 2003; **6:** 182–6.

20. Gilling PJ *et al*. Holmium laser resection v transurethral resection of the prostate: results of a randomized trial with 2 years of follow-up. *J Endourol* 2000; **14:** 757–60.

21. Wilson LC *et al*. A randomised trial comparing holmium laser enucleation versus transurethral resection in the treatment of prostates larger than 40 grams: results at 2 years. *Eur Urol* 2006; **50:** 569–73.

22. Bouchier-Hayes DM *et al*. KTP laser versus transurethral resection: early results of a randomized trial. *J Endourol* 2006; **20:** 580–5.

Chapter 13
Andrology

Jas Kalsi, Asif Muneer and Suks Minhas

ERECTILE DYSFUNCTION

Q. A 65-year-old man has had worsening erectile function for one year. He is now avoiding sexual intimacy. His wife is very concerned and asks him to see his GP. The GP tells him not to worry as it is a normal part of the ageing process. After a further 6 months, as the situation gets worse, the patient goes to see another partner in the practice who refers him to the urologist. How would you define erectile dysfunction?

A. It is defined as the persistent inability to achieve or maintain an erection sufficient for satisfactory sexual performance.

Q. Can you describe the different phases of penile erection?

A. In animal studies five distinct phases have been demonstrated:
- 0, flaccid
- 1, latent
- 2, tumescence
- 3, full erection
- 4, rigid erection
- 5, detumescence (initial, slow and fast phases).

Q. Can you explain the physiological process of penile erection?

A. Penile erection is the result of a complex and delicate interplay between many physical and psychological processes. The cavernous smooth muscle and the smooth muscle of the arteriolar and arterial walls play a key role in the erectile process. In the flaccid state, these smooth muscles are tonically contracted, allowing only a small amount of arterial flow. Sexual stimulation triggers the release of neurotransmitters from the cavernous nerve terminals, resulting in relaxation of these smooth muscles and the following events:
1. dilatation of the arterioles and arteries by increased blood flow in both the diastolic and systolic phases
2. trapping of the incoming blood by the expanding sinusoids
3. compression of the subtunical venular plexuses between the tunica albuginea and the peripheral sinusoids, reducing the venous outflow

4. stretching of the tunica to its capacity, which encloses the emissary veins between the inner circular and the outer longitudinal layers and further decreases the venous outflow to a minimum

5. an increase in intracavernous pressure (maintained at around 100 mmHg), which raises the penis from the dependent position to the erect state (the full-erection phase)

6. a further pressure increase (to several hundred millimetres of mercury) with contraction of the ischiocavernosus muscles (rigid-erection phase).

Q. **What mechanisms allow the penis to achieve a full rigid erection?**

A. During the full-erection phase, partial compression of the deep dorsal and circumflex veins between Buck's fascia and the engorged corpora cavernosa contribute to glanular tumescence. In the rigid-erection phase, the ischiocavernosus and bulbocavernosus muscles forcefully compress the spongiosum and penile veins, which results in further engorgement and increased pressure in the glans and spongiosum.

Q. **Can you describe the arterial supply of the penis?**

A. The main source of blood supply to the penis is from the internal pudendal artery. However, accessory arteries may arise from the external iliac, obturator, vesical and femoral arteries. The internal pudendal artery becomes the common penile artery after giving off a branch to the perineum.

The three branches of the penile artery are the dorsal, bulbourethral and cavernous arteries:

- cavernous artery – tumescence of the corpus cavernosum. Gives off many helicine arteries which supply the trabecular erectile tissue and the sinusoids. These helicine arteries are contracted and tortuous in the flaccid state, and become dilated and straight during erection
- dorsal artery – engorgement of the glans penis during erection
- bulbourethral artery – supplies the bulb and corpus spongiosum.

Distally, the three branches join to form a vascular ring near the glans.

Q. **Can you describe venous drainage of the penis?**

A. The venous drainage from the three corpora originates in tiny venules leading from the peripheral sinusoids immediately beneath the tunica albuginea. These venules travel in the trabeculae between the tunica and the peripheral sinusoids to form the subtunical venular plexus, before exiting as the emissary veins.

Outside the tunica albuginea, the venous drainage is dependent on the area of drainage as follows:

- skin and subcutaneous tissue – multiple superficial veins run subcutaneously and unite near the root of the penis to form superficial dorsal vein(s), which in turn usually drain into the saphenous veins
- emissary veins from the corpus cavernosum and corpus spongiosum – drain dorsally to the deep dorsal, laterally to the circumflex, and ventrally to the

periurethral veins. Beginning at the coronal sulcus, the prominent deep dorsal vein is the main venous drainage of the glans penis, the corpus spongiosum, and the distal two-thirds of the corpora cavernosa. It runs upward behind the symphysis pubis to join the periprostatic venous plexus

- emissary veins draining the proximal corpora cavernosa – form cavernous and crural veins. These veins join the periurethral veins from the urethral bulb to form the internal pudendal veins.

Q. Why should erectile dysfunction be investigated?

A. The correct assessment of men presenting with ED can identify the following:

- diabetes (ED may be the first symptom in up to 20% of cases)
- occult cardiac disease (ED in an otherwise asymptomatic man may be a marker for underlying coronary artery disease)
- dyslipidaemia
- presence of hypogonadism.

Q. What questions would you ask in the history?

A. I would see the patient in my specialist sexual dysfunction clinic, with discussions in the presence of his partner if possible. First, I would confirm that this is really ED (see the above definition), rather than some other problem such as Peyronie's disease or ejaculatory dysfunction. I would then ascertain the following points in the history:

- Was the onset of ED sudden or gradual?
- Does the patient have early-morning erections or not?
- Does ED occur in all situations (with different partners, masturbation)?
- What is the severity (objectively assessed with the IIEF five-part questionnaire)?
- Has previous treatment been successful?
- What are the patient's (and his partner's) needs and expectations?

Q. How would you assess the severity of the condition?

A. I would use a validated questionnaire such as the International Index of Erectile Function (IIEF) or the validated shorter version, the IIEF-5. These are helpful in assessing sexual function domains as well as the impact of treatments and interventions. The questionnaire is used to make an assessment over the previous 6 months (see Table 13.1).

The overall score allows the severity to be assessed objectively as follows:

- 1–7 severe ED
- 8–11 moderate ED
- 12–16 mild to moderate ED
- 17–21 mild ED
- 22–25 no ED.

Table 13.1 International Index of Erectile Function (IIEF-5) questionnaire

1. How do you rate your confidence that you could get and keep an erection?		Very low	Low	Moderate	High	Very high
		1	2	3	4	5
2. When you had erections with sexual stimulation, how often were your erections hard enough for penetration (entering your partner)?	No sexual activity	Almost never/ never	A few times (much less than half the time)	Sometimes (about half the time)	Most times (much more than half the time)	Almost always/ always
	0	1	2	3	4	5
3. During sexual intercourse, how often were you able to maintain your erection after you had penetrated (entered) your partner?	Did not attempt intercourse	Almost never/ never	A few times (much less than half the time)	Sometimes (about half the time)	Most times (much more than half the time)	Almost always/ always
	0	1	2	3	4	5
4. During sexual intercourse, how difficult was it to maintain your erection to completion of intercourse?	Did not attempt intercourse	Extremely difficult	Very difficult	Difficult	Slightly difficult	Not difficult
	0	1	2	3	4	5
5. When you attempted sexual intercourse, how often was it satisfactory for you?	Did not attempt intercourse	Almost never/ never	A few times (much less than half the time)	Sometimes (about half the time)	Most times (much more than half the time)	Almost always/ always
	0	1	2	3	4	5

Q.   What would you assess on a physical examination?

A.   A focused physical examination should be performed on every patient with ED. This should include an emphasis on the neurological, vascular and reproductive systems. Height, weight, body mass index and blood pressure should be recorded.

In particular, it is important to examine for the following:
- thyroid evaluation, pulmonary status and cardiac rhythm
- abdominal exam with waist circumference recorded
- penile exam (note any plaques or lesions)
- testis exam (note size and any irregularities)
- rectal exam (sphincter tone, prostate evaluation).

Q. **Would you perform any other tests?**

A. I would usually perform the following:
- urinalysis
- fasting glucose
- fasting lipids
- total testosterone
- prostate-specific antigen (after appropriate counselling)
- prolactin.

Q. **This patient is a non-insulin-dependent diabetic, he has had a gradual onset of ED, and he has an IIEF-5 score of 8. All blood tests other than fasting glucose are normal. How would you manage this patient?**

A. I would identify and treat any curable causes of ED such as poorly controlled diabetes. I would also initiate lifestyle changes (including exercise and weight loss) and seek to modify any associated risk factors. I would then offer him a trial of an oral PDE5 inhibitor if there are no contraindications.

Q. **How do PDE5 inhibitors work? Can you draw the diagram?**

A. Nitric oxide (NO) enters the smooth muscle cell, where it activates the soluble form of the enzyme guanylate cyclase (sGC), which catalyses the conversion of guanosine triphosphate (GTP) to the active intracellular second messenger cyclic guanosine monophosphate (cGMP). In turn, cGMP leads to activation of a number of intracellular events, which eventually bring about penile smooth muscle relaxation (*see* Figure 13.1), mainly via a reduction in intracellular calcium levels. The action of cGMP is terminated by its metabolism to GMP by phosphodiesterases (PDEs). Drugs that inhibit the action of PDEs (such as the PDE5 inhibitors) facilitate NO-induced smooth muscle relaxation within the penis by causing an accumulation of intracellular cGMP.

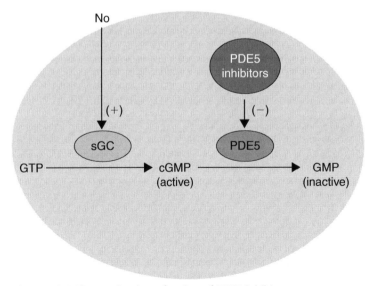

Figure 13.1 The mechanism of action of PDE5 inhibitors.

Q. Which PDE5 inhibitors are you aware of?

A. There are currently three agents available, namely sildenafil (Viagra®), tadalafil (Cialis®) and vardenafil (Levitra®).

Q. What are the differences between them?

A. The major difference is that sildenafil and vardenafil are relatively short-acting drugs, having a half-life of approximately 4 hours, whereas tadalafil has a significantly longer half-life of 17.5 hours. Furthermore, tadalafil is not known to have its bioavailability reduced by fatty foods.

Q. How would you counsel the patient and initiate therapy with a PDE5 inhibitor?

A. First, I would ensure that there are no contraindications to treatment with oral PDE5 inhibitors. In my practice, the specific choice of first-line medication is patient-driven. It depends on whether the couple wish to have unplanned sex (in which case use tadalafil) or planned sex (in which case use sildenafil or vardenafil). I then explain that my patient will need to have the maximum dose of the drug at least 1 hour before sex (*see* Table 13.2), ideally on an empty stomach and, importantly, that the medication will not work without appropriate sexual stimulation. I then also explain the potential side-effects and briefly the relevant pharmacology of the chosen drug, in layman's terms (*see* Table 13.2). When I have informed him of all these factors, the final choice is made by the patient.

Table 13.2 Characteristics of the different PDE5 inhibitors

	Sildenafil	*Vardenafil*	*Tadalafil*
Onset of action	15 min to 1 hour	15 min to 1 hour	15 min to 2 hours
Half-life	3–5 hours	4–5 hours	17.5 hours
Bioavailability	40%	15%	Not tested
Effect of food	Reduced absorption with fatty foods	Reduced absorption with fatty foods	None
Dosages	25, 50, 100 mg	5, 10, 20 mg	5, 10, 20 mg
Side-effects	Headache, dyspepsia, facial flushing, blurred/blue vision, rare cases of backache, myalgia	Headache, dyspepsia, facial flushing, rare cases of backache, myalgia and blurred/blue vision	Headache, dyspepsia, facial flushing, backache, myalgia, rare cases of blurred/blue vision
Contra-indications	Nitrates	Nitrates, anti-arrhythmics	Nitrates

Q. What are the common side-effects associated with PDE5 inhibitors?

A. All PDE-5 inhibitors produce side-effects that are usually associated with peripheral vasodilatation, including nasal congestion, facial flushing, headache and dyspepsia. Tadalafil has been linked to back pain in up to 10% of cases. Vardenafil has been shown to slightly prolong the QT interval. Optical neuropathies have been reported. However, the actual incidence of optical neuropathy is rare.

Q. The patient has recently been started on an antihypertensive by his GP. He feels that this has made his ED worse. What other medications are known to be associated with ED?

A. Diuretics and other antihypertensives are known to be associated with worsening ED. Other medications that are associated with ED include antidepressants, anti-anxiety and anti-epileptic drugs, antihistamines, non-steroidal anti-inflammatory drugs, Parkinson's disease medications, anti-arrhythmics, histamine H2-receptor antagonists, muscle relaxants, prostate cancer medications and chemotherapy medications.

Q. **Unfortunately, despite maximum doses of the PDE5 inhibitor, the patient does not get a satisfactory response. How would you manage this patient?**

A. I would explain to him that approximately 25% of patients do not respond to PDE5 inhibitors. I would recommended that he should try at least four of the highest tolerated dose of at least two drugs (taken sequentially, not concurrently), with adequate sexual stimulation. If there is still no benefit, re-education about the effect of modifiable factors, such as dose, timing of medication, alcohol consumption, adequate sexual arousal, and interaction with fatty foods is required. I would make sure that he is not hypogonadal. If he is, I would commence testosterone replacement together with the PDE5 inhibitor therapy. In patients who are hypogonadal, testosterone replacement may result in a general improvement in sexual function, improved erection and enhanced responsiveness to PDE5 inhibitors.

Q. **Despite optimisation, the patient still does not get satisfactory erections. What alternative treatment options are available?**

A. If patients do not benefit from PDE5 inhibitors or the latter are contraindicated, the need for second-line agents should be assessed. These include the following:
- *Alprostadil intraurethral suppositories*: a non-injectable prostaglandin pellet, which improves vascular flow by causing vasodilatation by increasing levels of cyclic AMP.
- *Intracavernosal injections*: local injections of one or a combination of alprostadil, papaverine and phentolamine.
- *Vacuum constriction devices*: these are effective in most patients and can be purchased with or without a prescription.

Third-line therapy includes the following:
- *Penile prostheses*: surgically placed non-inflatable (semi-rigid) or inflatable devices.
- *Penile vascular reconstruction*: reserved for specific young patients who have suffered from pelvic trauma involving the penile vasculature.

Q. **Which patients are entitled to erectile dysfunction treatment on the NHS?**

A. In 1999 the Secretary of State for Health restricted the availability of treatments for ED in the NHS. ED associated with certain medical conditions was deemed to qualify for prescription at NHS expense (endorsed as SLS–Schedule 11). These conditions include the following:
- diabetes
- multiple sclerosis
- Parkinson's disease
- poliomyelitis
- prostate cancer

- prostatectomy (including TURP)
- radical pelvic surgery
- renal failure treated by dialysis or transplant
- severe pelvic injury
- single-gene neurological disease
- spinal cord injury
- spina bifida.

In addition, there are two other qualifiers:
1. patients who were receiving a course of NHS drug treatment on 14 September 1998
2. patients who are suffering 'severe distress' on account of their ED.

The decision about referral to specialist services is based on the clinical judgement of the GP.

Q. **Which specialist tests are you aware of and when are they used?**

A. Specialist investigations include nocturnal penile tumescence testing, cavernosometry or cavernosography, and Duplex ultrasound. Most patients do not require further investigations. However, some patients wish to know the aetiology, and in others specialist investigations are required. These include:
- young patients who have always had difficulty in obtaining and/or sustaining an erection
- patients with a history of trauma
- cases where an abnormality of the testes or penis is found on examination
- patients who are unresponsive to medical therapies and who may desire surgical treatment for ED.

Q. **What is shown in Figure 13.2? How does it work and what is it used for?**

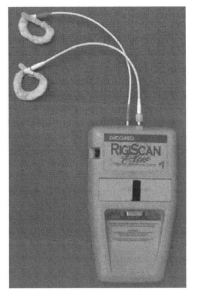

Figure 13.2

A. This is a Rigiscan device, which is used to provide a nocturnal penile tumescence (NPT) trace. It contains two rings which are placed around the tip and base of the penis, respectively. They are used to measure the number, duration and rigidity of nocturnal erections. Nocturnal and early-morning erections are a normal physiological event in all men, and are associated with the REM pattern of sleep. This test is used to differentiate between organic and psychogenic causes of ED.

Q. What is shown in Figure 13.3?

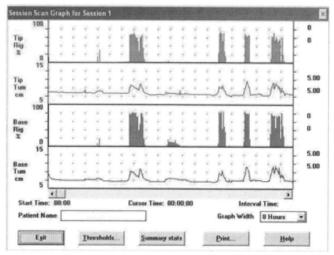

Figure 13.3

A. This is a normal NPT trace. A normal trace shows greater than 60% rigidity at the tip for longer than 10 minutes.

Q. Is there a role for duplex ultrasound in the investigation of ED? What are the important values?

A. This test is used if there is a suspected vascular cause of the ED. This investigation measures blood flow before and after intracavernosal injection of prostaglandin (PGE1). The normal values are a peak systolic velocity of > 35 cm/second and an end diastolic velocity of < 5 cm/second.

Q. What is the test shown in Figure 13.4 and how is it performed?

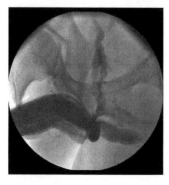

Figure 13.4

A. Figure 13.4 shows a cavernosogram. In cavernosography, an artificial erection is created followed by the injection of contrast into the penis. Imaging and blood flow is performed in order to identify any venous leaks. This image demonstrates a venous leak, although the pathological entity of venous leak is controversial.

Q. **What is shown in Figure 13.5 and how does it work?**

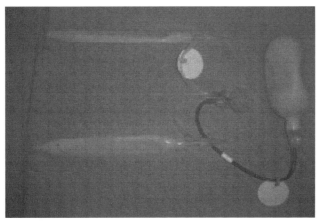

Figure 13.5

A. This is a three-piece inflatable penile implant. It consists of a reservoir that is implanted in the abdomen, a pump that is placed in the scrotum, and a pair of cylinders that are implanted in the penis. The reservoir is placed in an extra-peritoneal position. The pump is placed in the scrotum and pumped up to allow inflation. A small button is pressed on the pump to allow deflation. Penile prostheses should be offered to all patients who are unwilling to consider, failing to respond to, or unable to continue with medical therapy or external devices. All patients and their partners should be counselled pre-operatively. They should be shown and allowed to handle all of the available devices, and if possible they should have the opportunity to speak to other patients who have had surgery. Penile prostheses are particularly suitable for those with severe organic ED, especially if the cause is Peyronie's disease, or post priapism. All patients should be given a choice of either a malleable or inflatable prosthesis.

Q. **What are the possible complications of penile prosthesis surgery?**
A. The long-term risks include infection (5%), erosion (5%), and mechanical failure (4%) which may need re-operation. The initial cost is high, but the manufacturers do offer a lifetime guarantee. These risks are higher in patients who are diabetic.

Q. **What are the long-term success rates of penile prosthesis surgery?**
A. Long-term success and satisfaction rates of nearly 90% have been reported. These high rates are due to the improved mechanical reliability of the new devices and careful pre-operative counselling.[1] The advantages of a penile prosthesis include long-term efficacy with a high satisfaction rate, the fact that there is no need for medication, and the improved ability to lead a more normal sexual life.

INFERTILITY

Q. A 32-year-old man is referred to you for infertility. He has never fathered children, but has been married for 5 years. His wife is 37 years old. They have been actively trying to have children for 15 months. How would you define infertility?

A. The inability of a sexually active, non-contracepting couple to achieve pregnancy within 12 months.

Q. What is the baseline background fertility rate?

A. The probability of a normal couple conceiving is estimated to be 20–25% per month, 75% by 6 months, and 90% by 1 year. The baseline pregnancy rate is 1–3% per month (in non-azoospermic couples).

Q. Is infertility usually caused by a problem in the female partner?

A. Approximately 20% of cases of infertility are entirely due to a male factor, with an additional 30–40% of cases involving both male and female factors. Therefore a male factor is present in around 50% of infertile couples.

Q. When would you begin investigation, if at all?

A. Of those infertile couples who do not undergo treatment, 25–35% will conceive at some time by intercourse alone. In the past it was recommended that patients should not be investigated until after 12 months of attempted conception. However, with the advancing age of infertile couples, a basic, simple, cost-effective evaluation of both partners may be initiated at the time of presentation.

Q. How would you assess this man with infertility?

A. I would first make sure that his wife is also thoroughly screened. This is often most conveniently done in a joint clinic, with a gynaecologist. Then I would establish if this is actually infertility (see above definition). If infertility is confirmed, I would try to establish the causative and prognostic factors by taking a focused urological history and clinical examination, and by requesting relevant investigations.

Q. What would you ask about when taking the history?

A. I would ask about the duration of infertility, the details of previous pregnancies, methods of birth control used in the past, the couple's frequency of sexual intercourse, and the timing of coitus. Both erectile and ejaculatory function should be assessed, and the use of any vaginal lubricants during intercourse should be noted, as these may affect sperm quality.

The developmental history of the patient should be noted, including any history of cryptorchidism, age at puberty, and secondary sexual characteristics. The patient's past surgical history may be of particular importance, such as a previous history of orchidopexy, torsion of testis or inguinal hernia surgery.

The patient should be questioned about a history of urinary tract infections or sexually transmitted diseases as well as post-pubertal mumps.

A history of previous chemotherapy or radiation therapy may further impair testicular function.

A history of chronic upper respiratory tract infections should be actively sought.

Anabolic steroid abuse by athletes may result in hypogonadotropic hypogonadism.

Q. **What would you be looking for in the physical examination of this patient?**

A. On examination, the patient's habitus (obesity) as well as the pattern of virilisation should be noted. After this a focused uro-genital examination is performed. The penis should be examined for evidence of hypospadias and severe chordee, as both may interfere with proper deposition of semen. The scrotal contents should be examined with the patient standing in a warm room to allow for relaxation of the cremasteric muscle. The testes should be carefully palpated to determine consistency and to rule out the presence of an intra-testicular mass. The dimensions of the testes should be measured. Palpation of the epididymis should determine the presence of the head, body and tail. The possibility of epididymal obstruction is suggested by the presence of induration or cystic dilatation of the epididymis. Palpation of the vas deferens is performed to ensure its presence. Examination of the spermatic cords should be performed to identify the presence of a varicocele. A careful rectal examination should be performed to evaluate the prostate.

Q. **What initial tests would you perform on this patient?**

A. Semen analysis remains the cornerstone of the laboratory evaluation of the infertile male patient. All patients should have at least two semen analyses performed. If the semen analysis is abnormal, testosterone, FSH and LH should be sent to exclude an endocrine cause.

Q. **How would you counsel this patient about performing a semen analysis?**

A. An accurately performed semen analysis remains an important tool for the evaluation of the infertile male patient. In order to compare different semen samples from the same patient with accuracy, it is important to maintain consistency in the duration of sexual abstinence before collection of the specimen. It is recommended that the patient abstains for 3–5 days before providing the sample. The sample should be provided into a clean, wide-mouthed container either at the laboratory or at the patient's home, but must be delivered to the laboratory within 1 hour. It is recommended that specimens produced at home should be brought to the laboratory by placing the container in a shirt pocket next to the body to keep it warm during transit.

I would inform the patient that the specimen should be obtained by masturbation without the use of latex condoms, as these may interfere with the viability of sperm, due to the presence of spermicides. The specimen should be examined in the laboratory within 1–2 hours of collection. A label on the container should state the patient's name, the date, the time of collection, and the abstinence period.

Q. **Can the specimen be produced using coitus interruptus?**

A. Although interrupted coitus may be used as an alternative method for obtaining specimens, this is not recommended because the initial portion of the ejaculate may be lost, and bacteria and acidic vaginal secretions may contaminate the specimen, leading to false results.

Q. **What are the normal characteristics of the semen analysis?**

A. The World Health Organization (1999) has defined the reference values as follows:

volume:	≥ 2.0 ml
pH:	≥ 7.2
sperm concentration:	$\geq 20 \times 10^6$ sperm/ml
total sperm number:	$\geq 40 \times 10^6$ or more spermatozoa per ejaculate
motility:	$\geq 50\%$ with progressive motility (grades > 2)
	or
	> 25% with grade 4 motility
morphology:	$\geq 15\%$ of normal forms
viability:	$\geq 75\%$ or more of sperm viable
white blood cells:	< 1 million/ml.

Q. **The patient in question has a semen analysis performed. The following are his results on two occasions:**

volume:	**2.4 ml**
pH:	**7.5**
sperm concentration:	**6×10^6 sperm/ml**
total sperm number:	**14.4×10^6 spermatozoa**
motility:	**20% with > grade 2**
	and
	11% with grade 4
morphology:	**7% of normal forms**
white blood cells:	**< 1 million/ml.**

His hormone profile is normal. What is this man's diagnosis?

A. Combined defects in sperm density, motility and morphology are known as oligoasthenoteratospermia or OAT syndrome.

Q. **What are the potential causes of OAT syndrome?**

A. In most cases, OAT syndrome can be associated with a clinical varicocele. Other causes include cryptorchidism, temporary insults to spermatogenesis such as heat, drugs or environmental toxins, or idiopathic causes. A heat effect may be either environmental or endogenous (e.g. caused by a fever).

Q. **Physical examination in this man revealed a large left varicocele. What is a varicocele and how are these graded?**

A. Varicocele is defined as abnormal tortuous dilatation of the pampiniform plexus of spermatic veins. Varicoceles are graded (Hudson classification) according to their physical characteristics as follows:

- grade III – palpable and visible
- grade II – palpable on standing only, not visible
- grade I – palpable on Valsalva manoeuvre, not visible
- grade 0 – subclinical (ultrasound diagnosis only).

Q. **How common are varicoceles?**

A. Their prevalence is up to 15% in the healthy general population. However, they are present in 20–40% of men who present with infertility.

Q. Why do patients develop varicoceles?

A. Approximately 90% of varicoceles are left-sided. Differences in the venous drainage patterns of the right and left testicular veins may account for this left-sided predominance. The left testicular vein normally drains directly into the left renal vein, whereas the right testicular vein drains into the inferior vena cava. In addition, absence of the venous valves is more commonly found on the left side than on the right. Finally, the left renal vein may be compressed between the superior mesenteric artery and the aorta. This 'nutcracker phenomenon' may result in increased pressure in the left testicular venous system.

Q. Are varicoceles associated with infertility?

A. Semen samples from infertile men with varicoceles demonstrate decreased motility in 90% of patients and sperm concentrations of < 20 million sperm/ml in 65% of patients.

Q. Why are varicoceles associated with infertility?

A. Oligospermic patients with varicoceles are associated with higher intrascrotal temperatures (0.6°C higher). Other causes may include reflux of renal and adrenal metabolites from the renal vein, decreased blood flow, and hypoxia.

Q. When should varicoceles be treated in the context of fertility?

A. In adolescent patients with grade II/III varicoceles with reduced ipsilateral volume, and in sub-fertile patients with severe male factor infertility after full counselling.

Q. How would you manage the varicocele in this patient?

A. Improvement in seminal parameters is demonstrated in approximately 70% of patients after surgical varicocele repair. Improvements in motility are most common, occurring in 70% of patients, with improved sperm densities in 51% and improved morphology in 44% of patients. Semen characteristics usually improve between 3 months to 1 year after surgery.

There have been many studies reviewing the effect of varicocele on fertility. Conflicting results have been obtained, with most studies being uncontrolled.

The Evers meta-analysis suggests that varicocele treatment does not improve pregnancy rates.[2] However, this meta-analysis included trials of patients with sub-clinical vericoceles and patients with normal semen parameters. When these are excluded, a further meta-analysis reported pregnancy rates of 36.4% in the treated group, compared with 20% in the untreated group. The recommendations of the Joint Committee of the American Urological Association and the American Society for Reproductive Medicine did not acknowledge the conclusions of the Cochrane meta-analysis, and consider varicocele treatment to be suitable for patients with palpable varicocele and abnormal semen parameters.

The NICE guidelines recommend that men should not be offered surgical treatment for varicocele because it does not improve pregnancy rates.

Q. What would you recommend to this couple?

A. I would recommend that they are seen in a joint clinic by a urologist with a special interest in male infertility and by an expert in assisted reproduction techniques (ART). They should be appropriately counselled about the relative success rates of all of the available options, which would include either a varicocele ligation or ICSI/IVF, depending upon their personal circumstances.

Q. **Which assisted reproduction techniques are you aware of?**

A. ART involve the manipulation of sperm or ova, or both, in an attempt to improve the likelihood of conception and resultant live birth rates. They include the following:

- intrauterine insemination (IUI)
- *in-vitro* fertilisation (IVF)
- intracytoplasmic sperm injection (ICSI)
- microsurgical epididymal sperm aspiration (MESA)
- percutaneous sperm aspiration (PESA)
- testicular sperm extraction (TESE)
- testicular sperm aspiration (TESA).

Q. **What is TESE?**

A. It is testicular sperm extraction. The optimal technique for sperm extraction should be minimally invasive and avoid destruction of testicular function, without compromising the chance of retrieving enough spermatozoa with which to perform ICSI. Microdissection testicular sperm extraction is an advanced version of TESE, in which microsurgical techniques are applied to the retrieval of sperm from the seminiferous tubules. It results in the removal of a minimal amount of testicular tissue with maximal sperm yield, and reduces the negative impact on testicular function.

    The conventional TESE technique requires multiple, blind testis biopsies with excision of large volumes (> 500 mg) of testicular tissue, which can result in permanent damage to the testis. The microdissection TESE technique of sequential excision of microdissected seminiferous tubules (10–15 mg, or 2 mm in length, of seminiferous tubule) has been shown to be more successful, compared with the results achieved by conventional TESE or random biopsies of testicular tissue. However, long-term follow-up of endcrinological function is still recommended in these patients.

Q. **What is IVF and how is it performed?**

A. Usually gonadotropins are used to recruit multiple oocytes to each cycle. Follicular development is monitored ultrasonically, and ova are harvested before ovulation with the use of ultrasound-guided needle aspiration. *In-vitro* fertilisation is performed by mixing processed sperm with recovered oocytes. In standard IVF, when fertilisation occurs, the developing embryos are incubated for 2 to 3 days in culture and then placed trans-cervically into the uterus. Using this technique, 20–30% of transferred embryos will implant and produce clinical pregnancies. More than 90% of inseminated oocytes are routinely fertilised when sperm function is normal. However, fertilisation rates are reduced significantly when a male factor is present.

Q. **What is ICSI and when is it used?**

A. With IVF combined with ICSI, single sperm are injected into individual ova. This allows for fertilisation with extremely low numbers of sperm. IVF with ICSI is indicated in cases of severe male factor infertility, in couples with prior failed or poor fertilisation during regular IVF cycles, or in cases in which the sperm demonstrate significant defects in fertilising ability. In 2006, ICSI represented 47% of all IVF treatments in the UK.

Q. **What are the success rates of ICSI?**

A. The clinical pregnancy rates achieved by IVF and ICSI average 20–37% per initiated cycle. The female partner's age has a significant effect on pregnancy rates with IVF or ICSI. Pregnancy rates of 36.9% in women aged < 35 years and 10.7% in women aged > 40 years have been reported. In the UK, the Human Embryo Fertilisation Authority (HEFA) reports a mean take-home baby rate of 23.1%, with a rate of 31% for women under the age of 35 years.

Q. **Is there a difference in malformation rates between IVF and ICSI?**

A. Children born as a result of ICSI may have an increased risk of malformations (6.2%) compared with those born as a result of IVF (4.1%). However, only the rates between ICSI children and the control group was statistically significant. Furthermore, a recent meta-analysis has suggested a small significant increase in the rate of malformations in children born as a result of ART, compared with controls. A malformation rate of 6.2% has been shown with ART, compared with 4.4% in normal pregnancies.

Q. **Are there any specific concerns when treating patients with severe male factor infertility with ART?**

A. Patients who are considered to be candidates for ART with severe oligospermia or azoospermia may have associated defects in Y-chromosome microdeletion. This may result in this defect being transmitted to the offspring, so these patients should be offered chromosome analysis before starting assisted reproduction.

Q. **A further patient is referred to see you. He is 26 years old and has recently married. This is his first sexual relationship. He has already been to a private laboratory and performed two semen analyses 3 months apart. The results are presented below:**

volume:	2.7 ml
pH:	7.4
sperm concentration:	none seen
total sperm number:	nil
motility:	not assessed
morphology:	not assessed
white blood cells:	< 1 million/ml.

Would you perform any other tests?

A. After taking an appropriate history and conducting a focused physical examination, I would perform a baseline hormonal profile. I would also consider performing genetic analysis studies.

Q. **His testosterone is 7 nmol/l, and both his FSH and LH levels are significantly elevated, with the FSH concentration more than three times normal. What is his differential diagnosis?**

A. This man is likely to have a non-obstructive azoospermia. This may be secondary to hypogonadotrophism (Kallman's syndrome, pituitary tumour) or abnormalities of spermatogenesis (chromosomal abnormalities, toxins, orchitis, previous torsion).

Q. **What would you be specifically looking for on examination?**

A. I would be looking specifically for secondary sexual characteristics, body habitus, the presence of gynaecomastia, the size and consistency of the testis and whether the vas were palpable.

Q. **This patient has small soft testes with scars in both groins. Figure 13.6 is the biopsy from his testis. What does it show? What is the likely diagnosis?**

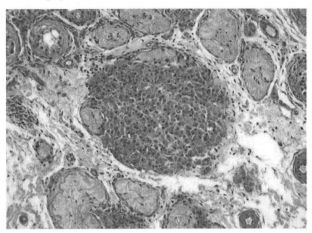

Figure 13.6

A. This testicular biopsy shows small hyalinised seminiferous tubules and pseudo-adenomatous clusters of Leydig cells. The likely diagnosis is Kleinfelter's syndrome, in which patients present with a non-obstructive azoospermia, a high FSH with a low testosterone level, small soft testes and bilateral undescended testes. This can be confirmed by genetic testing.

Q. **Upon genetic testing the patient is also found to have Y-chromosome microdeletion. What is the relationship between male infertility and Y-chromosome microdeletion?**

A. Patients with these microdeletions are usually phenotypically normal, with the only apparent abnormality being a defect in spermatogenesis. The defect occurs in one of three non-overlapping regions of the long arm of the Y chromosome, referred to as AZFa (proximal), AZFb (middle), and AZFc (distal). Although there is no strict correlation between the deletion and histological phenotype on testis biopsy, the following are associated:
- micro-deletion AZFa – Sertoli cells only
- micro-deletion AZFb – maturation arrest
- micro-deletion AZFc – severe oligozoospermia (no histological pattern).

Q. **Why is it important to test patients for microdeletions?**

A. It is important because these deletions will be transmitted to male offspring. Couples in whom the male partner has Y-chromosome microdeletions should be offered genetic counselling before embarking on a course of ART.

Q. **Another 26-year-old man with azoospermia has a normal hormone analysis and a normal testicular examination on his first visit. What do you suspect?**

A. He is likely to have an obstructive cause for his azoospermia. However, maturation arrest cannot be excluded without a testicular biopsy.

Q. **What would have been important in his examination?**

A. It is important to establish the presence of vas deferens. If there are no palpable vasa, the patient may have congenital bilateral absence of vas deferens (CBAVD). CBAVD is a clinical diagnosis based on physical examination, and is caused by an abnormality in the *CFTR* gene. This may occur in the absence of any respiratory symptoms.

Q. **What is the level of spermatogenesis in these patients and how would you manage them?**

A. Most of these patients have normal spermatogenesis. A scrotal exploration is now usually reserved for cases where a reconstruction is planned and access to sperm preservation is available. The diagnosis is made clinically along with genetic testing.

Q. **What is the role of testicular biopsy in azoospermic patients?**

A. The purpose of a diagnostic testicular biopsy is to differentiate between obstructive and non-obstructive azoospermia. Patients with clinical findings which are pathognomonic for either obstruction, such as CBAVD, or testicular failure do not require a testicular biopsy to establish the cause of azoospermia. Thus a diagnostic testicular biopsy is needed only in those patients in whom ductal obstruction is suspected based on the presence of a relatively normal serum FSH and testicular volume.

The other role of testicular biopsy is in the management of patients with non-obstructive azoospermia for sperm retrieval and IVF. In this setting, a testicular biopsy may be performed to simultaneously obtain prognostic information and harvest sperm for cryopreservation. Testicular biopsy is not indicated in patients with oligospermia, because the results will not alter therapy.

Q. **The patient has a testicular biopsy taken. How is it evaluated?**

A. The commonest system used to classify spermatogenesis on testicular biopsy is the Johnsen score (*see* Table 13.3).

Table 13.3 Johnsen score count

Score	Description
10	Complete spermatogenesis – organised epithelium
9	Many spermatozoa – disorganised epithelium
8	< 10 spermatozoa
7	No spermatozoa, but many spermatids
6	No spermatozoa, but < 10 spermatids
5	No spermatozoa or spermatids, but many spermatocytes
4	< 10 spermatocytes
3	Spermatogonia
2	Sertoli cells only
1	No cells, tubular fibrosis

Q. Figure 13.7 is the biopsy slide. What does it show?

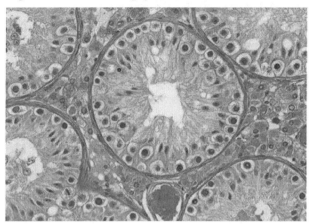

Figure 13.7

A. Figure 13.7 shows maturation arrest.

Q. **If the biopsy showed normal spermatogenesis, what would you do next?**

A. I would perform a vasogram to determine the site of obstruction in azoospermic patients who have active spermatogenesis documented by testis biopsy. Vasography should ideally be performed in conjunction with reconstructive surgery, because this procedure carries an inherent risk of vasal injury that could complicate future reconstructive surgery, if performed separately.

Vasography is performed at the level of the straight portion of the scrotal vas deferens by needle puncture with an orange needle on a 2.5-ml syringe containing injection of non-ionic contrast agent.

Q. **What is a normal vasogram?**

A. A normal vasogram is documented when contrast agent is visualised throughout the length of the vas deferens, seminal vesicles, ejaculatory duct and bladder. Proximal patency of the epididymis is documented by microscopic (× 400) visualisation of sperm in the intravasal fluid.

VASECTOMY AND REVERSAL

Q. **A 29-year-old man has been referred to you by his GP for consideration of a vasectomy. How would you assess him?**

A. I would see him in my routine urology outpatient clinic. Before seeing him, I would send him my patient information sheet on vasectomy. I would recommend that he attends the clinic with his partner.

The important points in the history relate to the patient's age, marital status, number of previous children, previous contraceptive history, previous surgery on the inguino-scrotal region, and why he wants to have a vasectomy. I would also ask whether he and his partner have considered other contraceptive methods.

Q. **What would you be looking for specifically on examination?**

A. As well a general examination, the important specific points on examination would relate to the laxity of the scrotum, whether the vasa are palpable, and whether there is any other scrotal pathology that might make the operation more difficult and a general anaesthetic advisable.

Q. **How would you counsel him for a vasectomy?**

A. I would provide written information on the procedure and invite the patient's partner to be involved in the decision-making process. I would explain why the procedure is being done, what the alternatives are, what the success rate is and what complications may occur. Specifically I would warn the patient that the procedure is essentially irreversible. Importantly, the couple must continue their current method of contraception until the patient is declared azoospermic post-operatively (see below). I would explain that failure may occur early (1 in 200 cases due to surgical error) or late (1 in 2000 cases due to recanalisation). I would counsel the patient that no one technique ensures 100% success, and that the early side-effects include bruising and swelling (common), haematoma (2%) and infection (3–4%). Long-term effects include chronic testicular or epididymal pain (1–10%) and sperm granuloma (10–15%). Around 60–80% of patients have detectable levels of serum antisperm antibodies.

Q. **You find out that the patient is not married, and has no partner and no children. What would you do?**

A. He fits one of the categories in which patients often change their mind or are dissatisfied. These patients require careful counselling, and an operation should only be performed after a full discussion with their GP and an undertaking that the patient does not want children in the future. Other groups that require careful attention are young couples, couples with two or fewer children, patients from lower socio-economic classes, and cases where it is possible that the operation is being requested for financial or emotional reasons, or that the male partner may be ambivalent about it.

Q. **The patient is adamant that he wants a vasectomy. What would be your recommendation?**

A. I would make sure that the case is fully discussed with the patient's GP. I would provide a written patient information sheet and a copy of the written consent. I would ask for a period of time to elapse between the consent and the operation, so that the patient has sufficient opportunity to make a fully informed choice. If after all this he is still convinced that this is what he wants, and he is supported by his GP, he would then be eligible for a vasectomy after careful counselling.

Q. **What vasectomy techniques are you aware of?**

A. Single, bilateral or no incision techniques.

Q. **What methods of vasal occlusion are you aware of? Do they have different success rates?**

A. Suture ligation is still the most commonly employed method worldwide, but it may result in necrosis and sloughing of the cut end distal to the ligature. If both ends slough, recanalisation may occur. Vasectomy failure occurs in 1–5% of patients when ligatures alone are used for occlusion. Recent evidence suggests that the use of Vicryl is associated with a higher rate of failure than is the use of catgut.

Vasal occlusion using two medium haemoclips on each end results in a failure rate of less than 1%.

Intraluminal occlusion with needle electrocautery, or battery-driven thermal cautery set at a power sufficient to destroy mucosa but not high enough to cause transmural destruction of the vas, reduces recanalisation rates to less than 0.5%. Using this technique it is recommended that at least 1 cm of the lumen should be cauterised in each direction.

Q. How would you perform a vasectomy?

A. Unless there are any contraindications, I perform vasectomy under a local anaesthetic. I use a mixture of 1% plain lidocaine and 0.5% bupivacaine in a 1:1 ratio. I perform the procedure in a warm room and with warm preparation solution to relax the scrotum. I use bilateral small incisions. Each vas is isolated from the spermatic cord vessels and manipulated to a superficial position under the scrotal skin. The vas is then firmly trapped between the middle finger, the index finger and the thumb of the left hand. The local anaesthetic is injected into the skin and then advanced into the peri-vasal sheath. One cm bilateral transverse incisions are carried down through the vas sheath until bare vas is exposed. The vas is delivered, and the vasal artery, veins and accompanying nerves are dissected free of the vas and spared. A 1 cm segment is removed and sent for pathological verification. The ends are occluded by using intra-luminal cautery, and the ends are separated in different fascial planes. I then close the skin with 4-0 Vicryl rapide. Fluffed up blue gauze dressings are held in place using a scrotal support.

Q. Please explain why you use this technique.

A. I use a bilateral incision technique because this reduces the likelihood of dividing the same side twice, and it is also easier to divide the vas far from the testis with bilateral incisions. Furthermore, longer testicular vasal remnants increase the success rates of a vasectomy reversal if this is required in the future. I use intra-luminal cautery and fascial interposition to reduce the incidence of vasectomy failure by re-canalisation.

Q. When would you send the patient a semen analysis and why?

A. The British Andrological Society (BAS) has recommended that patients should be instructed to ensure that they have had at least 24 ejaculations and preferably wait at least 16 weeks before submitting a first semen sample for examination. This reduces the number of false-positive samples and thus minimises both patient inconvenience and the need for repeat laboratory assessment.[3]

The Royal College of Obstetricians and Gynaecologists and Family Planning Association guidelines state that at least two azoospermic consecutive samples 2 to 4 weeks apart (in our practice at 12–14 weeks and 16 weeks post-vasectomy) must be obtained before contraceptive precautions can be dispensed with. However, it is known that there is significant non-compliance with regard to producing semen analyses by patients post-vasectomy (28% if two samples are requested).

Q. What is special clearance?

A. Traditional clearance is based on the production of two azoospermic samples more than 16 weeks after vasectomy. However, the finding of persistent non-motile spermatozoa in the initial two ejaculates is not uncommon, with studies reporting up to 33% non-azoospermic samples at 3 months, and 10% of ejaculates containing non-motile sperm at 6 months.

Special clearance is based on the finding of two consecutive sperm counts of < 10 000/ml with no motile sperm a minimum of 7 months after vasectomy. Discussion in the literature has suggested that the risk of pregnancy occurring from these non-motile sperm is small, and is probably no more than the risk of pregnancy occurring after two azoospermic semen samples, as a result of spontaneous recanalisation.

These men with low numbers of persistent non-motile spermatozoa in their ejaculate (i.e. after 7 months and at least 24 ejaculations) may be given 'special clearance' by their clinician to discontinue other contraceptive precautions following appropriate oral counselling and written advice about the risk of pregnancy.

Using these criteria, only 1 of 50 men who were examined at least 3 years after vasectomy had sperm in their analysis, the others being azoospermic. Furthermore, no pregnancies occurred during the 3 years of follow-up.

Q. **The patient returns 3 years later and is furious because his wife is now pregnant. What do you think has happened and how common is this?**

A. It is likely that he has had a late failure of vasectomy which is caused by recanalisation. It is defined as the re-appearance of sperm after two documented analyses showing azoospermic semen. The quoted incidence is around 1 in 2000.

He needs to undergo a further semen analysis to make sure that this is the correct diagnosis. If late failure has occurred, he should be offered a scrotal exploration, identification of the vasa and further occlusion. The patient should use alternative forms of contraception until he has had a further exploration and documented azoospermia.

Q. **A 55-year-old man is referred by his GP with secondary infertility. He had a vasectomy 22 years ago, and he now wants a reversal. How would you assess him?**

A. During the initial consultation, I would want to assess both partners with regard to their previous health and reproductive histories. I would examine the patient with regard to the size and consistency of the testis and epididymis as well whether the vasa are palpable. I would ask the patient to undergo a semen analysis if it has not already been performed. I would explain to the patient that the likelihood of success (patency or pregnancy) is based on the personal experience of the surgeon, the patient's health history, and the age and reproductive potential of his partner.

Q. **Is it common for patients to ask for a reversal?**

A. Approximately 6% of men who have undergone a vasectomy will subsequently request a reversal. The reason most frequently given by men requesting a vasectomy reversal is divorce and remarriage, with a desire to have children with their new partner.

Q. **What techniques can be used for the reversal?**

A. • Micro-surgical, magnified vision using loupes or macroscopic techniques.
 • Multi-layer vasovasostomy – standard.

- Modified single-layer vasovasostomy – an easier technique, which may be equivalent in outcome.
- Inguinal vasovasostomy – if obstruction of the vas is within the inguinal canal (i.e. after hernia repair).
- Epididymo-vasostomy is required in 20–30% of cases.

Q. **What are the important surgical principles required for a successful reversal?**

A. There should be sufficient mobilisation of both ends of the vas deferens to prevent any tension on the anastomosis.

The perivasal adventitia must remain intact, as stripping of the adventitia surrounding the cut ends of the vas increases the risk of excising an important blood supply to the vas, and may lead to ischemia and ultimate narrowing and occlusion of the anastomosis.

Precise approximation of the cut lumens is mandatory to avoid sperm leakage and formation of a sperm granuloma that may disrupt the lumen and result in a failed procedure. It is prudent to ensure that sperm retrieval is performed at the same time, so that if the reversal is not a success other options are available to the couple.

Q. **How would you perform it?**

A. I use a micro-surgical technique under a general anaesthetic. With the patient supine, the vas deferens is identified above the previous vasectomy. Two bilateral high 1- to 1.5-cm-long incisions are made directly over the vas. The vasal gap is identified. The vas is then dissected both proximally and distally to the vasectomy site, allowing sufficient length for the freshly cut ends of the vas to slightly overlap one another once they are positioned for anastomosis. The opposite side is then isolated in a similar fashion. When both vasa have been dissected free, they are held in a vasectomy reversal clamp above skin level.

The vas above and below the vasectomy site is then transected into a supple, normal area. After the vas has been cut, the ends are inspected and gently dilated with forceps.

A few drops of fluid from the testicular end of the vas lumen are placed on a sterile glass slide and examined by light microscopy. If there are sperm or sperm parts (e.g. sperm heads, sperm with partial tails) in large numbers, or the fluid is clear and copious with no visible sperm, vasovasostomy is generally indicated.

The cut ends of the vas deferens are positioned next to one another. A modified double-layer technique is used with six interrupted 9-0/10-0 sutures passed through the lumen, and six interrupted 9-0 sutures through the muscularis and the adventitia layers. The technique is then repeated on the other side.

Q. **Can all patients be treated with a vasovasostomy?**

A. Unfortunately, some patients will require a vaso-epididymostomy rather than vasovasostomy, because of a secondary obstruction in the epididymis. This appears to be a time-related phenomenon, such that the longer the time since the vasectomy, the greater the likelihood of an epididymal obstruction. More recently a model to pre-operatively identify patients who may require vaso-epididymostomy was created which is based on time since vasectomy and patient age. The predictive model provides 84% sensitivity for detecting patients who may require vaso-epididymostomy during vasectomy reversal (58% specificity). This model more accurately predicts the need for vaso-epididymostomy than using a specific duration from vasectomy cut-off alone.

Q. How would you decide which patients require a vaso-epididymostomy?

A. The decision to perform a vaso-epididymostomy is based on the quality of fluid found in the proximal vas deferens at the time of surgery. Fluid obtained from the proximal vas lumen should be examined under × 400 magnification with a light microscope. I would consider performing a vaso-epididymostomy if:
- the material coming from the proximal vas lumen is thick and devoid of sperm
- the fluid is creamy and contains only debris
- there is no fluid whatsoever when the vas is milked towards the cut end
- irrigation of the proximal vas with 0.1–0.2 ml of saline with a plastic angio-catheter attached to a tuberculin syringe fails to wash out any sperm.

Q. What are the success rates of the reversal?

A. If a vasovasostomy is performed, the success rates (patency rate and pregnancy rate) vary depending on the time interval between the vasectomy and its reversal (*see* Table 13.4). This is based on a large study of 1469 men who underwent microsurgical vasectomy reversal procedures at five institutions.[4]

Table 13.4 Patency and pregnancy rates according to time interval between the vasectomy and its reversal

Interval between vasectomy and its reversal (years)	Patency rate (%)	Pregnancy rate (%)
< 3	97	76
3–8	88	53
9–14	79	44
≥ 15	71	30

Q. Are there any other factors that are important with regard to success?

A. More recently, pre-operative factors that have been associated with a successful outcome include the same female partner as well as a short obstructive interval. Intra-operative factors included the use of surgical clips rather than suture at vasectomy, the presence of sperm granuloma and the presence and quality of the vasal fluid.

Q. Does the age of the female partner matter?

A. In a recent study using the microsurgical vasovasostomy technique it was reported that the pregnancy rate for couples in which the female partner was 40 years of age or older was significantly lower than that for couples in which the female partner was 39 years or younger (14% vs. 56%). The age of the female partner is therefore important in the counselling process, and it may not be cost-effective to perform vasectomy reversals in couples where the female partner is over 40 years of age.

Q. Does it matter which technique you use?

A. There is controversy as to whether or not microsurgery, loupes or macroscopic techniques are equally effective. However, most experts believe that the results of microsurgical vasectomy reversal are superior to the results of non-microsurgical techniques in terms of patency and pregnancy. Micro-surgery does require more training and experience to obtain the best results. Patency and pregnancy rates do not appear to be significantly different if a multi-layer anastomosis is performed as opposed to a modified single-layer technique, but the success is physician-dependent.

Q. **The patient returns 1 year after the reversal. He is upset because he and his new partner have been unable to conceive. Does he have any other options?**

A. It is important to establish whether he does indeed have sperm in his semen or not, and to determine the fertility potential of his partner. If he still wishes to have his own biologically related children, his other option is to either use his sperm (if there are enough in the semen) or undergo sperm extraction in conjunction with IVF and ICSI. He also still has the options of donor sperm and adoption.

Q. **The couple now decide that they would like to be referred for IVF on the NHS. They ask whether they have to pay for IVF treatment.**

A. Some NHS-operated fertility clinics offer free *in-vitro* (IVF) fertilisation treatment to people who have been sponsored by their primary care trust (PCT). The couple need to contact their local PCT to find out how to qualify for sponsorship.

The availability of IVF treatment on the NHS is subject to guidelines that were issued by the National Institute for Health and Clinical Excellence (NICE). These recommend that patients should be offered up to three cycles of IVF if:
- they are 23–39 years of age at the time of treatment, and
- one or both of them has been diagnosed with a fertility problem, or
- they have been infertile for at least 3 years.

Some PCTs have additional criteria that may affect the couple's eligibility for funding. For example, some PCTs will not provide funding for couples if one partner already has a child.

Unfortunately, waiting lists for NHS-funded IVF treatment will vary depending on the particular PCT. Unless the couple are exempt, they will still have to pay prescription charges for any medicines that they require.

EJACULATORY DYSFUNCTION

Q. **A 36-year-old man is referred under the urgent 2-week rule with a 3-month history of haematospermia. He is otherwise well. He is now abstaining from sexual contact as his partner is suspicious that he may have a sexually transmitted infection. Does he require urological evaluation?**

A. Haematospermia is commonly seen after a prolonged period of sexual abstinence. It almost always resolves spontaneously. However, if it persists beyond several weeks, the patient should undergo further urological evaluation, as it can occasionally be a result of an underlying significant urological pathology.

Q. **How would you investigate the patient?**

A. A careful history should be taken to exclude the presence of haematuria, a past history of TB and a family history of prostate cancer. Other important features in the history include recent trauma, infection and a history of bleeding disorders. A careful examination should include a blood pressure measurement, a genital and rectal examination should be performed to exclude the presence of tuberculosis, and a prostate-specific antigen (PSA) and a rectal examination should be performed in men over 50 years of age to exclude prostate carcinoma. The penis needs to be examined to exclude any lesions that may bleed and contribute to the ejaculate, and a thorough palpation along the course of the vas is required to ensure their presence and rule out any nodularity. Furthermore, an MSU and urinary cytology are sent to exclude the possibility of transitional-cell carcinoma of the prostate and the presence of sterile pyuria, respectively. In younger men, urethritis should be considered in the differential diagnosis and urethral swabs should be obtained.

Q. **Are there any features in the history which would suggest that the patient may require further evaluation?**

A. The three factors that dictate the extent of the evaluation and treatment are the patient's age, the duration and recurrence of the haematospermia, and the presence of any associated haematuria.

Q. **What are the common urological causes of haematospermia?**

A. The common urological causes include infections and inflammatory disorders (up to 40% of cases).

- Infectious causes include TB, HIV and CMV.
- Patients with symptoms of a sexually transmitted infection are commonly found to have titres positive for herpes simplex, *Chlamydia*, *Enterococcus* or *Ureaplasma*, allowing appropriate treatment to be initiated.
- Prostatitis (up to 30% of cases).
- Post-TRUS biopsy of the prostate (9–45%).
- Prostate cancer (up to 2%).
- Urethritis/urethral stricture is a recognised cause in younger men.
- Acquired and congenital cysts of the seminal vesicles.
- Systemic disorders (hypertension, chronic liver disease, amyloidosis, lymphoma and bleeding disorders).

Q. **All of the patient's investigations are negative, and he has persistent haematospermia. How would you investigate him further?**

A. I would request a transrectal ultrasound scan (TRUS). TRUS may reveal the presence of abnormalities in up to 95% of patients. Commonly seen abnormalities include prostatic calcifications (42%), ejaculatory duct calculi (39%), dilated ejaculatory ducts (33%), benign prostatic hyperplasia (33%), dilated seminal vesicles (22%), calcifications in seminal vesicles (20%), ejaculatory duct cysts (11%) and mullerian duct remnants (7%).

Q. **Are any further investigations warranted?**

A. If there is persistent haematospermia in a patient over the age of 40 years, especially if associated with haematuria, a cysto-urethroscopy is required.

Q. **TRUS and cystoscopy do not reveal any abnormalities. The haematospermia continues. What is your management plan?**

A. The most important goal in the management of such patients is to allay their anxiety. If they have been fully investigated and no cause can be identified, they can be reassured. In younger patients it is important to exclude infective causes, and a referral to a genito-urinary clinic is useful.

Q. A 37-year-old man attended the clinic together with his 34-year-old wife. They have been trying to conceive for 3 years without success. He has already undergone two semen analyses which show the following:

    volume: 0.4 ml

    pH: 8.3

    sperm concentration: < 1 x 10^6 sperm/ml

    motility: non-motile

How would you investigate him further?

A. I would investigate him with standard work-up including a focused history and examination, and baseline blood tests, including a hormone profile.

Q. In the history he says that he has a normal orgasm but complains that when he passes urine the first time after he ejaculates the urine is cloudy. What do you think is the diagnosis?

A. I suspect he is suffering from retrograde ejaculation.

Q. How would you confirm this?

A. A post-ejaculate urine examination should be performed to look for the presence of sperm.

Q. What are the known causes of retrograde ejaculation?

A. The commonest cause is retroperitoneal lymph node dissection, followed by diabetes mellitus, bladder neck surgery, trauma, medications such as alpha-blockers, urethral strictures, spinal cord injury, and post TURP.

Q. What treatment options does he have?

A. Medical treatments can be used to try to close the bladder neck and prevent retrograde ejaculation. Sympathomimetics, such as pseudoephedrine and ephedrine, can help to close the bladder neck and enhance antegrade ejaculation. Imipramine, a tricyclic antidepressant that has mixed anticholinergic and sympathomimetic properties, may also be used. At best medical treatments are successful in 50–60% of patients.

Q. What other options are available?

A. If medical therapy fails, sperm can be retrieved from an alkalinised post-ejaculate urine specimen and used for intrauterine insemination or IVF.

Q. How would you arrange for the patient to provide an alkalinised post-ejaculate urine specimen?

A. The normally acidic urine is considered to be spermicidal. The patient is instructed to alkalinise their urine by ingesting 1 g of sodium bicarbonate the night before and a further 1 g on the morning of collection of the specimen. He is then asked to empty his bladder before masturbating. He is instructed to obtain the post-ejaculatory urine specimen as quickly as possible after ejaculation, and to deliver the sample immediately to the laboratory. More recently a solution of sodium bicarbonate and sodium chloride (Liverpool solution) has been shown to be safe for use in units treating couples with retrograde ejaculation. It is a non-invasive and inexpensive regimen that may optimise urinary pH and osmolarity for sperm survival after retrograde ejaculation.

Q. Can alkalinised urine be used in combination IVF?

A. Yes, ICSI can be performed with spermatozoa retrieved from post-ejaculatory urine. Using this technique, the fertilisation rate has been reported to be as high as 51%, with 7 of 16 couples achieving clinical pregnancies and 3 live offspring delivered.

Q. A 42-year-old man is referred by his GP with erectile dysfunction. However, when you see him in the clinic you find that his main complaint is that he ejaculates within a minute of sexual intercourse. He is very embarrassed about the problem and he has just broken up with his first girlfriend. He has never had this problem before. What is the diagnosis?

A. He is suffering from premature ejaculation.

Q. What is the definition of premature ejaculation?

A. There is no absolute definition. However, most physicians use the definition given by the American Psychiatric Association's *Diagnostic and Statistical Manual of Mental Disorders (DSM-IV-R)*, namely 'persistent or recurrent ejaculation with minimal stimulation before, on, or shortly after penetration and before the person wishes it.'

Q. The patient asks you how long he should be able to last before ejaculation.

A. The ejaculatory latency has been measured by the intra-vaginal ejaculatory latency time (IVELT), which is defined as the time between vaginal intromission and ejaculation. The International Society for Sexual Medicine (ISSM) defines it as a male sexual dysfunction characterised by ejaculation which always or nearly always occurs before or within about 1 minute of vaginal penetration.

Q. He is concerned that there is something anatomically wrong with him. What would you say to him?

A. Premature ejaculation is classified as being either lifelong or acquired. As it is usually lifelong premature ejaculation that is associated with a biological cause, it is very unlikely that this patient has a biological or anatomical cause. His history suggests the need to address relationship issues, and the condition is unlikely to be secondary to a biological cause.

Q. What are the key points in the history?

A. The essential components in the history for a diagnosis of premature ejaculation include a short ejaculatory latency time, a lack of control and sexual dissatisfaction.

Q. How would you investigate this patient?

A. I would take a detailed medical and sexual history, perform a physical examination, and order appropriate investigations. The key to investigation is to establish the true presenting complaint, and to identify obvious biological causes such as medication or recent pelvic surgery, so that an optimal treatment plan can be instituted.

Q. What is the cause of premature ejaculation?

A. A number of theories have been proposed about the causes of premature ejaculation. They are divided into psychogenic and biological causes:

- *Psychogenic causes:* anxiety, early sexual experience, infrequent sexual intercourse, poor ejaculatory control techniques, evolutional.

- *Biological causes:* penile hypersensitivity, hyperexcitable ejaculatory reflex, hyperarousability, endocrinopathy, genetic predisposition, 5-HT-receptor dysfunction.

Q. **What can be done to help this young man?**

A. He can be treated with either behavioural therapy or pharmacological therapy, or a combination of the two.

Psychological/behavioural methods

- Advantages: neither harmful nor painful, with few side-effects, and this approach encourages open communication.
- Disadvantages: time-consuming, may be expensive, requires the partner's cooperation, and produces mixed results.
- There are two main strategies:
  - stop–squeeze method
  - stop–pause method.

Both methods suppress the urge to ejaculate by stopping sexual stimulation.

Pharmacological treatments

- SSRIs (citalopram, fluoxetine, fluvoxamine, paroxetine and sertraline). Daily treatment can be undertaken with paroxetine (20 to 40 mg), clomipramine (10 to 50 mg), sertraline (50 to 100 mg) or fluoxetine (20 to 40 mg). A meta-analysis of drug treatment studies has demonstrated that paroxetine produces the strongest delay in ejaculation. Ejaculation delay with daily treatment usually manifests itself at the end of the first or second week. With the exception of fluoxetine, SSRIs should not be withdrawn acutely, but gradually over a period of 3 to 4 weeks. It has been reported that clomipramine (25 mg), if taken on an on-demand basis about 5 hours before intercourse, can delay ejaculation in men with lifelong premature ejaculation.
- Topical local anaesthetics. The use of topical local anaesthetics such as lidocaine and/or prilocaine as a cream, gel or spray is well established. However, side-effects include significant penile hypoanaesthesia and possible transvaginal absorption and vaginal numbness.
- More recently, it has been reported that the application of SS cream results in a significant improvement in up to 89% of patients. SS cream is a natural compound made with extracts from nine herbs, some of which have a local anaesthetic property.
- PDE-5 inhibitors. Several authors have reported the use of sildenafil (Viagra) as a treatment for premature ejaculation. However, its major role appears to be in the treatment of acquired PE secondary to erectile dysfunction, rather than lifelong or acquired PE without erectile dysfunction. However, it may be used successfully as an adjunct to other therapies in the treatment of premature ejaculation.

Q. **A 22-year-old man attends clinic with a 1-year history of worsening inability to ejaculate. He was involved in a road traffic accident 3 years ago, but is otherwise well. How would you investigate him?**

A. After taking a full history and examining him I would like to know how severe his spinal injuries are and what the level of spinal cord injury is. In addition, I would like to ask him specifically about his bowel and bladder function.

Q. What do you think is wrong with him?

A. I suspect that he has anejaculation. I would confirm this with a semen analysis which would show complete absence of antegrade ejaculation and the absence of fructose and sperm in a post-orgasmic urine analysis.

Q. What are the commonest causes of this problem?

A. The commonest causes are spinal cord injury, followed by retroperitoneal lymph node dissection. In some patients the problem has psychological causes, and this should be suspected in patients who are suddenly unable to ejaculate, in those who can still masturbate to completion, and if no other causes of ejaculatory dysfunction can be identified.

Q. What is the instrument shown in Figure 13.8 and what is it used for?

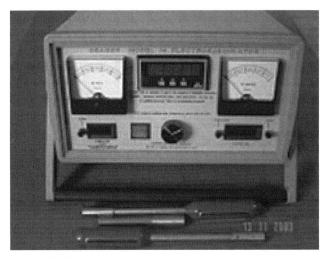

Figure 13.8

A. It is a Seager electro-ejaculator. It may be used to perform electro-ejaculation on spinal-cord-injured patients.

Q. How is electro-ejaculation performed? What precautions should be taken?

A. Electro-ejaculation involves the use of a rectal probe to stimulate the perirectal, periprostatic sympathetic nerves electrically. Patients without a spinal cord injury and those with low or incomplete spinal cord lesions require general anaesthesia. During electro-ejaculation, spinal-cord-injured patients with lesions above T6 or a history of autonomic dysreflexia should have their blood pressure monitored frequently for signs of autonomic dysreflexia and severe hypertension.

Q. When electro-ejaculation is performed, what is the quality of sperm retrieved?

A. Sperm obtained from electro-ejaculation have been shown to be of a poorer quality, with poor motility and impaired fertilising capacity. As a result, low pregnancy rates have been reported in patients undergoing electro-ejaculation and subsequent intrauterine insemination.

Q. Are there any other options available for patients who do not wish to have electro-ejaculation?

A. In infertile men with anejeculation, sperm retrieval can be performed using a percutaneous vasal sperm aspiration technique. The sperm can then be used for either intrauterine insemination (pregnancy rate of 73.1%) or IVF (pregnancy rate of 71.4%).

PEYRONIE'S DISEASE

Q. A 43-year-old man is referred by his GP with a 2-month history of penile pain, penile deviation and a lump on the dorsum of the penis. He is referred under the 2-week rule. How would you assess him?

A. I would take a detailed subjective history, including the duration of the symptoms, the presence or absence of pain, the degree of erectile function, the amount of curvature (degree and direction), the ability to penetrate, and any previous treatment modalities. I would use a validated questionnaire, such as the IIEF, to assess erectile function. I would ask specifically about any risk factors for erectile dysfunction, such as diabetes, hypertension and hyperlipidaemia, and for a past history of penile trauma.

During the physical examination I would note the size and location of the plaque/mass, the presence or absence of a foreskin, and whether there were any stigmata of previous trauma. I would specifically measure the penile length in both the stretched and flaccid state. Unless the patient has brought in a photograph showing the degree and direction of the curvature, I would perform an artificial erection using PGE1. I would then perform an examination of the extremities to identify any coexisting Dupuytren's contracture.

Q. What diagnosis is shown in Figure 13.9?

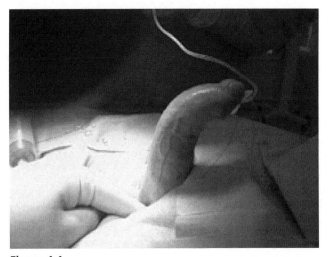

Figure 1.1

A. Figure 13.9 shows an image of Peyronie's disease.

Q. What are the cardinal features of this disease?

A. It is characterised by the development of a fibrous plaque or scar tissue within the tunica albuginea of the penis. It can present with one or a combination of symptoms, such as curvature, indentation, buckling, penile pain and penile shortening. It can also result in erectile dysfunction due to altered haemodynamics of cavernosal blood flow.

Q. What is the cause of Peyronie's disease?

A. The cause of this disease is not known. However, the most widely held hypothesis is that recurrent micro-traumatisation of the tunica albuginea during sexual intercourse leads to small lesions that activate processes of wound healing and the development of fibrotic plaque. Transforming growth factor beta seems to have an important role in this process, as it is over-expressed in the plaque.

Q. Is Peyronie's disease known to be associated with any other diseases?

A. Up to 30–40% of men with Peyronie's disease will also have Dupuytren's contracture. Other conditions associated with Peyronie's disease include plantar fascial contracture (Ledderhose's disease), tympanosclerosis and post-penile trauma.

Q. Which cytokines are implicated in the pathogenesis of Peyronie's disease?

A. There appears to be an imbalance between pro- and antifibrotic cytokines. Research suggests that there is overexpression of TGF-beta1 in penile plaques. Furthermore, fibrin and plasminogen activator inhibitor-1 (PAI-1) levels have also been shown to be increased in these plaques.

Q. How common is this condition and what is the natural history?

A. It has a prevalence of 0.4–3.2% and usually occurs in men aged 40–70 years. If it is managed conservatively, complete, spontaneous resolution occurs in 14% of patients, and progression of the disease occurs within 1 year in 40% of patients.

Q. What disease stages are you aware of?

A. There are two stages of the disease. Initially, a third of patients present with painful erections during the acute phase. This period can also be characterised by worsening deformity of the penis. The second stage of Peyronie's disease is characterised by a stabilisation of the deformity. Pain with erections generally subsides as the chronic phase begins.

Q. Does the patient require any further evaluation?

A. If the history and examination are characteristic, no further evaluation is required. However, objective evaluation may include penile duplex Doppler ultrasonography after the administration of an intracavernosal injection of a vasoactive agent to stimulate an erection. This test is also useful in cases where patients have erectile dysfunction with Peyronie's disease, and also if surgery is to be performed. The test can also demonstrate the presence of hourglass deformities and any hinge defects that may lead to buckling with axial loading.

Q. Are there any medical treatments available?

A. There are several options for the medical management of Peyronie's disease, including oral medical therapy, topical and intralesional injection therapy, extracorporeal shock-wave therapy and iontophoresis. Many of these therapies have not undergone rigorous evaluation in controlled clinical trials, and most of the relevant studies are retrospective and provide little more than anecdotal evidence to support the use of the agents studied.

The oral medical therapies that have been investigated include vitamin E, tamoxifen, para-aminobenzoate (POTABA), colchicines, L-arginine and pentoxifylline. Intra-lesional agents include steroids, verapamil and interferons.

Q. **The patient states that he has already had ESWL for renal stones in the past. He was impressed with the results of this. He would like to have ESWL for Peyronie's disease. Why was ESWL used for Peyronie's disease and what are the success rates?**

A. ESWL was used because it was thought that initiating an inflammatory reaction through direct damage to the plaque would result in plaque resorption. However, multiple randomised studies that were designed to evaluate the efficacy of shock-wave therapy have failed to demonstrate any improvements in curvature or plaque size. Furthermore, the NICE guidelines in the UK do not recommend it unless the patient has been informed of the low success rate and appropriate arrangements for audit and research are in place.

Q. **The patient decides not to undergo any treatment for the present. He returns 9 months later. The pain has settled, and the curvature is stable at 45 degrees dorsally. What is important in the history?**

A. It is important to establish whether the patient has erectile dysfunction and whether he can have penetrative sexual intercourse.

Q. **He is unable to penetrate and has no erectile dysfunction. What are his options?**

A. His options are either to be treated conservatively or to undergo a surgical straightening procedure.

Q. **Which patients should undergo surgery for Peyronie's disease?**

A. Surgical treatment is indicated in patients who have failed medical therapies and in those who have complex curvatures which make penetration difficult or impossible, or who have hinging effects or significant erectile dysfunction. Surgery should be reserved for patients with stable Peyronie's disease.

Q. **What surgical straightening procedures are you aware of?**

A. The surgical treatment involves either penile shortening or potentially penile maintaining procedures. Penile shortening procedures involve plication techniques, such as the Nesbit procedure or the 16-dot technique. Penile maintaining procedures involve incision of the plaque with subsequent grafting.

Q. **Which patients are candidates for a plication technique?**

A. Penile plication procedures are typically employed in patients with essentially normal erectile function and mild to moderate curvature (< 60 degrees). Also, these patients should have no hourglass deformities or destabilising hinge effect.

Q. **What types of plication technique are you aware of?**

A. Penile plication involves shortening the convex side of the penis. The patient must be thoroughly counselled about this expected postoperative penile shortening.

There are several methods for performing the plication.

- The Nesbit procedure involves excising an elliptical portion of tunica albuginea on the convex side. Studies have shown a success rate of 82% (penis straight), all patients had penile shortening and 1.2% developed post-operative erectile dysfunction.[5]
- The Yachia procedure involves no excision of tunica. Longitudinal incisions in the tunica are closed horizontally, thereby straightening the penis.
- The Essed–Schroeder procedure involves no excision or incision of the tunica albuginea. Plicating sutures are simply placed on the convex side of the curvature.

Q. **The patient is concerned about penile shortening. What other options are available?**

A. An alternative to plication procedures involves extending or lengthening the concave side of the curvature. This is generally done by incising the plaque with placement of graft over the defect in the tunica albuginea. Regardless of the shape of the incision, the goal is to completely relax the tunica and to cover the tunical defect with graft material.

Q. **Should the plaque be incised or excised?**

A. It is not recommended that the plaque be completely excised, as this may compromise the veno-occlusive mechanism and increase the risk of post-operative erectile dysfunction.

Q. **How would you counsel the patient about a plaque incision and grafting procedure?**

A. After making sure that the operation is appropriate for the patient, I would inform them of the success rate (a straight penis in 86% of patients) and of any important potential risks (bleeding, bruising, infection, circumcision, loss of > 1 cm in length in 26% of patients, erectile dysfunction 15%). Some authors recommend the use of penile traction devices post-operatively, as well as penile rehabilitation with PDE-5 inhibitors in order to decrease the risk of curvature recurrence and penile shortening.

Q. **What types of graft have been used? Which one is best?**

A. The grafts can be categorised as follows:
- autografts (tunica vaginalis, fascia lata)
- allografts (cadaveric pericardium)
- xenografts (porcine small intestine submucosa)
- synthetic grafts (Pelvicol, Dacron mesh, polytetrafluoroethylene).

No graft has been shown to be superior. For example, the results obtained using a fascia lata graft are similar to those obtained with an autologous vein graft.

Q. **By the time the patient returns for surgery he is complaining of severe erectile dysfunction. Would you still go ahead with surgery?**

A. After detailed counselling, I would cancel his operation and then discuss the alternative option of penile prosthesis insertion. This is indicated for patients with Peyronie's disease and concomitant severe erectile dysfunction.

Q. How does this technique differ from the standard penile prosthesis insertion?

A. After insertion and inflation of the penile prosthesis, the plaque is incised and patched, if necessary, or the penis is bent in the opposite direction to the curvature, thus breaking the plaque. This technique, which is described as modelling, has resulted in long-term satisfaction rates of up to 90%.

HYPOGONADISM

Q. A 52-year-old man who has been referred by his GP is complaining of worsening fatigue, moodiness and decreased libido. How would you assess him?

A. I would take a full medical history and perform a full physical examination, including height, weight and waist circumference. I would then ask for baseline blood tests, including a fasting glucose, lipids and hormone profile.

Q. You find that he has no history of previous medical problems and is not currently taking any medication. He stopped smoking 10 years ago. The family history is positive for hypertension and a father who died of a myocardial infarction at the age of 62 years. The patient's body mass index is 30.8 kg/m², his waist circumference is 104 cm, his blood pressure is 143/87 mmHg, and cardiorespiratory examination is unremarkable. Which hormone tests would you request and when?

A. Hypogonadism can be confirmed by checking a testosterone level. Morning values are preferred to afternoon blood samples because testosterone is secreted in the morning. This should include total testosterone, free testosterone, LH and FSH.

Q. Would you request an oestradiol level?

A. Not routinely. Oestradiol is useful when the patient has a higher body mass index, as in this case. Prolactin and a thyroid profile can also be useful when diagnosing secondary causes in selected cases.

Q. The patient's laboratory test results are as follows:

fasting plasma glucose:	6.2
HbA1c:	6.2%
total cholesterol	6.7 nmol/l
triglycerides	3.1 nmol/l
creatinine	78 µmol/l.

His total testosterone level in an early-morning sample is 7.2 nmol/l. How would you manage this patient?

A. I would seek the advice of an endocrinologist. The European Atherosclerosis Society suggests that total cholesterol levels in the range 5.2–6.5 nmol/l require dietary advice and correction of other risk factors. As his level is greater than 6.5 nmol/l, I would counsel the patient about starting regular exercise, and I would consider initiation of therapy with a statin through his GP. As his morning testosterone level is below 8 nmol/l, I would also consider starting testosterone replacement.

Q. What is your diagnosis?

A. This man has late-onset male hypogonadism. This is defined as a symptom complex resulting from the age-related decline in testosterone levels in men.

Q. What are the common causes of this condition?

A. Hypogonadism is failure of the testes to produce normal levels of testosterone and/or sperm. Primary causes of hypogonadism are commonly due to testicular failure, while secondary causes are due to pituitary or hypothalamic disorders (Kallman's syndrome), and combined hypogonadism is due to a combination of the decreased pulsatility of the pituitary gonadotropins and the decreased response of the testicular Leydig cells. Hypogonadism is more common in older men who have passed through their reproductive stage.

Q. What are the common signs and symptoms of this condition?

A. Hypogonadism in the adult commonly results in changes in sexual function, behaviour and muscle mass, and loss of secondary sexual characteristics. The patient may also report changes in mood and behavioural symptoms (depression, irritability and loss of motivation), in addition to complaints of lethargy or loss of energy. Physical examination may demonstrate some regression of secondary sexual characteristics, such as hair loss and possible loss of muscle bulk, in addition to the finding of softer smaller testes.

Q. On examination you find that the patient has bilateral gynaecomastia. How would you explain this?

A. Obesity can lead to the aromatisation of testosterone in fatty tissue to oestradiol, leaving less testosterone available for maintenance and virilisation functions. As a result of lowered testosterone levels, a clinically obese man may demonstrate evidence of feminisation, such as gynaecomastia.

Q. How would you treat this condition?

A. The most definitive treatment is weight loss, but some patients may also respond well to treatment with clomiphene citrate, a synthetic non-steroidal anti-oestrogen or tamoxifen.

Q. How common is late-onset hypogonadism?

A. It may occur in up to 18.4% of men over 70 years of age, regardless of ethnic background.

Q. Why is a dual-energy X-ray absorptiometry (DEXA) scan relevant in patients with hypogonadism?

A. Height loss, low-trauma fractures and lowered bone mineral density are more common in older male patients. Testosterone deficiency is more common in men who have experienced a hip fracture. Therefore it is important to use a DEXA scan to check bone mineral density in men who are recognised as being hypogonadal.

Q. On further questioning, the patient also admits to suffering from erectile dysfunction for 2 years. What percentage of patients with erectile dysfunction also have hypogonadism?

A. Overall, fewer than 10% of men who present with erectile dysfunction are found to have testosterone deficiency.

Q. **What is the relationship between ageing and testosterone levels?**

A. Several population-based studies have demonstrated that serum testosterone levels decrease with age.

Q. **What is the relationship between testosterone levels and sex-hormone-binding globulin?**

A. Free and albumin-bound testosterone is the portion of the circulating testosterone that is thought to be available to peripheral tissues. Testosterone that is bound to sex-hormone-binding globulin (SHBG) is tightly bound and not available to these tissues. This portion constitutes approximately 45% of the total circulating testosterone in healthy young men. Numerous factors can alter SHBG and thus total testosterone without affecting the bioavailable testosterone.

Q. **What factors may increase the level of SHBG?**

A. SHBG levels are increased by ageing, hepatic cirrhosis, hyperthyroidism, use of anticonvulsants, use of oestrogens, and HIV infection.

Q. **Should SHBG be measured in all patients?**

A. No. It should only be measured in cases where there is a low total testosterone level or conditions known to affect the SHBG concentration such as ageing. The age-related fall in serum testosterone levels may underestimate the fall in free and bioavailable testosterone levels because SHBG levels increase with age.

Q. **How would you manage this patient?**

A. After I had fully evaluated the patient and made sure that there were no contraindications, I would treat him with testosterone replacement therapy.

Q. **Are there any contraindications to testosterone treatment?**

A. The presence of active prostate or breast cancer is an absolute contraindication to treatment.

Polycythaemia, or an excessive increase in the number of red blood cells, may be observed in some men over 50 years of age who have been treated with testosterone replacement therapy. Therefore pre-existing polycythaemia is a contraindication, as an increase in the haematocrit above 54–55% is associated with increased blood viscosity and decreased blood flow.

Hypogonadal men who are treated with testosterone may develop or may have an exacerbation of sleep apnoea. Sleep apnoea should be treated and testosterone levels evaluated again before considering testosterone replacement therapy.

Testosterone is an anabolic agent that increases the retention of nitrogen, sodium, potassium and water. Men who have diseases such as congestive heart failure, liver failure or renal failure, which cause fluid retention, may experience a worsening of these conditions when treated with testosterone. Therefore testosterone replacement therapy should be avoided in men with stage III or IV heart failure or severe renal or liver failure.

Q. **What delivery systems are you aware of?**

A. When testosterone is administered orally, it is metabolised by the liver on the first pass, too rapidly for it to have an effect. In order to render it clinically useful, the chemical structure of testosterone has been modified or reformulated for alternate routes of administration (*see* Table 13.5).

Formulations of testosterone are now available for oral administration, intramuscular injection, transdermal administration by gel or patch, or subcutaneous implantation in the form of testosterone pellets.

Table 13.5 Formulations of testosterone therapy

Route	Dose
Oral	
Testosterone undecanoate*	120–160 mg once daily for the first 2–3 weeks, then 40–120 mg daily
Buccal T system	30 mg every 12 hours
Intramuscular injections	
Testosterone cypionate/enanthate	100–200 mg every 2 weeks
Testosterone undecanoate†	1000 mg every 6 weeks for the first 12 weeks, then 1000 mg every 3 months
Transdermal	
T gel	5–10 g daily (5–10 mg testosterone)
T patch	5–10 mg daily
Subdermal	
T pellets	4 (200 mg) pellets every 5–7 months

Q. How would you monitor the testosterone replacement therapy?

A. It is important to measure serum testosterone levels in patients who are receiving replacement therapy in order to determine whether treatment is raising the level to the desired range. Furthermore, the clinical signs and symptoms that initially caused the patient to be diagnosed and treated for testosterone deficiency should be monitored. In addition, it is useful to assess bone mineral density prior to treatment, and this may require re-evaluation at regular intervals.

In the older man it is very important to monitor for potential adverse effects of testosterone treatment and for delivery-system-specific adverse effects. The most common adverse effect is an excessive rise in the haematocrit (> 54%). If this occurs, treatment should be stopped to allow the haematocrit to normalise, after which treatment should be resumed at a lower dose.

The most serious safety concern is the potential for stimulating an occult prostate cancer to become a clinical prostate cancer. One should also consider using shorter-acting delivery systems when initiating testosterone treatment in older men. Should the patient develop a significant rise in haematocrit or PSA, or an abnormal digital rectal exam, it would be easier to stop treatment while further evaluation was undertaken. This is usually of less concern after a patient has been on testosterone replacement therapy for 3 months.

Q. What is the relationship between testosterone levels, replacement and prostate cancer?

A. Prospective epidemiological studies have not found a positive correlation between either total or bioavailable testosterone levels and prostate cancer. However, there are reports that men with low testosterone levels are more likely to have prostate cancer, and perhaps a higher grade of prostate cancer than men who are eugonadal. These findings have not been duplicated in population-based studies. There is also some evidence that low testosterone levels may cause some reduction in prostate-specific antigen (PSA) levels, and that replacement therapy will consequently be associated with some increase in PSA levels. The relatively small clinical trials that have been conducted have not shown an increase in clinical prostate cancer in the testosterone groups compared with the placebo groups, but the small size of these trials and the short follow-up periods do not provide enough data for definitive conclusions to be drawn about the safety of testosterone replacement therapy in relation to prostate cancer.

Q. **What are the common side-effects of testosterone treatment?**

A. Younger men who are receiving testosterone replacement therapy may experience acne, increased oiliness of the skin, gynaecomastia, suppression of fertility, and some testicular atrophy. These changes may also be seen in older men, but they rarely limit therapy.

ANDROLOGICAL EMERGENCIES

Q. **A 20-year-old man attends casualty with a 7-hour history of a painful erection. How would you assess him?**

A. A prolonged erection of this duration is a priapism and is a urological emergency. I would see him without delay in casualty. I would ensure that he has adequate analgesia, including a local anaesthetic penile block, and intravenous access. I would then perform baseline blood tests which would include an full blood count and sickle-cell screen if indicated, renal function and electrolytes. I would then enquire as to whether this is the first or a recurrent episode of the problem. An accurate history is required in order to establish whether this is an ischaemic or non-ischaemic priapism.

Q. **What is important in the history?**

A. In the history the important features are whether the erection is related to sexual stimulation or not (this is unlikely if it has lasted for 7 hours), the onset and duration of the erection, and whether it is painful. It is then important to ask about any specific risk factors such as pelvic, genital or perineal trauma which may precede this episode by several weeks, therapy for erectile dysfunction (both oral and intracavernous injections), other medications (particularly antipsychotics), and any history of haematological disease (such as sickle-cell disease or leukaemia). This may be a first episode, in which case the pre-existing erectile function should be documented. However, in a proportion of patients a priapism episode is preceded by shorter self-limiting erections known as 'stuttering priapism'.

Q. **What is important in the examination?**

A. It is important to ensure that analgesia is given before examining the patient. The baseline blood pressure and pulse must be recorded.

A focused urological examination is performed to assess for any signs of trauma or infection which may have precipitated the event. The genitalia, perineum and abdomen should be carefully examined to assess for evidence of trauma and to ensure that there is no obvious intra-abdominal lesion. Older patients should have a careful PR examination to exclude an underlying advanced pelvic malignancy. The degree of rigidity of the corpus cavernosum and glans may indicate the priapism subtype.

Q. **What types of priapism are you aware of?**
A. The two common types of priapism are ischaemic (low flow) and non-ischaemic (high flow). A more uncommon subtype is stuttering priapism.

Q. **How would you distinguish between the two types of priapism?**
A. On the basis of the history and examination, and with the aid of diagnostic investigations such as a cavernous blood analysis and radiological investigations such as Doppler ultrasound.

Q. **How would you manage the patient in casualty?**
A. After ensuring adequate analgesia, taking a focused history and examining the patient, I would send off baseline blood tests, including a full blood count and sickle-cell screen or haemoglobin electrophoresis, renal function and electrolytes. I would then perform a penile block and aspirate blood from the corpus cavernosum using a large-gauge butterfly needle, and send a sample for blood gas analysis and if possible glucose analysis. I would then continue to aspirate blood (up to 100 ml) from the corpus cavernosum until the penis was detumesced.

Q. **The blood gas analysis is shown below. The blood was dark when aspirated. What type of priapism is this likely to be?**

pO_2:	12 mmHg
pCO_2:	72 mmHg
pH:	7.1
glucose:	0.2 mmol/l.

A. The blood gas analysis is consistent with ischaemia, as there is evidence of hypoxia, acidosis and glucopenia. Therefore this is an ischaemic (low-flow) priapism.

Q. **What is the success rate of cavernosal aspiration in low-flow priapism?**
A. A literature review suggests a success rate of 24–36%, but this is dependent on the duration of priapism and the techniques used.

Q. **When is aspiration alone successful in the management of priapism?**
A. When it is done at an early stage, generally within 24 hours.

Q. **Are there any alternative ways of differentiating between low- and high-flow priapism without cavernosal aspiration?**
A. Yes, colour duplex ultrasound may be utilised as an alternative to differentiate the type of priapism. Patients with ischaemic priapism have little or no flow in the cavernosal arteries on duplex ultrasound, whereas non-ischaemic priapism shows high peak velocities.

Q. **The priapism responds to cavernosal aspiration but then 2 hours later reoccurs. What would you do now?**
A. A step-wise approach is recommended. I would move the patient to an area where he can be monitored haemodynamically. I would repeat the aspiration using a 20G butterfly needle in 50-ml portions and also wash out the corpus

cavernosum. If the priapism still persisted, I would inject an alpha-agonist such as phenylephrine. I would also ensure that the haemoglobin level was normal and that this was not a manifestation of a sickle-cell crisis.

Q. **How would you administer the phenylephrine?**

A. Phenylephrine is available as 10 mg in 1-ml aliquots. I would dilute the phenylephrine in 19 ml of saline so that the concentration becomes 0.5 mg/ml. I would then inject 0.5-ml aliquots (250 µg) every 5 minutes until detumescence occurred. Careful monitoring of the blood pressure and pulse would be required.

Q. **If the patient was to present with an ischaemic priapsim of more than 24 hours' duration which has not responded to corporal blood aspiration and α-agonists, what would you do?**

A. I would then proceed to perform shunt surgery.

Q. **What types of shunts are you aware of?**

A. Proximal and distal shunts.

Q. **What types of distal shunts are you aware of?**

A. I am aware of the Winter shunt (large biopsy needle) and the Ebbehoj shunt (scalpel), where a fistula is created between the glans and corpus cavernosum through the glans. There is also a T-shunt described by Lue, again using a scalpel through the glans and into the corporal tip followed by a 90° rotation.

Q. **What is the shunt shown in Figure 13.10?**

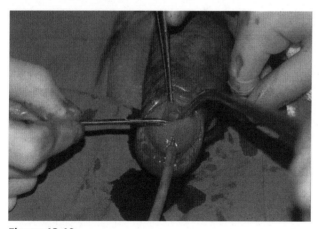

Figure 13.10

A. This is a picture of an El-Ghorab shunt where a piece of the tunica albuginea is excised at the tips of the corpora cavernosa via a dorsal transverse incision (on each side) distal to the coronal ridge.

Q. **A Winter shunt is performed bilaterally. However, this again fails to relieve the priapism. What would be your next step of management?**

A. I would seek the advice of a specialist centre. If distal shunting has failed, I would consider performing a proximal shunt after full discussion with the specialist centre and the patient.

Q. What types of proximal shunt are you aware of?

A. I am aware of the Quackels (corporo-spongiosal) and the Grayhack (corporo-saphenous) procedures.

Q. Is there any circumstance in which you might use a proximal shunt in preference to a distal shunt?

A. Yes, rarely, in cases where there is severe distal penile oedema or tissue damage.

Q. What are the success rates of shunt procedures and are there long-term problems?

A. The literature suggests success rates of 73–77% for the shunt procedures, but these depend on the duration of the priapism. Although shunt procedures may succeed in detumescence, there is a high rate of long-term erectile dysfunction (over 90%).

Q. Despite a proximal shunt procedure the priapism persists. It is now 72 hours since the priapism began. What is your plan now?

A. I would again discuss the case with a specialist centre. It is likely that the patient will require transfer to a tertiary centre.

Q. The patient is transferred to a tertiary centre. What do you think they will plan for him and why?

A. It is likely that they will explore the patient surgically and take a cavernosal smooth muscle biopsy to determine whether necrosis has already occurred. This would allow any patient with prolonged ischaemic priapism with non-viable tissue to be treated with the immediate insertion of a penile prosthesis, rather than shunt surgery, to minimise penile shortening and allow adequate rigidity for sexual function.

Q. What is the role of penile prosthesis insertion?

A. Prolonged ischaemic priapism using conservative measures or shunt surgery may result in cavernosal fibrosis, penile induration and shortening. Unfortunately, the resulting erectile dysfunction is usually severe and the subsequent placement of a penile prosthesis into a fibrotic penis can be extremely difficult and is associated with a higher complication rate. It is now recommended that in cases of severe prolonged low-flow priapism, a penile prosthesis is inserted early in order to maintain penile length and avoid further fibrosis.

Q. Another 36-year-old patient attends casualty with a persistent erection of more than 8 hours' duration. What is important in the history?

A. In the history the important features are whether the erection is related to sexual stimulation or not, the onset and duration of the erection, and whether it is painful or not. It is then important to ask about any relevant risk factors such as pelvic, genital or perineal trauma, therapy for erectile dysfunction or other medications, a history of haematological disease such as sickle-cell disease or leukaemia, and any previous history of neurological disease. This may be the first or a recurrent episode. It is imperative to ask about previous erectile function, as priapism may result in erectile dysfunction.

Q. The patient is in pain but the pain is in his perineum. What is important in his examination?

A. It is important to ensure that analgesia is given before examining the patient. The baseline blood pressure and pulse must be recorded.

A focused urological examination is performed to assess for any signs of trauma or infection which may have precipitated the event. In this case it is important to assess the genitalia, perineum and abdomen carefully for evidence of trauma. Again the degree of rigidity of the corpus cavernosum and glans may indicate the type of priapism that is present.

Q. **The patient has severe bruising of his genitalia. He was involved in a motorbike accident earlier in the evening but did not attend casualty as he was not seriously injured. How would you manage him?**

A. I would make sure that he was comfortable, and I would then send off baseline blood tests and ensure intravenous access. It is important to exclude any other coexisting injuries. Once this had been done, I would ask a radiologist to perform a penile duplex ultrasound scan on him.

Q. **Would you aspirate the corpus cavernosum?**

A. As the history and examination are highly suggestive of a high-flow priapism I would not do so. In cases where the history and examination are not consistent with high-flow priapism, I would aspirate the corpus cavernosum for diagnostic purposes only.

Q. **Would you inject sympathomimetic agents into the corpus cavernosum?**

A. I would not do so, as there is no evidence that this has therapeutic efficacy. Indeed it may result in significant adverse systemic effects.

Q. **The duplex ultrasound scan has confirmed high-flow priapism. How would you manage this patient?**

A. This is not a urological emergency and the patient can be managed conservatively. If a fistula is demonstrated on the duplex ultrasound scan, compression can be applied.

Q. **The patient is discharged home after a full skeletal survey. His priapism persists and he returns after 1 week. He requests treatment. How would you manage him?**

A. The site of the vascular injury may be diagnosed by pudendal arteriography with immediate embolisation if required. Super-elective embolisation can now be performed with success, using absorbable material.

Q. **What type of material would you recommend that the patient is embolised with?**

A. Non-absorbable materials used during embolisation pose a greater risk of erectile dysfunction (39%) than absorbable materials (5%). It is therefore recommended that autologous clots and absorbable gels are preferable to coils and permanent chemicals.

Q. **How successful is embolisation for high-flow priapism?**

A. The literature suggests that the success rate is 74–78% regardless of whether absorbable or non-absorbable materials are used.

Q. **Unfortunately the embolisation fails. The patient has now had persistent priapism for 6 weeks. What would you do?**

A. I would ask for a further colour duplex ultrasound. If this demonstrates a thick-walled cystic mass, I would counsel the patient about an open penile explo-ration and direct ligation. However, this is the option of last resort.

Q. **What is the success rate and the risk of complications?**

A. The literature suggests that open exploration and ligation is successful in 63% of cases, but is associated with a very high risk of erectile dysfunction (up to 50% of cases).

Q. **You are asked to see a 86-year-old man in casualty. He has a long-term catheter *in situ* and is from a nursing home. You are told that he has scrotal swelling (*see* Figure 13.11). What are you most concerned about?**

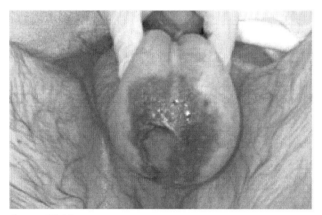

Figure 13.11

A. Figure 13.11 shows Fournier's gangrene, which is a form of necrotising fasciitis, affecting the perineum and male genitalia.

Q. **What are the important aspects in the history?**

A. It is important to ascertain the age of the patient, whether this condition has appeared suddenly or insidiously, and how long it has been present. It is also important to enquire about risk factors such as the following:
- any recent instrumentation of the urinary tract
- any recent surgery in the ano-genital area (or gynaecological procedures if this had been a female patient)
- whether a long-term catheter is present
- whether there is reduced mobility, in particular whether the patient is wheel-chair-bound, paraplegic or bedbound
- whether the patient is normally continent
- whether there are any comorbidities which may result in immunosuppres-sion (e.g. diabetes, alcohol abuse).

Q. **What is important in the clinical examination?**

A. It is important to first resuscitate these patients aggressively, as they are often very sick.

It is also important to record the vital observations such as body tempera-ture, blood pressure, O_2 saturations, pulse, peripheral circulation, sensorium and urine output to exclude signs of shock.

A focused uro-genital examination is required, including an evaluation of the perineum, the peri-anal region and the genitals. Specifically one is looking for any areas of skin necrosis and the presence or absence of crepitus of the anterior abdominal wall. Peri-anal involvement signifies an ano-rectal source, and the presence of skip lesions suggests more extensive involvement.

Q. **Where does the infection normally arise from?**

A. This infection most commonly arises from the skin, urethra or rectal region. There is an association between stricture disease and urethral instrumentation and the development of Fournier's gangrene. Predisposing factors include diabetes mellitus, local trauma, paraphimosis, peri-urethral extravasation of urine, perirectal or peri-anal infections, and surgery such as circumcision or hernia repair.

Q. **How are you going to manage this patient?**

A. Prompt diagnosis is critical because of the rapidity with which the process can progress. It may initially be difficult to differentiate the necrotising fasciitis from cellulitis, but the presence of marked systemic toxicity that is out of proportion to the local finding is often found.

I would then make sure that the patient is transferred urgently to a urological ward or ITU/HDU, depending on the clinical severity of the condition. There I would ensure that he is resuscitated with adequate intravenous hydration and antimicrobial therapy so that he may be suitably prepared for surgical debridement.

Q. **What investigations are required?**

A. I would ensure that baseline bloods tests are performed (full blood count, U&E, liver function tests, G&S and glucose) as well as blood gas analysis to exclude a metabolic acidosis. I would send cultures of the blood and urine as well as culture of any obvious pus from the region. In severe cases, I would ask the anaesthetist to insert appropriate lines for monitoring before surgery. If possible, a CT scan is useful pre-operatively to identify the possible source of infection.

Q. **Which organisms are usually responsible for this condition?**

A. There is a synergistic action, so normally multiple organisms are responsible. The commonest organism is *E. coli*. However, the infection is often mixed, containing facultative organisms (*E. coli, Klebsiella*, enterococci) together with anaerobes (*Bacteroides, Fusobacterium, Clostridium*, micro-aerophilic streptococci).

Q. **Which antibiotic would you plan to use?**

A. I would use an antimicrobial regimen recommended following discussion with the microbiologist. It would commonly include triple therapy such as augmentin or a parenteral third-generation cephalosporin such as ceftriaxone, together with gentamicin and metronidazole.

Q. **How would you consent the patient?**

A. These patients are often gravely ill and unable to give consent. It is therefore important to involve the family early on, and to emphasise that the patient needs an operation as a matter of extreme urgency. I would explain the gravity of the situation and that more than one procedure is likely to be required. I would also explain that we need to remove the subcutaneous gangrenous tissue, and that a urinary diversion with a suprapubic catheter is likely. In the longer term I would explain that large skin and subcutaneous tissue defects are likely, which may require plastic surgery for functional and cosmetic results. I would explain that the patient would be required to stay in the ITU/HDU, depending on their clinical condition, for optimal support.

Q. **Explain what you would do in theatre.**

A. An extensive incision should be made through the skin and subcutaneous tissues, going beyond the areas of involvement which show end arteritis until normal fascia is found and the subcutaneous tissue is bleeding. Necrotic fat and fascia should be excised, and the wound should be left open. A second procedure 24 hours later is always indicated. A suprapubic diversion should be performed in cases where urethral trauma or extravasation is suspected. Colostomy should be performed if there is colonic or rectal perforation.

Q. **Do these patients normally require an orchidectomy?**

A. Orchidectomy is almost never required, because the testes have their own blood supply independent of the compromised fascial and cutaneous circulation to the scrotum.

Q. **What is this patient's long-term prognosis?**

A. The literature suggests that the average mortality rate is around 20%. Higher mortality rates are found in diabetics, alcoholics, and patients with colorectal sources of infection who often have a less typical presentation, a longer delay in diagnosis, and more widespread extension.

Q. **Are there any scoring systems that can predict mortality and outcome in these patients?**

A. The mortality risk can be assessed using the Laor scoring system (Fournier's gangrene severity index), which looks at parameters on admission, including body temperature, heart rate, respiratory rate, sodium, potassium and creatinine levels, packed cell volume and whole blood cell count. A score of > 9 predicts mortality in 75% of cases.

Q. **Are there any adjunctive therapies which may be helpful in wound healing?**

A. The use of hyperbaric oxygen therapy in patients with Fournier's gangrene has been reported to give favourable results. Hyperbaric oxygen therapy has shown some promise in shortening hospital stays, increasing wound healing, and decreasing the gangrenous spread when used in conjunction with debridement and antimicrobial agents.

A recent small study suggests that vacuum-assisted closure (VAC) is as effective as conventional management in healing the wounds. However, with the use of VAC, patients had fewer dressing changes, less pain, fewer skipped meals and greater mobility, resulting in greater patient and physician satisfaction.

Q. **You are asked to see a patient on the ward who had a TURP 2 days ago. He has been complaining of penile pain. The nurse is asked to remove the catheter. What is the diagnosis shown in Figure 13.12?**

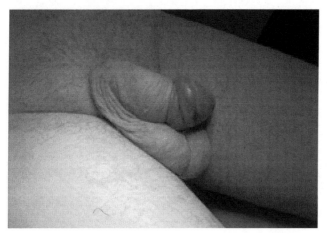

Figure 13.12

A.   This is a paraphimosis.

Q.   **How does it commonly occur?**
A.   It is often iatrogenic and frequently occurs after a well-meaning healthcare professional has examined the penis or inserted a urethral catheter and forgotten to replace the foreskin in its natural position. It develops when the tip of the foreskin retracts proximal to the coronal sulcus and becomes fixed in position and develops a constriction ring. Severe oedema of the foreskin occurs within several hours, depending on the tightness of the ring of the foreskin.

Q.   **What is your management plan?**
A.   In most cases, manual compression of the glans with placement of distal traction on the oedematous foreskin allows reduction of the paraphimotic ring.

Q.   **What is different about the dorsal band traction technique and how is it performed?**
A.   Most methods of reduction of paraphimosis focus on decreasing the oedema before reduction. This technique uses the basic surgical principles of traction and countertraction by applying a pair of Adson forceps directly to the band formed by the retracted preputial opening.

Q.   **What is the Dundee technique?**
A.   It is a technique in which the oedematous prepuce is first cleaned with an antiseptic cream and then a 26G needle (outer diameter 0.45 mm) is used to make about 20 puncture holes in the oedematous prepuce. Using gentle but firm pressure, the oedema fluid is then expressed from the foreskin until it has been completely decompressed, allowing easy reduction of the prepuce.

Q.   **What will you do once the foreskin is reduced?**
A.   If the tip of the foreskin is tight, there is a risk of recurrence. I would then list the patient for an elective circumcision. However, as the tissue planes can be difficult, it is advisable to wait until the oedema has settled completely. If all procedures fail, it is possible to perform a dorsal slit under a local anaesthetic.

REFERENCES

1. Mulcahy JJ. Penile implant infections: prevention and treatment. *Curr Urol Rep* 2008; **9:** 487–91.
2. Evers JL *et al*. Surgery or embolisation for varicocele in subfertile men. *Cochrane Database Syst Rev* 2004; **3:** CD000479.
3. Hancock P *et al*. British Andrology Society guidelines for the assessment of post-vasectomy semen samples (2002). *J Clin Pathol* 2002; **55:** 812–16.
4. Belker AM *et al*. Results of 1,469 microsurgical vasectomy reversals by the Vasovasostomy Study Group. *J Urol* 1991; **145:** 505–11.
5. Ralph DJ *et al*. The Nesbit operation for Peyronie's disease: 16-year experience. *J Urol* 1995; **154:** 1362–3.

Chapter 14

Technology in urology, principles of uroradiology and miscellaneous

John A Bycroft and Jim Adshead

ENDOUROLOGY TECHNOLOGY

Q. **What are the characteristics of the 'ideal' stent?**

A. The ideal stent would have the following characteristics:[1]
- good memory, with a configuration that prevents migration
- excellent flow characteristics
- radio-opaque
- biologically inert (biocompatible)
- resists biofilm formation, encrustation and infection
- made of a flexible material with a high tensile strength
- easy to insert
- easy to remove or exchange
- reasonable price
- minimal complications.

Q. **What are the indications for stent insertion?**

A. The indications can be divided into two categories – elective and emergency. Elective indications include the following:
- protection of anastomosis (pyeloplasty, ureteric reimplantation)
- to overcome extrinsic ureteric compression
- prior to chemotherapy to optimise renal function in obstructive uropathy
- pre-operatively (in gynaecological or colorectal surgery) to aid identification of the ureter.

Emergency indications include the following:
- relief of ureteric obstruction
- management of ureteric trauma.

Q. **What are the complications of ureteric stent placement?**

A. In addition to the complications of actual insertion, these can be divided into common and rare complications, as shown in Table 14.1.

Table 14.1 Common and rare problems associated with ureteric stent placement

Common problems	Rare problems
Trigonal irritation	Obstruction
Haematuria	Kinking
Fever	Ureteric injury/ureteric perforation
Infection	Stent misplacement
Inflammation	Stent migration
Encrustation	'Missed'/forgotten stent
Biofilm formation	Tissue hyperplasia

Q. **What are ureteric stents made of? Why are they radio-opaque?**

A. Ureteric stents are manufactured from a variety of polymers, such as polyure-thane and styrene-ethylene-butylene (C-flex). The radio-opacity of stents is increased by coating them with metals such as bismuth and barium.

Silicone stents are also manufactured. These are stiffer and therefore may cause more mucosal irritation, but can be left *in situ* for up to 1 year (in contrast to conventional polyurethane stents, which need to be changed every 6 months) Stents are generally 22–30 cm in length and are usually of the 'double-pigtail' variety. Sizes are generally in the range 4.7–8.0 Fr.

Metallic ureteric stents are increasingly being used for malignant ureteric strictures, e.g. the Memokath™ ureteric stent, which is made of nickel-titanium memory-shape alloy (Nitinol).

Q. **What are the different types of ureteric guidewires available?**

A. Many forms of ureteric guidewires have evolved over the years. Most guidewires are of the order of 0.035–0.038 inches in diameter, and approximately 150 cm long. Various configurations exist, and wires are commonly coated with PTFE (polytetrafluoroethylene) and have flexible tips of various lengths. Variations include hydrophilic wires (such as the Terumo wire), guidewires with a hydro-philic tip (e.g. the Sensor wire) and stiff wires (e.g. the Amplatz Super Stiff).

Q. **What are the various baskets available for ureteroscopic surgery?**

A. A large number of ureteroscopic baskets are commercially available. They may be either 'tipped' or 'flat wire', as used in semi-rigid ureteroscopy, or 'tip-less', as used in flexible ureterorenoscopy. The tipless variety may allow easier access using the flexible scope, and avoid trauma to the collecting system (eas-ily inserted into the renal calyx if necessary). Baskets are commonly made of nickel-titanium memory-shape alloy (Nitinol), and range in size from about 2 Fr to 3.2 Fr. Baskets are available that open in different ways (e.g. 'parachute' and 'helical').

Q. **Describe how a modern telescope, as used in cystoscopy, works.**

A. Originally, before the work of Professor Harold Hopkins, telescopes consisted of fine lenses cemented into long metal cylinders separated by long air spaces. That system was replaced by the Hopkins rod–lens system in the 1950s. This system, which is still in place today, essentially consists of a series of long glass rods in a metal cylinder separated by 'lenses' of air. Therefore internally it is a series of relatively long glass rods separated by air, as opposed to small lenses separated by long air spaces. The advantages of this include durability, superior light passage and image quality, reduced diameter of the instrument (permitting parallel access channels), colour reproduction, and the ability to 'document' images with photography or video.

Light is transmitted by optic-fibre bundles running from an external light source (note that this is usually a halogen external light source, which emits 'yellowish' light – thus the need for white balancing; neon light sources are expensive but do not require white balancing).

Q.   How does an optic fibre work? What are the two main applications of optic fibres in urology and how do they differ?

A. Optic fibres are flexible glass (or plastic) fibres that allow light to pass through them via a process termed *total internal reflection*. Optic fibres are grouped together in a parallel fashion and protected by external plastic sleeves.

They have two main uses in urology:
- *Transmission of a light source.* 'Light leads' transmit light from an external source to endoscopes. These leads consist of *non-coherent* fibres, and are relatively inexpensive to produce.
- *Transmission of images.* Image transmission (e.g. from a camera) relies upon *coherent* bundles of optic fibres. In this case, the orientation of the fibres at the proximal end must be the same as the orientation at the distal end to prevent image distortion.

Q.   How is the size/diameter of surgical instruments (e.g. cystoscopes, catheters, etc.) expressed?

A. The 'French gauge' (Fr) is used. This was developed by Charrière in the nineteenth century. The French gauge corresponds to three times the diameter (in mm). For example, a 21 Fr cystoscope sheath has an external diameter of 7 mm.

Q.   What are the approximate lengths, diameters and working channel configurations of the major endo-urological instruments?

A. *Semi-rigid ureteroscopes.* These vary in size depending on the manufacturer and the working channel configuration. It should be remembered that they use fibre optics for image transmission, rather than the rod–lens system of traditional rigid instruments, and therefore have a relatively small diameter that usually obviates the need for formal ureteric dilatation. The working element is of the order of 34 cm long, with the tip approximately 7–10 Fr (i.e. about 3 mm in diameter). If one working channel is present it is usually about 3.4 Fr, whereas if two are present they are about 2.3 Fr each.

Flexible ureteroscopes (ureterorenoscopes). The configurations vary depending on the age and model of the instrument. The distal end of the instrument is less than 9 Fr, and modern instruments may be even smaller (5.4 Fr, i.e. < 2 mm in diameter). Lengths vary, but are usually around 70–80 cm. Working channels are approximately 3.6 Fr, permitting the passage of instruments such as biopsy forceps up to 3 Fr and laser fibres. The endoscope may be inserted by means of a hydrophilic access sheath placed over a guidewire. These sheaths are approximately 45 cm and 10–14 Fr. They may have dual lumens to permit parallel instrument passage.

Cystoscopes. Adult cystoscope sheaths are generally in the range 17–25 Fr, and approximately 30 cm long. The components of the cystoscope are the telescope (rod–lens), bridge, obturator and sheath. The telescopes themselves are angled for various procedures, and are generally 0 degree (for urethrotomy, etc), 30 degree and 70 degree (for cystoscopy). Telescopes are colour coded with bands around the light-lead connector (e.g. green, red and yellow for 0, 30 and 70 degree, respectively).

Resectoscopes. These again vary in size depending on the manufacturer and the configuration. Common external sheath diameters are 26 Fr and 28 Fr.

STERILISATION AND DISINFECTION

Q. What is the difference between sterilisation, disinfection and cleaning?

A. Sterilisation is defined as the complete destruction of living organisms (including spores and viruses). This differs from disinfection, which is a process that is used to remove most viable organisms, but which does not necessarily inactivate some viruses and bacterial spores. Cleaning is a process that physically removes contamination but does not necessarily destroy microorganisms.

Q. How is autoclaving performed?

A. Autoclaving is a process that combines heat and pressure to sterilise instruments. By combining pressure with heat the temperatures of liquids such as water may be raised above their usual boiling points to facilitate the process. The autoclave is thus a form of 'pressure cooker.' The three variables used in autoclaving are therefore pressure, temperature and time. Typical cycles include 134° Celsius for a 'hold time' of 3 minutes, and 121° Celsius for a 'hold time' of 15 minutes. The actual timing of the whole process is longer than these values, of course, as the machines need to safely heat up and cool down.

Q. How is disinfection carried out?

A. Flexible instruments (e.g. flexible cystoscope) would generally be unable to withstand the conditions of autoclaving. They are therefore processed by high-level disinfection. They are manually cleaned with brushes and detergent, and then disinfected in an automated manner. Ultrasound is used in some devices to facilitate the cleaning process. Automated machines use a cycle whereby the flexible endoscope is disinfected with solutions of a chemical such as chlorine dioxide ('Tristel').

Q. How would you determine the level of disinfection required for reusable medical instruments?

A. These instruments are divided into three classes according to the Spaulding classification, namely critical, semi-critical and non-critical.

- Critical instruments are those that penetrate normally sterile tissue (i.e. surgical instruments). They generally require sterilisation before and after use.
- Semi-critical instruments are those that come into contact with mucous membranes or non-intact skin (e.g. cystoscopes).
- Non-critical items are those that only come into contact with intact skin (e.g. blood pressure cuffs).

Q. **What would you use for scrubbing and skin preparation prior to surgery?**
A. • Scrubbing:
  – 4% chlorhexidine (Hydrex)
  – 7.5% povidone–iodine (Betadine or Videne).
• Skin preparation:
  – inguinoscrotal: 10% aqueous povidone–iodine (Betadine or Videne)
  – genital: chlorhexidine 0.015% cetrimide 0.15% (Travasept solution).

Q. **What are the ideal climate conditions for an operating theatre?**
A. 21° C and 55% relative humidity.

DIATHERMY

Q. **What does Figure 14.1 show?**

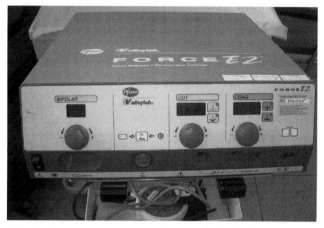

Figure 14.1

A. This is an image of a diathermy machine.

Q. **What is diathermy?**
A. It is the passage of high-frequency alternating current, in the range 400 kHz to 10 MHz, through body tissue. Where the current is concentrated, a temperature of up to 1000° C is produced, allowing the cutting or coagulation of tissue.[2]

Nerves and muscles are not stimulated with such a high-frequency alternating current (400 kHz to 10 MHz), as there is no time for the cell membranes of nerve and muscle to become depolarised (they are stimulated at lower frequencies only).

Q. **What type of diathermy do you use in theatre, and how does it work?**
A. The main types of diathermy used in an operating theatre are monopolar and bipolar.

Monopolar diathermy involves the delivery of high-frequency current from a diathermy generator to the active electrode (diathermy forceps or standard resectoscope loop or ball). High current density at the active electrode, which has a small surface area, results in heat at the point of contact with tissue. Current density then spreads from this point, throughout the body, returning

329

to the diathermy generator via the patient electrode plate (earth plate), which is the diathermy pad placed on the patient. Low current density at this electrode plate, due to its large surface area (70–150 cm²), results in no heat formation. Importantly, the patient electrode plate should be over a well-vascularised area away from any prosthesis, and the underlying skin should be free of scarring or hair to allow good contact of the plate with the patient.

With bipolar diathermy, current passes down one limb of forceps (active electrode) and back to the diathermy generator via the other limb (patient electrode plate). The advantage of bipolar diathermy is that there is no need for a plate to be placed on the patient. The disadvantages are that there is no cutting facility, the forceps need to be kept apart, and there is less power.

Q. **What is the difference between cutting and coagulation?**
A. The differences are listed in Table 14.2 and Figure 14.2.

Table 14.2 Differences between cutting and coagulation

Cutting	Coagulation
Continuous output (sine wave)	Pulsed output (interrupted sine wave)
100% on	6% on
0% off	94% off
(see Figure 14.2)	(see Figure 14.2)
Low voltage	High voltage
Non-contact mode: vaporisation and cutting	Non-contact mode: fulguration
Contact mode: dessication (coagulum)	Contact mode: dessication
Intense heat (1000° C)	Less heat
Charring/spread: low	Charring/spread: high
Power 125–250 W	Power 10–75 W
Typical diathermy machine setting: 150–160	Typical diathermy machine setting: 40–70

Note: The 'blend' facility only works in cutting mode – pulsed output (50% on and 50% off).

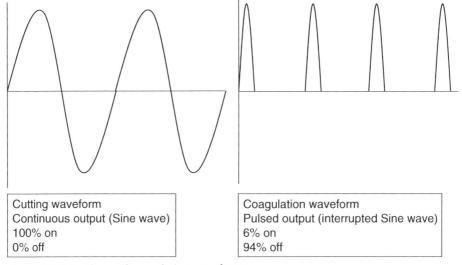

Cutting waveform
Continuous output (Sine wave)
100% on
0% off

Coagulation waveform
Pulsed output (interrupted Sine wave)
6% on
94% off

Figure 14.2 Cutting and coagulation waveforms.

Q. What are the potential complications and precautions with regard to diathermy?

A. The complications and precautions are as follows:
- Burns:
  - due to misapplication of the patient electrode plate
  - metal prosthesis or implants should not be touched directly with the active electrode or the patient electrode plate
  - use of inflammable preparatory solution may result in superficial burns on skin or in cavities.
- Explosions:
  - in obstructed hollow viscera
  - if inflammable volatile anaesthetic agents (e.g. ether) are used.
- High-voltage electrocution:
  - of the patient or the surgeon because of faulty cables.
- Obturator kick.
- End artery necrosis:
  - especially with monopolar diathermy, during penile surgery.
- Pacemakers:
  - diathermy needs to be used with caution in patients with pacemakers (see below).

Q. How are diathermy burns avoided?

A. Inflammable liquids (e.g. those containing alcohol) should be avoided. The patient electrode plate should be at least 70 cm² in size, and placed appropriately (see above). The patient should not be in contact with any other metal objects (e.g. drip stands). In addition, touching other instruments with the diathermy probe (either inadvertently or deliberately) should be avoided (to prevent direct coupling).

Q. You are in the middle of a TURP when the diathermy stops working. How would you resolve the situation in order to complete the procedure?

A. I would perform a series of checks, as follows:
1. Make sure that the machine has not been switched off inadvertently.
2. Check that the diathermy cable is still connected to the diathermy machine.
3. Ensure that the diathermy cable has not broken.
4. Make sure that the diathermy cable is properly connected to the working element of the resectoscope.
5. Ensure that the loop is not broken.
6. Check that the irrigating fluid is still glycine (1.5%).
7. Make sure that the patient electrode plate is appropriately attached to the patient and that the return cable to the diathermy machine is still connected.

Q. You are contacted by your junior colleague about a 78-year-old patient who is due to have a TURP in 2 weeks' time. The doctor suspects that the patient has a pacemaker, and wishes to seek advice. What are the potential risks?

A. The main risks with pacemakers and implantable cardioverter defibrillators (ICDs) are pacemaker inhibition, phantom reprogramming and ventricular fibrillation.

- *Pacemaker inhibition*: the high frequency of the diathermy current may simulate cardiac electrical activity, thus inhibiting the pacemaker. If the patient is pacemaker-dependent, the heart may stop beating.
- *Phantom reprogramming*: the high frequency of the diathermy current may simulate the radio-frequency impulse by which pacemakers are reprogrammed. As a result, the pacemaker may start to work in an entirely different mode.

Q. What precautions should be taken before, during and after the operation?

A. All information about the pacemaker/ICD should be available, including the type of device (pacemaker/ICD), serial numbers, the date of implantation, the hospital that implanted the device, the indication for the device, and the date and result of the last check. The patient should have a card displaying this information. The cardiac clinic should be contacted to determine the precise indication for the device, and to determine whether the device is due for replacement.

In general, diathermy should be avoided in the first instance in such patients, and an alternative treatment strategy should be considered. If the surgical procedure is deemed unavoidable, the following points should be considered.

Prior to the surgery, carefully consult the cardiologist, pacemaker clinic and cardiac technician in elective cases (see above). Most devices will not need to be adjusted pre-operatively. However, advice should still be sought, as the consequences may otherwise be life-threatening. ICDs are generally set to 'monitor only' to prevent inadvertent activation, and should of course be switched back after the operation. Consider whether the procedure can be performed with bipolar diathermy (e.g. TURP).

During the procedure, the patient plate electrode should be sited so that the current path does not pass right through the pacemaker. Furthermore, it is important to ensure that it is properly applied. Avoid inappropriate grounding through ECG leads. The diathermy machine should be positioned well away from the pacemaker (> 15 cm). The patient's heart rate should be continuously monitored, and a defibrillator should be immediately available, as well as an external pacemaker. Surgically, short bursts of diathermy should be used and the operative time should be short as possible. Antibiotic prophylaxis should be given, and fluid overload should be avoided in these cases.

Clinical magnets may be secured over ICDs to prevent inadvertent shocks and to allow pacemakers to function at a fixed rate. However, they are very rarely used in current practice, because of the risk of phantom reprogramming.

In emergency situations, pre-operative checks may not be possible. However, the device should be checked post-operatively as soon as is practicable.[3]

EXTRACORPOREAL SHOCK-WAVE LITHOTRIPSY (ESWL)

Q. Describe the various components of the shock-wave lithotripter.

A. Whatever the device that is used, the lithotripter will have four main components. These are an *energy source*, a *medium for transmission of energy* (e.g. water), a *focusing device* and an *imaging modality*.

The first machines to be used were the Dornier lithotripters. These used electrohydraulic energy to perform electrohydraulic lithotripsy (EHL), whereby a spark is produced between two electrodes under water, which results in the rapid expansion and collapse of a gas bubble and subsequent energy transmission. A metal hemi-ellipsoid reflector is used to focus the energy. This modality produces the most effective shocks, but can be painful, and the intensity of the shock wave is variable. An example of such a machine that is used today would be the Dornier lithotripter S II.

A second type is the electromagnetic lithotripter. This relies on a cylindrical electromagnetic source, and energy is focused by an acoustic lens. An example of this would be the Storz Modulith SLX-F2.

Thirdly, piezoelectric technology may be used to produce the energy. Piezoelectric materials consist of ceramic or crystal elements that produce an electrical discharge under stress or tension (the direct effect). Energy transmission in this lithotripter relies on the 'converse piezoelectric effect', whereby energy is produced via the movement of the source when electricity is passed through it. An example of a piezoelectric lithotripter would be the EDAP LT 02.

The acoustic shock wave that is produced has two main phases. First, a short *positive phase* causes erosion at the entry and exit points of the calculus. The stone also shatters internally due to the compressive effect of the wave. The effect of compression/tension-induced cracks is sometimes referred to as 'spallation'. Secondly, a longer *negative pressure phase* component of the wave results in the formation of microbubbles, and the collapse of these microbubbles causes further erosion of the stone surface via the formation of 'microjets'. The two phases are illustrated schematically in Figure 14.3.

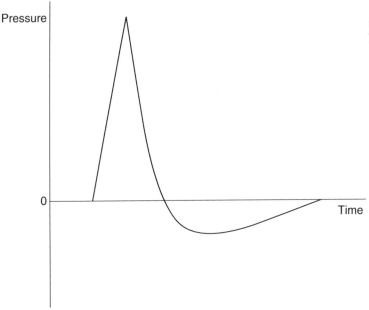

Figure 14.3 The two phases of a shock wave (shock-wave pressure profile).

Q. What are the indications for ESWL?

A. The indications are as follows:
- renal pelvis stones < 20 mm
- lower pole stones < 10 mm
- upper ureteric stones < 10 mm
- sandwich therapy in conjunction with percutaneous nephrolithotomy (PCNL).

Q. What are the contraindications to ESWL?

A. The contraindications can be divided into absolute and relative.
- Absolute contraindications include the following:
- uncorrected coagulopathy
- sepsis or active UTI
- distal obstruction
- pregnancy.

Relative contraindications include the following:
- hard stones (cystine or calcium oxalate monohydrate)
- morbid obesity (> 135 kg)
- abdominal aortic aneurysm
- abdominal pacemaker.

Q. How would you consent a patient for ESWL?

A. Informed consent for ESWL would involve a description of the procedure, discussion of the alternative treatments, and an explanation of the potential complications.[4]

Common complications
- Haematuria.
- Renal/ureteric colic.
- UTI requiring antibiotic treatment.

Occasional complications
- Stones will not break because they are too hard, so an alternative treatment is required.
- Repeated ESWL treatments may be required.
- Recurrence of stones.

Rare complications
- Perinephric haematoma.
- Steinstrasse.
- Severe infection that requires intravenous antibiotics with or without nephrostomy.
- Adjacent organ damage (in patients with diabetes).
- Hypertension.
- Arrhythmias.

INTRACORPOREAL ENERGY FORMS

Q. A 53-year-old man who has an 8 mm mid-ureteric stone and JJ stent *in situ* presents for ureteroscopy. Can you tell me what you would use to fragment this ureteric stone?

A. I would use a lithoclast. The lithoclast is known as a contact-type intracorporeal lithotripter. The device allows pneumatically generated energy to be delivered as kinetic energy to the stone. Compressed air delivered from an external supply fires a projectile in the handpiece of the lithoclast into a probe (similar to a jackhammer), and the energy is thus transmitted to the calculus (the probe must be in contact with the stone to fragment it). The probe tends to 'bounce' off the wall of the ureter, minimising trauma, and is considered a safe modality in the ureter, although ureteric perforation may still occur if it is used without care. A disadvantage of the device is that the stone may be retrogradely propelled higher up the ureter or into the kidney.

Lithoclast energy is delivered by a rigid probe, and this therefore limits its use to rigid endoscopes. In addition to fragmentation of ureteric stones, the lithoclast can be used to fragment renal stones during percutaneous nephrolithotomy (PCNL). (During PCNL the lithoclast can be combined with the *hollow* ultrasound probe, which is able to suck up stone fragments, e.g. as in the Swiss LithoClast Master.)

Q. What alternative forms of energy could you use for a ureteric stone?

A. An alternative modality to the lithoclast in the ureter would be laser, such as the holmium laser. LASER is an acronym for **L**ight **A**mplification by **S**timulated **E**mission of **R**adiation. The three characteristics of laser light are its coherence (the light is parallel), its monochromacity (the light is all of the same wavelength) and the fact that it is in phase (Collimation). Laser is formed by applying energy to a lasing medium, a process that is known as 'pumping.' The energy may be light, chemical or even another laser, and the medium may be a solid, liquid or gas. The laser chamber itself is fully reflective apart from an aperture that is able to let light escape when it reaches a certain intensity. Photons are released from the medium when energy is applied, and this in turn leads to the release of more photons from the medium. The light is therefore amplified, and a state known as 'population inversion' occurs whereby more light is released than is absorbed. The wavelength of holmium laser is 2140 nm, and it is therefore invisible. A secondary red aiming beam is utilised. The depth of penetration is 0.4 mm (holmium laser). Laser works primarily via a photo-excitation/photothermal effect (i.e. heat production). Different fibres sizes exist. It is recommended that 200-μm fibres should be used with the flexible ureterorenoscope and 365-μm fibres (or less) with the semi-rigid ureteroscope.

Electrohydraulic lithotripsy (EHL) should be avoided in the ureter due to the risk of ureteric damage (although it may be used in the bladder). Similarly, the use of ultrasonic energy should be avoided in the ureter because of thermal side-effects (i.e. high temperature at the tip of the ultrasound probe).

Q. How does electrohydraulic lithotripsy (EHL) work?

A. An underwater spark plug is generated by applying voltage/current to two concentric electrodes with different voltage polarities, which are 1 mm apart and separated by insulation. This electrically generated spark at the tip of the probe results in the momentary production of heat in a localised area, and a small amount of irrigant (which is typically water) surrounding the electrode is vaporised, forming a gas bubble. Subsequent expansion and collapse of the gas bubble generates a hydraulic shock wave in 1/800 second, which impacts on the stone.

Collapse of the cavitation bubble can be symmetrical (around 1 mm from stone) or asymmetrical (around 3 mm from stone). The symmetrical aspect results in the production of a strong secondary shock wave, whereas the asymmetrical part results in the formation of high-speed microjets. Both of these then result in stone breakage in a similar mechanism to ESWL (see above).

The probe should be placed on or not more than 1 mm from the stone.

EHL is delivered using a flexible probe (via cystoscope) and is generally used to fragment bladder stones.

EHL should never be used in the ureter, as it may result in ureteric perforation.

Q. **How does ultrasound lithotripsy work?**

A. Ultrasound waves, produced by an ultrasound generator, are transmitted down a hollow probe resulting in vibration of the probe tip. This vibration, when in contact with the stone, produces a drilling or grinding action leading to stone fragmentation. Ultrasound is used in PCNL, often in combination with a lithoclast (as the ultrasound probe is hollow, it is able to suck up small stone fragments). In addition, this energy form is used for disintegration of bladder stones. As it is a rigid probe it is used with rigid endoscopes only.

Ultrasound must not be used in the ureter, as vibration of the tip results in high temperatures and therefore there is a significant risk of ureteric perforation.

Q. **How would you ensure laser safety in theatre?**

A. • Make sure that the theatre doors are closed throughout the procedure.
   • Ensure that a warning sign is displayed at the theatre entrance doors, and that a warning light at these doors comes on when the laser is being used.
   • The theatre that is used should have a non-reflective coating on the walls.
   • Minimise the number of staff who are present in theatre.
   • The Laser Safety Officer should be present.
   • The surgeon and staff handling the laser should have been trained on a certified laser course.
   • Appropriate eye protection (goggles) should be worn, depending on the wavelength of the laser being used.
   • Laser should be placed on standby when not in use.
   • The laser pedal should have a guard.

Q. **What is the device shown in Figures 14.4a and 14.4b and how does it work?**

Figure 14.4a   **Figure 14.4b**

A. Figure 14.4a shows the generator for the Swiss LithoClast Master.

Figure 14.4b shows the foot pedals used to activate the Swiss LithoClast Master.

The Swiss LithoClast Master has both a lithoclast and an ultrasound probe and is used for PCNL. During this procedure the lithoclast is combined with the *hollow* ultrasound probe, which is able to suck up stone fragments.

PRINCIPLES OF URORADIOLOGY

Q. What is the machine shown in Figure 14.5 and how does it work?

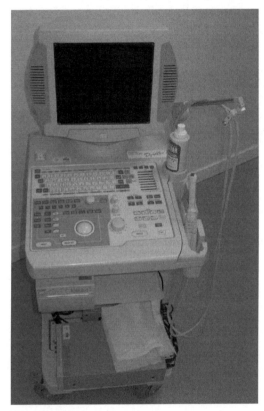

Figure 14.5

A. This is an ultrasound machine. It can be used as either a diagnostic or therapeutic tool in medicine. High-frequency sound waves are produced by the passage of current through a piezoelectric transducer, and are subsequently focused. Medical ultrasound waves have frequencies in the range 2–18 MHz. Lower frequencies are used to look at 'deeper' tissues, as the attenuation of sound waves is greater at higher frequencies. For example, a transrectal ultrasound (TRUS) probe works at about 7 MHz, and transabdominal ultrasound works at around 3.5 MHz. Ultrasound waves pass into the body via an interface consisting of the soft rubber coating on the transducer and gel. The sound waves are deflected back to the transducer, depending on an appropriate density change within the

337

tissues. Large density changes (e.g. fluid and stone) produce a greater 'echo', and the time taken for the waves to come back to the transducer can determine the depth of the tissue.

Q. **What are the main therapeutic applications of ultrasound?**

A. The main current therapeutic applications of ultrasound are lithotripsy (extra-corporeal, during percutaneous nephrolithotomy and intracorporeal) and high-intensity focused ultrasound (HIFU), which is used in the treatment of prostate cancer. Ultrasound as a modality can guide other therapies such as prostate brachytherapy, cryotherapy and extracorporeal shock-wave lithotripsy.

Q. **A 55-year-old man attends with acute loin pain and dipstick haematuria. His renal function is normal and there are no contraindications to intra-venous contrast administration. What is your radiological investigation of choice and why?**

A. See the chapter on urinary stone disease.

Q. **A 62-year-old woman presents with possible renal/ureteric colic. She has non-insulin-dependent diabetes with a normal serum creatinine level. The casualty officer has arranged an IVU which revealed a 6-mm vesico-ure-teric junction stone. The patient has been handed over to your care. What are the concerns about this management and how would you deal with it?**

A. See the chapter on urinary stone disease.

Q. **What are the general contraindications to administration of intravenous contrast media?**

A. The contraindications to intravenous contrast media are as follows:
- allergy to media
- impaired renal function (creatinine concentration > 130 μmol/l)
- metformin usage (see chapter on urinary stones)
- untreated hyperthyroidism and myelomatosis.

Q. **A 64-year-old man is referred for an MRI following the diagnosis of pros-tate cancer. He has previously had intracranial surgery following a stroke, and he works as an electrical engineer. What would be your concerns?**

A. In this particular case, my concerns would be that the patient may have an intracranial clip (e.g. for an aneurysm), or that he may have an intra-ocular fer-rous foreign body (secondary to his job). Imaging should not be performed on patients with intra-cranial clips unless one is absolutely certain that they are MRI compatible. Patients who may have metal foreign bodies in their eyes should have radiographs of their orbits performed prior to MRI scanning. Radiographs can pick up objects ≥ 0.1 mm in size, and ferrous foreign bodies below this size are not thought to be dangerous.

Other implanted devices that are contraindicated include ICDs, pacemak-ers, cochlear implants, dental implants, neurostimulators, ocular implants, tissue expanders and prosthetic heart valves (depending on the type).

Extra-cranial surgical clips (e.g. following abdominal surgery) are generally encased in fibrous tissue, However, they may cause artefact, and scanning should be deferred for 6 weeks post-operatively.

Q. Briefly describe the physics behind magnetic resonance imaging. What is the difference between T1 and T2 images?

A. Magnetic resonance imaging utilises the nuclei of hydrogen atoms (protons). The protons usually spin in a random fashion, However, on entering the MRI scanner they align with the magnetic field in the longitudinal plane (the magnet in an MRI scanner is always 'on'!), and produce a secondary spin (precession) at the same frequency, which will vary according to the strength of the magnet. A radio-frequency (RF) pulse is applied, which gives the nuclei the energy to move out of alignment and into the transverse plane, and to precess in phase with one another. When this pulse is removed, the atoms release their energy in two ways. First, energy is released back into the surrounding environment, causing magnetic movements to relax and realign back into the longitudinal plane, a process referred to as *T1 relaxation*. Secondly, nuclei then lose their precessional coherence and dephase, due to energy loss between adjacent nuclei, and this process is referred to as *T2 decay*. The release of energy is picked up in the transverse plane as an electrical voltage by a receiver coil, and this is the MR signal.

T1 relaxation occurs more rapidly in fat, as the size of the molecules enables them to return energy to the environment more quickly. This means that there is a greater degree of transverse magnetisation following the next RF pulse, resulting in a very bright signal from fat on T1 weighted images, whereas fluid remains dark. These scans are excellent for viewing anatomy, due to the good tissue differentiation.

T2 weighted images rely on the process of T2 decay, which occurs more slowly in water, and therefore maintains transverse magnetisation for longer, resulting in a higher signal. Consequently, water has a very bright signal on these images, producing a scan which is more useful for demonstrating pathology.

Q. What is nephrogenic systemic fibrosis? How may this be related to MRI investigations?

A. Nephrogenic systemic fibrosis (NSF) is a condition of unknown cause that affects patients with renal disease. It causes tightening of the skin of the extremities and sometimes of the trunk. It can be fatal, and 5% of patients develop the fulminant form. Causes of death are related to respiratory complications, clotting abnormalities and fractures/falls, among others. There is no consistently successful treatment for NSF, although various strategies, including steroids, plasmapheresis and renal transplant, have been used.

Recent reports have linked the use of gadolinium-containing contrast agents to the development of NSF in patients with renal impairment. Until further information is available, gadolinium-containing contrast is used with great caution in patients with a GFR of < 60 ml/min/1.73 m^2, including dialysis patients. The Royal College of Radiologists has recommended that if patients must receive these agents, they should be specific 'highly stable' agents, and that the use should not be repeated within 7 days. The smallest dose possible should be used. Specific agents (Omniscan, Magnevist and Optimark) should *not* be used.

Q. You have requested an MAG3 scan on a 29-year-old man whom you suspect has a PUJ obstruction. What is MAG3, how is it handled by the kidney, and what should the patient know prior to the test?

A.   MAG3 stands for mercaptoacetyltriglycine. MAG-3 is attached to the radioactive tracer technetium 99m, an isotope with a short half-life (approximately 6 hours) that is used for other nuclear medicine scans, such as DMSA. MAG3 is principally excreted by tubular secretion (90%), although approximately 10% is filtered at the glomerulus. Radioactivity is recorded via a gamma-camera (as with DMSA).

The patient will be asked to attend the nuclear medicine unit, and before the investigation they will have to empty their bladder. Their usual medications should not be stopped, and the patient should be well hydrated. Children should not be brought along for the scan due to the potential radiation risk. A cannula is inserted, and a diuretic is injected (usually 15 minutes prior to the test, although protocols vary). The patient does not need to undress, although metal objects should be removed. The patient sits on a chair while the MAG3 is injected through the cannula. They then have to sit still for approximately 20 minutes while images are recorded. The patient is asked to keep well hydrated after the test.

Please also refer to the chapter on paediatric urology.

Q.   **A 2-year-old girl requires an MAG3 scan to investigate a unilateral hydronephrosis. The parents are concerned about the process surrounding the scan and the risk of radiation. How would you reassure them?**

A.   Although the investigation is associated with radiation exposure, the overall dose is low (approximately 0.7 mSv). This is equivalent to about 4 months of background radiation. By comparison, air travel (at 26 000 feet) provides approximately 3 μSv per hour at temperate latitudes, and approximately 1 μSv per hour around the equator. Therefore no investigation involving radiation is entirely without risk. However, the benefits of the investigation need to be weighed up against the risks.

Children should eat and drink as normal before the scan, and should not stop any regular medications. The child should attend the ward in a well-hydrated state, and the paediatrician will insert a cannula after the application of anaesthetic cream. Occasionally the child may need some sedation. Diuretic may be injected prior to the isotope injection. The child must lie on a bed for approximately 20 minutes. They do not need to be undressed, but will have to remove any metal objects. After the scan they should be kept well hydrated and empty their bladder regularly.

Please also refer to the chapter on paediatric urology.

Q.   **You have requested a DMSA scan on a 34-year-old woman to look for the presence of renal scarring suggested on an ultrasound scan. What is DMSA, and how is the scan performed?**

A.   DMSA stands for dimercaptosuccinic acid. It is attached to the radio-tracer technetium-99m (see above). DMSA is a cortical scanning agent that localises in the proximal tubule. It is minimally excreted, and its presence is a reflection of functioning renal tissue and nephrons.

An important difference between the 'patient experience' of DMSA compared with that of MAG3 is that patients may be in the hospital for many hours during a DMSA renogram. If a female patient suspects that she may be pregnant, she should inform the department before attending, and should not be accompanied by children. A cannula is inserted into the patient, and the isotope is then injected. The static images are taken after an interval of approximately 2–4 hours post-injection. The patient is not required to undress, but any metal objects should be removed. During the actual scan they will have to lie still on a couch. The gamma 'camera' is placed close to the kidneys but not touching the patient. After the scan the patient is asked to keep well hydrated and to empty their bladder regularly.

Q. **What steps are necessary to ensure X-ray safety in theatre?**

A. First, I review the case in question, justifying my use of radiation exposure. In female patients of childbearing age a pregnancy test is performed prior to leaving the ward. In theatre suite, I make sure that the theatre doors are closed throughout the procedure. In addition, I ensure that the warning sign is displayed at the theatre entrance doors, and that a red warning light at these doors comes on when X-rays are being used. Personal protection, in the form of lead aprons and thyroid shields, is available to all personnel. X-rays are then used according to the ALARA (As Low As Reasonably Achievable) principle. The X-ray source (on the lower stem of the C-arm) is placed as close to the operating table as possible, in order to decrease radiation scatter. One should attempt to keep a good distance from the radiation source, as radiation exposure is inversely proportional to distance from the source. Intermittent screening is preferred to continuous screening. The alarm on the machine sounds when the radiation dose limit is reached.

MISCELLANEOUS
Renal failure and transplantation

Q. **Outline the main complications of chronic renal failure.**

A. The main complications that affect patients symptomatically are fluid overload, anaemia, renal osteodystrophy, pericarditis anaemia and the effects of cardiovascular disease. Hypertension, dyslipidaemia and the metabolic complications of acidosis and hyperkalaemia are factors that can lead to progression of the above.

Q. **Describe what you see in Figure 14.6. What is the composition of this solution?**

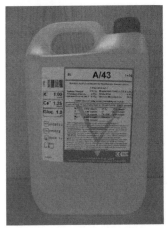

Figure 14.6

A. Figure 14.6 shows a dialysate solution. It consists of water, sodium (132–155 mmol/l), potassium (0–4 mmol/l, i.e. sub-physiological concentration), calcium, magnesium, chloride, bicarbonate (or acetate – as a buffer) and glucose. The pH is in the range 7.1–7.3.

Q. **What is the device shown in Figure 14.7? What are the principal differences between haemodialysis and haemofiltration?**

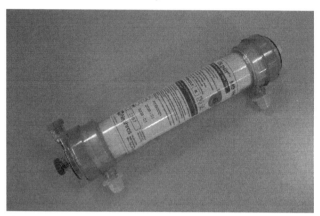

Figure 14.7

A. This device is a haemodiafiltration (HDF) filter. HDF is a process that combines dialysis and haemofiltration.

Haemodialysis works by two main mechanisms, first and principally the *diffusion* of solutes across a semi-permeable filter (made of modified cellulose or synthetic material), and secondly the principle of *ultrafiltration*, which is caused by the convective flow of solutes and liquids. The negative pressure that is necessary to allow this to occur is produced via the outlet pump of the dialysis machine. Haemofiltration does not use a dialysate solution, and relies on a hydrostatic pressure gradient alone to produce ultrafiltration. Fluid is replaced either before or after filtration. Haemodynamic stability of patients is thought to be better maintained by utilising filtration alone rather than diffusion.

Q. **How may permanent venous access be created, and what are the complications?**
A. Permanent access is provided principally via either radial or brachial fistulae. The arteries are anastamosed to the cephalic vein. Brachial fistulae are associated with a higher risk of 'steal' syndrome due to the higher flow rates. Alternatively, the arteries and veins may be linked with a 'bridging graft.'

Common complications include thrombosis of the fistula or graft, stenosis (usually occurring at or distal to the fistula or graft), ischaemia of the digits, infection (of grafts), aneurysm/pseudoaneurysm formation, superior vena cava obstruction or extravasation into limbs.

Q. **What are the principles of peritoneal dialysis? What are the different types of peritoneal dialysis? What complications may occur?**
A. Peritoneal dialysis uses the peritoneum as the 'dialysis membrane', and dialysis fluid is instilled into the peritoneal cavity. Solutes move via diffusion down a

concentration gradient, and fluid transfer occurs via osmosis, 'dragging' some molecules with it.

There are two main systems of peritoneal dialysis, namely continuous ambulatory peritoneal dialysis (CAPD) and automated peritoneal dialysis (APD).

CAPD originally used glass bottles that had to be disconnected and reconnected. This was superseded by a method that used plastic bags, the disadvantage of this being that the patient had a plastic bag continuously attached to them. Modern methods rely on a 'two-bag' system with a 'Y' connector. This is associated with lower rates of peritonitis and allows the patient to be free from a bag while not performing fluid exchanges. Typically patients exchange 2 litres of solution four times in 24 hours. The solution consists of sodium, potassium, calcium, magnesium, lactate and bicarbonate. The pH is low (approximately 5.5). The tonicity of the fluid is increased by the addition of either dextrose, icodextrin (a glucose polymer produced from the hydrolysis of starch) or amino acids.

APD is not dissimilar, but facilitates an automated system whereby fast exchanges can be performed overnight.

Access to the peritoneal cavity is via a semi-permanent catheter, such as the Tenckhoff catheter. This uses a 'double-cuff' method to reduce the likelihood of infection. Catheters are placed using the Seldinger technique under local anaesthesia, or placed surgically either by open surgery or laparoscopically.

Complications associated with peritoneal dialysis may occur at the time of insertion of the catheter, and include visceral injury (to bladder and bowel), haemorrhage, leak or infection. General complications of peritoneal dialysis include local infections around the catheter (and ultimately tunnel infection). One of the most serious complications is peritonitis. Although potentially fatal, this is often treatable by administering antibiotics intraperitoneally. An uncommon complication is sclerosing peritonitis, in which the peritoneum becomes sclerosed and fibrosed. Filtration is greatly affected. The aetiology is ultimately unknown, but is associated with long-term peritoneal dialysis usage and recurrent infections. An even rarer complication is sclerosing encapsulating peritonitis, which results in bowel obstruction and intestinal failure.

PREGNANCY

Q. **Outline the main maternal renal tract changes during pregnancy.**

A. Pregnancy results in generalised relaxation of smooth muscle (due to the effects of progesterone), which in addition to mechanical factors such as dextro-rotation of the uterus contributes to the hydronephrosis of pregnancy commencing in weeks 6 to 10. Hydronephrosis is seen particularly on the right, probably due to the uterine dextro-rotation. By 28 weeks of gestation, 90% of pregnant women will have hydronephrosis.

Pregnancy is associated with an increase in renal blood flow (up to 75%) and an approximately 50% increase in GFR. Creatinine clearance is therefore increased in pregnancy, and this is reflected in relatively reduced levels of serum creatinine and urea. Proteinuria increases up to 3 g/day, and glycosuria is very common.

Q. A 24-year-old woman is referred to you by the obstetricians. The patient is 21 weeks pregnant and has acute left loin to groin pain, a normal serum creatinine level, and no evidence of sepsis either clinically or biochemically. What imaging modalities are available to you diagnostically?

A. Ultrasound is the least invasive investigation, but is not particularly sensitive in the detection of ureteric calculi, and is obviously operator-dependent. Hydronephrosis, as mentioned above, is not a specific marker for obstruction and stones. However, a dilated ureter *below* the iliac vessels may be more suggestive of a stone or other obstruction. The presence or absence of ureteric jets may also be helpful.

IVU is feasible, but carries an inherent risk of radiation exposure, so this modality is not commonly utilised. However, the absolute risk of a (limited) IVU is low. The contrast medium itself carries no specific risk to the pregnancy.

With regard to cross-sectional imaging, CT is avoided due to the relatively high radiation risk. The safety of MRI in pregnancy has not been fully elucidated. However, an experienced radiologist may be able to detect the stone as a filling defect within the ureter, and this imaging modality is therefore sometimes used.

Q. The above patient is found to have a left lower ureteric stone with moderate hydronephrosis on MRI and ultrasound. How should this patient be treated medically?

A. There should be close consultation with the obstetric team. In addition, those who are unfamiliar with prescribing in pregnancy should refer to the *British National Formulary*. Simple analgesia such as paracetamol or co-dydramol may be used, but non-steroidal anti-inflammatory drugs should be avoided (particularly in the third trimester), due to the risk of premature closure of the patent ductus arteriosus in the unborn. Maternal use of opiates such as pethidine and morphine is associated with respiratory depression in the newborn.

Q. What are the options for antibiotic usage in pregnant women with urinary tract infection?

A. Again one should refer to the *British National Formulary*. In general, penicillins or cephalosporins are safe in the non-allergic patient. Antibiotics that are commonly used in non-pregnant patients may have adverse effects. Trimethoprim's mechanism of action is to interfere with bacterial dihydrofolate reductase and the production of folic acid. There is therefore the possibility of teratogenicity, particularly if this drug is used during the first trimester. Quinolones, such as ciprofloxacin, are contraindicated in pregnancy due to the risk of arthropathy in the fetus. Finally, gentamicin has been found to lead to an increased risk of auditory or vestibular nerve damage during the second and third trimesters.

OTHERS

Q. How would you ensure correct site surgery (e.g. in patients undergoing radical inguinal orchidectomy or nephrectomy)?

A. I use the pre-operative marking recommendations as set out by the National Patient Safety Agency and the Royal College of Surgeons of England.[5]

During consent the correct side should be marked by the operating surgeon.

A checklist is attached to the patient notes and then completed sequentially by the multi-disciplinary team prior to leaving the ward, on arrival in the theatre suite, in the anaesthetic room, and then finally in the operating theatre immediately before the start of surgery. Each check is only dealt with once the previous one has been completed and signed off.

Appropriate radiological investigations must also be available in theatre and be viewed by the surgeon prior to commencing the surgery.

In addition, more recently I have also become aware of the recent World Health Organization Surgical Safety Checklist which is being introduced into most NHS trusts.

Q. What precautions would you take when inserting a prosthesis (e.g. AUS, penile)?

A. In my practice, steps to reduce the risk of infection begin prior to the surgical procedure itself. The patient is advised to have Hibiscrub (chlorhexidine) washes or showers for 24–48 hours and Naseptin cream. Any other focus of infection that is detected pre-operatively is also treated prior to consideration for surgery. At induction of anaesthesia, prophylactic broad-spectrum intravenous antibiotics to cover skin commensals are given. Shaving of the surgical site is performed in theatre prior to surgery. During the procedure itself, I ensure that the lowest number of theatre staff possible are present in the operating room, and that their movement in and out of theatre is minimised. I ensure meticulous haemostasis at the time of surgery. Antibiotic solutions (e.g. gentamicin) can be applied to the prosthesis once it has been removed from the sterile packaging, as well as irrigation of the wound with antibiotics prior to placement. When inserting the prosthesis, fresh gloves are applied and a no-touch technique is used. Typically, I would use a small swab to handle the prosthesis. After the procedure, antibiotic treatment is continued according to local policy.

Q. How would you manage a patient who begins to experience difficulty breathing following scrotal injection of lignocaine, prior to vasectomy under local anaesthetic?

A. This should be treated as an emergency, as the patient is likely to be having an anaphylactic reaction (due to allergy to lignocaine). Initially assess the patient and confirm the diagnosis, and request a nurse or colleague to fast bleep the 'Arrest' team. While waiting for the emergency team to arrive, follow ALS principles and check the airway, breathing and circulation. Oxygenate the patient and gain intravenous access.

From the resuscitation trolley give 0.5 ml of 1 in 1:1000 adrenaline intramuscularly. Give 200 mg of intravenous hydrocortisone and 10 mg of intravenous chlorpheniramine (Piriton).

REFERENCES

1. Tolley D. Ureteric stents, far from ideal. *Lancet* 2000; **356:** 872–3.
2. www.valleylab.com/education/poes/index.html
3. www.mhra.gov.uk/home/groups/dts-bi/documents/websiteresources/con2023451.pdf

4. www.baus.org.uk/information_links/procedure_specific_consent_forms.phtml
5. National Patient Safety Agency and Royal College of Surgeons of England. *National Patient Safety Alert 06*. Joint Commission on Accreditation of Healthcare Organizations, April 2003; www.npsa.nhs.uk

Chapter 15
Commonly asked viva questions

ONCOLOGY
- How would you manage a patient who has a PSA of 200 and a positive bone scan with a biopsy proving Gleason 8 adenocarcinoma of the prostate?
- How would you explain to a GP how to start LHRH analogue treatment?
- When can you give the first LHRH injection?
- How would you manage bone pain in metastatic prostate cancer?
- What are the 2-week guidelines for referral of suspected malignancy?
- How would you investigate a 50-year-old man with painless haematuria?
- How would you investigate a 3 cm mass in the kidney detected on renal ultrasound scan?
- How would you manage a newly diagnosed pT1G3 tumour in the bladder?
- What if the patient with a pT1G3 bladder tumour also has CIS?
- What is the TNM classification for bladder cancer?
- Draw the transverse appearance of the prostate as it would appear on TRUSS.
- Discuss the role of interferon-α in the treatment of RCC?
- What are the complications of radical prostatectomy?
- What are the complications of radiotherapy for carcinoma of the prostate?
- What are the risks of ureterolysis?
- What is the role of finasteride in prostate cancer prevention?
- How would you investigate a female patient with painless haematuria who is on methotrexate treatment?
- How would you administer mitomycin C?
- Tell me about the Bosniak classification.
- Describe the technique of TRUSS and prostate biopsy.
- What are Partin's tables?
- Tell me about prostate brachytherapy.
- What happens to PSA levels after radiotherapy treatment?
- What is the aetiology of carcinoma of the bladder?
- What is an acceptable GFR prior to undergoing chemotherapy?
- What is accelerated MVAC?
- How common is cord compression in advanced carcinoma of the prostate?
- What is the half-life of PSA?
- What is the significance of a high PSA nadir following LHRH analogue treatment?

- What chemotherapy can be used in advanced prostate cancer?
- Tell me about VHL.
- What is the incidence of upper tract TCC? How often would you image the upper tract in a patient with a history of bladder cancer?
- How would you manage a T3b RCC? What is the prognosis?
- A 37-week pregnant woman presents with haematuria. What would be the investigation and treatment?
- A 73-year-old man presents with LUTS and is noted to have a PSA of 140 and an obvious prostate cancer on DRE. How would you discuss the findings with the patient? How would you manage this patient?
- When would you start hormone treatment in the above patient? Why does a flare response occur? What are the side-effects of LHRH analogues? How would you avoid osteoporosis?
- How many cores should you take on a TRUSS biopsy of the prostate? What is the benefit of increasing the number of cores?
- What are PSA density, PSA velocity and free:total PSA?
- Classify PIN. What is the incidence of CaP and PIN. What would you do if PIN was found on a prostate biopsy?
- What are the different types of testicular tumour?
- How would you counsel a patient about orchidectomy?
- How many cycles of chemotherapy are used in stage I seminoma and teratoma?
- A 40-year-old man has a renal mass diagnosed. What are the indications for partial and radical nephrectomy?
- What are the surgical approaches to the kidney?
- What are the indications for nephron-sparing surgery?
- How would you investigate a caval thrombus?
- A patient presents with a testicular tumour. Does it make any difference whether you perform orchidectomy through the scrotum or the inguinal region?
- How would you follow up a patient with a T1b renal-cell carcinoma post-operatively?
- What is the role of neoadjuvant chemotherapy in carcinoma of the bladder?
- What investigations would you perform before giving cisplatin therapy?
- What are the autocrine mechanisms of carcinogenesis?
- What is the management of a 65-year-old man with a PSA of 5?
- What do you understand by the term 'age-related PSA'?
- How would you counsel a patient for biopsy of the prostate?
- Discuss the significance of a negative prostate biopsy in a patient with a PSA of 5.
- What is a tumour suppressor gene?
- What is the impact on the management of prostate cancer with seminal vesicle involvement?
- What are the indications for adjuvant treatment post radical prostatectomy?
- What do you know about anti-angiogenic therapy for cancer and monoclonal antibodies for cancer?
- What are the BAUS guidelines for metastatic prostate cancer?
- What is the PRO7 trial?
- What do you know about zoledronic acid? What is the evidence for the use of zoledronic acid and what are the complications?
- How would you manage adenocarcinoma at the dome of the bladder?

- What is the management of urachal carcinoma? The margins are positive. What further treatment is required?
- What do you know about familial prostate cancer? What is the relevance of breast cancer?
- How does the androgen receptor work?
- What is the management of keratinising squamous-cell metaplasia? What is the risk of progressing to SCC?
- What is malakoplakia of the bladder?
- What is the management of a 6 cm angiomyolipoma?
- What is the evidence for performing an extended lymphadenectomy for invasive bladder cancer?
- What is the role of neoadjuvant chemotherapy for invasive bladder cancer?
- What is an oncogene? How does *ras* oncogene cause a malignant phenotype?
- What is a mutation?
- What are the indications for a partial nephrectomy? How would you perform a partial nephrectomy? What is the warm ischaemia time?
- What is the management of metastatic renal cancer?
- What is the literature for adjuvant treatment of renal cancer?
- What is the management of classical seminoma?
- What is the toxicity of BEP?
- What is a tumour suppressor gene?
- What is the evidence for post-operative intravesical mitomycin C?
- What percentage of people with a normal PSA have underlying prostate cancer?
- What is the pick-up rate of prostate biopsy?
- Tell me about the European screening programme for prostate cancer.
- What are the predisposing conditions for carcinoma of the penis? What are the metastatic sites?

PAEDIATRIC UROLOGY
- What is the classification of VUR?
- What associated abnormalities are found with VUR?
- How would you manage grade III VUR?
- How would you measure GFR?
- How would you perform a renogram?
- Describe how you would perform an orchidopexy.
- What is the management of an undescended testicle?
- How would you perform a Whitaker test?
- What are the indications for and how would you perform a pyeloplasty?
- How does isotope renography work?
- What are the phases in a renogram? How long would you wait before scanning?
- What are the symptoms of PUJ obstruction? Which renogram would you perform? What are the treatment options?
- What is the incidence of undescended testes?
- Describe the Fowler–Stephens procedure.
- What is the differential diagnosis of the acute scrotum?
- What is the management of a 2-year-old with cryptorchidism?
- Describe the descent of the testes.

- What is the natural history of cryptorchidism?
- What is the fate of undescended testes?
- What is the fate of bilateral undescended testes?
- A 3-year-old girl with a first UTI has been treated and makes a complete recovery. When would you organise the DMSA? If photopenic areas are found, what would you do?
- What prophylactic antibiotic would you use in the above case?
- Define reflux and what classification is used.
- Draw the glomerulus. What happens to the GFR when the efferent and afferent arterioles constrict?
- What is the presentation of a ureterocele? Describe the treatment and complications.
- How would you perform a laparoscopic pyeloplasty?
- What other methods of pyeloplasty do you know?

ANDROLOGY
- What are the side-effects of sildenafil?
- What are the contraindications to sildenafil?
- Draw the NO/cGMP pathway.
- What are the differences between high- and low-flow priapism?
- How would you manage a penile fracture which presents within 24 hours?
- A man wants to undergo a vasectomy. How would you counsel him?
- What would you do if persistent sperm are seen following a vasectomy?
- How would you assess a man with erectile dysfunction (ED)? What tests would you ask for?
- What are the side-effects of a PDE5 inhibitor?
- What is the incidence of chronic scrotal pain post vasectomy?
- Tell me about haemospermia.
- What are the indications for varicocele repair in adolescent males?
- What is the evidence that varicocele repair improves semen parameters?
- What are the approaches available for varicocele repair?
- In which patients would you scan the upper tracts when presented with a varicocele?
- What is the risk of ED in a patient presenting with a fractured penis?
- How would you treat high-flow priapism?
- Tell me about Peyronie's disease.
- Tell me about the testosterone pathway.
- How is testosterone released from the adrenals?
- What is testosterone bound to?
- What happens to testosterone during the day?
- When should a testosterone assay be performed?
- How is testosterone converted to DHT?
- What is the rate of infection of a penile prosthesis?
- What is the risk of priapism for someone using intracavernosal prostaglandin?
- Classify priapism. What are the investigations and treatment?
- What precautions would you take in order to minimise the risk of infection when inserting a penile prosthesis?
- Describe the Lue procedure for the management of Peyronie's disease.
- Give an anatomical description of a hydrocele.

STONES AND UTI

- How would you manage a 1.5 cm lower pole calyx stone?
- What are the contraindications to ESWL?
- What is the management of a 6 mm stone in the upper third of the ureter?
- Draw an obstructed renogram curve.
- What is Homsy's sign?
- What is the incidence of asymptomatic bacteriuria in pregnancy?
- What is the incidence of pyelonephritis in pregnancy?
- Which antibiotics are contraindicated in pregnancy?
- How would you define urinary tract infection?
- Describe the concept of bacterial adherence.
- Where did the 10^5 cfu definition arise from?
- What is the epidemiology of urinary tract calculi?
- What is the composition of stones and their frequency?
- What is the management of a 3 mm distal ureteric stone?
- What is the role of α-blockers in the management of ureteric stones?
- What is the management of first-time stone formers?
- How would you perform a 24-hour urine analysis in a recurrent stone former?
- What is the effect of calcium restriction on stone disease?
- What is the definition of a UTI?
- What are the causes of stone formation? How would you treat hypercalcaemia?
- What is the management of a child with a large distal ureteric stone?
- What analgesia would you use for ESWL? What type of machine do you use in your department?
- How would you locate the stone?
- Which energy level do you start at?
- What are the contraindications to performing an IVU?
- What conditions cause calcified cysts in the kidney?
- What are virulence factors?
- What is the dosing regime for gentamicin?
- How does gentamicin work?
- Describe the various lithotripters and how they work.
- What type of antibiotic is trimethoprim?
- Define recurrent UTI.
- What are the risk factors for UTI? What investigations would you perform?
- How would urine dipstick help in UTI?
- What defences against *E. coli* are there?
- What is the role of *Lactobacillus* in preventing *E. coli* colonisation?
- What does *P. fimbriae* attach to?
- What is the Stamey test?
- What is the classification of prostatitis?
- How would you treat prostatitis medically?
- What are the risks of PCNL?
- What is the management of post-PCNL bleeding via the nephrostomy?
- What is the prevalence of UTI before and after starting sexual activity?

FEMALE AND RECONSTRUCTIVE UROLOGY AND BLADDER DYSFUNCTION

- How would you treat interstitial cystitis?
- How would you investigate a female patient with incontinence?
- How would you manage a 20-year-old woman with urgency and frequency?
- How does tolterodine XL work as extended release?
- What are the problems associated with ileocystoplasty?
- How would you manage chronic pelvic pain syndrome?
- A 55-year-old woman with MS is bedbound with a problematic catheter. What is the investigation and management of this patient?
- How would you perform a bladder neck closure?
- What is Ulmstein's integral theory of continence?
- What is Delancy's hammock theory?
- What are the complications of TVT and TOT?
- What do you understand by types I and III incontinence?
- How does Botox work in the bladder and what are the risks?
- What changes occur in the urinary tract during pregnancy?
- How would you manage loin pain and hydronephrosis in a 35/40 pregnant woman?
- What is Fowler's syndrome?
- Draw the neurophysiology of micturition.
- What are the complications of an ileal conduit?
- What are the principles of reservoir reconstruction?
- What is Laplace's law?
- How would you perform a video cystogram?
- What are the causes of painful urinary retention in a 25-year-old woman?
- What are the urodynamic findings in a patient with MS?
- What are the risk factors for upper tract deterioration in a neurogenic bladder?
- What is the management of OAB in MS?
- How would you perform a Boari flap and a Psoas hitch?
- What are the causes of a urethral stricture?
- What are the narrowest parts of the urethra?
- How would you deal with a post-TUR bulbar stricture?
- What is the value of urethrography in stricture disease?
- What do you understand about interstitial cystitis?
- How would you diagnose interstitial cystitis?
- What is a Koch pouch?
- What is a Mainz 2 pouch?
- What are the provocative manoeuvres during urodynamics?
- What is the stop test?
- What is PSA? What causes PSA elevation?
- How would you consent for TRUSS and what are the side-effects of the procedure?
- What is the definition of detrusor instability? What is the medical and surgical treatment?
- How many times should a patient cough during urodynamic evaluation?
- Which types of neobladder do you know using small bowel?
- How does trospium chloride work?
- What types of Botox are there?

- How many types of DSD are there?
- How would you diagnose a urethral diverticulum?
- Why does a urethral stricture give a flat curve?
- What is the evidence for ISC in urethral stricture management?
- What is the significance of mast cells in a biopsy from a patient with interstitial cystitis?
- How is interstitial cystitis classified? What are the disadvantages of this classification?
- How would you perform a colposuspension?
- Which antibiotic prophylaxis would you use in a colposuspension?
- How would you manage a pelvic haematoma post colposuspension?
- What are the risks of nephrostomy insertion in a pregnant woman?
- Why do you detubularise the ileum in pouch formation?
- What end-fill pressure on urodynamics would be significant for a neuropathy with reduced compliance?
- What is the Mitrofanoff principle?
- What are the metabolic consequences of a continent pouch? What happens to serum calcium?
- What is the risk of UTI in CISC?
- How common is bacteriuria in patients with an ileal conduit?
- What is the commonest urethral stricture?
- Where are strictures most commonly located post TURP and why?
- What is the calibre of the urethra?
- Draw a diagram of the bulbar urethra and corpus spongiosum.
- What makes bladder muscle contract?
- Where is the sacral micturition centre?
- How do sympathetic fibres get to the bladder?
- What is the nerve supply and structure of the urethral sphincter?
- How do the sphincter arrangements differ in female patients?
- What sensations can you feel in the bladder?
- What is DSD? Where is the site of the lesion?
- Which sensory neurotransmitters are in the bladder?
- What injuries would you get with an open-book pelvic fracture?
- Explain a urethral distraction defect.
- Draw a diagram of the micturition pathway.
- Who described the pontine micturition centre?
- Where is the social control of voiding?
- What happens to micturition with lesions above the pons and below the pons?

UROLOGICAL EMERGENCIES
- How would you take your SHO through insertion of a suprapubic catheter?
- What are the advantages of a suprapubic catheter over a urethral catheter?
- You are called to the gynaecology ward to see a patient who is 3 days post hysterectomy and has clear fluid draining vaginally. What would you do?
- What would you do with a 12-year-old boy with an acutely painful scrotum?
- How would you classify acute scrotum diagnosis according to age group?
- How would you diagnose idiopathic scrotal oedema?

- How would you manage a ureteric injury which occurs during aneurysm repair?
- A patient arrives having been involved in a road traffic accident, and presents with haematuria. What is the subsequent management?
- How would you perform a urethrogram in a patient with a fractured pelvis?
- What is the management of a patient with pelvic fracture and urethral and bladder trauma?
- Classify renal trauma.
- What is shock?
- What is the relationship between the uterine artery and the ureter?
- What is the definition of SIRS? What is septic shock? What are the clinical features of shock?

TECHNOLOGY IN UROLOGY

- What types of contrast media do you know?
- What do we worry about with contrast media?
- What are the components of a cystoscope?
- How is a cystoscope constructed?
- What is the physics behind the Hopkins lens system?
- What does 'laser' stand for?
- What are the settings for your diathermy machine when performing a TURP?
- Draw the circuit diagram for diathermy.
- Show the waveform for diathermy.
- Tell me about green light laser.
- What are the advantages and disadvantages of laser?
- How would you perform a sphincter EMG?
- How would you perform a flexible cystoscopy?
- Which local anaesthetic agent would you use?
- What angle lens is used in a flexible cystoscope?
- What is a DEXA scan?

BPH

- What is the meaning of F (in terms of catheter size)?
- What is the role of urodynamics in men?
- How would you set up a LUTS clinic?
- How many uroflows would you perform in each patient in a LUTS clinic?
- What do you understand by a frequency–volume chart?
- How can you improve patient compliance with a frequency–volume chart?
- Draw a uroflow showing normal male flow and one showing a male with BPH.
- What are the indications for TURP?
- How would you manage a diabetic patient undergoing TURP post-operatively?
- What are the pharmacotherapies used in BPH?
- How would you manage a patient who has been on combination treatment and presents with retention?
- How would you design a trial of laser prostate vs. standard TURP?
- What are the complication rates for TURP?
- What do you know about warfarin?

- A patient presents with haematuria and is on warfarin and bleeding secondary to BPH. What would you do?
- What are the surgical treatments for BPH?
- What is on the IPSS sheet?
- What is the disadvantage of the IPSS?
- Tell me about the concept of uroselectivity in alpha-blockers.
- Tell me about MTOPS. What are your recommendations for combination therapy?
- How do 5-alpha-reductase inhibitors work? What is the benefit of dutasteride?
- With regard to BPH, what are the messages from MTOPS?
- What is the difference between dutasteride and finasteride?
- What are the absolute indications for surgery in a patient with BPH?
- What is the IPSS? How is it used?
- What are the complications of bladder outflow obstruction?
- What types of flowmeter are there?
- How would you interpret a flow rate?
- How would you work out the voided volume on a flow rate?
- What is the mortality associated with TURP?
- Tell me about laser prostatectomy.
- What is the bladder outflow obstruction index?
- What irrigation fluid do you use during TURP?
- Why would you use 1.5% rather than 3% glycine?
- Tell me about TUR syndrome.
- How can you monitor for TUR syndrome during surgery?
- What are the risk factors for acute urinary retention?
- What are the treatment options for men with LUTS?
- Tell me about the BAUS guidelines for LUTS.
- How would you manage patients with acute urinary retention (AUR)?
- What is the efficacy of alpha-blockers prior to undergoing a trial without catheter?
- What is the significance of a residual volume during AUR?
- Tell me about chronic retention.
- What is the physiological basis of post-obstructive diuresis? Distinguish between pathological and physiological diuresis.
- Draw the zones of the prostate gland.
- Where does BPH originate?
- Describe the embryology of the prostate.
- How would you consent for a TURP?
- Tell me about the National Prostatectomy Audit.
- What is nocturnal polyuria?

Index